THE TIMETABLES OF ™
WOMEN'S HISTORY

A Chronology of the Most Important People and Events in Women's History

KAREN GREENSPAN

A TOUCHSTONE BOOK

Published by Simon & Schuster

New York   London   Toronto   Sydney   Tokyo   Singapore

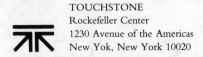

TOUCHSTONE
Rockefeller Center
1230 Avenue of the Americas
New Yok, New York 10020

First Touchstone Edition 1996

The Timetables of Women's History is a trademark of Simon & Schuster Inc.
The Timetables of Women's History is part of a best-selling series of books, including *The Timetables of Science, The Timetables of History, The Timetables of Technology, The Timetables of Jewish History,* and *The Timetables of American History.*

TOUCHSTONE and colophon are registered trademarks
of Simon & Schuster Inc.

Designed by Irving Perkins Associates
Manufactured in the United States of America

10 9 8 7 6 5 4 3 2 1

Library of Congress Cataloging-in-Publication Data

Greenspan, Karen.
    The timetables of women's history : a chronology of the most
important people and events in women's history / Karen Greenspan.
        p.   cm.
    Includes index.
        1. Women—History—Chronology.   I. Title.
HQ1121.G74   1994
305.4′09—dc20   94-41762   CIP
ISBN 0-671-67150-2
        0-684-81579-6 (Pbk)

ACKNOWLEDGMENTS

An undertaking of this magnitude must outstrip the expertise of any single scholar, as it has mine. Many hands have shaped this book. I am most grateful to the readers and consultants who generously offered much-needed guidance, criticism, and perspective: Steven Epstein, Elaine Handley, Penny Jolly, Robert Miner, Patricia Quinn, Jay Rogoff, and Philip J. West. I must also thank my excellent researchers, Carrie Giddens, Rodger Hurley, Deborah Jacobs, Jennifer Jolly, Deborah Lapin, Erica Lindgren, Rebecca Noel, Michele Niese, Carl Rabke, Sue Stein, and Erica Tolley, who helped to assemble and check much of the information in the book. Many others, colleagues, friends, and students, deserve my thanks for the help and encouragement they have extended along the way. Of course, I bear the responsibility for any errors the book might contain.

I want to thank Skidmore College's Office of the Dean of Faculty, the Associate Dean, and the Faculty Development Committee for their generous support of this project. Dr. Margery Sly of the Sophia Smith Collection at Smith College offered substantial assistance in acquiring illustrations, for which I owe her a great debt of gratitude. Finally, I must acknowledge the contributions of Bob Bender and Johanna Li, my editors at Simon & Schuster.

My greatest thanks go to the growing ranks of women's historians, whose groundbreaking studies made this work possible. I hope that future editions of this book will benefit from the increasing range and reliability of research in women's history.

Karen Greenspan
Saratoga Springs, NY
April 1994

LIST OF ESSAYS

LIST OF ILLUSTRATIONS

INTRODUCTION

Real solemn history, I cannot be interested in. . . . The quarrels of popes and kings, with wars on pestilences in every page; the men all so good for nothing, and hardly any women at all. —Jane Austen, *Northanger Abbey,* 1818

Human beings are a curious but credulous lot. We want to know all about ourselves—where we are going, where we have been, what makes us who we are—but we are willing to settle for a good story, even if it leaves out half the population. When information is missing, suppressed, or simply forgotten, we permit our expert storytellers—historians—to shape our vision of the past without it. We tend to assume that since history happens to everyone, everyone is included in it.

Why then should we need women's history? Women, after all, have lived, worked, and died just as men have. Female rulers, heroes, poets, gods, and saints appear in some of the earliest records. Do women, like nations, races, religions, and intellectual communities, really have a distinct history of their own? If we understand "women's history" to imply some experience or outlook or self-definition shared by all women of all times and all places that sets them apart from all men, our answer is no. If, on the other hand, we recognize that women have been as various as the times and cultures in which they lived, but that they have been excluded or misrepresented in a historical record constructed mostly by men, then we must with justice answer yes. Furthermore, the world's women have this in common: they have been important shapers of *human* history, not just of their own.

Most early and preindustrial societies left behind only sparse, uneven written records concerning women; in some, women do not appear at all. Their omission may mean that they were held in low esteem or that they did not contribute to the affairs judged important in their time. Or it may mean nothing more than that an incomplete record has survived or that chroniclers took women's active presence for granted. Some things are so commonplace that record keepers have no need to mention them; they assume that their readers already know. In contrast, later writings have quite a lot to say about Woman, though more often treating her as a problem and debating her nature than recording her deeds. The scarcity of women in histories written in the modern period results from the equation of political power with historical significance.

There is no history of mankind, there is only an indefinite number of histories of all kinds of aspects of human life. And one of these is the history of political power. This is elevated into the history of the world. —Sir Karl Popper, *The Open Society and Its Enemies,* 1945

Until recently, most historical writing made little mention of women, except when they acted upon the same stage as men. On that stage, the development of institutions and states took precedence over how ordinary people lived. Ignoring the influence of bedchamber, nursery, and convent, historians concerned themselves with the largest institutions and the most powerful classes: countries and conflicts, churches and kings. And upon that stage women have not, by and large, been able to accomplish as much as men. The characterization of women as ancillary and domestic because they have traditionally acted most often in the service of someone else (a husband, a child, a parent, a sibling) has meant that, well into our own time, they could rarely be regarded as significant actors in the world of male endeavor. In *that* world, famous or accomplished women were curiosities, like the woman preacher Samuel Johnson compared in 1753 to a dog walking on its hind legs: "It is not done well; but you are surprised to find it done at all."

But our ideas change, affected by intellectual trends as well as by individuals' selection and presentation of information. Contemporary historians have begun to study nontraditional materials, documenting those whose voices have been stifled, disregarded, or mute: peasants, ethnic minorities, homosexuals, children, and, of course, women. In our time, we have come to recognize the importance of the politically marginal world long inhabited by such groups. Scholars have begun to see the continuity—and interdependence—of the public and private spheres.

Over the last quarter century, as women's studies has matured as a discipline, scholars have discovered a wealth of information about women's lives and accomplishments. Some of this material appears in conventional historical sources: public documents like chronicles, legal codes, official biographies, ecclesiastical records. Other information comes from the study of popular or folk culture: artifacts, customs, practices, and social attitudes. Women's own writing has offered significant insight into both the real and the socially constructed shape of their lives. Social historians, by opening up private life to the same scrutiny once reserved for empires and wars, have probed the sources of feminine power in women's traditional province. Ever more exhaustive treatments of women's history appear on our shelves, but the task of finding, translating, interpreting, and publishing information about women remains daunting. We

11

have just begun to fill the enormous gaps in our knowledge of women's participation in history.

No biological, psychological or economic destiny can determine how the human female will appear in society. —Simone de Beauvoir, *The Second Sex*, 1949

In presenting the achievements of women in cultures all over the world, from ancient times to the present, *The Timetables of Women's History,* like its parent work, *The Timetables of History,*™ celebrates the full range of human endeavor in politics, arts and humanities, religion, science and technology, social advancement, philosophy, and private life. Like its sibling volumes, *The Timetables of Science,*™ *The Timetables of Technology,*™ *The Timetables of American History,*™ and *The Timetables of Jewish History,*™ *The Timetables of Women's History*™ sets its special subject in a general context, providing touchstones against which to measure women's achievement. Unlike earlier volumes, *The Timetables of Women's History* has broadened its focus to include the events and people of Africa, Asia, South America, and elsewhere. Though they are underrepresented, as are those of the premodern world, this is not by choice, but is rather a function of the availability and quality of sources. Future editions will benefit from the growing body of reliable scholarship in women's studies.

Given its enormous temporal and geographical scope, this volume cannot hope to include every woman of importance or every issue, event, and idea concerning women. We have tried to present major events and their chief participants. At the same time, we have indicated those trends, customs, beliefs, and practices that assisted or inhibited women's participation in the life of their times. From the long and lengthening list of historically important women we have had to select representatives to convey the magnitude of women's historical influence and achievement.

More than half the entries are biographical. Famous women appear alongside obscure ones, women who influenced their own time but have since disappeared from view, and women we now recall whose contemporaries ignored them. Most are listed under the year of their first notable achievement, with birth and death years, when known, in parentheses. Additional significant accomplishments are listed without birth and death years. When no other firm date is available, women appear under either their year of birth or their year of death, whichever we know more certainly.

While *The Timetables of Women's History* has striven for precision and accuracy, the book can only be as precise, complete, and accurate as the sources themselves. Nevertheless, some readers will quarrel with a date or a definition; most will miss something they expected to find. Readers are encouraged to send in their own entries (with sources) to the publisher for inclusion in the second edition. Errors and omissions aside, the editor hopes that every reader will delight in discovering much that is interesting and unfamiliar.

N.B. There will be very few Dates in this History. —Jane Austen, *The History of England,* 1791

Despite our associations of chronology with progress and periodization, women's history neither builds consistently upon achievement nor falls neatly into traditional periods or standard historical categories. Nevertheless, items in *The Timetables of Women's History* appear in chronological order. Because early records are sparse, we move first by 500-year periods, then by centuries, half centuries, decades, and, finally, year by year, as sources and dates become more abundant and precise. For a similar reason, the categories that organize items to reflect the major areas of women's activity are added as they become appropriate. By the 19th century, there are 10 categories:

General/Context. Historical context for women's achievements: world events, major figures, important discoveries, cultural practices, prevailing attitudes, intellectual trends, etc.

Daily Life/Customs/Practices. Health, household, children, marriage, dress, law, related innovations.

Humanities/Fine Arts. Fine arts, literature, scholarship, music, folk arts, architecture.

Occupations. Practice by women of law, medicine, commerce, and other occupations by which women earn their living.

Education. Founders and the founding of schools, teachers, students, first degrees, coeducation, etc.

Performing Arts/Entertainment/Sports. Acting, singing, instrumental music, performance art, professional and amateur sport of all kinds.

Religion/Philosophy. Institutions, reformers, practices and beliefs, theology, education.

Science/Technology/Discovery. Natural and social sciences, mathematics, invention, etc.; also women explorers, adventurers.

Statecraft/Military. Rulers, military leaders, objects and initiators of national and international activity; builders and destroyers of civilizations.

Reform. Women's rights, suffrage, abolition, temperance, peace, health, educational reform, human rights, etc.

Boxed essays focus on key individuals and events or give an overview of issues and trends in women's history that are difficult to classify or date. Like the chronological list, they do not attempt to cover everything; instead, they offer a representative selection of topics.

The index lists items by year and category (designated by letter).

THE TIMETABLES OF

WOMEN'S HISTORY

	General/ Context	Daily Life/ Customs/ Practices	Humanities/ Fine Arts	Occupations
–4000	Beginning of the Bronze Age in the Middle East, 4th millennium B.C. Sumerians found city of Ur in Mesopotamia (modern Iraq) Indo-European language and male gods introduced into east central Europe by invading Kurgan horsemen from southeastern Russia, displacing the matrilineal "Old Europeans," presumed makers of the female religious statues called "Venus figurines"			
–3500	Foundation of Egypt's First Dynasty, c. 3100 B.C. Introduction of bronze working, iron working in Egypt; wheels in Sumer and Assyria			
–3000	The epic of *Gilgamesh*, the first known written legend, in Sumerian cuneiform Egyptian Old Kingdom period, c. 2686–2181 B.C.	Egyptian monarchs of both sexes wear false metal beards as a sign of royalty In Crete, noblewomen wear bell-skirted dresses with corseted bodices to		Ka-Kum, the earliest recorded brothel, operates in the Sumerian city Erech, or Uruk, c. 3000 B.C. Merit Ptah, whose image can be found on a tomb

ARCHEOLOGICAL EVIDENCE OF WOMEN IN PREHISTORY

For feminist historians, European archeology offers tantalizing but ambiguous evidence of women's lives in prehistoric times. Some recent sources draw our attention to Stone Age artifacts found at Dolní Větsonice, Czechoslovakia, for instance. There, 26,000 years ago, someone fashioned an ivory portrait of a woman with a distinctive face; nearby, archeologists also found what might be her grave, containing a woman's skeleton buried with what seems to be great honor. Could this indicate that women held political or religious power at that time in Europe? Other artifacts from the period—popularly known as "venuses" because they depict women's bodies with an emphasis on their reproductive attributes—have been found all over the European continent, from Spain to Siberia. These suggest mere women, or perhaps female deities, might have played more important roles than standard history has recognized.

Late-19th-century scholars, under the influence of Darwin's theory of evolution, sought to explain or justify what archeology seemed to indicate had been a universal shift over time from matriarchal to patriarchal societies. Studies in the 20th century look for patterns rather than universal theories to account for societies' subordination of women. Archeological evidence indicates that human patterns of living have developed, for ecological or social reasons, in the direction of intergroup competition and warfare, favoring larger and stronger males.

Archeology has uncovered more weapons and bones—arti-

Performing Arts/ Entertainment/ Sports	Religion/ Philosophy	Science/ Technology/ Discovery	Statecraft/ Military	
	Sumerian goddess Nintu, also called Ninhurgad or Ninmah, is believed to have created human beings in six varieties, molding them from clay			**−4000**
	Erishkigal is the Sumerian queen of the underworld; like the Greek Persephone, she is said to have been carried off there, where she reigns for part of the year			
				−3500
	Nammu is the primeval earth goddess of Sumerian mythology		Si Ling-Chi, empress of China, develops the process by which the thread is removed from the cocoon of the silk worm; she establishes silk cultivation and weaving industries, 2640 B.C.	**−3000**
	Maat is the Egyptian goddess of truth, justice, and law; her symbol, an ostrich plume, appears on the god Osiris's scale of justice opposite a human heart			
	In Greek mythology, the Sphinx, a monster with a woman's face, a lion's body, and a bird's wings, stations herself outside Thebes in Egypt, asking a			

facts of hunting, a chiefly male activity—from earlier societies than artifacts of females' gathering baskets, say, or the remains of the overwhelmingly vegetable diets of most primitive peoples. Stone and bone hunting artifacts resist decay when fiber or wooden artifacts do not.

Around 6000 B.C. humans began to domesticate animals and to practice agriculture. Even though some have theorized that women's subordination followed the invention of private property, no clear evidence proves either the worship or the denigration of women in that period.

The first European states—Mycenae and Crete—again offer ambiguous clues about the status of women. Certain Mycenaean tablets seem to indicate equal status for women and men, but no clear evidence has yet established the worship of a goddess or women's overall status.

Our first written histories show a clear subordination of women; but all three early Western civilizations for which we have documentary evidence—Greek, Roman, and Hebrew—had already evolved into male-dominated warrior cultures. Until more definitive archeological finds are unearthed, we continue to wonder whether matriarchal or egalitarian societies existed in primitive times.

	General/ Context	Daily Life/ Customs/ Practices	Humanities/ Fine Arts	Occupations
−3000	Sumerians begin to develop cuneiform writing Egyptians build the Great Pyramid of Giza as a tomb for Pharaoh Cheops, c. 2900 B.C. Non-Semitic Sumerians reign in southern Babylonia	emphasize their exposed breasts Egyptians begin wearing wedding rings, c. 2800 B.C. Noble Babylonian ladies c. 2800 B.C. wear long-sleeved tunics with fringed capes, metal rings around the neck, and caps or fillets tying up the hair at the nape of the neck; the queen's richly ornamented garb included a tight-sleeved tunic, soft shoes, earrings, bracelets, and a diadem		in Egypt's Valley of the Kings, is the earliest known female doctor, c. 2700 B.C.
−2500	Dawn of the Iron Age in the Middle East Inauguration of China's 700-year Hsia dynasty, 2205–1766 B.C. Sumerians conquered by the Akkadians, 2360 B.C. Development of the loom in Europe Egyptian Middle Kingdom, c. 2050–1786 B.C.			
−2300			The first known female poet, Sumerian priestess Enheduanna composes the "Exaltation of Inanna," a hymn to the Great Goddess	
−2000	Development of potter's wheel, bellows, and discovery of glass in Mesopotamia; bathroom plumbing in Crete Mycenae, Crete, and Cyprus, Aegean and Phoenician cultures, 2000–500 B.C. Beads and faience begin to be manufactured in Egypt Bronze smelting introduced into Egypt	Mycenaean women c. 2000 B.C. wear frilled bodices, which leave the breasts exposed, flounced skirts over a loincloth, earrings, and diadems covered by a veil Bronze Age Teutonic girls' garments c. 2000 B.C. consist of a long linen tunic covered by a short outer tunic belted at the waist; older women wear a long, full tunic belted at the waist; hair is braided or bound in a net	Originally Greek goddesses of memory, the nine Muses become identified with individual arts and sciences whose practitioners they are said to inspire; they are Calliope, muse of epic poetry; Clio, muse of history; Erato, muse of love poetry; Euterpe, muse of lyric poetry; Melpomene, muse of tragedy; Polyhymnia, muse of sacred poetry; Terpsichore, muse of choral song and dance; Thalia, muse of comedy;	Articles 108–110 of the Code of Hammurabi regulate the business practices of women wine sellers

Performing Arts/ Entertainment/ Sports	Religion/ Philosophy	Science/ Technology/ Discovery	Statecraft/ Military	
				−3000
	riddle of passersby and devouring those who cannot answer it. When her riddle (what goes on four legs in the morning, two in the afternoon, and three in the evening?) is answered correctly by Oedipus (man, who crawls as an infant, walks upright in adulthood, and leans upon a staff in old age), she throws herself to her death in rage			
	Legendary Chinese emperor Fu Hsi, c. 2800, originates the yin and yang philosophy of nature, which says that health and tranquillity require perfect equilibrium of female (yin) and male (yang) principles; the male, according to Fu Hsi, is always dominant			
		Queen Semiramis links the Babylonian royal palace with the Temple of Jupiter by a tunnel under the Euphrates, the first tunnel built below a river, 2200–2101 B.C.		**−2500**
				−2300
	Persephone is regarded in Greek mythology as the queen of the underworld and the goddess of reborn crops; daughter of the goddess Demeter, she is believed to have been abducted by the god Hades, and brought by force to his underground realm; she and her mother are central to the Eleusian mysteries; her Roman counterpart is Proserpina		According to classical myth, Penthesilea (d. 1187 B.C.) is the queen of the Amazons, slain by Achilles when she comes to the aid of the Trojans after Hector's death; Achilles sincerely laments the death on account of her beauty and courage

Royal women, known as *fu*, of the Shang period in China play politically active roles, such as presenting tribute from areas they ruled, holding office | **−2000** |

	General/ Context	Daily Life/ Customs/ Practices	Humanities/ Fine Arts	Occupations
−2000	Horizontal loom used in Egypt Art of writing and of silk weaving known in the Far East Grape cultivation for wine and wine presses known in Egypt and Mesopotamia	Contraceptives appear in Egypt	and Urania, muse of astronomy	
−1900	Tin first used in Western Europe Avebury and Stonehenge circles built Hammurabi, ruler of the Babylonian empire, conquers Mesopotamia, imposing the oldest known legal compilation, the Code of Hammurabi; it encompasses family life, business and economic matters, criminal law, and ethics, c. 1792–1750 B.C.	Hagar of Egypt is the handmaid of the childless Sarah, sent by her to Abraham to produce an heir, 1898 B.C.; Hagar becomes the mother of Ishmael (Gen. 16, 21, 25)		
−1700	Abraham founds Jewish nation Shang, or Yin, the first historical Chinese dynasty, c. 1766–1122 B.C.	Rachel, Hebrew wife of Jacob, youngest daughter of Laban, mother of Joseph and Benjamin, dies in childbirth; so beloved is she that Jacob erects a monument to her near which the Messiah will be born		

THE LEGAL STATUS OF WOMEN IN THE ANCIENT WORLD

When agriculture replaced hunting as the primary means of food getting in primitive societies, women enjoyed a remarkable measure of economic autonomy. The earliest known written law code, the Babylonian Code of Hammurabi (c. 1792–1750 B.C.) sets forth a strong position of legal economic independence for women: a woman's dowry was bestowed upon her; she passed her land and property on to her children, over whom she and her husband exercised equal authority. In some cultures, women possessed greater economic power than men. In Sparta, for example, women owned two thirds of the land while Arab women owned the flocks that their husbands pastured for them. Records indicate that some Menominee Indian women owned as many as 1500 birch bark vessels. In ancient Egypt, too, women were equal to their husbands in law and business. They disposed of private property and even loaned their husbands money at a stiff interest rate.

In Rome women might wield economic power; some early Roman women freely managed their own finances, though such activities were not necessarily looked upon with

Performing Arts/ Entertainment/ Sports	Religion/ Philosophy	Science/ Technology/ Discovery	Statecraft/ Military	
	Worshiped under many names, Greek goddess Rhea, a Titan, is the mother of many of the Olympians, most of whom are swallowed by their father to prevent his own overthrow; by means of a ruse, she enables Zeus to depose his father and free his siblings		in the Shang government, leading armies, regulating agriculture, and supervising religious activities	**−2000**
Figurine in Indus Valley depicts a female dancer				**−1900**
	Sarah (sometimes Sarai), wife of Old Testament patriarch Abraham, gives birth to Isaac in her old age, as promised by Jehovah, whereupon her name is changed to Sarah Leah, the daughter of the Syrian Laban who deceived Jacob into marriage, has six sons, named as heads of six of the tribes of Israel, and a daughter, Dinah (Gen. 29-31; 33-35; 46; 49; Ruth 4:11)		Dinah, only daughter of the patriarch Jacob, is seduced by Canaanite prince Shechem, but her brothers Simeon and Levi prevent their marriage, tricking the Canaanites and massacring them, 1732 B.C. (Gen. 34, 46:15)	**−1700**

favor. In 195 B.C., Roman women demanded repeal of the Oppian Law, which had limited their right to purchase expensive goods. Their demands caused a scandal for which the women were ridiculed for acting solely in the cause of vain luxury; nevertheless, the law was repealed.

As the power and wealth of empires and city-states were consolidated, though, women lost status before the law. Assyrian law between 1450–1250 B.C. steadily ate away at women's rights. Assyrian wives could not be seen unveiled in public; their fidelity (not their husbands') was strictly en-forced. Hebrew law required women to be virgins upon marriage, though their husbands were not censured for visiting prostitutes. Divorce was the husband's privilege alone. Women in Athens during the Golden Age could not buy or sell land, make contracts, or bring legal action. Their marriages were arranged by parents. Only men could inherit property; widows could not even inherit from their husbands. In the ancient world, to the degree that societies became more prosperous, by so much were women's legal rights circumscribed.

	General/ Context	Daily Life/ Customs/ Practices	Humanities/ Fine Arts	Occupations
−1600	Egyptian New Kingdom period, 1570–1085 B.C.	Both men's and women's fashions in the Egyptian New Kingdom, c. 1530 B.C., require a thin tight-fitting garment that leaves one shoulder bare		
−1500	Kingdom of Assur on upper Tigris, c. 1500 B.C.	Assyrian women c. 1500 B.C. wear fringed shirts and mantles thrown over one shoulder Bedouin women c. 1500 B.C. wear woven multi-colored mantles fastened on one shoulder, fillets in their hair, and shoes made of one piece of leather	In Greek mythology, Scylla is a female monster who endangers ships in the Strait of Messina; Scylla, who sits on a rock on the Italian side and barks like a dog, has 12 feet, six heads each with three rows of sharp teeth, each on a long neck; she is reputed to have been a nymph changed into a monster by the jealous sorceress Circe; on the other side of the strait sits Charybdis, a male monster who swallows the waters and casts them up again three times a day—a whirlpool	
−1400	The Iron Age begins in Asia Minor Mycenaeans settle in Greece and lay the foundations of Greek civilization, c. 1400 B.C. Assyrians begin their rule in Mesopotamia, c. 1350–1251 B.C.	Egyptian queens c. 1350 B.C. customarily wear a sacred-vulture headdress and carry a scourge, part of the royal paraphernalia; the queen, head of the gods' harem of living noble ladies, bears the attributes of the wife of a god: plumes, solar disk, diadem, neck ornaments, handle cross, and lotus scepter; she wears a tight-fitting tunic that widens		

EGYPTIAN QUEENS

Aristocratic women in ancient Egypt enjoyed privileges and rights that most women in other cultures of the time did not. Egyptian women played a part in more aspects of religious, economic, and social activities than in any other early civilization we know about. Court women, trained for roles in international relations, helped promote the scientific and cultural knowledge of the day. Women enjoyed equal legal status with men of the same social class.

While not consistently true in practice, in theory the right to succeed to the throne passed through the female line. Sister often married brother, following the example of the goddess Isis and the god Osiris, to keep the throne and fortune within the family. In most cases, queens who ruled did so at the end of a

Performing Arts/ Entertainment/ Sports	Religion/ Philosophy	Science/ Technology/ Discovery	Statecraft/ Military	
			Queen Aahhotep I rules in Egypt, c. 1570–1546 B.C., she helps to quell an uprising in Thebes, helping to unite Egypt under one rule	**–1600**
			Queen Aahmes Nefertari (Ahmose I) rules in Egypt, c. 1580–1557 B.C.	
Egyptian harem women are trained as dancing girls and musicians	Semele becomes pregnant by the disguised god Zeus; she is persuaded by his jealous wife, Hera, to ask him to reveal himself in his true form; regretfully, he appears to her as a thunderbolt and burns her up, but not before their unborn child, the god Dionysus, is rescued by Hermes; Semele is later rescued from Hades by Dionysus and her raising, symbolizing the return of spring, is widely celebrated		Breaking a 2000-year old tradition, Hatshepsut I (d. 1469 B.C.) becomes Egypt's first female pharaoh, ruling peacefully for 20 years; she always wears men's clothes and is addressed as His Majesty; she rules as queen from c. 1490–1469 B.C.); her reign marks an era of peace and rebuilding for New Kingdom Egypt	**–1500**
	Egyptian Queen Hatshepsut erects two obelisks at Karnak, 1485 B.C.; she has built a magnificent temple on the west side of the Nile, whose walls she has decorated with pictures of an expedition she sent to the land of Punt			
	The Eleusinian mysteries, performed in honor of the goddess Demeter and her daughter Persephone, become the most famous mysteries in the Greek and Roman world; they continued to be celebrated well into the Christian era; their secret was so well guarded that little is known of them beyond the fact that they centered on the abduction			**–1400**

dynasty, usually in a last-ditch attempt to keep the family in power. They exercised power in the name of an enfeebled husband or a son; some even took a masculine name.

Hatshepsut, one of the most famous queens, declared herself both a man and a god. Her 20-year reign was known for maintaining peace and for establishing trade routes. Nefertiti, renowned for her great beauty, ruled as queen while believing in one god—this in a traditionally polytheistic country. The most famous Egyptian queen, Cleopatra, had legendary beauty, intelligence, and feminine wiles. As the last queen of independent Egypt, she seized the throne to prevent the Roman annexation of her kingdom. Her celebrated reign and fierce independence helped establish a literary tradition of the manipulative female ruler.

	General/ Context	Daily Life/ Customs/ Practices	Humanities/ Fine Arts	Occupations
−1400	Foundation of Phoenician sea power city of Tyre on the east coast of the Mediterranean, c. 1400 B.C.	below the knees and leaves the breasts exposed		
−1374				
−1300	Alphabetic script develops out of cuneiform writing in Mesopotamia Led by the prophet Moses and his brother Aaron, a 40-year migration of Israelites begins, 1275 B.C. after 300 years of Egyptian oppression		Miriam sings with Moses at the parting of the Red Sea; her song of praise after the defeat of the Egyptians is one of the earliest pieces of Hebrew poetry (Ex. 15:20–21); she is the probable leader of the women of the migration out of Egypt	

WOMEN IN EARLY JEWISH SOCIETY

The Jewish religion departed dramatically from other ancient religions. While the known cultures of antiquity worshiped many gods and goddesses, the monotheistic Hebrews, or Jews, believed exclusively in a male divinity who had no wife or consort. The Jewish religion contributed to the patriarchal tradition in Western lands; its Ten Commandments, believed to have been handed down from God, formed the moral basis for Western culture.

Ancient Judaism placed women in a clearly subordinate position. Rabbinical literature refers to women as social and religious inferiors to men; their function was to maintain the home, abide by Jewish law, and instruct the children in the Jewish tradition.

Men made up the membership of the covenant community, symbolized by the rite of circumcision. Women sat separately from men in the synagogue, forbidden to read aloud or hold public positions, and prohibited from studying the Torah and Talmud. Though they lighted the Sabbath candles, they were not permitted to say prayers blessing the bread and wine. As justification Hebrew scholars pointed to the creation myth in Genesis, wherein Eve's disobedience to God in eating from the tree of knowledge branded women as the source of sin and death in the world.

Girls raised under the strict rule of their fathers found that authority passed on to their husbands. A wife referred to her husband as "master"; he in turn considered her his property. If she produced no children, her barrenness could supply grounds for divorce—the husband's exclusive right. Hebrew law also gave a husband the right to kill both his adulterous wife and her partner. But as long as he did not choose another man's wife,

Performing Arts/ Entertainment/ Sports	Religion/ Philosophy	Science/ Technology/ Discovery	Statecraft/ Military	
Minoan women are shown participating in bull leaping as catchers and leapers	and return of Persephone by Hades, god of the underworld Naomi, whose name means "beauty," is the wife of Elimelech, mother-in-law of Ruth, and grandmother of Obed, who is grandfather of David, 1312 B.C. (Ruth 1–4); she is remarkable for her tolerant, loving reception of the Moabite Ruth into her family, especially when she returns from Moab to Bethlehem			**–1400**
	Under the influence of his wife Nefertiti, Egyptian king Amenhotep IV introduces monotheism, establishing a new cult of the sun god Aten and opposing the priests of Amen			**–1374**
	Zipporah, the devoted wife of Moses, is venerated on the seventh day of the Hebrew month of Adar Rahab, a harlot of Jericho, shelters Jewish spies and hides them from the king in exchange for safety for herself and her family during the coming battle; to give thanks, she converts to Judaism and becomes a model of fidelity and discretion			**–1300**

a husband could have sexual relations outside of marriage.

While early Hebrew law and custom placed woman under the control of man, she could be honored not only for fulfilling her roles as wife and mother, but also for transcending them. The Hebrew Bible tells of the prophets Miriam (Exod. 15:20), Deborah (Judg. 4:4), Huldah (II Kings 22:14), and Noadiah (Neh. 6:14), for example, who served as authoritative channels for divine truth. Revered as one of the great leaders and judges of the tribes of Israel, Deborah vanquished the armies of the Canaanite enemy Sisera. When Sisera escaped, her contemporary, the brave but treacherous Jael (Judg. 4:17-22), welcomed him into her tent, offered him hospitality—and smashed his head in. Deborah's famous song tells of their triumph.

Disobeying the Egyptian king who ordered them to kill the male babies they delivered, the midwives Shiphrah and Puah claimed that the hardy Hebrew women gave birth before they could reach them (Exod. 1:15). The stories of Vashti and Esther, though traditionally interpreted to show the importance of female submission, demonstrate the women's wisdom and courage in the face of masculine unreason: Vashti defied her husband's demand that she display her beauty before his drunken guests (Esth. 1, 2) while Esther, at great personal risk, interceded for the Jews, who were about to fall victim to the irrational anger of her husband's prime minister.

Examples of female perfidy and of women's undisguised oppression (like the gruesome story of the woman sacrificed to save her husband from the lust of the Benjaminites in Judges 19) abound in the Hebrew Bible. Nevertheless, Jewish women were accorded respect for performing their daily duties well and they were praised for their valor—at least in song and story.

	General/ Context	Daily Life/ Customs/ Practices	Humanities/ Fine Arts	Occupations
−1200	The city of Troy falls to Greek forces after a 10-year siege, 1183 B.C.; according to Homer, the war was caused by the kidnapping of Greek High King's wife, Helen, by Paris of Troy Foundation of the Chou dynasty, 1122–221 B.C., in China The Iron Age begins in Europe in Greece The Hittites rule over Asia Minor as far as Syria from the second millennium; their loose empire breaks up c. 1200 B.C.		Penelope, wife of Odysseus in the *Odyssey*, is besieged by suitors while her husband is away; she fends them off for 10 years until he returns and slays them; her name is synonymous with the wifely virtues of patience and faith The 12th-century B.C. poet Phautasia, daughter of Nicanchus of Memphis in Egypt, writes poems on the Trojan War and Ulysses, from which Homer copied the greater part of the *Iliad* and the *Odyssey*	
−1100		Rizpah, daughter of Aiah, sits vigil over her dead sons' bodies day and night until David takes pity on her and inters the bodies; she becomes a figure for the tenderness of woman's love		
−1000	Building of the Great Temple of Jerusalem, 961 B.C. The oldest books of the Old Testament are set down in writing David of Hebron is annointed King of Judaea, 1010–970 B.C. Urban societies beginning in China	Mesopotamians wear long rectangular pieces of fabric draped around their bodies; men's are wrapped counterclockwise, women's clockwise		
−950		King Solomon of Judaea's household includes 700 wives and 300 concubines The House of the Forest of Lebanon, an armory, judgment hall, and palace for his wife, pharaoh's daughter, is completed by Solomon		

Performing Arts/ Entertainment/ Sports	Religion/ Philosophy	Science/ Technology/ Discovery	Statecraft/ Military	
Egyptian papyri refer to a class of professional women musicians in Egypt; Assyrian and Babylonian women, too, practice as professional musicians around this time		Penthesilea, queen of the legendary Amazons and successor to Osythia, fights and is killed by Achilles at the siege of Troy; Pliny says she invented the battle-ax	Fu Hao is a royal consort and lady general in the Hunan province of China, 1199 B.C. Abigail, wife of Nabal and known for her beauty and wisdom, saves her family's fate; David asks the wealthy Nabal for help in fighting Saul, but when Nabal refuses, he prepares to destroy Nabal's family and possessions; Abigail saves them by sending David what he wants and by her famous blessing and admonition (I Sam. 25:24-31); Nabal dies in shock 10 days later after hearing of the fate he escaped, and Abigail marries David Queen Twosre rules as pharaoh of Egypt	**–1200**
	Michal, daughter of Saul, is the only woman in the Bible to take the initiative in getting her own husband; she marries David, but later publicly mocks him for playing with the servants and dancing before the Ark of the Covenant when it is brought from Shiloh to Jerusalem, 1042 B.C. (II Sam. 6:16-23)			**–1100**
Greek myth tells of Atalanta, the renowned virgin huntress who is the swiftest mortal alive; she joins the famous hunt for the Caledonian boar, where she wins the admiration of her male companions				**–1000**
				–950

	General/ Context	Daily Life/ Customs/ Practices	Humanities/ Fine Arts	Occupations
−900	Rise of the earliest Hebrew prophets Purple fabric dyes developed by Phoenicians Composition of the *Odyssey* and the *Iliad*, Greek oral epics ascribed to Homer (fl. c. 850 B.C.)	Absalom, son of King David of Judaea, kills his half brother in revenge for the rape of his sister, Tamar, and is banished		
−800	The first Greek Olympic Games are held in 776 B.C.; women are not permitted to attend The traditional date for the foundation of Rome is 753 B.C. Slavery first recorded in Greece Temple and palace architecture begins to be developed in Greece	Greek women c. 800 B.C. dress their hair elaborately for special occasions, with locks and plaits, some produced with a curling iron; ordinary styles are much simpler, hair parted and knotted at the back of the neck, sometimes held with headbands, fillets, or kerchiefs		
−750	Kingdom of Asurnazirpal (Ashurbanipal) unites with Babylonia, 729 B.C.	At about this time, both Greek men and women wear the *chiton*, two rectangular pieces of fabric sewn up the sides, with holes left for the head and arms Etruscan women c. 750 B.C. wear long close-fitting dresses, laced shoes made of one piece, conical headdresses, long embroidered cloaklike garments pulled over the shoulders from the back, and large plate earrings; they are depicted attending banquets as well as entertaining flautists and jugglers		
−700	Development of horseshoes in Europe The Dorians supplant Mycenaeans in Greece			

Performing Arts/ Entertainment/ Sports	Religion/ Philosophy	Science/ Technology/ Discovery	Statecraft/ Military	
	Assyrian Queen Sammu-ramat (811–807 B.C.), known to legend as Semiramis, rules the Assyrian Empire for five years after the death of her husband, King Shamshi-Adad V, 811 B.C.; she is regent for her son, but inscriptions indicate that she held the actual power; she introduces the worship of the Babylonian god Nebo into the Assyrian constellation of gods; successful in the wars against the Medes and the Chaldean, she remains influential through several reigns		In the 10th century, Balkis, queen of Sheba (a region in southern Arabia), makes her celebrated visit to King Solomon

Known for her cruelty and ruthlessness, Athaliah, daughter of Jezebel and the king of Samaria and widow of the king of Judah, slays all her grandchildren after her son dies, and becomes queen, 884 B.C.; slain in 878 B.C. by the order of the high priest after she enters the sacred enclosure of the temple (II Kings 8:26; 11:1-20; II Chron. 22:2-24:7) | **−900** |
| | The reigning high priest in Thebes (Egypt) is a woman | | | **−800** |
| | | | According to legend, Numa Pompilius (715–672 B.C.), second king of Rome, is taught the lessons of wisdom and law, which he incorporates into his institutions, by the nymph Egeria

Arab ruler Queen Zabibi is required to send tribute to King Tiglath-pilesar III of Assyria after his victory over a coalition of Middle Eastern states, 738 B.C.

Queen Samsia rules southern Arabia while Assyrian ruler Tiglath-pilesar III attacks Damascus, 732 B.C. | **−750** |
| | The most ancient oracle of the Greeks, the oracle of Zeus at Dodona, is tended by priestesses known as pigeons who brazenly beat gongs and interpret messages delivered through the leaves of a sacred oak, the cooing | | Queen Naqi'a becomes regent of Assyria while her husband, King Sennacherib, is at war, 689 B.C.; she plays an important role in the kingdom, particularly in its building program, and her influence continues into the | **−700** |

27

General/ Context	Daily Life/ Customs/ Practices	Humanities/ Fine Arts	Occupations
–700			
–650 Destruction of Ninevah, 612 B.C. Birth of Lao-tzu (c. 604–531 B.C.), founder of Taoism		Greek lyric poet Sappho (fl.600 B.C.) of Lesbos leads women dedicated to the cult of Aphrodite; the affection she expresses for them in her poetry is the origin of the term "lesbian"; fragments of seven books of poetry survive; a poetic meter, the "Sapphic," is named for her; she was much admired and copied in the ancient world and is recognized as one of the greatest poets of all time	
–600 Iron welding invented in Greece, c. 566 B.C. The Assyrian Empire falls, 606 B.C. Gold coin or bars first used in China First map of the world, inscribed on clay, made at Ninevah	By about 600 B.C., Minoan women usually wear metal corsets Phrygian women c. 600 B.C. wear full-length long-sleeved patterned dresses with a mantle and the so-called Phrygian cap, a long hoodlike hat that curves forward toward the brow	Panthea, wife of Abradatus, king of Susa, is taken captive by Cyrus, king of Persia; Zenophon's account of her history is said to be the "first extant . . . prose love story in European literature"	

WOMEN IN ANCIENT GREECE

The position of women in the Greek family is still debated; it varied depending on their status, the city-state, and the time in which they lived. What little we do know is based on records left by the upper class. Greek literature is plentiful in its misogynous tales, and Greek society, as evidenced by that literature, was clearly patriarchal. Yet many powerful female characters appear in the Greek myths.

Subservience and seclusion seemed to have been important ideals for real Greek women, except in Sparta, where women enjoyed great liberty. Spartan girls were educated with boys, could engage in physical training and competitions. Some won Olympic victories. Spartan women also had effective control over wealth.

However, the Western world based its classical ideal of woman on Athenian values, and in Athens women's lives were more circumscribed. Marriages tended to be arranged, with love hoped for as a result of a union. The purpose of marriage was procreation, and a male heir was considered essential. If no male children were produced, then an adult male was adopted who would be obliged to marry one of the daughters. A fertile wife was a most valuable asset, but control of the number of children prevented the family wealth from being spread too thin.

In the ancient world, families were relatively small and life expectancy was short, usually no more than 30 years. Between ages 14 and 17, women married husbands

Performing Arts/ Entertainment/ Sports	Religion/ Philosophy	Science/ Technology/ Discovery	Statecraft/ Military	
	of the pigeons nesting in it, and the sounds of the nearby brook		reign of King Esarhaddon (c. 681–669 B.C.)	**–700**
	When a scroll written like the Torah is found in the Holy Temple in Jerusalem, King Josiah sends sages to the prophetess Huldah to inquire whether to consider the book holy; with her approval, the book Deuteronomy is added to the Torah		The legendary rape of the Sabine women, c. 735–600 B.C. Romans invite neighboring tribes to celebrate the newly founded city so that the young men can carry off the local girls; this leads to war, then peace and intermarriage	
	Huldah, Jewish prophetess, wife of Shallum, and keeper of the royal wardrobe, makes an impressive prophecy to the king of Judah, Josiah, warning him that God's day of reckoning is approaching, delayed only by his piety and desire for reform, 624 B.C. (II Kings 22:14; II Chron. 34:22)	Acca Laurentia (fl. c. 634 B.C.), Roman nurse famed for healing abilities and for her beauty	Pheretima, wife of Battus, king of Cyrene and mother of Arcesilaus, comes to rule Cyrene, 624 B.C.; when her son is assassinated, she recovers the kingdom with the help of the king of Egypt; she causes all the assassins to be rounded up and crucified around the walls of Cyrene, and hangs about them the amputated breasts of their wives; it is said she was devoured by worms	**–650**
		The second wonder of the ancient world, the hanging gardens of Babylon (c. 605–562 B.C.), are built for Queen Amuhia by her husband, Nebuchadnezzar		**–600**

about 15 years older. In addition to disease and malnutrition, the high status given to male homosexuality and widespread sex with courtesans and slaves account for the low population.

A wife's duties entailed raising the children, directing domestic slaves, and running the household in her husband's absence. The purpose of the household and the Athenian wife was to meet the man's daily needs. Religious organizations did provide women with some respite from domestic seclusion. Groups dedicated to the worship of the mother-goddess existed in Greece and Asia during the Hellenic period.

Educated and artistic women came primarily from families that specialized in those fields. Literacy for women was a privilege; most girls found it enough to learn domestic skills from their mothers. Athenian women were not permitted to participate in government or war. They also were not allowed to act in plays; men took female roles. In Greek drama, however, women were often portrayed as strong and sometimes heroic. Centuries later, with an admittedly incomplete understanding of upper-class Greek women's lives and little knowledge about slaves' existences, we are left to ponder the ambivalent attitudes the Greeks seemed to have had for their women, and to wonder how much of that ambivalence has been passed down through the ages.

	General/ Context	Daily Life/ Customs/ Practices	Humanities/ Fine Arts	Occupations
–600		Nitocris, wife of a king of Assyria and contemporary of King Nebuchadnezzar (perhaps his wife), contributes much to the improvement of Babylon; inscription on her tomb reads that her successors would find treasure within if they were in need of money, but their labor would be ill repaid if they opened it without need; Cyrus opens it out of curiosity and finds within it only these words: "If thy avarice had not been insatiable, thou never wouldst have violated the monument of the dead"		
–550	Birth of Confucius (c. 551–479 B.C.), Chinese philosopher and founder of Confucianism Siddhartha Gautama Buddha (c. 563–c. 483 B.C.) establishes Buddhism Pythagoras of Samos, Greek mathematician and philosopher, flourishes, c. 550 B.C. First codes of law issued in China, 526 B.C.	Greek women c. 550 B.C. wear a stiff chiton, or tunic of wool, decorated with patterned ornamental bands, reaching down to the feet, girded at the waist; it is sewn, meant to be pulled on over the head; chest and shoulders are covered by a short jacket or kerchief or by pulling the extra fabric through the girdle and draping over the upper body; these are fastened with pins or brooches Vashti, wife of Ahasuerus, king of Persia, refuses to reveal herself wearing the crown royal to drunken guests, and is repudiated by her husband even though she has broken no law		In Babylonia, the earliest known female lawyer wins a case she pleads against her brother-in-law, c. 550 B.C.
–500	Age of Pericles (c. 495–429 B.C.); during this time, the Parthenon, a temple on the Athenian acropolis dedicated to the virgin goddess of wisdom and war, Athena, is rebuilt Steel smelted in India	Persian women c. 465 B.C. wear a veil over the mouth, still customary in Armenia today Early Greek vase painting c. 500 B.C. shows the Amazon warrior wearing a short tunic with long hose, high laced boots, and a Phrygian cap, carrying a battle-ax, small shield, and often a bow The Greek chiton c. 500 B.C. becomes softer and fuller, made of linen rather than wool; women also begin to wear the	Caryatids, columns carved in the shape of women that support a roof or beam on their heads, are meant to recall the defeat of Caria in which the men were killed and women enslaved Many of the tragedies written by Greek playwright Euripides (c. 484–406 B.C.) attack conventional Athenian attitudes, such as the subordination of Greek women (*Alcestis*) as well as foreign women (*Medea*)	

Performing Arts/ Entertainment/ Sports	Religion/ Philosophy	Science/ Technology/ Discovery	Statecraft/ Military	
				–600
	Esther (521–485 B.C.) is the biblical savior of the Israelites; she is venerated on Shabbat Shira The Buddha grants the request of his aunt Maha-prajapati to found an order of nuns that frees women from family life and gives them the same opportunity as men to pursue a spiritual path		Tomyris, queen of the Massagetae (a powerful tribe of the Araxes River region in southwest Asia), defeats the invading Cyrus the Great, ruler of the Persian Empire, 529 B.C.	**–550**
The legends of Clytemnestra and her daughter Iphigenia become the source material for the leading Greek dramatists Archaic Greek figurines show women workers led in song and dance by a female flautist; work songs become a particularly feminine genre in Europe and Africa over the next millennium Greek women in the early classical period are given athletic and gymnastic training to promote	*Rakshas*, Hindu evil spirits, haunt cemeteries, devour human flesh, and assume any shape at will; though some are hideous, others, especially female *rakshas*, entice humans by their beauty		Queen Artemisia I, ruler of Halicarnassus and Cos (a Greek city-state in southwestern Anatolia), assists Xerxes, ruler of the Persian Empire, in his attack on the Greeks by commanding a force of warships in the naval Battle of Salamis, c. 480 B.C.; Herodotus records that she was a valuable adviser to Xerxes Athaliah, queen of Judah, seizes control of the country upon the death of her son, 480 B.C.; she promotes the worship of	**–500**

General/Context	Daily Life/Customs/Practices	Humanities/Fine Arts	Occupations
−500	himation, a loose cloak that is sometimes drawn over the head	Corinna, fifth-century B.C. Greek poet of Tanagra in Boeotia, is considered a rival and critic of Pindar	
−450 Celts overrun the British Isles Greek historian Herodotus (c. 484–425 B.C.) composes his *History* Birth of Thucydides, Greek historian (c. 470–c. 400 B.C.) Peloponnesian Wars between Athens and Sparta begin 431 B.C. and end 404 B.C. with Spartan victory The Parthenon, a temple dedicated to the goddess Athena, is built, c. 447–432 B.C. Birth of Plato, Greek philosopher (427–347 B.C.)	Mistress of Athenian statesman Pericles, Aspasia of Miletus is famous for her intellectual achievements in a period when most Greek women were uneducated; hosting his political associates, she in effect conducts the first salons; tradition states that she was unsuccessfully prosecuted for impiety in 431 B.C. Greek women c. 450 B.C. bind their breasts with a wide band or girdle before dressing The oath of the Greek physician Hippocrates (Hippocratic Oath) states that "I will not give a pessary to a woman to cause abortion"	Highly cultivated Greek courtesans known as hetaerae are often freed women or women of free birth; among the most famous are two named Laïs; one was the most beautiful woman of Corinth; the other was so beautiful that the women of Thessaly pricked her to death; Phryne of Athens, a contemporary, was so wealthy that she offered to rebuild the walls of Thebes, only if she could inscribe upon them: "Alexander destroyed them, but Phryne the hetaera rebuilt them" The comedy *Lysistrata* by Greek playwright Aristophanes (c. 448 B.C.–c. 380 B.C.) is first performed c. 415 B.C.; its subject is a sexual strike by the women of Athens and Sparta to force their warring men to make peace	

LEARNED WOMEN IN ANTIQUITY AND THE MIDDLE AGES

Despite cultural restrictions on their education, women have taught and been taught for millennia. Many scholarly women became teachers and advocates for the education of women. In Egypt, a caste of scribe-priestesses served the goddess of the alphabet; others became the "mistress of the house of books." An ancient Vedic text refers to female scholars, poets, and seers who displayed their knowledge in public disquisitions. In Greece, women philosophers and scholars flourished, and some taught important Greek thinkers. Aristoclea taught the mathematician Pythagoras, who married Theano, a teacher who wrote about mathematics, physics, medicine, and child psychology at the school founded by her husband. Socrates studied with the Arcadian prophetess Diotima; both he and Plato learned from the renowned Aspasia of Miletus, Pericles's mistress, known as the first lady of Athens.

In the centuries following the fall of Rome, learned women were chiefly to be found in monasteries; the majority of secular women during the Middle Ages had little access to education.

Performing Arts/ Entertainment/ Sports	Religion/ Philosophy	Science/ Technology/ Discovery	Statecraft/ Military	
health and beauty; in Crete they take part in ritual bull leaping; Ionian women participate in boar hunts; Spartan girls train as athletes, wrestling naked with young men			Baal and tries to eliminate all her grandsons, who are rivals to the throne; one survives and leads a revolt against her; an opponent of the prophet Elijah, she is executed c. 437 B.C.	−500
			Lucretia, wife of Tarquinius Collatinus, is raped by Sextus, son of Tarquinius Superbus; after confessing the assault to her husband, she stabs herself to death, leading to a successful uprising against the Tarquins, 508 B.C.; the legend of the heroic Lucretia has undergone many incarnations in Western art, literature, and music	
Fifth-century Greek warrior-poet Telessilla rallies the women of the besieged city of Argos with war hymns and chants			Parysatis is the wife of Darius II Orchus, king of Persia, and mother of Artaxerxes Mnemon and Cyrus, whom she loves so dearly as to commit great injustices and barbarities to further his interests; poisons Statira, the wife of Artaxerxes, 423 B.C.	−450

Girls of noble birth were typically schooled by nuns in courtly manners, household management, and reading in their vernacular, though those who were expected to rule in their husbands' place usually studied with their brothers. In fact, until the 12th century and the rise of universities, which excluded women entirely, aristocratic girls and boys received a comparable education. In the later Middle Ages, authors of books on the proper upbringing of girls advised that only those who were destined to be nuns should be educated. Nevertheless, some women of the rising middle class were taught to read and write by nuns or male tutors.

Women in convents, on the other hand, who were free from the demands of child rearing and running a home, in many ways lived lives of sanctioned independence. They were the great teachers of women during the Middle Ages. As nurturers of intellectual communities they kept alive the arts, sciences, and the study of languages at a time when many believed that women's mental capacity was greatly inferior to men's.

	General/ Context	Daily Life/ Customs/ Practices	Humanities/ Fine Arts	Occupations
−400	Socrates (c. 470–399 B.C.), Athenian philosopher, is tried, accused of corruption, and condemned to poison himself, 399 B.C. The Greek philosopher Plato founds the Academy in Athens, 387 B.C.; it continues as a philosophical school until suppressed by the Emperor Justinian in 529 A.D. Mayan astronomy at its peak; accurate calendar calculated, c. 400–100 B.C. Birth of Aristotle (384–322 B.C.), Greek philosopher The umbrella is first recorded in Greece, 340 B.C.	Greek women c. 400 B.C. wear softer chitons made of linen, crepe, byssus, or cotton, arranging the thin fabric in narrow pleats and folds produced by stitching or ironing; the himation is worn over head and shoulders Though the citizenship laws of Athens restrict women's freedom in social activities, citizen-women take active part in such matters as making wills and family councils The law of *epikleroi* puts girls of 14—the age at which many are expected to marry—in legal possession of their property Xenophon (430?–?354 B.C.) comments that Greek girls are treated less generously than boys, brought up on a diet low in meat and only occasionally given well-watered wine; though they are taught to read and write, they are generally less well educated than their brothers	Legendary princess of Colchis in Asia Minor and priestess of the goddess Hecate, Medea is said to have fallen in love with the Greek hero Jason, assisting him in stealing the Golden Fleece; committing several murders on the way, she returns to Corinth with Jason and marries him; when he later repudiates her in order to make a political marriage to a younger woman, she slays the bride and her own two children, escaping to Athens in a winged chariot drawn by dragons	Middle-class Greek women work in the house, overseeing slaves, working wool, mixing flour, and weaving; poor citizen-women hold a privileged place in the marketplace, where they sell garlands, ribbons, and food, or paint vases, or run inns and taverns; older women act as midwives, carry messages, and take part in funerals as professional mourners
−350	Alexander the Great (356–323 B.C.) succeeds his father, Philip of Macedon, in 336 B.C. as leader of the Greek confederation; he begins a career of conquest that extends Greek civilization eastward as far as India, 336 B.C.	Thucydides, in his *History of the Peloponnesian War,* points out that the wives of defeated warriors are sold into slavery Sisygambis, mother of Persian commander Darius, commits suicide upon hearing of Alexander the Great's death (323 B.C.), unwilling to survive so generous an enemy		
−300	Completion of the Colossus of Rhodes, one of the Seven Wonders of the World, 280 B.C.	By the late Zhou period in China, women occupy no political roles, though some legends and historical documents suggest that women were thought to		

Performing Arts/ Entertainment/ Sports	Religion/ Philosophy	Science/ Technology/ Discovery	Statecraft/ Military	
Greek playwright Aristophanes satirizes women's assumption of male roles in his comedy *Ecclesiazonsae* (*The Congresswomen*)	The cult of Cybele, the great mother-goddess of Phrygia, comes to Greece; she is worshiped in ecstatic rites, including a ritual bath in the blood of a sacrificed bull; her worship is brought to Rome in 204 B.C.

In his *Republic*, Plato recommends that women be given the same training as men, including gymnastics, music, wrestling, and the arts of war, in order that male and female "guardians" might share state duties equally; he models his plan on an idealized view of contemporary Spartan customs | | Artemisia II, queen of Caria (?–350 B.C.), assumes the rule of the country in her own right after the death of her husband in 352 B.C.; famed as a botanist and medical researcher, she is a powerful political leader, suppressing a revolt by the inhabitants of the island of Rhodes

Orchomenus revolts against Thebes; following a siege, all the males executed, women and children sold, 363 B.C. | **−400** |
| | Byzantines adopt the crescent symbol of the goddess Hecate as the symbol of their empire, c. 340 B.C.

Aristotle advises abortion for parents with too many children and argues that "neglect of an effective birth control policy is a never failing source of poverty which in turn is the parent of revolution and crime" (*Politics*, c. 335 B.C.) | | Ada, queen of Caria in southern Anatolia, assumes the rule of the city-state Halicarnassus after the death of her husband-brother the king, 344 B.C.; in 341 B.C. she loses her position to her younger brother, but in 334 B.C. she returns to power after making an alliance with the invading Alexander the Great

When Macedonia's regent is overthrown by Cassander, he seizes Olympias, mother of Alexander the Great, and has her executed, 316 B.C.; he then marries Alexander's half sister, with whom he rules for almost 20 years | **−350** |
| | According to Greek legend, Philomela, daughter of the king of Attica, is brought by her brother-in-law Tereus to visit her sister Procne; on the way, | | Arsinoe II (316–271 B.C.), daughter of Ptolemy I of Egypt, marries King Lysimachus of Thrace, c. 300 B.C.; in an attempt to secure the in- | **−300** |

	General/ Context	Daily Life/ Customs/ Practices	Humanities/ Fine Arts	Occupations
–300	First Punic War 264–241 B.C. Sarmatian jewelry spreads in southern Russia, c. 300–100 B.C.	have ties to the supernatural, which might have allowed them behind-the-scenes political and social power In Greek vase painting c. 300 B.C., women are represented as tumblers wearing loincloths, playing stringed instruments, attending and serving at banquets Public calamities in Rome require that the goddess Juno be propitiated by 27 virgins or married women; in 207 B.C. and again in 214, unmarried girls in long gowns sing in Juno's honor; after a great fire in A.D. 64, married women are called upon to perform similar rites Statira, daughter of Darius and wife of Alexander the Great, is murdered after her husband's death by his other wife, Roxana, also a daughter of Darius		
–250	Egyptian medical science, supported by Ptolemy IV, flourishes in Alexandria Second Punic War, 218–201 B.C. Great Wall of China unified under Ch'un dynasty, 204 B.C.		Married to Ptolemy III of Egypt, Berenice (273–221 B.C.) dedicates a lock of her hair to her husband's safe return from war in Syria; her lock is commemorated in poems by Callimachus, Catullus, and, in altered form, in Alexander Pope's *Rape of*	

ARISTOTLE'S VIEW OF WOMEN

The Greek philosopher Aristotle (384–324 B.C.) was Plato's most brilliant student. His biological theories have influenced the course of Western scientific inquiry up to modern times. For example, his ideas about conception and embryology endured until the invention of the microscope in 1665 enabled scientists to observe the stages of the embryo's development. His description of women as defective or incomplete men, as quasi monsters, in fact, is still reflected in Freud's late-19th-century psychoanalytical theories about female sexuality.

Consistent with his theory that women were physically and psychologically incomplete, Aristotle maintained that men's superiority lay in their greater size, strength, agility, and power of intellect. Females, he believed, were mere matter; males were spirit and mind. Pregnant women were merely vessels, or pas-

	he rapes her, cuts out her tongue, and imprisons her, telling Procne that her sister is dead; Philomela sends a message woven in cloth to Procne and both revenge themselves upon Tereus by serving him the flesh of his little boy; all three turn into birds—Philomela a sparrow, Procne a nightingale, and Tereus a hoopoe; the story is retold by Ovid in *Metamorphoses*		heritance of her own children, she has his heir murdered; she flees to Macedonia in the resulting strife and there holds the city of Cassandrea until she is exiled to Samothrace by the new king of Macedonia; she eventually escapes to Egypt, where she marries her brother Ptolemy II (276 B.C.), ruling jointly with him from c. 276 B.C. until her death **−300**
	Sul, or Sulis, the Celtic goddess identified with Minerva (or Athena), is the patron of the city of Aquae Sulis, modern Bath in England; the baths remain in use until at least the fourth century A.D.		Bartare, "candace of Meroë" ("candace" is not a name, but a corruption of the Meroitic word for "queen"), is the first of the ruling queens of Meroë (in Nubia); she rules from c. 284 B.C. through 277 B.C.
	The goddess of the hearth, Vesta, is worshiped in every Roman household, but her official worship is carried out by six priestesses sworn to her service for 30 years, who tend a fire that is never allowed to go out; the Vestal Virgins served under a high priest, and the punishment for losing their virginity was to be buried alive; these practices continued into the fourth century A.D.		
			Laodice is the sister and wife of Antiochus II, king of Syria; by elaborate pretense, she places her son on the throne in 246 B.C. after she murders Antiochus; put to death by Ptolemy Euergetes of Egypt; city of Laodicea named for her **−250**

sive incubators, for the embryo, formed from the male seed alone.

Aristotle regarded women as unfit for freedom or political action, passive by nature, and subject to the rule of their husbands. He took for granted that women's proper sphere was the household; that they might assume political leadership was out of the question. Pointing to the fall of Sparta as proof of women's baneful influence on public affairs, he attributed the city's demise to the excessive freedom—in education, physical training, and civic responsibilities shared with men—enjoyed by Spartan women. The public/private polarization by which he justified withholding citizenship from Athenian women provided a rationale for maintaining women's second-class status in the West for many centuries.

	General/ Context	Daily Life/ Customs/ Practices	Humanities/ Fine Arts	Occupations
−250			*the Lock;* at her husband's death, she rules Egypt with her son Ptolemy IV until he has her assassinated When her husband King Syphax of Numidia is defeated by the army of Scipio Africanus, Sophonisba (or Saphanba'al) takes poison to save herself from being taken captive to Rome, 203 B.C.; her tragedy has been told by Livy, painted by Mantegna and Rembrandt, and dramatized by Corneille	
−221	Ch'in dynasty in China (221–207 B.C.)			
−206	Han dynasty in China (206 B.C.–A.D. 220)			
−200	Cleansing of the Great Temple by the Maccabees and restoration of Judaism in Jerusalem, 165 B.C.; the event is commemorated by Jews as the Feast of Dedication, or Hanukkah Manufacture of paper in China	Roman women march on the Senate to persuade the senators to repeal the Oppian Law, which forbids Roman women to wear jewels, purple or gold embroidery, and to drive in carriages, 195 B.C.; originally passed during the Punic wars as an economic measure, the law is still in force after the defeat of Hannibal in 202 B.C., but does not apply to men; the appeal is won by L. Valerius, who argues, "Give the women their baubles; these will satisfy their trivial minds and keep them from interfering in more serious matters"		Chinese women of the Han period work chiefly in the household, responsible for silk production, crop raising, and animal husbandry
−150	Third Punic War 149–146 B.C.	Roman women c. 150 B.C. wear the *tunica recta,* one piece of material wrapped around the body reaching down to the feet, usually fastened at the waist with a girdle; the undergarment is a long tight-sleeved tunic; they sometimes wear a *palla,* a mantle draped in various ways	Cornelia, daughter of Scipio Africanus, is known as the mother of the Gracchi, a model Roman matron; at the death of her sons, she retires to Misenum, where her home becomes a center of culture, c. 123 B.C.	
−100		Clodia, mistress of the Roman poet Catullus, is the subject of many of his poems, in which she appears as Lesbia, c. 60 B.C.; she then becomes mistress	Roman artist Iaia of Cyzicus is known for her carving and painting on ivory as well as for a self-portrait; she surpasses the most famous painters of	According to a contemporary account, Japanese women divers, able to hold their breath for up to three minutes, re-

Performing Arts/ Entertainment/ Sports	Religion/ Philosophy	Science/ Technology/ Discovery	Statecraft/ Military	
				−250
				−221
				−206
	Hebrew legend holds that Lilith was created simultaneously with Adam; refusing to be subordinated to him, she was expelled from Eden into a region of the air; Arabic legend adds that she married the devil and became the mother of evil spirits; because she is said to be dangerous to children and pregnant women, superstitious Jews lay coins inscribed with the names of Adam and Eve and the words "Avaunt thee, Lilith" in the room occupied by their wives		Lu Hou, empress of China, wife of Gao Zu, the first emperor of the Han dynasty, becomes the real ruler at his death, even though their son is nominally emperor; she rules through a succession of child emperors until rival factions have her killed in 180 B.C. Queen Shanakdakhete rules Meroë, 177–155 B.C.	**−200**
	When a Vestal Virgin is killed by lightning in Rome, a number of virgins are executed for unchastity; the Sibylline oracle orders the live burial of a Greek and Gallic couple		After the death of her husband Demetrius II Nicator, Cleopatra Thea, queen of the Seleucid Empire of Syria, rules the empire jointly with first one son, 125 B.C., then another, until her death in 120 B.C.	**−150**
	When the Sibylline Books, or prophecies, are destroyed in Rome, copies are made to replace them, 83 B.C.; these are collections of inspired		Salome Alexandra becomes ruler of the Maccabees following the death of her husband, King Alexander Jannaeus, 76 B.C.; she is proclaimed	**−100**

General/ Context	Daily Life/ Customs/ Practices	Humanities/ Fine Arts	Occupations
–100	of the politician Caelius; her sexual indiscretions served as an unfailing source of gossip in Rome	her day, working faster and receiving higher prices than her top competitors	trieve food from the sea floor
	Roman ladies of rank c. 60 B.C. keep several slave girls to dress their hair in complicated fashions, interlacing the parted, curled, waved, and braided hair with ribbons, fillets, hair nets, and diadems; simpler styles consist of parted hair gathered in a knot at the neck in the Greek fashion	Chinese author and civil servant Liu Hsiang writes the first collection of biographies of women, *Biographies of Famous Women*, 80 B.C.	

WOMEN IN ANCIENT TIBET

Ancient Chinese historiographers describe a perhistoric "women's kingdom" in southeastern Tibet where women held political power with male warriors and servants were subordinate. Greek legends include another women's kingdom in western Tibet, the Amazon land that even Alexander the Great could not conquer.

By the time of recorded history, these vanished matriarchal societies had left a tradition of maternal influence over Tibetan emperors. In ordinary families, women were in charge of material resources and decisions required their consent. Ignoring marital fidelity, they enjoyed the same sexual freedom as men and included illegitimate offspring in their families. Divorce was frequent and could be initiated by either party. Property was divided equally; male

<table>
<tr><td></td><td>utterances by Greek prophetesses known as Sibyls; they were kept by special priests and consulted only by order of the Roman Senate in times of great need; last consulted in the fourth century A.D., they were soon afterward ordered burned

Increased participation by women in Buddhism contributes to the positive view of women in the Mahayana movement, which recognizes the spiritual potential of nuns and laywomen</td><td></td><td>king herself and her eldest son is appointed high priest; favors the sect of the Pharisees, bringing the founders of rabbinic Judaism to power, 79 B.C. she rules until her death in 67 B.C. —100</td></tr>
</table>

king herself and her eldest son is appointed high priest; favors the sect of the Pharisees, bringing the founders of rabbinic Judaism to power, 79 B.C. she rules until her death in 67 B.C. **−100**

Queen Amanerinas rules Meroë from c. 99 B.C. to c. 84 B.C.; a dedicatory inscription to her and her son survive on the Great Stele in a Meroitic temple

Livia (56 B.C.–A.D. 29), wife of Emperor Augustus and mother, by her first husband, of Emperor Tiberius; a woman of intelligence and power, she was given the title Julia Augusta by her husband's will; she exerted considerable political influence until her death; her house, famous for its murals, still stands on the Palatine hill in Rome

Monima, native of Salonica, is ordered killed by Mithridates the Great along with all his other wives lest they fall into the hands of Lucullus, his conqueror

Phaedyma is the wife of Smerdis the Magian and the daughter of Olanes, one of the seven Persian lords who conspired against Smerdis; she discovers that her husband is not a son of Cyrus the Great because his ears have been cut off by Cambyses

---

children went with their fathers while female children went with their mothers. Remarriage for both parties was the norm.

The dominant religion of the Tibetans, Mahayana Buddhism, which emphasizes female symbols, considers women to have a spiritual potential, which the male needs. It also asserts that in Buddhism natural differences between male and female are irrelevant. Buddhist nuns, excluded from the formal study of Buddhist philosophy, were under the supervision of monks, but they excelled in tantric practice. Nuns were advisers to nobility and to cabinet ministers. Many became famous for their spiritual achievements.

	General/ Context	Daily Life/ Customs/ Practices	Humanities/ Fine Arts	Occupations
−50	Jesus of Nazareth is born c. 4 B.C. Introduction of the Julian calendar, 46 B.C. Assassination of Julius Caesar, 44 B.C. Octavian (Augustus) becomes the first emperor of Rome, 27 B.C. Virgil (70–19 B.C.), Roman poet, writes the great Roman epic the *Aeneid* between 30 B.C. and 19 B.C.	Calpurnia, wife of Julius Caesar, warns her husband against attending the fateful meeting of the Senate on the Ides of March, according to Plutarch; she is remembered for the warmth of her devotion to her husband Death of Fulvia, 40 B.C., an ambitious woman of no integrity, who participated in the political disputes between her third husband, Mark Antony, and Octavian; Cicero singled her out in his speeches against Antony and she is said to have advocated his assassination; it is reported that, when his head was brought to her after his murder, she drove a needle through its tongue in revenge for his nasty comments about Antony in his *Philippics*		

Performing Arts/ Entertainment/ Sports	Religion/ Philosophy	Science/ Technology/ Discovery	Statecraft/ Military
			Ptolemy XIII and his sister Cleopatra become co-rulers of Egypt, 51 B.C.; he deposes her in 49 B.C. **−50**
			Cleopatra is restored to the Egyptian throne by Julius Caesar, 48 B.C.; she bears him a son and lives in Rome until his death
			Cleopatra rules Egypt with her son, Ptolemy XV, 44 B.C.
			Octavia, sister of Octavian, is divorced by Mark Antony, finally destroying relations between the two leaders, 32 B.C.
			Cleopatra and Roman leader Mark Antony begin a love affair that leads to Antony's unpopularity in Rome; following the defeat of their forces in the Battle of Actium (31 B.C.) and Mark Antony's suicide, Cleopatra kills herself by the bite of an asp, a snake sacred to the Egyptian sun-god, 30 B.C.
			Cheng-Chuan, empress of China during the Han dynasty, is the de facto ruler of the empire, first with her husband, Emperor Yuan Ti, and then with a succession of heirs from 48 B.C. until her death in A.D. 13
			Queen Anula assumes the throne of Sri Lanka upon the death of her husband in 47 B.C. and rules first through a succession of lovers and then on her own until succeeded by her son, King Kutakanna Tissa, in 42 B.C.
			Queen Amanishakete rules Meroë from c. 41 B.C. to 12 B.C.; her reign is marked by prosperity, an extensive building program, and widespread trade and iron working
			Nominally emperor of China, Ch'eng Ti's domain is actually ruled by his mother, widow of Emperor Yuan Ti, with

General/ Context	Daily Life/ Customs/ Practices	Humanities/ Fine Arts	Occupations
–50			
–10			
1	According to the New Testament, Sapphira and her husband, Ananias of Jerusalem, are struck dead for lying about the amount of the proceeds from the sale of a piece of land they donated to the church; their names come to signify, respectively, a female and a male liar (Acts 5) Roman Emperor Augustus attempts to prevent adultery by depriving the guilty of half their inheritance and prohibiting them from marrying their lovers		

Performing Arts/ Entertainment/ Sports	Religion/ Philosophy	Science/ Technology/ Discovery	Statecraft/ Military	
			her nephew Wang Mang, c. 37 B.C.	**−50**
			Cleopatra of Cyrene, daughter of Mark Antony and Queen Cleopatra VII (69–30 B.C.), assumes the rule of Cyrene in Lybia, 33 B.C.; she is deposed when Octavian (Augustus) triumphs in the battles of 31 B.C.	
			Mariamne, daughter of Alexander, second wife of Herod the Great, and mother of Alexander, Aristobulus, and two daughters, attempts to murder her husband and is executed for it in 28 B.C.; Herod's great remorse over the execution drives him insane for a time and is later commemorated in Lord Byron's *Herod's Lament*	
			Amanitere, queen of Meroë, begins her joint rule with King Natakamani, 12 B.C.–A.D. 12; they oversee the greatest building program known in ancient Meroë, including the restoration of the great temples of Amon in the principal cities of Meroë and Napata	**−10**
	According to the New Testament, Salome, daughter of Herodias, pleases her stepfather, Herod Antipas, governor of Judaea, so well with her dancing that he promises her "whatsoever she would ask"; following her mother's advice, she demands the head of John the Baptist, imprisoned for denouncing Herodias's divorce and remarriage, on a platter (Matt. 14:6-11)			**1**
	Mary, a chaste Jewish girl betrothed to the carpenter Joseph, is said to have been and remained a virgin before and after the birth of her son, Jesus of Nazareth; she later bears four sons and at least two daughters to Joseph			
	Anna, daughter of Phanuel, bears witness with			

	General/ Context	Daily Life/ Customs/ Practices	Humanities/ Fine Arts	Occupations
1				
25				
30				
40	The Romans establish the trading center of Londinium (later London), c. A.D. 43 St. Paul writes his earliest Epistles (c. 47–49)	St. Paul instructs husbands: "Let your women keep silence in the churches: for it is not permitted unto them to speak; but they are commanded to be under obedience. . . . And if they will learn anything, let them ask their husbands at home: for it is a shame for a woman to speak in the church" (I Cor. 14:34-35)	Pan Chao (c. 50–112), a celebrated woman scholar, is historian to the court of Emperor Ho, a poet laureate, and teaches Empress Teng; her *Lessons for Women* urges humility, subservience, housewifely duties and avoidance of lustful intimacy in marriage	
50		A professional poisoner, Lucusta lives in Rome, where she is hired by Agrippina to poison Claudius and by Nero to poison Britannicus; she is put to death by Emperor Galba; her name has come to signify a person who murders those whom she is supposed to look after		

Performing Arts/ Entertainment/ Sports	Religion/ Philosophy	Science/ Technology/ Discovery	Statecraft/ Military	
	Simeon, her husband, to the unborn Messiah carried by Mary			1
			Roman aristocrat Agrippina I (c. 13 B.C.?–A.D. 33) blames Tiberius for her husband Germanicus's death and is the center of a group opposing him; he has her arrested and banished to Pandateria, where she dies of starvation, A.D. 29	25
	Photina, the first-century biblical "woman of Samaria," is martyred with her sons in Carthage The legendary St. Martha (first century), a friend of Christ, is venerated as a preacher and dragon killer at Tarascon, France Crucifixion of Christ; on his way, St. Veronica offers comfort; an image of his face is said to have appeared on the handkerchief with which she wiped his brow; she ends her days as a recluse in Soulac, France		Vietnamese sisters Trung Nhi and Trung Trac organize a revolution against their Chinese overlords; they succeed in ejecting the Chinese and rule as co-queens of an independent Vietnam from A.D. 30 to A.D. 42; that year a massive Chinese force invades and the sisters, unable to defend their country, kill themselves; they are still venerated in temples in Vietnam	30
	Phoebe, a deaconess from Cenchrae, is the bearer of St. Paul's Epistle to the Romans and seems to have given financial support to the Christian community in Corinth		Agrippina II (15–59), empress of Rome; at one time exiled, she returns to marry her uncle Claudius, emperor of Rome, in A.D. 49; she later has him killed in order to make her son, Nero, emperor, who in turn has her murdered Messalina the Elder, wife of Roman Emperor Claudius, plots with her lover to overthrow him; she is put to death when her numerous plots and infidelities are exposed	40
Greek writer Athenaeus records 3000 hetaerae (educated courtesans) working as musicians in Athens	The son of Euphemia, first-century queen of Ethiopia, is said to have been raised from the dead by St. Matthew Philo Judaeus describes a Jewish monastic community of "aged virgins," living an ascetic life near Alexandria, who study philosophy and the Scrip-	Mary the Jewess is an early alchemist in Alexandria, working on the chemistry of metals; devises apparatus for distillation and sublimation, invents the water bath, which is said to be named after her (not the Virgin Mary); the *bain-marie*, known to every domestic cook, is a dish of hot wa-	Octavia, daughter of Emperor Claudius and Messalina, marries Nero, A.D. 53; they divorce in A.D. 62 so he can marry Poppaea; he first banishes her, then has her executed on a trumped-up charge of treason	50

	General/ Context	Daily Life/ Customs/ Practices	Humanities/ Fine Arts	Occupations
50				
60	Flavius Josephus, Jewish general and historian, writes *History of the Jewish War*, A.D. 68 First Jewish Revolt (66–70) against the Romans in Judaea Boadicea (or Boudicca), queen of the East Anglia Celtic tribe the Iceni, rises in rebellion against Roman annexation of her kingdom, A.D. 61; she sacks Colchester, London, and Verulamium before she is defeated by General Suetonius Paulinus, and takes poison	Messalina the Younger, wife of Emperor Nero of Rome, unlike many of her predecessors a woman of reasonably good character, holds a high position in Roman society after her husband's death		
70	Destruction of Jerusalem by Rome Fall of Masada (Israel), A.D. 73			Roman scholar Pliny the Elder mentions several Greek women painters, including Timarete, Eirene, Kalypso, Aristarete, Iaia, and Olympias, none of whose works survive

ANCIENT WOMEN WARRIORS

From myth and earliest antiquity, some women have excelled in that traditionally masculine pursuit, warfare. Greek myth tells of Athena, goddess of war, a woman "born of no woman," springing instead from Zeus's forehead, to lead men into battle.

In the era between myth and history numerous stories arise of the Amazons, a society of women warriors, thought by the Greek historian Herodotus to have come from Asia and to have laid siege to Athens twice. The Amazons were said to need to kill a man before they could marry, keep only their female babies, and amputate their right breasts to facilitate their use of bow and arrow.

Roman accounts tell of warrior women like Zenobia of Palmyra and Boadicea of the Iceni of Britain, women who fought against Rome. Queen Boadicea led a revolt in Britain against the Roman procurator who had assaulted her and raped her daughters. Defeated in A.D. 62, she avoided the humiliation of marching in a Roman triumphal parade by taking poison.

Just before the time of Boadicea, two Vietnamese sisters, Trung Trac and Trung Nhi, led the first of many Vietnamese uprisings against the Chinese. Trung Trac, a titled widow whose husband was murdered by the Chinese, was herself raped by them. Another legendary woman fighter arose during that

	tures with the same dedication as men; they are the earliest examples of permanent sexual asceticism among women in antiquity, apart from Rome's Vestal Virgins	ter in which pans containing the substance to be heated are placed	**50**

Empress Poppaea Sabina, murdered by her husband, Roman emperor Nero
Photograph courtesy Württembergische Landesbibliothek Stuttgart

60

Berenice (28–after 75) becomes the mistress of Emperor Vespasian's son Titus and supports the Romans in the Jewish War A.D. 67; he dismisses her when he becomes emperor in A.D. 79; daughter of Herod Agrippa, she is present at St. Paul's defense before her father

Poppaea Sabina (d. A.D. 65) becomes Emperor Nero's mistress, then his wife in A.D. 62; Jewish historian Flavius Josephus says that she had an interest in Judaism, though not Jewish herself; she is accused by Tacitus of influencing Nero to murder his mother and divorce Octavia

Dowager empress during the Eastern Han dynasty, Tou Hsien rules China from A.D. 88 to A.D. 97

Queen Amanikhatashan of Meroë begins her 32-year reign in A.D. 62

70

rebellion: the pregnant Phung Thi Chinh, who stopped fighting just long enough to give birth, strapped her baby to her back, and hacked her way out of danger. The third-century virgin warrior Trieu Au, sometimes called the "Joan of Arc of Vietnam," raised thousands of troops again to fight the Chinese.

In Africa, where traditions of women leaders were not uncommon, 15th-century Queen Amina led widespread conquests in what is now Nigeria. Perhaps best known to Westerners was Queen Jinga (Nzinga), who lived from 1582 to 1663. She fought the Portuguese slavers and managed to live a long, independent, warlike life. She relished her ferocious reputation, executing and cannibalizing captives and encouraging infanticide to keep her followers unfettered by domestic obligations. The 19th-century English explorer Richard Burton testified to the endurance of the African woman warrior tradition in the modern world: he witnessed in battle the king of Dahomey's fabled all-woman armies—who were said to be unusually muscular and to fight better than the men.

These fierce women, and many others whose deeds have gone unrecorded, created a fighting tradition that would be upheld by women in the ages to follow.

General/ Context	Daily Life/ Customs/ Practices	Humanities/ Fine Arts	Occupations
100 Composition of books of the New Testament, canonized as sacred by the fourth century Trade begins along the Old Silk Road between China and Europe	Romans introduce small, individual wedding cakes as fertility symbols to be thrown at the bride by the guests Appearance of *The Kama Sutra*, an account of the art of erotic love by the Indian sage Vatsyayana Roman women, like their husbands, sleep with their clothes on: loincloth, brassiere, corset, tunic, and sometimes a mantle; when they arise, they put on slippers and a robe to await their bath		
110	Plotina Pompeia, wife of the Roman emperor Trajan, accompanies him through the Parthian wars, sharing both his triumphs and his responsibilities, c. A.D. 116		
120 Roman historian Suetonius composes *Lives of the Caesars,* A.D. 121			
130 Second Jewish Revolt (132–135) against the Romans results in banishment of Jews from Jerusalem		Five of Julia Babilla's epigrams are carved on the Colossus of Memnon	

WOMEN IN ANCIENT INDIAN SOCIETY

Between 200 B.C. and A.D. 528, the decentralization of authority in the Indian states revolutionized Indian society. In a process similar to feudalization in Europe, the Brahmins and Kshatriyas (the two highest Hindu castes) obtained legal power over peasants and aboriginal peoples. The Laws of Manu, particularly those pertaining to governing castes and women, reduced women to a heretofore unknown subservience.

Manu, the mythic supreme law giver of Hindu society, maintained that a woman was legally dependent upon and subordinate to the adult males in her family. Denouncing romantic love, Manu stipulated that women must submit themselves to marriages that they could not revoke, although a husband could cast off his wife if she refused to obey him. Women could not remarry if widowed, and initially had no property rights, although customs evolved that allowed

Performing Arts/ Entertainment/ Sports	Religion/ Philosophy	Science/ Technology/ Discovery	Statecraft/ Military	
	St. Priscilla establishes the first Roman catacomb, c. A.D. 98		Roman Emperor Domitian, a notable persecutor of Christians, is assassinated by his wife on account of his cruelty, A.D. 96	**90**
	Beruyah is an influential first-century Talmudic scholar whose opinions on matters of the law are still respected by scholars of the 20th century Dorcas, or Tabitha, an early convert to Christianity who lived outside Jerusalem, is said to have been raised from the dead by St. Peter; Dorcas Societies are named after her The *Acts of Thecla* tells of a woman from Iconium in Asia Minor who, renouncing marriage and sexuality and following the Apostle Paul, becomes a Christian teacher; the biography is regarded by some as legitimizing women's ability to teach and baptize			**100**
	Queen Helena is recorded in the Talmud as having set a legal precedent regarding the height of the *sukka*, a hut built for the harvest festival *Sukkoth*			**110**
				120
				130

women at least partially to maintain themselves, if they had borne no sons. The law sanctioned suttee, or widow burning.

By A.D. 500, women's only instruction came in the form of two epic poems, the *Mahabharata* and the *Ramayana,* moral stories central to Indian culture that represent all the tribes and peoples of the subcontinent. The *Mahabharata* tells of a power struggle between two families over land rights, and asserts that a woman's dharma, or duty, is to serve her husband, even to the point of death. The *Ramayana* is a searing tale of wifely submission, loyalty, and chastity that idealizes female courage and long-suffering. The principles of Hinduism together with the doctrines and beliefs about a woman's place became firmly entrenched both in Indian society and in the minds of the women who heard these poems repeated all their lives long.

	General/ Context	Daily Life/ Customs/ Practices	Humanities/ Fine Arts	Occupations
140	Rome destroys Carthage in A.D. 46			
160	Great Plague throughout Roman Empire, A.D. 167	Faustina the Elder, wife of Emperor Antoninus Pius, and her daughter Faustina, wife of Emperor Marcus Aurelius, are reputed on little evidence to have been faithless and promiscuous; Faustina the Younger accompanied her husband on his northern campaigns, and in his *Meditations* he expresses real love for her		
165	A Jewish revolt led by Judas Maccabaeus frees the Temple in Jerusalem from the Syrians in A.D. 165			
190	Tertullian (Quintus Septimius Florens Tertullianus), an early Church father, converts to Christianity; a prototypical misogynist, he admonishes women, "And do you not know that you are Eve? God's sentence hangs still over all your sex and His punishment weighs down upon you. You are the devil's gateway"	The Lex Julia, A.D. 198, stipulates that a wife may not bring criminal accusations of adultery against her husband, even though men have this privilege; at the same time, women found guilty of adultery lose half their dowries, a third of their estates, and must be banished to an island		
200		The Germanic Goths initiate the tradition of "best man," taking their best fighters to abduct brides from neighboring villages Though formerly the only recognized family relationship had been established through the male line, Roman law now recognizes descent through the female line, even beyond legitimate marriage The Roman custom of marriage *cum manu,* transferring the woman from the hands of her father to the hands of her husband, is replaced by marriage *sine manu,* in which the woman is made the ward of a legitimate guardian; such guardians become		

Performing Arts/ Entertainment/ Sports	Religion/ Philosophy	Science/ Technology/ Discovery	Statecraft/ Military	
			Empress Liang rules China as regent for a succession of child emperors from A.D. 144 through A.D. 150	**140**
Gladiatrices—female gladiators—fight both publicly and privately for the entertainment of Roman spectators; combats in which women fight in companies against each other or individually against dwarfs are eventually banned	Roman matron Pudentiana is known for protecting the poor who buried martyred Christians			**160**
				165
			Pimiku, the first known ruler of Japan, holds power until her death in A.D. 247; though she never married, she has a daughter in 234; she is reputed to have built the Shrine of Ise, the most important Shinto shrine in Japan	**190**
	St. Perpetua of Carthage is martyred by the Romans along with a slave girl, St. Felicity, and four male companions, A.D. 203; the *Passion of Ss. Perpetua and Felicity,* written in part by Perpetua herself, is one of the most impressive authentic narratives of the early Christian martyrs Apuleius tells the myth of Psyche ("soul"), beloved of the disguised god Cupid (Eros), who bids her never to seek his identity; one night, overcome by curiosity, she takes a lamp to look at him and, realizing by his wings who he must be, trembles, spilling a drop of hot oil on his shoulder; he flees and she searches for him, becom-		Empress Jingo-kogo (c. 169–269) becomes regent of Japan at her husband's death; during her 69-year regency, she sends a vast fleet to invade Korea; the Koreans capitulate immediately and offer tribute; she fights off all challenges to her rule	**200**

General/ Context	Daily Life/ Customs/ Practices	Humanities/ Fine Arts	Occupations
200	less and less powerful as gradually married women with children are no longer required to have one, even to draft a will Galen identifies the ovaries, calling them "female testicles"		
220	Six Dynasties period in China, 220–589; rise and fall of 29 significant dynasties in all, but six successive dynasties had their capital at Nanking		
240			

WOMEN'S POSITION IN EARLY CHRISTIANITY

Christian belief is based on the life and teachings of Jesus of Nazareth as they are represented in the Gospels of the New Testament of the Bible. Jesus, raised as a Jew, preached the equality of all souls before God, rejecting the traditional view of women as intellectually and spiritually inferior to men. He spoke directly to women about religious doctrine, often teaching through parables in which women could see themselves, or using women to illustrate his teachings. Women in the Gospels served as important models for women in later centuries.

In the years immediately following Jesus' death, women acted as men's equals in the burgeoning Christian Church. The Acts and Epistles of the New Testament make many references to women as important leaders and evangelists for the new religion. In the communal life and the consequent struggle to keep Christianity alive, both men and women were recognized as having gifts of the Holy Spirit necessary for the success of the community. St. Thecla of Ioconium, for example, was an apostle, an ordained preacher of the Gospel, and a companion of St. Paul of Tarsus.

Stories of women saints and martyrs offer some of the most powerful images from the early days of Christianity. Until the fourth century A.D., more than 100,000 Christians were persecuted by the Roman Empire, which tried to squelch the new cult that taught pacifism at a time when Rome was recruiting soldiers. Martyrs like Saints Catherine, Barbara, Margaret, and Perpetua of Carthage became models for Christian humility and strength, illustrating a way to salvation available to all.

Although early Christianity was relatively egalitarian, after its institutionalization it grew to restrict women's participation and behavior. The Christian Church structured itself on the Jewish synagogue, which was governed by groups of elected male elders. The new religion adopted the patriarchal traditions of

200

ing the slave of Venus, who treats her cruelly; eventually she is reunited with Cupid and becomes immortal

The third century St. Zenobia is martyred with her brother on a red-hot iron bed

Roman matron Cecilia, patron saint of the blind and of musicians, supposedly the inventor of the organ, is martyred in the third century

St. Christine, a teenage Roman girl, is killed by her father for distributing some of his wealth among the poor

220

240

Vietnamese resistance leader Trien Au (222–248) raises an army to fight the Chinese, but is defeated after six months and commits suicide rather than surrender; a temple consecrated to her memory stands in present-day Vietnam

churches throughout the Greco-Roman world. Theological reasons for the subordination of women as well as advice on appropriate behavior for women appeared in many of the letters of the New Testament. The analogy of Christ as the head and the Church as the body was used to illustrate the relationship of husband and wife. As the religion spread, virginity came to represent the ideal state for women.

Because churchmen so feared women's power to arouse lust, chastity was promoted as the most prized of feminine virtues. Virgins who chose the monastic life had opportunities that their married counterparts did not: communal life offered an alternative to the dangers of childbearing and a relatively secure life in an often dangerous society. Monastic life sometimes allowed women to travel, to become literate, and to have intellectual pursuits. Monastic communities flourished in Europe from the fourth century on; some abbesses wielded authority and leadership within the Church, controlling double houses of monks and nuns. Until the 11th century, such abbesses took charge of the clergy and laypeople who resided on the monastery's land. Like bishops, some abbesses sat in parliaments and signed official Church decrees; they answered to the pope in Rome, rather than to a bishop or abbott.

The impact of Christianity on the treatment of women in late antiquity is still a matter for debate. The new religion, in founding itself upon existing ideas and traditions, naturally came to reflect the attitudes of the times in which it was born. Yet the strong current of equality for women that characterized Christianity in its earliest years ran counter to those traditions and was destined to resurface again and again throughout Christianity's long history.

General/ Context	Daily Life/ Customs/ Practices	Humanities/ Fine Arts	Occupations
240			
250			
260			

East Mexican figurine whistle in the form of a standing woman wearing a quechquémitl *(cape), skirt, and headdress, late preclassic to early classic,* A.D. *150-300*
Photograph courtesy Moreen O'Brien Maser Memorial Collection of Art, Skidmore College

270		Chinese calligrapher Wei Shuo (272–350) writes a textbook for calligraphy, *Diagram of the Battle Array of the Brush*	
300	Mayan civilization flourishes in Mexico fourth to 16th centuries	Roman men and women both wear togas Women in the early Christian period in Europe add color and Christian initials as decorative elements to classical Roman styles; they adopted the eastern Roman dalmatic, a long, ample tunic with full sleeves, under which another tunic might be worn; or they might wear the *casula*, a midlength curved mantle shaped like a priest's robe, over the long tunic The garb of the Byzantine Empire is characterized by heavy use of silk, gold, jewelry, patterns, brocades, and bright colors; women wear the dalmatic and mantles like those of the West, but far richer	

Performing Arts/ Entertainment/ Sports	Religion/ Philosophy	Science/ Technology/ Discovery	Statecraft/ Military	
			23-year-old Vietnamese peasant Trieu Thi Tinh (b. 225) leads thousands in a revolt against the Chinese, committing suicide when the revolt fails, A.D. 248	240
	St. Agatha is martyred for rejecting the advances of a man named Quintian, A.D. 251; because she is represented iconographically as carrying her breasts, which resemble bells, on a plate, she is the patron saint of bell founders			250
			Zenobia, queen of Palmyra, becomes sole ruler on the death of her husband, A.D. 267, whose murder she may have arranged; in 271, she breaks off from the Roman Empire, but in 272 is defeated by the Emperor Aurelian's forces; she is exhibited in Rome by Aurelian, then pensioned off in a villa in the suburbs	260
	The Roman martyr Mustiola is beaten to death with leaden scourges, A.D. 275			270
By this century, female instrumentalists and singers are in such short supply in Athens that their male patrons fight in the streets for their services	St. Agnes is martyred for insisting upon remaining a virgin instead of marrying a wealthy non-Christian; she is executed at the age of 12 or 13 by being stabbed in the throat, c. A.D. 304

German St. Afra is arrested on a trumped-up charge of prostitution, but is martyred for being a Christian; she is burned to death on an islet in the river Lech, A.D. 304

Syncletica, the prototypical Christian desert mother, retreats to the desert of Scete

Alexandra, a.k.a. Serena, wife of the Roman Emperor Diocletian, is converted to Christianity by the bravery of St. George, c. A.D. 302 | | | 300 |

General/ Context	Daily Life/ Customs/ Practices	Humanities/ Fine Arts	Occupations
300			
310	On the Feast of St. Valentine (Feb. 14), newly adopted by Roman Christians, young men draw the names of eligible young women from a box as part of the festivities, A.D. 313		

Performing Arts/ Entertainment/ Sports	Religion/ Philosophy	Science/ Technology/ Discovery	Statecraft/ Military	
	Fourth-century Euphemia of Abyssinia popularizes devotion to the Archangel Michael			**300**
	Abbess and desert mother Sara remains in the desert at Scete for 40 years			
	Legendary British St. Ursula and her 11,000 companions are supposed to have been martyred at Cologne, Germany			
	Early Christian martyr Antonina is dispatched at Nicaea by being sewn into a sack and thrown into a pond, c. A.D. 306			
	Yazdandocta, a fourth-century Persian matron, ministers to 120 Christian martyrs at Seleucia			
	The legendary Christian martyr Pelagia of Tarsus is roasted to death			
	Martyred in Syracuse, A.D. 303, St. Lucy is patron saint of those afflicted in the eyes; she is said to have responded to a suitor who admired her eyes by tearing them out and presenting them to him, saying, "Now leave me to live in God"; she is represented iconographically as carrying her eyes on a platter			
	Execution of Saints Rhipsime, Gaiana, Marianne, and their 35 companions, protomartyrs of the Armenian church, by Roman Emperor Diocletian, A.D. 312			**310**
	St. Catherine of Alexandria, a martyr whose body was carried to Sinai, is represented iconographically as carrying a wheel, the instrument of her martyrdom; she is known for her intelligence and high level of education			
	Flavia Julia Helena, born in Britain c. 280, is converted to Christianity and persuades her son, Constantine the Great, to do the same, A.D. 312			

320

330

350

	St. Augustine of Hippo defines marriage as a blessing instituted solely "for the purpose of begetting offspring" (*City of God*)		

Hypatia of Alexandria: Mathematician and Philosopher

Of the few early women philosophers and scientists about whom anything is known—among them Hipparchia of Athens (third century B.C.), or Beruyah of Jerusalem (second century A.D.)—we know the most about Hypatia of Alexandria (c. 370–415). Her father, the mathematician Theon, instructed his extraordinarily gifted daughter in mathematics. Scholasticus says that Hypatia surpassed both contemporaries and later thinkers in mathematics; others refer to her as a philosopher. She is reputed to have lectured on Plato, Aristotle, and other important philosophers, to have attracted crowds of students, and to have lectured at public expense. She conducted her discussions in the center of the city, without reserve or embarrassment before male officials, pupils, and colleagues. Described as beautiful and well proportioned, Hypatia customarily wore the tattered cloak favored by ancient philosophers; she seems never to have married.

Seven letters written to her by her most famous pupil, Synesius of Cyrene (later bishop of Ptolemais), survive; in them, Synesius addresses her as "mother, sister, teacher, and benefactress"; he remarks that philosophy in Egypt is nourished by her fecundity. In one letter, he asks her to send him a hydrometer, and in another describes an astronomical instrument he de-

	Called the "Mother of Monasticism," St. Macrina the Younger (c. 330–379) succeeds her mother, St. Emmelia, as the head of a small religious community in Pontus; the philosophy of the type of monasticism she pioneered is apparent in the monastic rule of her younger brother, St. Basil of Caesaria; her life was written by another of her younger brothers, St. Gregory of Nyssa, who also authored a Socratic-style dialogue with her called "On the Soul and Resurrection"			**320**
	By proclamation of the Emperor Constantine, the Saxon celebration of Eastre, goddess of spring, is converted to a Christian holiday celebrating Christ's resurrection, A.D. 325			
	Eusebius of Caesarea writes that the monument of Miriam, sister of Moses, stands near the city of Petrae and is still considered a sacred spot			**330**
			Jingo, regent empress of Japan, begins her 24-year reign, A.D. 356	**350**

signed with her help. Though we have no trace of her own works, contemporaries record that she "wrote a commentary on Diophantus, the Astronomical Table, and on Apollonius's *Conics* a commentary."

In 412, Hypatia's associate Orestes, the city's prefect, came into conflict with Archbishop Cyril of Alexandria, who engineered violent conflicts between the city's Jews and Christians. Hostilities escalated for several years until Cyril's monks confronted the prefect in the street and beat him. He was saved by the people of Alexandria, who captured one of the monks, tortured, and executed him.

In March 415, Cyril's monks took revenge on Hypatia, who they thought persuaded Orestes to turn his back on Cyril. They dragged her from her chariot into the cathedral, stripped and killed her, then hacked her back into pieces, which they burned.

We do not know whether Cyril ordered her death, nor is it clear that she would have been murdered had she not been a woman. As her city's outstanding representative of pre-Christian traditions, though, she provided a natural focus for the archbishop's hostility to the old order.

General/Context	Daily Life/Customs/Practices	Humanities/Fine Arts	Occupations
370		The first woman to have written on mathematical subjects, mathematician, astronomer, and philosopher Hypatia of Egypt (c. 370–415) is one of the most popular and admired teachers of the Hellenistic world	
380	Christianity becomes the official religion of the Roman Empire, A.D. 380		
390	The Roman Empire is divided into eastern and western halves, A.D. 395

Last Olympic Games, A.D. 393; they are forbidden in 394 | | |

GALLA PLACIDIA: THE PERSONAL IS POLITICAL

The princess Galla Placidia lived in the very vortex of the collapse of the Roman Empire. Throughout her life, she associated with some of the most notorious Romans and barbarians. Her first appearance in history was in the year 408, when the Senate consulted her about the political reliability of her cousin Serena; she advised them that she should be strangled. Soon after, when Alaric sacked Rome, he carried Placidia off as part of his booty.

After Alaric's death, his successor, Ataulf, married Placidia.

His wedding gift to her was 50 handsome youths, each carrying two platters; the platters were loaded with spoils from the sack of Rome.

In 415, Placidia lost both a son and a husband. Two years later, she was unwillingly married to a distinguished general, Constantius. After her marriage, she and her brother, Emperor Honorius, scandalized the court by their amorous behavior in public. Whether or not as a result of their closeness, in 421, Placidia became Augusta and her husband be-

Performing Arts/ Entertainment/ Sports	Religion/ Philosophy	Science/ Technology/ Discovery	Statecraft/ Military	
	St. Emmelia, wife of St. Basil, has 10 children who also become Christian saints			**370**
	Ss. Paula (d. 404), Eustochium, and other religious Roman women join St. Jerome in his exile in the Holy Land, A.D. 386; with Paula's money, they build a monastery for men and three communities for women at Bethlehem		Empress Galla Placidia (c. 388–450) rules the Western Roman Empire as Augusta; she lives to see her son become Emperor Valentian III The troops of Queen Mavia of the Bedouin Saracens (ruled c. 370–380) defeat a Roman army; Mavia makes an honorable peace and her daughter marries a Roman commander in chief under the eastern Emperor Valens	**380**
	Destruction of the temples of the Delphic Oracle by the Goths, A.D. 396; the most important oracle in Greece, it was sacred to Apollo and presided over by a young priestess, called the Pythia, through whom the oracles were delivered in an ecstatic trance; she took her title from the python, a snake or dragon thought to have been killed by Apollo		Eudoxia, daughter of a Frankish military ruler, marries the Byzantine Emperor Arcadius, A.D. 395; the de facto co-ruler with the weak emperor, she participates fully in the political struggles of the time; designated "Augusta" in 400, she dies of a miscarriage in 404 Queen Prabhāvatī Gupta becomes regent over the Deccan region of India from the death of her husband, King Rudrasena II, until A.D. 410; she is noted for introducing the Gupta culture of northern India to the Vākāta Kingdom	**390**

came Augustus, joint ruler with Honorius of the western empire.

However, Placidia became a widow again and, after quarreling with Honorius, was exiled to Constantinople. When Honorius died in 423, Placidia's four-year-old son, Valentinia III, was his rightful heir. Placidia's nephew ruled Constantinople, and his army pressed the child's claim. In 425, the little boy was clothed with the imperial robes in Ravenna. His position remained more or less secure until 432.

Placidia's political and familial crises were not yet over, though. In the year 450, her daughter Honoria fell in love with a butler. Placidia had the butler executed, deprived Honoria of royal rank, and arranged a marriage for her. As strong-willed as her mother, Honoria again rebelled, promising her hand to the devastating leader of the Huns, Attila, who was making ready to invade Rome. No sooner had the indomitable Placidia died, still refusing to allow Honoria to marry him, than invade Rome he did.

400

*Dancing Apsaras, late Chola or e
Vijayanaga period bronze, 13th t
14th centuries, south India*
Photograph courtesy Moreen
O'Brien Maser Memorial Collec
of Art, Skidmore College

410

420

430

450   Vandals sack Rome, A.D.
      455

Performing Arts/ Entertainment/ Sports	Religion/ Philosophy	Science/ Technology/ Discovery	Statecraft/ Military	
	St. Brigid, abbess at Kildare c. 450–525, is the patron saint of Ireland Fifth-century desert mother St. Athanasia, wife of St. Andronicus, disguises herself in order to live as a hermit in the desert Mary the Egyptian, a fifth-century prostitute, becomes a penitent and hermit in the Jordanian desert Two fifth-century Druid women, Ethnea and Fedelmia, convert to Christianity and are said to have died of joy as a result The fifth-century historian Palladius mentions almost 3000 women living as hermits in the Egyptian desert		Celebrated in plays and poetry, Hua Mu-Lan is the most famous of Chinese women warriors; legend claims that she won a sword fight with her father, allowing her to take his place in battle for 12 years, disguised as a man; she so impressed her commanding officer that he offered her his daughter in marriage During the time of the Sanhedrin (dissolved in the fifth century), Jewish law's supreme court, Jewish women are known to have served as queens, having the same rights and duties as kings	**400**
	Disciple of St. Jerome renowned for her asceticism, Marcella is the first Roman desert mother	Murder of Hypatia of Egypt at the hands of Christian monks who, at the behest of Archbishop Cyril of Alexandria, drag her into the cathedral, strip and kill her, cut her body into pieces and burn them, A.D. 415	Pulcheria (399–453), empress of the Eastern Roman Empire, begins her reign with her brother, Theodosius II, A.D. 414; an exemplary religious figure, she is eventually canonized by the Greek Orthodox Church	**410**
	Death of St. Euphrasia, a relative of Emperor Theodosius I known for her meekness and humility, who gave up her rank and wealth to join a convent of nuns in Egypt			**420**
	Denial that Mary is the mother of Jesus and therefore the mother of God is condemned by the Third General Council at Ephesus, A.D. 431			**430**
	While Attila the Hun advances through Gaul, A.D. 451, St. Genevieve (422–c. 500) encourages Parisians not to abandon their city, but instead to pray for divine assistance; though many regard her suggestion with scepticism, she is vindicated when Attila changes his course away from the city; St. Genevieve is thus			**450**

	General/ Context	Daily Life/ Customs/ Practices	Humanities/ Fine Arts	Occupations
450				
460				
470	Fall of the Western Roman Empire, A.D. 476			
490	Clovis, king of the Salian Franks, converts to Christianity, embracing its hierarchy and laws, A.D. 496 Visigoths capture Rome			
500	The French penal code, the Salic Law (Pacis Legis Salicae), is committed to writing	The (Burgundian Law code) Leges Burgundionum decrees that the property of women who give themselves voluntarily into marriage becomes the property of their husbands; under the same law, however, women's desire to be guardians of their children has priority over other claims The Visigoth legal code permits widows to assume guardianship over their minor sons If a bridegroom drinks of St. Keyne's well in Cornwall before his bride, it is said that he will be master in his house; if she drinks first, she will dominate The Salic Law declares that women may not inherit land; eventually interpreted as prohibiting women from occupying the French throne	Chu Ching-Chien is a calligrapher listed as one of the "teachers of great influence" in sixth-century *Biographies of Famous Chinese Nuns*	
510			Hu, queen of the Toba, sends the Buddhist Sung Yün to India to fetch some documents, A.D. 515; he leaves a notable account of Central Asia in the sixth century	
520	St. Benedict's establishment of the monastery of Monte Cassino in Italy marks the beginning of Western monasticism, A.D. 529			

Performing Arts/ Entertainment/ Sports	Religion/ Philosophy	Science/ Technology/ Discovery	Statecraft/ Military	
	revered as the patron saint and savior of Paris			450
	St. Dwynwen, Welsh founder of a religious house at Anglesey, is the patron saint of true lovers			460
				470
				490
Popular women's dance songs flourish in Europe though Church councils speak out against them	Sixth-century Welsh saint Keyna, daughter of King Brychan Brycheiniog, leaves her family to become a hermit; she founds oratories in England and Wales St. Dymphna, an Irish recluse at Gheel, is martyred by her depraved father Galla, sister-in-law of Boethius, is a bearded nun at the monastery of St. Peter in Rome In Norse mythology, Skuld, one of the three Norns, or Fates, represents the future; a veiled figure holding a scroll, she faces the future; her name is related to the English word *shall*			500
			Queen Hu, the last most vigorous ruler of her line, takes over at the death of her husband, A.D. 515; her reign ends in 528	510
			Amalswinthe (498–535), daughter of King Theodoric the Great of the Ostrogoths, becomes regent for her young son upon the deaths of her husband and father, A.D. 526; in 533, she puts	520

Funerary figurine of a Chinese court lady, Six Dynasties period, 265-589 Photograph courtesy Moreen O'Brien Maser Memorial Collection of Art, Skidmore College

	General/ Context	Daily Life/ Customs/ Practices	Humanities/ Fine Arts	Occupations
520				
540				
568				
570			During the lifetime of Muhammad (570–632), Muslim women participate in poetry competitions as well as in warfare, where they serve as nurses, as chanters encouraging the fighters, and occasionally as combatants themselves	
580	Sui dynasty in China, 589–618			
590				

Performing Arts/ Entertainment/ Sports	Religion/ Philosophy	Science/ Technology/ Discovery	Statecraft/ Military	
			down an attempted rebellion; in 534, she becomes co-ruler upon her son's death; in the ensuing power struggle, she is banished to Tuscany and killed	520
	St. Scholastica (d. 543), St. Benedict's sister and by some accounts his twin, founds and rules a convent in the neighborhood of her brother's foundation at Monte Cassino; Benedict confers with her regularly about spiritual matters; she is considered the mother of the Benedictine order			540
	Bavarian Queen Theolinde (568–c. 628) is famous for defending the Christian faith against Arian heretics			568
	Death of one of the foremost women saints of Ireland, St. Ita (a.k.a. Ida or Mida), who founded a community of virgins in County Limerick, where she conducted a school for small boys, among them the future abbot and missionary, St. Brendan	Matches are invented by women of northern Ch'i province in China for starting fires for cooking and heating, c. A.D. 577		570
	St. Radegunde (518–587) appoints her disciple Agnes (d. 586) first abbess of Sainte Croix at Poitiers, France, A.D. 588; both women are addressed in verse by the poet Venatus Fortunatus Queen Theodelinde and King Authari convert the Lombards to Roman Catholicism, A.D. 589			580
	Bertha of France (d. 612) agrees to marry Ethelbert, King of Kent, on the condition that she is able to continue worshiping as a Christian, A.D. 596; founds St. Martin's Church in Kent, and influences the spread of Christianity in England through her protection and the endorsement of St. Augustine		Empress Suiko-Tenno (554–628) begins her 36-year reign of Japan, A.D. 592, marked by increased contact with Korea and China and by the encouragement of Buddhism Death of Fredegund, Frankish queen of Neustria (in modern-day France), A.D. 597; one of the most bloodthirsty queens in European history, she rises to power	590

	General/ Context	Daily Life/ Customs/ Practices	Humanities/ Fine Arts	Occupations
590				
600		Anglo-Saxon law sets forth a schedule of fines relating to the disposition of women: a man lying with a maiden belonging to the king must pay 50 shillings in compensation; for a grinding slave, he must pay 25 shillings; if she is of lower status, he need pay only 12 shillings; laws concerning marriage stipulate sums for buying maidens with a bride payment and endowing women who have borne live children with half the husband's goods; kidnap and rape are also subject to monetary penalties Kentish law mandates a scale of compensation to be made to the guardian of any woman violated or seduced by another man Gallic women c. A.D. 600 wear long unbelted blouses over long skirts		
610	The Chinese T'ang dynasty, 618–907, affords women their greatest degree of autonomy until modern times; they practice many professions,			

Performing Arts/ Entertainment/ Sports	Religion/ Philosophy	Science/ Technology/ Discovery	Statecraft/ Military	
			by becoming King Chilperic I's wife; she carries on a bitter rivalry with Queen Brunhilde of the Frankish kingdom of Austrasia, complete with multiple political assassinations ordered by both queens	**590**
	Daughter of an Irish king, the seventh-century St. Bega, or Bee, establishes the monastery of St. Bee in Copeland, England; she is widely venerated in Northumbria as the patron of victims of exploitative northern lords and Scottish raiders		Khaula, an Arabian army commander in the Battle of Yermonks, is befriended by another female chief, Wafeira, and together they rout the Greeks, who are unnerved by these fierce women	**600**
	The seventh-century nun Heiu is the first nun in Northumbria; she founds religious houses in Hartlepool and Tadcaster			
	Florentina de Ecija is the seventh-century superior of 40 Spanish convents and 1000 nuns			
	Fatima (606–632) is the daughter of Muhammad by his first wife, Khadija, and the wife of Ali, the fourth caliph; a virgin, she gives birth to three sons who, along with her husband and grandsons, become the 12 holy ones who rule the hours of the day; she is revered in all branches of Islam; according to the Koran, she is one of the four perfect women: Khadijah, Muhammad's first wife; Mary, daughter of Imran; and Asia, wife of the pharaoh drowned in the Red Sea			
	Female symbolism and women practitioners (*siddha*) are prominent in Buddhism's tantric tradition; women are depicted as skilled spiritual guides and companions of men on the tantric path			
	Birth of Ayesha Bint abu-Bakr (611–678), Arab spiritual leader and authority on the Muslim tradition		For the 40 years of her reign, Brunhilde (c. 550–613), queen of the Frankish kingdom of Austrasia (part of modern-day France, Belgium, and	**610**

	General/ Context	Daily Life/ Customs/ Practices	Humanities/ Fine Arts	Occupations
610	arts, and crafts, some for- merly reserved for men, such as medicine, building and design, music, paint- ing, poetry, hunting, polo, calligraphy, and chess			
620	Muhammad is expelled from Mecca in 622 and flees to Yathrib (now Medina); his flight, called the hegira, marks the be- ginning date of the Is- lamic calendar			
621	Buddhism becomes Ja- pan's state religion, A.D. 621			
630	The Muslim Empire (632–945) is formed through the unification of most of Arabia	Seclusion and veiling be- come common practices for Muslim women; dur- ing Muhammad's lifetime,		

WOMEN IN EARLY ISLAM

Like Judaism and Christianity, Islam is a monotheistic religion. It was founded in the seventh century in the Arab region known as Mecca by the prophet Muhammad. The Koran, the Muslim holy book of injunctions handed down to Muhammad from God, forms the basis of Islamic law.

While many basic tenets of Islam (meaning "submission to" or "peace with God") are similar to those of Judaism and Christianity, Muslims have five inviolable duties: to profess faith in one God, to pray five times a day facing Mecca, to give alms to the poor, to fast during Ramadan (the month in the lunar calendar in which Muhammad received his first revelation), and to make at least one pilgrimage to Mecca. Forbidden practices include handling and eating pork, con-

suming alcohol, gambling, and making images of divine figures.

According to the Koran, women and men have equal responsibilities to God, though in the traditional Arab society of Muhammad's day, women remained subservient to men. Muhammad sought to introduce some equality to male/female relationships by outlawing female infanticide, allowing girls as well as boys to be educated, and reforming the economic position of married women. Upon marriage men were to pay women a dowry—insurance against divorce or widowhood—which women were permitted to manage themselves. They might also retain other personal income for their own use and bequeath it to family members as they wished when they died.

Performing Arts/ Entertainment/ Sports	Religion/ Philosophy	Science/ Technology/ Discovery	Statecraft/ Military	
			Germany), plays a major role in the bloody rivalries of the Frankish world, at one point uniting Austrasia and the Frankish kingdom of Neustria under her rule; she is finally overthrown and sentenced to death by being dragged behind a wild horse	**610**
			Wu Zitian rules as empress of all China during a period of increased power and prestige for women of royal, aristocratic, and official families; during the same period, the influence of famous concubine Precious Consort Yang, beloved of Emperor Xuan Zong, attains power and wealth for her family; both women are celebrated in literature as heroines, but reviled as examples of the misuse of political power by women	
	St. Gertrude of Nivelles (626–659), abbess and liturgist, is venerated as the patron of travelers and as a protector against mice, rats, and madness			**620**
				621
	After her husband's death, Ayesha, the third of Muhammad's nine wives and the daughter of the first	During her reign, Queen Sonduk builds the first known observatory in the Far East, Ch'omsong-dae	Queen Sonduk rules Korea from 632 to 647 because the male line of the Silla dynasty has died out;	**630**

If widowed, a wife inherited part of her husband's property and was assured of being supported by her sons. Moreover, she was theoretically allowed to choose her own spouse, though most girls were barely 10 years old when they were betrothed. Realizing that a cooperative wife was the best guarantee of a stable marriage, Muhammad gave women the right to state conditions of their own in the marriage contract.

Other stipulations were less liberal, in particular the religious injunctions concerning female modesty and obedience. Muhammad described marriage as a condition of servitude for women. Single women (and men) were cursed, considered a threat to the social order. To care for the large population of war widows, men were encouraged to take several wives. A man could divorce any of his wives without showing cause as long as he provided them some financial compensation. Violators of women were believed to be punished in the afterlife; women were punished on earth, usually by their husbands.

After Muhammad's death in A.D. 632, the rights he had granted to women began to erode. Within several years, women were no longer permitted to worship in the mosque; soon after, they were forbidden to go alone on the annual pilgrimage to Mecca. As Islam grew, women lost their political clout as well. However, their marital and financial rights as established by Muhammad remained. Within the home, women still wielded considerable power.

	General/ Context	Daily Life/ Customs/ Practices	Humanities/ Fine Arts	Occupations
630		only his wives were se- cluded and veiled in order to guard them from the importunities of his fol- lowers; the practice did not exist before that time		
640			Al-Khansā (600–675) and her daughter Amra write elegiac verses in Arabic, A.D. 645	
650	Composition of the Ko- ran, the sacred book of the teachings of Muham- mad	The Koran accounts for the hierarchy of the sexes thus: "Men are superior to women on account of the qualities with which God hath gifted the one above the other, and on account of the outlay they make from their substance for them" (Sura IV: 38) One of the oldest books on Muslim law, *Majmu'al- Fiqh*, stipulates that if a girl is betrothed by her father or grandfather be- fore she reaches puberty, she may not refuse the marriage, but if she is betrothed after puberty and does not like the match, she may refuse it; another tract on law, the *Sahih* of al-Bukhari, says that women who have been married may not be betrothed except at their own demand; even a vir- gin must be asked for her consent—which she signi- fies by her silence		
658				
660				

Performing Arts/ Entertainment/ Sports	Religion/ Philosophy	Science/ Technology/ Discovery	Statecraft/ Military	
	caliph, abu-Bakr, supports her father rather than Muhammad's son-in-law, Ali, in the struggles for power, c. A.D. 656; she is revered as the "Mother of Believers"; she is also called "the Prophetess"— like "Sultana," a title of honor	(Tower of the Moon and Stars); the tower lasts through the twentieth century	at age seven she explained to her father why a peony should have no smell, and when she was proved right the king predicted, "My wise little daughter! She shall reign when I am gone"	**630**
	Ethelburga is the abbess of the abbey built for her by her brother in Barking, England; three years following her death she becomes its patron saint			**640**
	St. Hilda (614–680), praised by the Venerable Bede in his *Ecclesiastical History of the English People,* founds the monastery of Whitby, a double monastery that houses men and women, in 657; she is responsible for teaching England's first vernacular poet, Caedmon, to write; a major religious figure of her time, she participated in the Synod of Whitby in 663, one of the great events in English church history

According to an old Scottish legend, Winifride flees the unwanted attentions of a prince, who cuts off her head; her uncle puts her back together and brings her to the local church, where Winifride had already determined to devote herself as a nun; she lives there until her real death c. 659 | | Empress Wu Chao (625–705) rules China for 50 years, 15 de facto and 35 de jure, from A.D. 655 to A.D. 605; daughter of a general, she starts adult life as one of the emperor's concubines; marries the crown prince when he becomes emperor, takes over his administration, takes over China's longstanding war against Korea and wins by a victory at sea, survives many plots, and takes up various lovers and companions until her death at 80; notorious for her favorites at court and for utter ruthlessness, she nevertheless rules extremely well, giving China decades of peace and prosperity, and leaving her grandson the wherewithal for a reign that was to be a golden age and high point of T'ang poetry and art | **650** |
| | St. Waltrudis founds and becomes abbess of a monastery at Mons, Hainaut, A.D. 658 | | | **658** |
| | Queen Bathildis, English wife of Clovis II, founder of the abbey of Chelles, France, becomes a nun when her son Clotaire is old enough to reign by himself, A.D. 665; she takes the veil from the hands of St. Bertilla (d. 705?), the first abbess of Chelles | | | **660** |

General/ Context	Daily Life/ Customs/ Practices	Humanities/ Fine Arts	Occupations
670			
680			
690			

Performing Arts/ Entertainment/ Sports	Religion/ Philosophy	Science/ Technology/ Discovery	Statecraft/ Military	
	Death of St. Hunna, a noblewoman of Alsace known as the Holy Washerwoman, A.D. 679		Sexburga reigns as queen of Wessex, 672–674	**670**
	The Northumbrian Queen Etheldreda (630?–679), who became a nun contrary to her husband's wishes, returns to her native East Anglia and establishes a church and double monastery on the Isle of Ely, A.D. 673; she cares for the poor and practices medicine; her burial place becomes a shrine famous for its miraculous powers of healing			
	Death of St. Waldtrudis, A.D. 688, member of a saintly family that included her mother, St. Bertilia, her sister, St. Aldegundis of Maubeuge, and her daughters, the abbesses St. Aldetrudis and St. Madelberta	Empress Wu Tse-t'ien (683–705) of China builds a cast-iron column weighing about 1325 tons to commemorate the Chou dynasty; in 688, she builds a 294-foot cast-iron pagoda	Empress Jito-tenno (625–701) assumes the rule of Japan following the death of her husband; her reign is marked by administrative reforms, agricultural development, and the encouragement of both the Buddhist and Shinto religions; in 697 she abdicates in favor of her nephew	**680**
			Chinese Empress Wu Tse-t'ien removes T'ang heir-apparent in favor of her son	
	St. Irmina, a German princess, becomes a nun when her betrothed falls off a cliff in a struggle with a rival for her hand; she supports the missionary labors of St. Willibrord by giving him property on which to found the famous monastery of Echternach. Her sister, St. Adela, founds a monastery near Trier, Germany, becoming its first abbess; a letter addressed to her by Abbess Aelffled of Whitby has been found among St. Boniface's correspondence			**690**
	Women frequently head powerful double monasteries, such as Saint-Denis, Faremoutiers, Chelles, and Andely in Frankish Gaul, and Whitby, Barking, Coldingham, Ely, Wenlock, Winbourne, and Beverly in England			

	General/ Context	Daily Life/ Customs/ Practices	Humanities/ Fine Arts	Occupations

700

Humanities/Fine Arts: Princess Abbassa wanders throughout Arabia, reciting her life story in poetry; some of her Arabic verses are still extant, and six lines are preserved in a book written by Ben Abon Haydah

710

General/Context: The Shinto religion of Japan, with its worship of natural objects, ancient deities, and national heroes, coexists with Buddhism; Buddhism incorporates many Shinto gods into its own pantheon

Nara, the first Japanese historical period, 710–

	At the request of St. Boniface, Abbess Tetta of Wimbourne sends St. Lioba of Wessex (c. 700–c. 780) to help Boniface with his missionary work in Germany; some of her correspondence with him survives; she is buried next to him at Fulda, Germany		The kahina (the "prophetess" or "sorceress") unites the Byzantine and Berber forces against the invading Arabs during the struggle for Byzantine Africa (modern Tunisia); she maintains an independent Berber kingdom for a considerable time until her death in battle against the Arabs	**700**
	Anglo-Saxon martyr St. Osith, whose husband Sighere, king of the Saxons, is more interested in hunting than in women, is allowed to remain a virgin and enter a convent; she is beheaded by pirates attempting to carry her off during a raid; her memory is preserved in such local place names as St. Osith's Well and in the village of St. Osith, England		Empress Gemmyo of Japan begins her 21-year rule, A.D. 703	
			Chinese warrior Nieh Yin-niang is reputed to have been a one-woman Robin Hood, aiding the weak and wreaking vengeance on criminals; she was taught swordsmanship by a nun, C. A.D. 700	
	Komyo (701–760), a devout Buddhist and member of Japan's Fujiwara family, marries Emperor Shomu and is the mother of Empress Koken; in Nara, an early capital of Japan, she founds many famous temples and charitable institutions for the sick and starving and encourages the use of Chinese medicine rather than charms and talismans; it is said she personally washed 1000 poor people		Empress Wei is regent of China from A.D. 705 to A.D. 712	
	The late-eighth-century *siddha* Yeshay Tsogyal comes to symbolize nondualistic wisdom in female form in Buddhist tantric tradition; she is known as *de chen rgyal mo,* the "Great Bliss Queen"			
	Patron of Brussels, St. Gudula, (d. 712) godmother of St. Gertrude of Nivelles, is renowned as a wonder-worker			**710**

	General/ Context	Daily Life/ Customs/ Practices	Humanities/ Fine Arts	Occupations
710	794, characterized by the flowering of Buddhist learning and the assimilation of Chinese culture Moors invade Spain in 711			
720		Byzantine *Ecloga*, based on emperor Jushnan's legislation, declares that marriage requires the consent of both parties: it is not a matter of simple cohabitation; should the husband predecease his wife, the dowry and prenuptial gifts revert to her, as does the custody of the children		
730	Charles Martel's army defeats Islamic forces in the Battle of Tours at Poitiers in 732, halting the westward expansion of Islam			
740	First printed newspaper appears in China			
750	The Arabs learn the art of papermaking from the Chinese			
760				
770			A Buddhist prayer for Japanese Empress Shotoku is the earliest known surviving piece of printing	
780		The Saxon legal code does not allow widows to assume guardianship over their minor children; instead, male kinsmen, preferably the husband's, take on the responsibility	Berthe *aux grands pieds* (Bertha of the big feet, d. 783), wife of Pepin the Short and mother of Charlemagne, wields great influence at court until her death	

Performing Arts/ Entertainment/ Sports	Religion/ Philosophy	Science/ Technology/ Discovery	Statecraft/ Military	
				710
				720
	A disciple of St. Boniface, St. Adela is the daughter of Dagobert II, king of the Franks; she becomes a nun on the death of her husband, Alberic, and is the founding abbess of a monastery at Pfalzel near Trèves, c. A.D. 734			**730**
				740
	Relindis, Benedictine abbess at Masseyk, Netherlands, is a colleague of St. Boniface in the Christianization of Europe		Komyo rules Japan on behalf of her daughters following her husband's death in 756	**750**
			Empress Shotoku (assumed name of empress Koken) rules Japan, 764–770	**760**
	One of St. Boniface's missionaries, Hugeberc of Hildesheim, writes the first Anglo-Saxon account of the conversion of the Franks and the Germans as well as a life of Bishop Willibald combined with a guide for pilgrims to the Holy Land, A.D. 778; she exemplifies the central role played by women in missionary activity and in Christianity in northern Europe			**770**
	English abbess of Heidenheim, St. Walburga serves as one of St. Boniface's missionaries on the European continent; she is the saint after whom Walpurgisnacht, the witches' festival, is named		Beginning of the reign of Irene (752–803), empress of the Byzantine Empire; she rules until 802, suppressing iconoclasm and thereby encouraging the great flowering of Byzantine religious art	**780**

	General/ Context	Daily Life/ Customs/ Practices	Humanities/ Fine Arts	Occupations
800	Frankish King Charlemagne (742–814) is crowned emperor of the West by Pope Leo III in A.D. 800	Sunni law governing the family throughout the premodern era permits polygamy and the keeping of concubines, though the practice is confined to the wealthy; divorce and remarriage are not only permitted but frequent; women have a legal right to sexual satisfaction in marriage; contraception and abortion are permitted, if not encouraged Saxon and Thuringian legal codes (c. A.D. 800) demand that free women who marry without consent of their guardians forfeit all claims to their own property *Droit du Seigneur* (the lord's right), also known as *jus prima noctis* (law of the first night), is established by Ewen III of Scotland; the law establishes the lord's right to deflower the bride of each of his retainers and serfs; vassals who consummate their marriages within three nights of the wedding are declared blasphemous, while those who deflower their brides before the lord has his turn face legal penalties		
830	First reference to a printed book in China, A.D. 835			
840				
850	The first European medical school is founded in Salerno, Italy; it closes in 1817		According to medieval legend, Pope Joan, a woman disguised as a monk, is said to have succeeded Pope Leo IV; her sex was discovered when she gave birth to a child	

Performing Arts/ Entertainment/ Sports	Religion/ Philosophy	Science/ Technology/ Discovery	Statecraft/ Military	
	St. Theocleta the wonder-worker is venerated in the Greek Orthodox Church			**800**
	Born in Byzantium, the aristocratic Kassiane the Nun (b. c. 805) is the most famous woman hymnographer of the Eastern Orthodox Church; author of 23 hymns incorporated into the liturgy, she is known for "The Troparion of Kassiane"			
				830
	St. Irene is a miracle worker, prophet, and abbess of the convent of Chrysobalant at Constantinople			**840**
	Dhouda, countess of Septimania in southern France, composes a Latin treatise for the instruction of her elder son; offering ethical and moral advice, the work is remarkable for its literary grace and clear moral position			
				850

	General/ Context	Daily Life/ Customs/ Practices	Humanities/ Fine Arts	Occupations
850			during the ceremony of her enthronement Japanese Princess Irge is born; her writings enjoy great repute in Japan	
860				
890		The law code of Alfred, king of West Saxons (Alfred the Great, 849–899), establishes a schedule of fines for offenses against women		
900	Alfred the Great dies in Winchester	Frankish women c. A.D. 900 dress themselves in long-sleeved tunics with gaily decorated borders, mantles fastened at the breast with a brooch, and soft pointed leather shoes in the Roman fashion; a noblewoman might wear a loose embroidered tunic over a tight-sleeved one A 10th-century *takkanah*, or enactment, of a new Talmudic law makes polygamy illegal for Ashkenazi Jewish men Byzantine law and custom deny women the right to give evidence in contractual matters; in "purely feminine" affairs, however, like childbirth and "other things which only the female eye may see," they are allowed to testify Under Byzantine law, a man who commits adultery with another man's wife will have his nose slit, as will the woman; she, however, will be forced to leave her husband's house, be branded a whore, and will have to give up her children	Known for her fine embroidery, Anglo-Saxon Queen Aelflaed (909–916) might have supervised making of the finest surviving examples of early medieval embroidery, the stole and maniple of St. Cuthbert A Chinese calligrapher by trade, Lady Li Fu-jen (c. 907–960) is probably the first exponent of bamboo painting The 10th-century Spanish nun Ende is one of the few women painters of the Middle Ages whose name and work have survived; a manuscript illuminator, she is followed by a few whose names and work are known, like the 12th-century German nuns Guda and Claricia, and by many more whose work was anonymous	
910				

Performing Arts/ Entertainment/ Sports	Religion/ Philosophy	Science/ Technology/ Discovery	Statecraft/ Military	
				850
	The Greek Orthodox monastic founder Athanasia serves as adviser to the empress in Constaninople, c. A.D. 860			**860**
			Death of Engelberge, queen of the Franks, who presided over the court of her husband, Louis II, Charlemagne's grandson, A.D. 891; she went on military campaigns with him, negotiated over territory with his uncles, and arranged his reconciliation with the pope	**890**
Queen Gormfhlaith composes many laments and elegies after the death of her third husband, the high king of Ireland; at least 11 attributed to her survive	The 10th-century Irish nun Sunnifa is shipwrecked in Norway, where she founds monastic houses		St. Ludmila of Bohemia (c. 860–921) undertakes the upbringing of her grandson, the future St. Wenceslaus; she prepares him to take up the reins of government, but is later murdered by anti-Christian nobles who support his mother, Drahomira	**900**
			Through the 10th and 11th centuries, the Hausa States (modern-day Nigeria), are ruled by the Habe queens: Kufuru, Gino, Yakumo, Yakunya, Walzana, Daura, Gamata, Shata, Batatume, Sandamata, Yanbamu, Gizirgizir, Innagari, Jamata, Hamata, Zama, and Shawata	

Seated Parvati with Ganesha, 10th-century Kashmiri bronze
Photograph courtesy Moreen O'Brien Maser Memorial Collection of Art, Skidmore College

	Mercian leader Lady Ethelfleda (870–918) founds St. Alkmund's church in 911; in 917 she		Ethelfleda rules the Anglo-Saxon kingdom of Mercia, first with her husband and then on her	**910**

	General/ Context	Daily Life/ Customs/ Practices	Humanities/ Fine Arts	Occupations
910				
940				
950		Byzantine divorce can be had on several grounds: adultery by the woman, impotence in the man, plotting to kill one's spouse, leprosy, insanity, and conspiracy against the emperor		
960	Otto I is crowned the first Holy Roman Emperor, A.D. 962 Sung dynasty in China (960–1279)	During the Sung dynasty in China, women's activity is restricted to the home; chastity becomes their most important virtue; foot binding becomes fashionable among the elite		
970			The Spanish Apocalypse manuscript preserved in Gerona Cathedral contains the first known illuminations signed by a woman	
980				
990		Anglo-Saxon noble-women controlled their own property and at times had to litigate in their own defense; c. 992 Wynflæd charges Leof-wine with illegally seizing land given her by the earl Ælfric; 14 of her 25 witnesses are women; the case is decided in her favor: Leofwine must com-		

Performing Arts/ Entertainment/ Sports	Religion/ Philosophy	Science/ Technology/ Discovery	Statecraft/ Military	
	wins back for the Saxon English much of the territory annexed by the Danes		own after his death in A.D. 911; she is acclaimed in the chronicles as a great fortress builder and defender of her people against the Vikings and the Welsh	910
			Drevelians revolt against taxes imposed by Igor of Russia and kill him, A.D. 945; his wife, Olga, succeeds him as regent, raising an army and compelling Drevelians to pay tribute.	940
				950
	St. Adelaide (931–999) becomes empress of the Holy Roman Empire when her husband, Otto the Great, is crowned in Rome; she founds and restores monasteries, urges the conversion of the Slavs, and is renowned as a peacemaker			960
	Queen Olga, grandmother of St. Vladimir, is an early convert to Christianty in Kiev		Elfrida, widow of Edgar the Saxon king, has her stepson King Edward the Martyr murdered in order to put her own son Ethelred on the throne in Wessex	970
	Comba Osorez, Benedictine abbess at Archas, Portugal, is martyred by the Saracens		Otto III, grandson of St. Adelaide, is a baby when his father, Otto II, dies; his mother, the Byzantine princess Theophano, becomes regent, A.D. 983; when she dies suddenly in 991, St. Adelaide returns to serve as regent	980
	The abbess of Winchester, Wilfrida (d. 988), is seduced by King Edgar of England			990

	General/ Context	Daily Life/ Customs/ Practices	Humanities/ Fine Arts	Occupations
990		pensate her for rents and other payments she has lost while he had possession of the land, which is handed over to the bishop before being restored to Wynflæd		
1000			Lady Murasaki Shikibu (978?–1026?) composes *The Tale of Genji (Genji monogatari)*, c. 1020, considered the greatest single work in Japanese literature German nun Hrosvitha (935–c. 1002) is one of the first to adapt classical dramatic forms to Christian ends; her compositions include narrative poems and a poetic epic celebrating the rule of Otto I Sei Shōnagon, a lady-in-waiting in the Heian court, writes *The Pillow Book;* she has many lovers in the court, so much of the book is amorous reminiscence	
1010			Ealdswith (1016–1035), granddaughter of Brihtnoth, is given a village by the abbey of Ely where she and her woman could produce their embroidery Queen Aelgiva, wife of Edward the Confessor, embroiders an altar frontal so richly embellished with gems, pearls, and thread of gold that it resembles a mosaic, c. 1016	
1020				

WOMEN ARTISTS IN THE MIDDLE AGES

During the Middle Ages most art was produced in monasteries. Noblewomen who were sent to convents for their education often contributed to the foundation's support by learning to copy and sometimes decorate manuscripts. Though sometimes the lack of training and competitive standards left their artistic abilities inadequately developed, some of the age's most prolific *scriptoria* (workshops for producing manuscripts) were staffed by nuns who copied text in beautiful hands, drew the initials, and painted the illustrations.

Besides copying and illuminating books, women of the Middle Ages are most famous for the great religious and secular embroideries and tapestries. Being free of the laborious business of running a medieval household, nuns and aristocratic women had the leisure to pursue artistic projects of enormous scale, like

990

1000

The Latin comedies of Terence are read aloud in the convent of Gandersheim, though whether the plays of Hroswitha are given dramatic readings at this time is still debated

The 11th-century Tibetan mystic Machig Lapdion dies at the age of 99

French churchman Roger de Caen writes *Carmen de contemptu mundi (Song of Contempt for the World)* in which he associates women with all that is fleshly and warns Christian men to avoid them; his work is part of a continuing debate, the *Querelle des femmes,* on women's nature, particularly the dimensions of their sexuality

1010

St. Adelaide of Bellich (d. 1015), the daughter of a count in the region of Bonn, Germany, rules two convents founded by her father and founds a third herself; she insists on her nuns' learning Latin, an unusual requirement in her day

Saxon noblewoman Aelgifu (d. c. 1040), mistress of Canute of Denmark, is appointed regent of Norway by him, 1010; her cruelty and harshness cause an uprising in 1035; returning to England after Canute's death, she persuades the nobles to recognize her son Harold "Harefoot" as king

1020

St. Cunegund (d. 1033) gives up her position of empress of the Holy Roman Empire to become a nun, 1024; she and her

the Bayeaux Tapestry. This hanging depicting the 11th-century Battle of Hastings was designed to circle the chapel at Bayeaux, France. It is a work not only of consummate artistry in the use of woolen thread on linen, but also of great imagination and complexity. In typical medieval fashion, the names of most of the women who created needlework art remain unknown to us. Projects like tapestries, manuscripts, liturgical garments, embroideries, and even panel paintings tended to be done cooperatively by groups of women, none of whom could rightfully take sole credit for the final product. Unlike Renaissance and modern women artists, medieval women worked comfortably within a tradition of artistic anonymity.

	General/ Context	Daily Life/ Customs/ Practices	Humanities/ Fine Arts	Occupations
1020				
1030		The law code of Anglo-Saxon King Canute (995–1035) demands that a woman discovered in adultery must forfeit all she possesses to her husband and must lose both her nose and her ears; a widow of less than a year who marries again loses all goods she gained from her previous husband; if she waits a year, she may dispose of herself and her property as she will	Queen Gisela of Hungary (d. 1043) commissions the gold and purple chasuble that becomes the coronation robe of Hungary	
1040	Between 1040 and 1049, Bi Sheng, an obscure Chinese commoner, invents movable type			
1050			Frankish women c. 1050 wear their outer tunic belted, together with a fur-lined mantle fastened at the neck with a cord	
1060	The Norman Conquest: William the Conqueror invades England and claims the throne, 1066	Anglo-Saxon needlewoman Aelfgyth is given an estate in Buckinghamshire by the king's sheriff, Godric, in return for teaching his daughter embroidery, c. 1066	Japanese author Lady Sarashima (c. 1008–1060) (a.k.a. Takasue-no-Musume—her real name is no longer known) writes *Sarashima Nikki,* in which she records her experiences	
1070				

Performing Arts/ Entertainment/ Sports	Religion/ Philosophy	Science/ Technology/ Discovery	Statecraft/ Military	
	husband, St. Henry of Bavaria, found the monastery and cathedral of Bamberg, Germany			1020
				1030
			Lady Godiva (d. 1080), wife of Earl Leofric of Mercia, asks her husband to lighten Coventry's taxes; he promises to do so if she will ride naked through the marketplace at midday; she does so, covered only by her long hair, and the earl makes good his promise	1040
			Emma of Normandy (d. 1052), wife of English kings Ethelred II and Canute, is deeply involved in the dynastic struggles of the late Anglo-Saxon period	1050
				1060
	St. Margaret (c. 1045–1093), daughter of Edward d'Outremer, marries King Malcolm III Mac-Duncan of Scotland; she acquires great influence over her husband, promoting religion and the arts of civilization in his realm; her children include Matilda, "Good Queen Maud," the wife of Henry I of England, and St. David of Scotland			1070

	General/ Context	Daily Life/ Customs/ Practices	Humanities/ Fine Arts	Occupations
1080	Tower of London built 1086 by William the Conqueror		Li Ch'ing-chao (1081–after 1141) is a celebrated Chinese woman poet and the exponent of lyrical poems of irregular length known as *tz'u*, designed to be set to music Hispano-Arabic poet Wal-lādah bint al-Mustakfi dies, 1087; her surviving works form a verse correspondence with her lover, the poet Ibn Zaydūn	The Domesday Book records that Eadgifu the Fair, an Anglo-Saxon woman, was a great land-owner during the reign of King Edward the Confessor (1042–1066); she is listed as holding more than 27,000 acres across England
1090	The First Crusade, (1096–1099), the first of several attempts by European Christians to wrest the Holy Land from Muslim hands, is launched by Pope Urban II and organized under Bishop Ademar and Count Raymond IV of Toulouse			
1100	The University of Paris is founded as a definite entity before 1170, although its roots go back to the early 1100s	Highborn German women at the time of the Minnesängers (love poets), c. 1100, wear close-fitting dresses with sleeves tight above and falling wide below the elbow Englishwomen, like their German counterparts, wear long-sleeved dresses,	Rise of the aristocratic literary notion of courtly love; at the same time, middle-class *fabliaux* (bawdy tales originating in France) represent the other extreme: women as lusty, greedy tricksters bent on satisfying themselves while fooling their husbands	

MEDIEVAL REGENTS AND QUEENS

The lives of medieval princesses, far from being the romantic existence of fairy tale and legend, were often far more constrained than those of their middle-class contemporaries. Princesses usually became queens following diplomatic marriages, betrothal negotiations often having begun before the girls were 10. Consequently, their public responsibilities as queens started early—the average age for English princesses was 14—and usually in a foreign country with a different language and customs. Their education, though, like their brothers', fit them for the social and political power they were to wield.

The best known woman ruler of that time is Eleanor of Aquitaine, perhaps the richest woman in the medieval world and one of the most powerful. Married at 15 to Louis VII of France, she accompanied him on Crusade and divorced him after 15 years. She married the ambitious and much younger Henry II of

England and, as heiress to half of southern France, precipitated some 400 years of war between France and England. Backing a rebellion of her sons against Henry II, she was held in honorable confinement by him—1173–1185—although she was able to keep him from divorcing her and seizing her kingdom. She was released by her son Richard after his accession in 1189 and lived on to rule England while he went on Crusade. Her interests were not merely political: she built up educational and religious institutions in France and England, creating courts that were centers for courtly manners and customs, and rearing her offspring—including the future English kings Richard the Lionhearted and John Lackland—to carry on her legacy.

Other eminent women rulers in Europe included Blanche of Castile, who during the 13th century served as regent of France, and was known for quelling anti-Semitism and freeing the poor

Performing Arts/ Entertainment/ Sports	Religion/ Philosophy	Science/ Technology/ Discovery	Statecraft/ Military	
	St. Margaret, queen of Scotland, builds St. Oran's Chapel; responsible for establishing Roman Catholism in Scotland			1080
	Christina of Markyate (c. 1096/7–1160) flees to a hermitage when her family betrothes her to a pagan; evidence points to her having commissioned the famous St. Albans Psalter St. Humbeline (1092–1135), the sister of St. Bernard of Clairvaux, is famous as a Cistercian prioress at Jully, France, and as Bernard's counselor and confidante		At the end of the 11th century, the last Habe queen marries the son of the king of Baghdad, Abayajidda, who becomes the first Habe king	1090
Renewed copying of the plays of Hroswitha of Gandersheim suggests that performances of her dramas anticipate by at least a century the earliest mystery and morality plays	St. Paulina, a hermit in Thuringia, Germany, founds the double monastery of Paulinzelle, 1107 Chana Bat Yoheved, daughter of the scholar Rashi (Rabbi Schlomo ben Isaac), teaches women Jewish law		Welsh heroine Maud de Valerie rebels against the oppressive regime of King John and dies as his prisoner	1100

from prison. Queen Bathild ruled France in the seventh century after her husband went insane. She helped link French and English convents and prohibited the sale of Christians as slaves. Another seventh-century ruler, Queen Bertha, worked to Christianize England after she converted her husband, King Ethelbert. Likewise, the 14th-century Queen Jadwiga, considered one of Poland's greatest rulers, continued the Christianization of Europe, successfully conducting peace negotiations, leading military actions, and founding the University of Cracow before her death at age 28.

In the Eastern Roman Empire some outstanding women ruled as well during this epoch. Pulcheria became the regent at age 16 in 414, ruling for 33 years. Her sister-in-law, Eudocia, who ruled with her, evidently wrote the law codes attributed to her husband. Irene, the wife of Emperor Leo IV, ruled after her husband's death in 775, before her son came of age. He later exiled her, but she returned and had him imprisoned and blinded. Ruling the empire alone, she fostered religious life, founded hospitals, and aided the poor. The royal sisters Zoë and Theodora governed the Eastern Empire with great success from 1028 to 1055 through the reigns of four emperors: they cleared both the government and the Church of corruption.

Longstanding historical conventions attributed major accomplishments to reigning kings, but female regents and queens helped shape the destinies of many medieval lands, at times ruling competently, even spectacularly, in an era when average women had little political power.

	General/ Context	Daily Life/ Customs/ Practices	Humanities/ Fine Arts	Occupations
1100		small belts, and mantles fastened by a cord at the neck	Chu Shu-chen is a Chinese poet who mourns her unhappy condition in *tz'u* poems of great delicacy; her name is synonymous with a kind of refined misery	
1110			Héloïse (1101–1164), niece of Canon Fulbert of Notre Dame Cathedral in Paris, is seduced by her tutor, theologian Peter Abelard, 1118; they marry secretly, but when news of it gets out, her uncle has Abelard castrated; the unwilling Héloïse becomes a nun, Abelard a monk	
1120			The first known woman to write poetry in German, Frau Ava (d. 1127) is possibly a nun at the Austrian abbey of Melk; she composed four religious poems	
1130				In France, brothels are officially sanctioned, but prostitutes are confined to certain streets and loca-

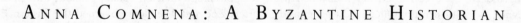

ANNA COMNENA: A BYZANTINE HISTORIAN

Anna Comnena (1083–post 1148) was the author of *Alexiad,* the life of her father, the eastern Emperor Alexius I Comnenus. An outstanding Byzantine historian, her work remains one of the most important in medieval Greek historiography. In her preface, she describes herself as "born and bred in the Purple," meaning that she was a royal princess. She was educated in Greek, rhetoric, philosophy, music, and science. Her motivation in writing the *Alexiad,* she says, is to keep from otherwise inevitable oblivion the deeds and character of even her most noble father. The result of her labors is an urbane, vivid, and highly readable document that many believe superior to any produced by her Latin contemporaries in the West.

Anna wrote the *Alexiad* in a melancholy period of her old age. She does digress. Overall, however, the narrative is vivid, fast-moving, and notable for shrewd character sketches. Anna's authorial individuality is unmistakable. She makes no bones

Performing Arts/ Entertainment/ Sports	Religion/ Philosophy	Science/ Technology/ Discovery	Statecraft/ Military	
	Flowering of Church misogyny; theologians blame humankind's fall on Eve and warn men against trusting women			**1100**
	Rise of the cult of the Virgin Mary in Europe; she gains new prominence in religious worship, venerated as the chief compassionate link between humans and God; she is often addressed in secular terms formerly used to describe the beauty, virtue, and desirability of noble ladies			
	The cult of Sitala, the Indian goddess of smallpox, arises			
				1110
			Eleanor of Aquitaine (1112–1204), daughter of William of Aquitaine, holds and administers property equaling one-third of present-day France; she participates in the Crusades, governs as royal regent, and marries the kings of England and France	**1120**
	Bavarian anchoress and artist Dietmut of Wessobrun (c. 1057–1130) is the patron of calligra-		Eleanor of Aquitaine marries Louis VII, becoming queen of France (1137–1151)	**1130**

about her prejudices against Armenians, Pope Gregory VII, Turks, and Latins in general. She is impressed by physical beauty but has no interest in fine architecture. She excels in descriptions of machines and instruments of war, such as the crossbow, whether invented by friend or foe. She projects a sincere religion that includes, however, no charity whatsoever for heretics.

The character of Alexius comes across as cunning, some-times harsh and uncompromising, but essentially an exponent of the honorable ruler. He appears courageous and mindful of his responsibilities. Anna's achievement therefore amounts to more than preserving her father's memory. It is a vindication of classical values associated with civil discipline and order, not only in her father's policies toward his subjects and victories over his military enemies, but also in the spiritual life of his realm.

	General/ Context	Daily Life/ Customs/ Practices	Humanities/ Fine Arts	Occupations
1130				tions; they are not al- lowed to inherit property and must often defend themselves against charges of theft and sorcery
1140	The Second Crusade (1147–1149) is preached by Bernard of Clairvaux The University of Bologna becomes the major European center for the study of law in the Middle Ages	The Bolognese jurist Gratian writes, "Woman's authority is nil; let her in all things be subject to the rule of man . . . neither can she teach, nor be a witness, nor give a guarantee, nor sit in judgment" *(Decretum Gratiani)*	Provençal *trobairitz* (woman troubador) Azalais de Porcairages (b. c. 1140) leaves behind two *vidas* (biographical sketches) and a poem, *Ar em al fregs temps vengut*	
1150				
1159				
1160	The Cathedral of Notre Dame is started in Paris, c. 1163			

HILDEGARD OF BINGEN: SAINT AND SCIENTIST

Known as the "Sibyl of the Rhine," the Benedictine nun Hildegard of Bingen possessed one of the greatest minds of her time. Scientist, composer, mystical theologian, playwright, and adviser to popes and kings, Hildegard admonished the highest and healed the lowest. Her authority came from her visions, which she claimed were divinely inspired.

Born into a noble German family distantly related to the Emperor Frederick Barbarossa, Hildegard spent all but the first seven years of her life in a convent, eventually becoming the founding abbess of the monastery on the Rupertsberg at Bingen. Since earliest childhood, Hildegard had been visited by visions no one else could see; she kept them to herself for many years, not knowing what to make of them. As she grew older, the visions grew more persistent and she, having been, as she says, persuaded to reveal them by means of a miraculous illness, had them written down. The pope and a committee of theo-

Performing Arts/ Entertainment/ Sports	Religion/ Philosophy	Science/ Technology/ Discovery	Statecraft/ Military	
	phers; 45 books, including two bibles, illuminated by her survive			**1130**
	St. Hildegard of Bingen (1098?–1179), the "Sibyl of the Rhine," composes her major visionary work, *Scivias (Know the Ways),* 1141, authorized by Pope Eugenius III, who gives her permission to publish her revelations, 1147 Gilbert of Sempringham founds the Gilbertine Order, the first medieval religious order originating in England, A.D. 1147; mainly a women's order, the houses were double, often ruled by an abbess		Mélisande becomes the queen of Jerusalem following the conquest of the crusaders, 1143	**1140**
Probably completed in 1158, St. Hildegard of Bingen's *Symphonia Harmoniae Celestium Revelationum* (Symphony of the Harmony of Heavenly Revelations) consists of 77 songs; they are performed by Hildegard and her sisters at Rupertsburg	St. Hildegard of Bingen embarks on a round of preaching tours (1152–1162) in the Rhineland, an almost unheard-of activity for a woman of her time		Eleanor of Aquitaine marries King Henry II, becoming queen of England (1152–1204); she is the mother of Richard I and King John; her right to Aquitaine in southern France sets off approximately 400 years of territorial wars between France and England	**1150**
			Eleanor of Aquitaine's claims to her French properties are supported by an English invasion of Toulouse, led by her husband's chancellor, Thomas à Becket; the English are routed	**1159**
	Death of St. Mechtildis of Diessen (1125–1160), kinswoman of Emperor Frederick I, healer, visionary, and, by the injunction of Pope	St. Hildegard of Bingen writes several works of natural science and medicine in the 1160s, including the two-part *Liber subtilitatum diversarum natu-*	Matilda, or Maude (1102–1167), empress of Germany and daughter of King Henry I of England, is a claimant to the English throne; after her	**1160**

logians ruled favorably on their authenticity. An account of 26 of these visions together with the beautiful if eccentric illuminations she commissioned to illustrate them comprise *Scivias.* Her other writings include medical and natural history treatises, hymns, canticles, homilies, and a morality play. She even composed a language of her own.

Hildegard advocated a more active role for women in the Church. She herself went on preaching tours, during which she not only spoke in public but also performed at least one exorcism—activities usually the province of male ecclesiastics. Her voluminous correspondence included letters to the Church hierarchy as well as men and women on every level of society both abroad and in Germany. Though greatly revered in her own time and studied today as one of her century's most important mystical writers, Hildegard was never canonized, though she is listed as a saint in the Roman martyrology.

	General/ Context	Daily Life/ Customs/ Practices	Science/ Technology/ Discoveries	Humanities/ Fine Arts	Occupations
1160					
1163	In Europe, dissection of the human body is discouraged by the Church				
1168	Oxford University in England is founded				
1170	Thomas à Becket, made Archbishop of Canterbury in 1162, is murdered in Canterbury Cathedral by agents of King Henry II				
1180	Kamakura period of Japanese history (1192–1333) The Third Crusade (1189–1191) follows the fall of Jerusalem (1187) to Saladin I				
1190	Islam spreads through the subcontinent of India			Herrad of Landsberg composes and illustrates an illuminated manuscript, the *Hortus deliciarum* (*Garden of Delights*), one of the greatest of the medieval pictorial encyclopedias, 1195	
1194					
1199					

Performing Arts/ Entertainment/ Sports	Religion/ Philosophy	Science/ Technology/ Discovery	Statecraft/ Military	
	Anastatius IV, abbess of Edelstetten in Germany German visionary St. Elisabeth of Schönau (1126–1164), whose visions, recorded by her brother, became popular reading in the Middle Ages, is famous for her contribution to the legend of St. Ursula and the 11,000 virgins	*rarum creaturum, Liber simplicis medicinae* or *Physica,* and *Liber compositae medicinae* or *Causa et Curae*	father's death she and her cousin Stephen jockey for power; she intermittently gains control but eventually loses to Stephen; her son becomes Henry II	**1160**
				1163
				1168
	Death of St. Hildegard of Bingen, 1179 Marie d'Oignies (1177–1213) is a visionary Beguine whose biography by Jacques de Vitry is widely read in the late Middle Ages		Eleanor of Aquitaine is imprisoned for 15 years for having backed the rebellion of her two sons against their father, Henry II, 1174; she is released at Richard's accession to the throne	**1170**
			Queen Tamara rules Georgia in Asia, 1184–1212	**1180**
				1190
	12-year-old St. Lutgardis (1182–1246), born in the Netherlands, enters a Benedictine convent because her dowry has been lost in a business speculation; a gifted visionary, she becomes one of the most beloved saints of the Middle Ages			**1194**
			At the death of Japanese shogun Yorito Minamoto, his widow, Masako, and her father assume leadership of the ruling council of 13	**1199**

	General/ Context	Daily Life/ Customs/ Practices	Humanities/ Fine Arts	Occupations
1200	The University of Paris receives its charter	Medieval Frenchwomen c. 1200 wear dresses with wide skirts and close-fitting bodices and sleeves The average age of marriage for noblewomen in the 13th and 14th centuries is 14 to 16; although female mortality in childbirth and male mortality in combat are both high, the average lifespan is 30 to 40 years, the wives often surviving their husbands	Swiss women specialize in the production of textiles—embroidery, laces, brocades, and tapestry; in the countryside, they produce furniture, tableware, and tiles French poet Marie de France is famous for her Breton *lais*, verse romances with Celtic, supernatural, and Arthurian elements; for her beast fables based on Aesop, she is known as Ysopet (little Aesop)	The female Japanese samurai Tomoe is said to be "a match for a thousand warriors and fit to meet either God or devil" In the 12th and 13th centuries, European girls serve as apprentices in craft guilds; some women attached to exclusively female corporations in the clothing industry hold legally defined rights and privileges, including the ability to negotiate contracts and control the guild's finances; according to the *Livre des métiers* of Etienne Boileau, Parisian women hold membership in at least 86 of the 150 trade and craft guilds
1203	Composition of Wolfram von Eschenbach's epic romance *Parzival*			
1204	The Fourth Crusaders (1202–4) sack Constantinople Establishment of the Latin Kingdom of Constantinople			
1208	The Albigensian Crusade is launched; the military might of Europe is directed against a small group of Cathar heretics in the south of France			
1209	Italian friar Giovanni Francesco Bernardone of Assisi, later St. Francis, founds the Franciscan Order (Friars Minor)			

MEDIEVAL MARRIAGE

In Europe during the High Middle Ages (c. 1100–1300) domestic life revolved around the institution of marriage. Men in their late twenties typically wed women in their teens. Only half of these young wives lived through their childbearing years, and many saw nearly half of their children die in infancy. Marriage, though, was a union essential for survival. Most couples spent their lives working the land on which their families' existence depended.

The Christian Church validated the nuclear family by making marriage a sacrament. In theory, the wedded couple mirrored in their own lives the relationship between God and humankind. According to St. Paul, "The head of the woman is the man. . . . For a man indeed ought not to cover his head, forasmuch as he is the image and glory of God: but the woman is the glory of the man." (I Cor. 11:3, 7-9). What man owed to God, woman owed to man. Nevertheless, married couples owed each other equivalent duties, chief among them sex. Considered a debt, each partner might demand sex of the other and expect immediate payment. Though the Church sanctioned only marital sex, and that only for procreation, it recognized that, in St. Paul's words, "It is better to marry than to burn." (I Cor. 7:9). To encourage a new couple's passion, wedding guests shouted obscenities during the ceremony. Nevertheless, the Church placed restrictions on the frequency of sexual inter-

Performing Arts/ Entertainment/ Sports	Religion/ Philosophy	Science/ Technology/ Discovery	Statecraft/ Military	
Lyrics in the 13th-century collection of Latin songs, Carmina Burana, refer to dance and the accompanying songs as feminine activities				**1200**
The *lais* (short musical narrative romances in French) of Marie de France are performed by itinerant singers before courtly audiences in France and England				
				1203
				1204
				1208
				1209

course. The dictate for continence during menses, pregnancy, nursing, and at intervals during the liturgical calendar, as well as before and after communion, kept intercourse at a minimum for most couples. A strictly observant couple might have sex no more than two days a week.

The goods of marriage, though, fell considerably short of the perfection of virginity and chastity. Widows were encouraged by their confessors and often by local law to remain chaste, at least for a time. A woman's desire to remarry argued for her sexual insatiability: why else would she submit herself to the acknowledged bondage of marriage? Ideally, a widow would spend her remaining years in chaste and modest conversation with God—and spend her remaining fortune on good works in the Church. Only in this way might she redeem herself from her loss of virginity; in the medieval hierarchy of female virtue, chaste widows outranked sexually active married women.

The Church's view of marriage, though far more fully documented than any other, did not necessarily reflect what secular people actually thought and did. Widows and widowers did remarry; people manifestly had sex for pleasure as well as to engender children. Many people of both sexes who lived monastic lives had no other choice; and many who married did so for political, financial, or social reasons—not just to avoid "burning."

General/Context	Daily Life/Customs/Practices	Humanities/Fine Arts	Occupations
1212 The Children's Crusade sets out for the Holy Land; slave dealers kidnap and sell one army of children in Egypt while the other army falls apart in Italy; at least 50,000 children are lost, many sold into slavery			
1213 Invasion of China by Genghis Khan			
1215 King John of England signs the Magna Carta Foundation of the Dominican Order (Order of Friars Preachers, or Black Friars) by Spanish-born priest St. Dominic			
1218 Pope Innocent III preaches the Fifth Crusade (1218–1221); it strikes at Egypt but fails Genghis Khan invades the Near East, destroying ancient centers of civilization, 1218–1222			
1219			

St. Clare of Assisi
Photograph © Buch-Kunstverlag Ettal

WOMEN'S WORK IN THE MIDDLE AGES

Women of all cultures throughout time have been doing much of the same work: caring for children, cleaning, cooking, sewing, taking care of the ill, and tending the dying. The universal everyday nature of this kind of work accounts for its historically low status and near invisibility in the historical record.

City women in early civilizations worked as laundresses, shopkeepers, dressmakers, midwives, hairdressers, and physicians. In the countryside, women were involved in all aspects of agriculture and homemaking, performing whatever work was needed to ensure family survival. Women often took in boarders, ran inns, preserved and sold food, spun and carded linen and wool, and took in sewing or produced other household goods to bolster the family economy. Through the ages, too, women and girls have followed armies, not just cooking, washing, and gathering fuel, but digging trenches, nursing the wounded, burying the dead, and, of course, selling their sexual favors.

Social class, then as now, dictated who did what work and under what conditions. In the Middle Ages, for example, servants or slaves performed many caretaking duties for aristocratic women. Nonetheless, noblewomen were not idle: their possessions, estates, and servants demanded their attention as their management often fell to wives whose husbands were away on Crusade. With their own hands they made tapestries and vestments; handled accounts; mediated quarrels; and graciously provided their husbands with a comfortable refuge.

Many women labored at jobs traditionally thought of as men's work. For instance, during the Middle Ages, German and Czechoslovakian women worked in the mines; in 14th-

Performing Arts/ Entertainment/ Sports	Religion/ Philosophy	Science/ Technology/ Discovery	Statecraft/ Military	
	Clare of Assisi, the 18-year-old follower of St. Francis, founds the Order of Poor Clares; though she asks for as stringent a rule as that of the friars, the pope permits only Clare herself to live a life of extreme poverty; he also mandates that the Poor Clares, unlike the mendicant friars who are permitted to travel freely and beg for their sustenance, lived enclosed in a cloister			**1212**
				1213
	St. Agnes of Assisi (1198–1253), the younger sister of St. Clare, is given the habit by St. Francis and sent to San Damiano; she establishes convents at Mantua, Venice, and Padua and supports her sister's struggle for apostolic poverty			**1215**
				1218
			Yoshitoke Hojo and his sister Masako wrest con-	**1219**

century Siena, Italy, they carried sand for the construction of the cathedral; and in Toulouse, France, they helped build the college of Périgord.

Craftsmen who worked in homes and shops were often assisted by their wives; many medieval widows inherited their husbands' businesses. Consequently, women practiced many trades that demanded responsibility and business acumen. Some were large-scale merchants involved in foreign commerce. More typically, medieval women worked with their husbands as butchers, chandlers, ironmongers, net makers, shoemakers, glovers, girdlers, haberdashers, purse makers, cap makers, skinners, bookbinders, gilders, painters, silk weavers and embroiderers, spicers, and goldsmiths.

Unmarried women had to support themselves; some married women carried out wage-earning work distinct from that of their husbands. Girls learned trades by being apprenticed, as did boys, although unlike boys they usually remained apprenticed only until marriage.

The earliest tax records show that women participated in retail guilds, selling a wide variety of goods. Guild privileges, bought with a license, entitled them to occupy choice market sites and buy from wholesalers. Throughout Europe women sold goods that were unrelated to their husbands' professions, and it was not unusual for unmarried or widowed women to support themselves this way. Guilds provided women with special opportunities: marriage to a guildsman provided women with status and financial security. Guildswomen enjoyed independence with their own income and protected craft.

	General/ Context	Daily Life/ Customs/ Practices	Humanities/ Fine Arts	Occupations
1219				
1221				
1222	The University of Padua, Italy, is founded			
1224	The University of Naples, Italy, is founded			
1225	Birth of St. Thomas Aquinas (c. 1225–1274), Catholic theologian and philosopher		The first 4000 lines of *Roman de la rose* (*The Romance of the Rose*) are composed by Guillaume de Lorris c. 1230; the remaining 17,000 lines by Jean de Meun c. 1275; the poem begins as an allegory of love and turns into a virulent antifeminist diatribe	
1226				
1227	Death of Genghis Khan			
1228	The Sixth Crusade (1228–1229), led by Holy Roman Emperor Frederick II, embarks for the Holy Land; Frederick			

Performing Arts/ Entertainment/ Sports	Religion/ Philosophy	Science/ Technology/ Discovery	Statecraft/ Military	
			trol of Japan from the Minamoto family; though they install their own shogun, the real power remains in their hands	**1219**
	Patron saint of queens, St. Elizabeth of Hungary (1207–1231) marries Louis of Thuringia at the age of 14; she lives a life of prayer and austerity, building hospitals and caring for the poor and the sick; at her husband's death in 1228, she renounces the world, becoming a Franciscan tertiary			**1221**
				1222
	St. Christina Mirabilis (the "Astonishing," 1150–1224) of St. Trond, Belgium, is known for her repeated returns from death, her repugnance for the smell of humans, and her remarkable physical feats			**1224**
				1225
			Known as the "wisest of all women of her time," Queen Blanche of Castile (1188–1252), mother of Louis IX of France (later St. Louis), becomes regent for her 12-year-old son at the death of her husband; through her courage, diligence, and political abilities she controls ambitious barons until her son attains his majority	**1226**
				1227
				1228

	General/ Context	Daily Life/ Customs/ Practices	Humanities/ Fine Arts	Occupations
1228	ends the Crusade the next year by signing a treaty with the Egyptian sultan The inquisition established at Toulouse by the Albigensian Crusaders forbids laypeople to read the Bible			
1229	Foundation of the University of Toulouse, France	The ancient Japanese custom of *ohaguro*, staining the teeth black, becomes widely accepted as a mark of beauty		
1231	Cambridge University in England is founded	In spite of the Japanese shogun's order not to sell children into slavery, Japanese farmers continue—for centuries—to sell their daughters		
1236			English embroiderer Mabel produces pearl-studded vestments for Henry III of England (1239–1241); later she is commissioned to make "a standard of ruby samite well embroidered with gold and with images of the Virgin and St. John" for Westminster Abbey	
1240	Birth of Bolognese poet Guido Guinizelli (1240?–?1274), who founds the *dolce stil nuovo* school of love poetry; its practitioners include Guido Cavalcanti and Dante Alighieri			
1244	Foundation of the University of Rome, Italy			
1246				
1248	The Seventh Crusade (1248–1250) called to recapture Jerusalem from the Egyptians, is led by King Louis IX of France; the Crusade fails and Jerusalem remains in Muslim hands until 1918			
1249				

Performing Arts/ Entertainment/ Sports	Religion/ Philosophy	Science/ Technology/ Discovery	Statecraft/ Military	
				1228
	The German convent of Helfta, famous for the intellectual and spiritual flowering brought about under its abbess Gertrude of Hackeborn (elected in 1251), is founded			1229
				1231
	St. Agnes of Bohemia (1205–1282) founds a house of Poor Clares in Prague; she is called the "half-self" of St. Clare of Assisi		Sultan Altamsh, of the Delhi slave dynasty, is succeeded by his daughter Raziy'yat-ud-din, who rules until she is assassinated by her Hindu followers four years later; she is the first Muslim woman to rule on the Indian subcontinent	1236
	Christina of Stommeln (1242–c. 1312) is a visionary and stigmatic whose life story becomes popular reading in the years following her death Anastasia is the Pomeranian founder of the Red Monastery at Spalato, Slavonia			1240
				1244
	St. Juliana of Mont Cornillon (1192–1258) founds the Feast of Corpus Christi at Liège			1246
				1248
			Shahar al-Dur ("spray of pearls"), the only woman	1249

107

	General/ Context	Daily Life/ Customs/ Practices	Humanities/ Fine Arts	Occupations
1249				
1250	Death of Holy Roman Emperor Frederick II (1194–1250)	Philippe de Navarre's treatise on conduct advises women not to learn to read unless they intend to become nuns, lest they encounter love letters that contain indecent language		
1252	The Inquisition (established by the Roman Catholic Church to investigate charges of heresy) employs torture for the first time in extracting confessions King Louis IX expels the Jews from France			
1253	The Sorbonne University is founded in Paris, France			
1258	In response to widespread famine and disease, a flagellant movement springs up in Europe; many women are attracted to these and other grassroots religious movements			
1261	The Latin kingdom of Constantinople falls			
1262			Fu-Jen Kuan (1262–1319) is one of the finest Chinese bamboo painters	
1264	Yuan, or Mongol, dynasty beings in China (1264–1368)			
1269				

Performing Arts/ Entertainment/ Sports	Religion/ Philosophy	Science/ Technology/ Discovery	Statecraft/ Military	
			to rule Egypt during the Islamic era, begins her reign by eliminating her son, a rival to the throne, 1249	**1249**
	German Beguine St. Mechthild of Magdeburg (b. c. 1207–1282) composes the first four books of her *Fliessende Licht der Gottheit* (*Flowing Light of the Godhead*) Persecution of witches begins in France; it continues with ever greater zeal until the mid-18th century	St. Thomas Aquinas describes reproductive biology; his Aristotelian ideas will exercise enormous influence in gender definitions for centuries to come		**1250**
				1252
				1253
				1258
	St. Gertrude the Great (c. 1256–1302) comes to the abbey of Helfta in Saxony; in her time, Helfta becomes a center of spiritual activity			**1261**
				1262
				1264
	The wealthy English noblewoman Dervorguila, Lady of Galloway (d. 1298), establishes a number of religious houses during the 13th century, including the Cistercian Sweetheart Abbey; following her husband's			**1269**

	General/ Context	Daily Life/ Customs/ Practices	Humanities/ Fine Arts	Occupations
1269				
1270	The Eighth Crusade is called off when its leader, Louis IX of France, dies in Tunisia			
1271	The Ninth and Final Crusade (1271–1272), led by Prince Edward of England, accomplishes little			
1275	Marco Polo reaches Yunnan, China, and enters the service of Kublai Khan			
1279	The Yuan dynasty in China, 1279–1368, is founded by Kublai Khan	Under the Yuan, Ming, and Qing dynasties, the chastity of widows is highly valued		
1282	The Sicilian Vespers rebellion precipitates a wholesale massacre of the French and a war that lasts for years			
1286				
1289		Francesca da Rimini (d.1285?) is put to death for her love affair with Paolo Malatesta, her husband's brother; the affair has become the subject of several important literary renditions		
1290	King Edward I expels the Jews from England Formation of the League of the Three Forest Cantons, the beginning of Switzerland	In medieval Spain, women at court often bleach their hair, which they wear long and flowing; they may wear loose-flowing robes and gowns in bright contrasting colors or gowns belted tightly under the breasts	Death of Beatrice Portinari (1266–1290), the beloved of Dante Alighieri, in whose *Divine Comedy* and *Vita Nuova* she symbolizes spiritual love and divine revelation; she was married to Simone de' Bardi	

Performing Arts/ Entertainment/ Sports	Religion/ Philosophy	Science/ Technology/ Discovery	Statecraft/ Military	
	death, she continues to support Balliol College, founded by her husband, John de Baliol, in 1263			1269
				1270
				1271
				1275
				1279
	The mystic Douceline founds an institute of Beguines at Marseilles Ingrid Elovsdotter becomes the first Swedish Dominican nun			1282
	St. Margaret of Cortona (1247–1297), Franciscan tertiary and former courtesan, is granted a charter by the bishop of Arezzo to establish a hospital and a house of nursing sisters, called the Poverelle; she also founds the Confraternity of Our Lady of Mercy to support the hospital and assist the poor			1286
				1289
	Death of St. Cecilia Romana (c. 1200–1290), the first Dominican nun of San Sisto in Rome	It is said of Claranna von Hohenburg, a Swiss nun in Kloster St. Kathrinen, Diessenhofen, that she was so advanced in scientific knowledge that she had not only read the books of Dionysius the Areopagite, but had understood them as well	The mysterious death of the child Queen Margaret of Scotland, known as the Maid of Norway (1283–1290), leaves Scotland without a monarch and precipitates a serious civil war over the Scottish succession	1290

	General/Context	Daily Life/Customs/Practices	Humanities/Fine Arts	Occupations
1292				The Paris census records the names of eight female physicians, in addition to the more usual midwives, apothecaries, and surgeons
1298	Earliest spinning wheel invented in Germany			
1300	Until this century, men and women of the feudal nobility receive approximately the same education—elementary instruction in reading and writing; the rise of universities, which deny admission to women, heightens the disparity between men's and women's opportunities for intellectual and professional activities	Among the feudal nobility of France, parents often arrange marriages for children still in the cradle in order to secure financial and social advantage Paolo da Certaldo's *Handbook of Good Customs* advises against women learning to read, unless they are to become nuns The most common accusations against women in northern European towns are brawling, cheating, beating servants, and robbing tavern customers, as well as more serious charges of adultery, murder, theft, arson, heresy, abortion, and infanticide	Legend identifies that the early 14th-century sculptor Sabina von Steinbach as the creator of some of the figures decorating Strasbourg Cathedral; unfortunately, the legend is based on a mistranslation During the 14th century, Philippa of Hainaut, Edward III's queen, backs coal mining on her estates in England, establishing the fortunes of the northeastern ports in England	By this year, the number of women in guilds has increased substantially in Paris; the tax roll lists 36 female silk spinners, up from eight in 1292
1304				
1305				
1308				
1309	Pope Clement V moves the papacy to Avignon in France, beginning the 78-year Babylonian Captivity			
1310				

Performing Arts/ Entertainment/ Sports	Religion/ Philosophy	Science/ Technology/ Discovery	Statecraft/ Military	
				1292
				1298
	The 14th-century saint Hugolina of Vercelli, Italy, lives for 47 years disguised as a male hermit European women enjoy greater opportunities for travel by this century, particularly on pilgrimages to holy shrines			**1300**
	St. Juliana Falconieri (1270–1340) draws up a code of regulations for women of the Servite order, called "Mantellate," not formally confirmed until 1424			**1304**
	Italian Benedictine Santuccia Terrebotti founds 24 convents in Italy while successfully persuading her husband to become a monk			**1305**
	At her death, the heart of St. Clare of Montefalco (b. c. 1268) is said to have an image of the cross imprinted on it			**1308**
				1309
	Marguerite d'Oingt, Carthusian prioress and			**1310**

	General/ Context	Daily Life/ Customs/ Practices	Humanities/ Fine Arts	Occupations
1310				
1313				
1317				
1320				In French cities, women earn a maximum of 68% of men's wages in all professions
1321	Foundation of the University of Florence, Italy			
1324				
1325				
1327			Some believe that Laura, the source, according to Petrarch, of his poetic inspiration, is the historical Laure de Noves of Avignon (1308–1348), but most regard her as a poetic fiction	

Performing Arts/ Entertainment/ Sports	Religion/ Philosophy	Science/ Technology/ Discovery	Statecraft/ Military	
	mystic at Poleteins, writes *The Mirror of St. Marguerite d'Oignt*, one of the most influential mystical works of the Middle Ages French Beguine Marguerite Porete is burned for heresy in Paris			1310
	St. Notburga (1266–1313), a German peasant who spent her life as Count Henry of Rattenberg's housekeeper, is renowned for her care of the poor			1313
			In France, the Estates General invoke the Salic Law to prevent the throne from reverting to the female line	1317
	Margaret of Città-di-Castello (b. c. 1287) a blind Italian Dominican tertiary and mystic, is venerated as the patron of the blind and of abused children			1320
				1321
	Petronilla of Meath is the first Irish woman to be burned for witchcraft in Dublin			1324
	St. Isabel of Portugal (d. 1336) is known for founding many charitable establishments prior to her entry into the religious life Arrested by the Inquisition, Lady Prous Boneta (c. 1290–1325) declares herself to have been given the Holy Spirit by God "as it had been given to the Virgin"; at her trial she declares that the pope and the sacraments have ceased to exist; she is burned at the stake			1325
			Queen Isabella of England and Roger de Mortimer depose King Edward II by having the Parliament force his abdication and replace him with his 14-year-old son	1327

	General/ Context	Daily Life/ Customs/ Practices	Humanities/ Fine Arts	Occupations
1330				
1333	The Black Death begins in China			
1337	Hundred Years War begins			
1338				
1341				
1342			Marie de Saint Pole, the pious widow of the earl of Pembroke, founds Pembroke College in Cambridge, England	
1344				
1346				
1347		In an effort to control venereal disease, Jane I, queen of the Sicilies and countess of Provence, opens a brothel in Avi- gnon, where prostitutes are required to be exam- ined weekly		
1348	The Black Death sweeps Europe			

Performing Arts/ Entertainment/ Sports	Religion/ Philosophy	Science/ Technology/ Discovery	Statecraft/ Military	
			Queen Isabella of England is put under restraint by her son, Edward III	1330
				1333
				1337
			Known as Black Agnes, Agnes Dunbar (c. 1312–1369), countess of Dunbar and March and granddaughter of the Scottish King Robert the Bruce, successfully defends her castle against a five-month siege mounted by King Edward III of England, eager to annex Scotland	1338
			Kasa (whose name means "queen" in the African language of Mandinke) rules the ancient empire of Mali in West Africa with her husband, King Mansa Sulaiman, until 1360	1341
				1342
	St. Bridget of Sweden's (1304–1373) visions and prophecies form *Revelations*, important sources of iconography in late-medieval and Renaissance art; founder of the Bridgettines, she is the patron saint of Sweden			1344
			Queen Philippa of Hainaut of England raises troops to defeat the Scots, who attack during the absence of King Edward III and his army	1346
				1347
	Joanna de Segni is famed for tending victims of the Black Death			1348

117

	General/ Context	Daily Life/ Customs/ Practices	Humanities/ Fine Arts	Occupations
1350	At about this time the Italian Renaissance begins and spreads slowly throughout Europe	Single women in towns can support themselves by spinning or brewing, by managing a shop, tavern, bakery, or barbershop, or by working as a seamstress, money changer, bathhouse attendant, maidservant, wet nurse, washerwoman, or entertainer		Philippa of Hainaut supports the wool industry in Norwich and fosters trading links between England and her native Flanders
1353			Giovanni Boccaccio completes his *Decameron;* the work reveals an unusual appreciation of women's intellectual and psychological abilities	
1355				
1358	The Jacquerie uprising of French peasants against their overlords			
1360			Elsbeth Stagel (c. 1330–1360), the first important Swiss female poet, composes *Lives of the Sisters in the Convent of Töss,* one of the finest works of mystical literature of the period	
1368	Ming dynasty in China (1368–1644)	Foot binding becomes so prestigious in aristocratic Chinese circles that the first emperor of the Ming dynasty forbids jokes about big feet, because they reflect on his wife's unbound feet		
1373				
1375				

Performing Arts/ Entertainment/ Sports	Religion/ Philosophy	Science/ Technology/ Discovery	Statecraft/ Military	
				1350
				1353
			King Alfonso IV of Portugal puts Spanish noblewoman Inés de Castro (c. 1320?–1355), mistress and later wife of Alfonso's heir, Pedro, to death; when Pedro becomes king in 1357, he has her body exhumed and placed upon a throne, so that his courtiers might render her the homage denied her during her life	**1355**
				1358
				1360
				1368
	Julian of Norwich (c. 1343–1413) is the author of *Revelations of Divine Love,* one of the first books in English written by a woman			**1373**
			Queen Margaret of Denmark, Norway, and Sweden (1353–1412), acts as regent for her son in Denmark	**1375**

	General/ Context	Daily Life/ Customs/ Practices	Humanities/ Fine Arts	Occupations
1378	The Great Schism, dividing the Catholic Church and setting up rival papacies in Rome and Avignon, begins			
1380		The French knight Geoffrey de la Tour Landry writes a book of advice to his daughters, recommending patience with their husbands' infidelity; if his daughters were to commit adultery, though, they would be subject to legal punishment		
1381	The Peasants' Revolt, the first popular uprising in England against oppressive taxes, is led by Wat Tyler			
1382				

CHRISTINE DE PIZAN: THE FIRST FEMINIST

Probably the first woman since antiquity to support herself as a professional writer, Christine de Pizan (c. 1364–c. 1430) was the daughter of a distinguished Italian astrologer-physician at the court of Charles V in Paris. Christine was given the elementary education permitted to young girls of her day. She was married at 15 to a notary with some university training, whose appointment as royal secretary exposed the young couple to the humanist crosscurrents of the French court. Left a widow at the age of 25, Christine had three children and an elderly mother to support; both her father and his patron, Charles V, had died. In desperation, she turned to what she knew best—the plume.

Some 10 years passed before Christine's career as a writer began, and we do not know for certain how she supported herself in the meanwhile. Most likely she took on work as a manuscript copyist, one of the few profitable occupations open to women, in Paris's flourishing book trade. If she did, she may have made copies for patrons of works that later served as sources for her own.

Christine's poetry seems to have come into vogue around 1402, when she assembled her *Cent balades* (*One Hundred Ballads*). Around the same time, she joined with some of the most important Parisian humanists in the debate over the misogynist satire in Jean de Meun's part of the *Roman de la rose,* a famous allegorical poem. Her spirited part in the debate—conducted through letters and tracts—made her famous as a defender of her sex.

Performing Arts/ Entertainment/ Sports	Religion/ Philosophy	Science/ Technology/ Discovery	Statecraft/ Military	
				1378
	St. Catherine of Siena (1347–1380) is best known for encouraging Pope Gregory XI to return to Rome from Avignon and for her letters to the pope and her written dialogues and revelations The visions of Lidwina (1380–1433), a religious sister at Schiedam in Belgium, are the source of inspiration for the 15th-century German mystic Thomas à Kempis, author of *Imitation of Christ*			**1380**
				1381
			Louis the Great of Hungary and Poland is succeeded in Hungary by his daughter Mary of Anjou and in Poland by his daughter Jadwiga Anne of Bohemia (1366–1394) marries King Richard II of England; she helps spread John Wycliffe's heretical doctrines and introduces Bohemian caps and sidesaddles to England	**1382**

Among other lengthy works, Christine wrote two important explorations of women's role in society, *Cité des dames* (*City of Ladies*) and its sequel, *Livre des trois vertus* (*Book of Three Virtues*). The first incorporates into biographies of famous women discussions of women's problems; the second, addressed to women of all classes, suggests how they might make the most of the opportunities available to them. Together, the works offer a clear explication of the problems and solutions women faced in late medieval French society.

In the wake of many works on subjects as diverse as history, education, politics, mythology, military strategy, and religion, Christine's last poem, written in 1429, celebrates Joan of Arc's victory at Orléans and the coronation of Charles II. The poem triumphantly expresses Christine's joy that a young girl could bring about such a miraculous reversal of France's fortunes—in a sense justifying Christine's 20-year defense of women. Though as far as we know she wrote nothing more, her works were widely copied and read well into the 16th century. Several of her works were translated into Middle English, Flemish, and Portuguese, and her audience included Margaret of Austria, Mary of Hungary, Louise of Savoy, Anne of Brittany, and Queen Leonora of Portugal. Unlike so many writers of either sex, she seems to have realized the ambition she expressed in her autobiographical *La vision de Christine*: to win renown for her true merits and accomplishments.

	General/ Context	Daily Life/ Customs/ Practices	Humanities/ Fine Arts	Occupations
1383				
1386			Geoffrey Chaucer (1340?–1400) writes *The Legend of Good Women,* nine verse narratives recounting the lives of women, and begins writing *The Canterbury Tales*	
1387				
1388				
1389				
1397				
1399			Christine de Pizan defends women against Jean de Meun's antifeminism in her *Epistle to the God of Love;* she writes a second defense in 1400	
1400		Burgundian fashion in noblewomen's headgear calls for high headdresses made of kerchiefs drawn over a frame, forming bull's horns, or draped with a veil; women's dresses become long and trailing, with short low-necked bodices, the outer garment trimmed with fur and draped to expose the gown beneath; middle-class women wear large linen headdresses that	Some medieval legends hold that the first roses appeared miraculously in Bethlehem when the burning brands meant to execute an unjustly accused "fayre mayden" turn into roses in response to her prayer Antoine de la Sale writes the satirical *Les quinze joyes de mariage* (*The Fifteen Joys of Marriage*), describing the trials men suffer in marriage	

122

Performing Arts/ Entertainment/ Sports	Religion/ Philosophy	Science/ Technology/ Discovery	Statecraft/ Military	
			When Portugal's Ferdinand I (b. 1345) dies without a male heir, his widow, Leonora, reigns as regent for their daughter Beatrix, who marries Juan of Castille; they are overthrown two years later	1383
				1386
			At her son Olaf II's death, Margaret of Denmark succeeds to both the Danish and Norwegian thrones	1387
			Margaret of Denmark is elected queen of Norway by the Norwegians	1388
			Margaret of Denmark and Norway is offered the Swedish throne: she defeats the Swedish king and takes him prisoner; she persuades the diets of the three countries to accept her grandnephew, Eric of Pomerania, as king	1389
			Queen Margaret of Denmark, Norway, and Sweden designs the Union of Kalmar uniting Denmark, Norway, and Sweden under a single monarchy	1397
				1399
A woman chosen to be Maid Marian (consort of the legendary Robin Hood) acts as the Lady of Misrule in British Yuletide revels; she is also associated with May Day revels				1400

	General/ Context	Structure/ Military	Daily Life/ Customs/ Practices	Science/ Technology/ Discovery	Humanities/ Fine Arts	Religion/ Philosophy	Occupations	Athletics/ Entertainment/ Sports
1400			completely cover their hair In the 15th century, a biographical dictionary lists 1763 notable Arab women, many of whom are scholars					
1406								
1412								
1413								
1415	The Battle of Agincourt shatters the French nobility							
1426								
1427			Mohnyinthado, king of Ava, marries Shin Bomai, making her his junior queen; he and his chief queen found the Burmese dynasty of Ava					
1429								
1430								

124

Performing Arts/ Entertainment/ Sports	Religion/ Philosophy	Science/ Technology/ Discovery	Statecraft/ Military	
				1400
	St. Colette of Corbie (1380–1447), over the course of 40 years, founds 17 new convents and reforms old ones in France, Savoy, Flanders, and Spain			**1406**
			Death of Queen Margaret of Denmark, Norway, and Sweden who has been known as the "Semiramis of the North"	**1412**
	Catherine de' Vigri (1413–1463), patron saint of Bologna and of artists, is known for her paintings, liturgical music, and spiritual autobiography, *The Seven Spiritual Weapons*			**1413**
A proclamation to the York Play demands that the acting guilds exclude people whose voices do not project, probably one of the reasons women are not permitted to act				**1415**
	Joan of Arc (La Pucelle, 1412–1431) begins to experience visions and voices, which urge her to join the French forces fighting the English			**1426**
				1427

Joan of Arc
Photograph courtesy Lauros-Giraudon/Art Resource

			With Joan of Arc at its head, the French army raises the English siege around Orléans; Joan stands by the dauphin as he is crowned Charles VII of France	**1429**
	German nun Magdalena Beutler of Freiburg			**1430**

General/ Context	Daily Life/ Customs/ Practices	Humanities/ Fine Arts	Occupations
1430			
1431			
1438 Johann Gutenberg develops the printing press in Mainz, Germany			
1440			
1442		*Champion of the Ladies* by Martin de France mounts a passionate defense of women against medieval misogyny	

MARGERY KEMPE: THE FIRST ENGLISH AUTOBIOGRAPHER

The first known autobiography in English was written by a woman: Margery Kempe, a 15th-century housewife from the town of King's Lynn. After bearing 13 children and running a mill and a brewery, she became an itinerant visionary, making pilgrimages to the Holy Land and dictating her life story to priestly scribes. Her richly textured *Book* offers an intimate view of her experiences and tells us much about the daily life of ordinary people in medieval England.

Margery Kempe was the daughter of the one-time mayor of King's Lynn; she married a merchant and lived happily with him for many years. Following the birth of her first child, though, she seems to have suffered from a violent postpartum depression, from which she was healed by a vision of Christ. Many years and children intervened before she gave up her fine clothes and social ambitions to become an ascetic, blessed with the "gift of tears"—bitter, loud weeping in church that disrupted the service and annoyed the congregation. Her neighbors, who knew her well, regarded her conversion skeptically, as did many strangers whom she sought to convert. Nevertheless, encouraged, she tells us, by frequent visions of Christ and Mary, she persisted in her holy life. Apprehended several times during her wanderings on the suspicion of heresy, she managed to persuade her inquisitors (including the bishop of Lincoln) of her orthodoxy.

Performing Arts/ Entertainment/ Sports	Religion/ Philosophy	Science/ Technology/ Discovery	Statecraft/ Military	
	(1407–1458) predicts that anyone witnessing her death will automatically gain salvation; on January 6, she is placed before the convent church's altar, where she is seen by the city's council, representatives of the regional Dominican authorities, and hundreds of believers; she is declared dead by the city doctor, and, on the command of her confessor, rises again; though most are satisfied by what they have seen, some believe her to be a witch; such public displays of piety were practiced by many nuns in contintental Europe			**1430**
	Margery Kempe (b. 1373) dictates her life story		After her capture by the English in May 1430, Joan of Arc is tried by an ecclesiastical court, which finds her guilty of heresy; she is burned at the stake in the marketplace in Rouen	**1431**
				1438
	St. Frances of Rome (1384–1440), founds the Oblates of Mary; the church of Santa Francesca Romana is named after her			**1440**
	St. Margaret of Ravenna (1442–1505) is the founder of the Congregation of the Good Jesus			**1442**

Margery patterned her conversion on a continental tradition of affective piety whose chief exponents had been women since the early 12th century. Her particular model was St. Bridget of Sweden, whose *Revelations* circulated in vernacular translations all over Europe. Women mystics like Bridget could pursue lives of risk, adventure, and spiritual exploration; Margery, in imitating such models, could break free of the ordinary tedium of her life, compel an audience, and command respect. Though illiterate, she understood the importance of committing her visions and revelations to writing in the services of those goals. She found herself a cleric to take dictation and, when he died, she found another.

Whether Margery was a real mystic or not has been hotly debated since the discovery of her manuscript in 1934. To some, she seems to be trying too hard, to be too calculating, too conscious of what she is doing. Others find her persuasive, arguing that her social and educational background, not her ambition, account for the homely quality of her narrative. However we regard her mysticism, *The Book of Margery Kempe* provides modern readers with intimate, confessional, authentic testimony of a medieval woman at once extraordinary and typical.

	General/ Context	Daily Life/ Customs/ Practices	Humanities/ Fine Arts	Occupations
1444		The beautiful Agnès Sorel (1422–1450), called Mlle. de Beauté, becomes the mistress of King Charles VII of France; she remains politically influential until her death		
1445				
1446			Italian Carmelite nun Antonia Uccello (1446–1491), daughter of Paolo Uccello, is admired for her extraordinary drawing talent	Margaret, duchess of Burgundy, sister of King Edward IV, is active in political affairs; she is the patron of William Caxton, the first printer of English books
1452				The first professional association for midwives is founded in Regensburg, Germany
1453	Hundred Years War ends			
1455				
1460			Suor Barbara Ragnoni, Italian artist, is credited with the painting of an adoration of the shepherds, a fine example of the Sienese school in the late 15th century	
1462				
1463				
1465		Around this time, European women adopt the chopine, a style of platform shoe; in some areas, ladies of fashion wear chopines up to 30 inches high	Margaret of Anjou and Elizabeth Woodville are the founders and benefactresses of Queens College in Cambridge, England	

Performing Arts/ Entertainment/ Sports	Religion/ Philosophy	Science/ Technology/ Discovery	Statecraft/ Military	
				1444
			Margaret of Anjou (1430–1482) marries English King Henry VI; rivalry between her and the duke of York leads to the War of the Roses	**1445**
				1446
				1452
				1453
	24 years after her execution, the trial and the verdict that condemned Joan of Arc as a heretic are overturned; she is completely rehabilitated			**1455**
				1460
			Queen Margaret of Anjou's army, under Pierre de Breze, launches an abortive raid on England	**1462**
	After 28 years of governing the duchy of Alençon, Margaret of Lorraine (1463–1521) becomes a Poor Clare at a convent she founds in Argentan, France			**1463**
				1465

	General/ Context	Daily Life/ Customs/ Practices	Humanities/ Fine Arts	Occupations
1469				
1470		Mid-15th-century Spanish women begin to wear *verdugados*, wide skirts reinforced with strips of wood Jane Shore (1445?–1527?) becomes the mistress of King Edward IV of England; wields so much political influence after Edward's death that his successor, Richard III, accuses her of witchcraft; she is imprisoned and dies in poverty and disgrace		
1473				
1474	William Caxton prints the first book in English			
1476				

MORE WOMEN WARRIORS

From the Middle Ages to modern times, the world has produced women warriors of exceptional caliber, although their exploits, with few exceptions, are not widely known. Such women were both active participants and pawns in men's wars.

Tamara of Georgia in Asia, an ascetic and an avid hunter with a flair for military strategy, was called "king" by the men she led into battle because she campaigned with them and suffered their hardships. By the time she died in 1212, she had conquered Turks, Persians, Russians, and Armenians who bordered Georgia and caused her country to flourish for 24 years as it never had before or since. Though canonized by the Georgian church, tales of erotic excess became attached to her legend. Odd as it may seem, the saint/voluptuary duality is common in Western legends of women warriors. Their violent deeds associate them in the popular imagination with maleness, in particular with aggressive sexuality and its converse, heroic abstinence. Such women are rarely perceived as "normal": they must represent one sexual extreme or another (or very often, both).

Some French women fighters became famous duelists while large numbers of others died fighting in the Crusades, unidentified and unhonored by history. The most famous of them was Joan of Arc, a peasant girl who crowned the king of France in Rheims Cathedral. Instructed by mystical voices to fight the English and save France, she donned men's clothing, cropped her hair, and offered her services to the dauphin. After a number of successes in battle against the English, she was captured and tried for heresy and witchcraft, charges supported by her men's garb and by the almost inconceivable fact of her virginity. How, her accusers asked, could she eat, sleep, and fight with men and not be raped if she were not a witch? Because she posed a threat to English victory, she was found guilty and burned at the stake.

In 15th-century Spain, Queen Isabella, known as the "crusading warrior queen," fought ruthlessly to unite Spain. A woman of exceptional stamina and horsemanship, Isabella directed battles against the Moors, then later, in the tradition of

Performing Arts/ Entertainment/ Sports	Religion/ Philosophy	Science/ Technology/ Discovery	Statecraft/ Military	
			King Ferdinand II of Aragon (1452–1516) and Queen Isabella of Castile (1451–1504) marry, consolidating the two kingdoms	**1469**
				1470
			Caterina Cornaro (1454–1510) rules the kingdom of Cyprus after the death of her husband, James II of Lusignan	**1473**
				1474
			Louise of Savoy (1476–1531) serves as regent of	**1476**

many male warrior leaders, oversaw the eradication of domestic enemies—in her case expelling the Jews from Spain and establishing the Inquisition to eradicate heresy from her Catholic land.

By the 17th and 18th centuries, the warlike exploits of more women began to be recorded. Christina Ross, for example, fought for 10 years as a British trooper until her sex was discovered. She was permitted to stay on in the army as a cook and became the legendary "Mother Ross." Women fought at sea as well, as pirates, like Ann Bonney and Mary Reade in the 1720s, and as sailors in the navy, like British tar Mary Anne Talbot (1778–1808).

Women fought in the American Revolution too. Among the best known was Mary Hayes, known as "Molly Pitcher," who earned her nom de guerre by supplying American soldiers with water and manning the cannon of her collapsed husband. Other women were active in prewar revolutionary terrorist organizations, including one group of five captured after terrorizing their neighborhood disguised as Indians. Meanwhile, the Matrons of the Iroquois League, among them one Mary Brant, played a major role in keeping the western tribes of the Six Nations allied with the British.

In the 19th century, the rani of Jhansi developed a legendary reputation with her enemies, the British, in India. She died in hand-to-hand combat leading troops in the Sepoy mutiny after ferocious engagements that gained her a sometimes gruesome, sometimes lurid reputation as "the most dangerous of rebel leaders" in India.

The image of an armed woman fighting beside and against men challenged the notion of women as the smaller, softer, weaker, gentler sex, the sex that needs to be protected. Suspected of being "unnatural" in more ways than their fighting ability, the existence of women warriors threatened socially constructed conceptions of gender. If women can fight and win, what can't they do?

	General/ Context	Daily Life/ Customs/ Practices	Humanities/ Fine Arts	Occupations
1476				
1478	The Spanish Inquisition is established			
1485		French ladies adopt the *barbette*, a hoodlike veil with a pleated kerchief in front		
1486			British noblewoman Juliana Berners (b. 1388?) is the author of what may be the first book by a woman to appear in print, *Book of St. Albans*	
1488				Mother Shipton (b. c. 1488?) survives accusations of witchcraft based on her claims of prophetic powers and lives to be 73
1490	As favorite daughter and confidante of Louis XI, Anne de Beaujeu becomes guardian of her brother Charles VIII	Middle-class Italian women of the early Renaissance wear high-bodiced dresses with tight sleeves German women of the middle class typically wear trailing gowns with laced bodices	Properzia de' Rossi (1490–1530) is cited by Giorgio Vasari as the first woman sculptor; she is celebrated for her complex sculptures	

THE GREAT WITCHCRAFT MANIA

Though the persecution of witches began in the Middle Ages, it increased dramatically after the Reformation. Initially, witchcraft was regarded as a form of heresy. Stereotypes inherited from antiquity were applied almost unaltered to medieval heretics; they included ritual fornication with a demonic beast, and destruction of the surrounding community by malicious magic. In the two centuries of the great witchcraft mania, these stereotypes were refined, applied principally to women, and associated with non-Christian, rather than unorthodox Christian, belief. While men were sometimes accused of witchcraft, the vast majority of accusations fell upon older lower-class women, especially widows who lived outside small villages.

Both Protestants and Catholics justified witch-hunts with theological arguments about the power of the devil and ancient assumptions about women's nature. Beginning in the late 15th century, printing presses poured forth sensational tracts encouraging superstitious terror of the putative power of witches. Meanwhile, religious and civil wars left people doubting authority and anxious about the stability of their world. Secular and religious rulers eager to restore stability found persecution of outgroups a useful means of turning the

Performing Arts/ Entertainment/ Sports	Religion/ Philosophy	Science/ Technology/ Discovery	Statecraft/ Military	
			France while the king is away	**1476**
			Empress Helena Sabla of Ethiopia (d. 1522) becomes regent for four successive child emperors after the death of her husband; as the ruler of a Christian state isolated in a Muslim world, she maintains a delicate balance of alliances to keep her country independent	**1478**
	Lady Margaret Beaufort founds and supports many academic and religious institutions; she writes books and lectures			**1485**
				1486
				1488
	Beatrice de Silva founds the Franciscan Order of the Conception of Our Lady after walling herself up for 40 years			**1490**

Finding the devil's mark
Engraving by T. H. Matteson; illustration courtesy Sophia Smith Collection, Smith College

focus of discontent away from their foundering institutions.

The witch-hunter's handbook, *Malleus Maleficarum* (*The Hammer of Witches*), written in 1486 by two German monks who had hunted witches themselves, instructed officials in the methods of identifying, trying, and executing witches. In accordance with the legal procedures they inherited from medieval jurisprudence, they recommended torture as a way of eliciting confessions.

By the mid-1500s, almost no one doubted the power of witchcraft; those who did could bring upon themselves accusations of heresy. Witchcraft trials became opportunities to rid society of people, both men and women, who had behaved in a socially or even politically objectionable way.

Between 1480 and 1700, a period associated with enlightened humanism and important Church reform, more people were prosecuted, convicted, and punished for witchcraft than at any other time, fully three quarters of them women. We estimate that more than 100,000 trials took place, resulting in somewhat fewer executions. Why misogyny should ignite an entire continent at this particular period remains a mystery. Like any other irrational mass behavior, its complex causes seem insufficient to account for its shocking effects.

	General/ Context	Daily Life/ Customs/ Practices	Humanities/ Fine Arts	Occupations
1491				
1492	Genoese navigator Christopher Columbus claims the New World for his Spanish backers, Queen Isabella and King Ferdinand of Spain Book publishing becomes a recognized profession Incan Empire is at its height under Topa Inca			
1497				
1499				
1500	English and French brides abandon the customary yellow and begin to wear white to symbolize their virginity	In Italy from the 14th to the 16th centuries, fair hair is preferred to dark; women shave their eyebrows and foreheads, sometimes up to the middle of the head, to produce the impression of an egglike molded brow Well-to-do Moorish women in Spain wear long baggy trousers under a pleated tunic A noble lady at the French court is likely to wear a barrel-shaped skirt over a hoop (*vertugade* or *vertugalle*) Turkish women of the 16th and 17th centuries wear wide baggy breeches, as do men; they also wear cotton or silk undergarments, one or two outer garments, and a tarboosh, or fez, which may be draped with a veil		

Performing Arts/ Entertainment/ Sports	Religion/ Philosophy	Science/ Technology/ Discovery	Statecraft/ Military	
			Anne of Brittany marries Charles VIII of France; the independent dukedom of Brittany, of which she had been sovereign, is annexed to France	**1491**
			Queen Isabella and King Ferdinand expel the Jews from Spain and confiscate their property	**1492**
			Queen Aissa Koli assumes the rule of the West African state of Kanem-Bornu; she relinquishes sole rule in 1504 when her younger brother turns 12, but continues as a close adviser during his reign	**1497**
			Diane de Postiers (1499–1566), mistress of Henry II of France until his death exercises great power over him	**1499**
	Caritas Pirckheimer (1467–1532), abbess of the Klara Kloster at Nürnberg, Germany, is known as the erudite friend and correspondent of many famous humanist scholars	Jakob Nufer of Switzerland performs the first recorded cesarean operation on a pregnant woman	According to Aztec legend, Paranazin, the sister of Montezuma, emerges from one of her frequent cataleptic trances to forecast the arrival of an army of foreign ships that would conquer the empire	**1500**

	General/ Context	Daily Life/ Customs/ Practices	Humanities/ Fine Arts	Occupations	Education
1502					Lady Margaret Beaufort establishes the Lady Margaret Chair of Divinity at Oxford; she establishes Cambridge University's Christ College in 1505 and St. John's in 1508; she herself studies medicine and theology, writing books and lecturing on the latter at Cambridge
1504					
1509					
1512			Sin Saimdang (1512–1559) is one of Korea's most gifted painters; she is a calligrapher, embroiderer, and poet and admired for her virtue		
1514					
1516	Machiavelli writes *The Prince;* Thomas More writes *Utopia*				
1517	The beginning of the Protestant Reformation; German theologian Martin Luther nails his *Ninety-five Theses* protesting Church corruption to a church door in Wittenberg	Katharina von Bora (1499–1552) is the celebrated wife of Martin Luther			

Performing Arts/ Entertainment/ Sports	Religion/ Philosophy	Science/ Technology/ Discovery	Statecraft/ Military	Reform	
					1502
			Juana la Loca (Joanna the Mad, 1497–1555) inherits Castile at the death of her mother, Queen Isabella of Spain; the death of her husband, Philip the Fair, two years later exacerbates her mental disorder, and she is sent away by her father, Ferdinand, while he rules as regent in her stead; contemporary rumors suggest that she was sane, the victim of her family's political manipulations		**1504**
			Henry VIII of England marries Catherine of Aragon		**1509**
					1512
	Death of Anne de Bretagne, wife of both Charles VIII and Louis XII; she was licensed by the pope to bless marriages				**1514**
					1516
					1517

	General/ Context	Daily Life/ Customs/ Practices	Humanities/ Fine Arts	Occupations	Education
1518					
1519	The Spanish invade Mexico				
1520		The *goller*, a short shoulder cape with a turned-up lapel, becomes fashionable in northern Switzerland; Swiss women of the middle class, like their peers in most Germanic countries, characteristically wear a belt or girdle with keys, knife, fork, sewing implements, a purse, and other items hanging from it	Italian sculptor Properzia de' Rossi wins a competition to produce marble sculpture for the church of San Petronio in Bologna; while it is not known with certainty which are hers, records indicate that she made at least three sibyls, two angels, and two bas-relief panels		
1524	Peasants' War (1524–1526) spreads throughout the Holy Roman Empire				
1525		French poet Louise Labé (1526–1566) has the first salon in France; she writes and			

EDUCATION OF WOMEN IN EARLY MODERN EUROPE

As Europe moved into the 16th century, women continued to be considered intellectually inferior to men. However, the rebirth of classical learning prompted some humanists, notably the Italian nobleman and writer Baldassare Castiglione, to argue for the education of women. A few outstanding women such as Louise Labé—a poet, linguist, musician, horsewoman, and head of the Lyons School of writing—provided models for women of intellectual ability.

Except in Spain and Italy, women in the early modern period were prohibited from attending universities. Nevertheless, women who were taught to read had more opportunities to

become educated. The invention of the printing press made books more available; in the Protestant movement women were encouraged to become literate so they could read scriptures.

During this era religious teaching orders were formed. As a complement to the Jesuit order, the English nun Mary Ward founded the Institutes of Mary for the education of women. One of the earliest proposals for a women's college, it was deemed too radical by the Catholic Church; she was imprisoned and her order dissolved, though eventually restored. Angela Merici (1470–1540), an Italian, founded the Ursulines in 1535, an unconventional order in which women took vows but

Performing Arts/ Entertainment/ Sports	Religion/ Philosophy	Science/ Technology/ Discovery	Statecraft/ Military	Reform	
			The formation of the Protestant Garrison, a brigade of 350 girls pressed into service to construct fortifications in the wars against the Emperor Maximilian (1459–1519) in Guienne, France		**1518**
	The Augustinian tertiary and recluse Marchesina Luzi is martyred in the mountains of Mambioa, Italy		Donna Marina (Malinche or Tenepal), the Aztec princess who becomes Cortes's translator, diplomatic adviser, and mistress, participates in the meeting of Montezuma and Cortes		**1519**
					1520
	By this year, the first two Franciscan convents have been built in Mexico City		The women of Marseilles, France, aid in the defense of their city against the Bourbons, forming the famous Rempart des Dames		**1524**
					1525

lived at home and taught in the community. Although she started with the support of the Church, by 1612 the order's members and activities were confined to convents. In Spain the Augustinians, Benedictines, Franciscans, Dominicans, Tertians, and Carmelites participated in educating girls.

Outside of convents, the sole source of education for women was a private tutor, possible only for the privileged. Mary Sidney, for example, was tutored along with her brother, Sir Philip Sidney. Sir Thomas More's three daughters were educated at home, as were the earl of Surrey's daughters. In Italy, aristocratic women like Isabella Gonzaga and Vittoria Colonna served

as patrons of great humanist scholars, often employing them as tutors and commissioning literary and philosophical works. In the same fashion French ladies conducted salons, where artists and thinkers of the day gathered to discuss literature, science, and philosophy. The 18th-century Enlightenment saw the rise of the great *salonistes,* highly educated women whose conversation was avidly sought by the likes of La Rochefoucauld, Voltaire, Pascal, and d'Alembert. While most people still thought of educated women as oddities, unnatural and not quite feminine, the evidence that women were fully as capable as men of sophisticated thought was growing.

	General/ Context	Daily Life/ Customs/ Practices	Humanities/ Fine Arts	Occupations	Education
1525		publishes several books of poetry			
1527		Mlle. St. Pather, chief almoner to Marguerite, queen of Navarre, has orders to act without delay in the face of need			Queen Marguerite of Navarre (Marguerite d'Angoulême, 1492–1549) establishes a foundlings school in Paris, the Maison des Enfants Rouges, so-called because of the scarlet dresses of the children
1528			Baldassare Castiglione writes *The Courtier*, a book promoting literacy and education for women that helps make women's participation in artistic, literary, and musical activities acceptable		
1529			Cornelius Heinrich Agrippa writes *De nobilitate et praecellentia femina sexus* (*Of the Nobility and Excellence of the Feminine Sex*), a widely translated work that argues for women's superiority		
1530	The spinning wheel is in general use in Europe				
1531					
1533	Ivan the Terrible becomes the first Russian czar				

Performing Arts/ Entertainment/ Sports	Religion/ Philosophy	Science/ Technology/ Discovery	Statecraft/ Military	Reform	
					1525
			Marguerite d'Angoulême marries Henri d'Albret, king of Navarre; also known as Marguerite de Navarre and Marguerite de Valois, she is sometimes referred to as *marguerite des marguerites* ("pearl of pearls")		**1527**
					1528
			Queen Margaret of Austria and Louise of Savoy, mother of Francis I of France, negotiate *La Paix des Dames* or The Peace of Cambrai; no war follows for six years		**1529**
			Daughter of King Henri and Queen Marguerite of Navarre, Jeanne d'Albret (1528–1572) is taken by Francis I, king of Spain, to Tours, France, to prevent her betrothal to the Spanish heir		**1530**
	A Native American, Juan Diego, sees the Virgin Mary four times on a hill outside Mexico City, begining the devotion to Our Lady of Quadalupe				**1531**
	Queen Marguerite de Navarre is called to the Sorbonne to answer charges of heresy for her poem *Le miroir de l'ame pécheresse* (*The Mirror of a Guilty Soul*); she ignores the summons		Catherine de Médicis (1519–1589), a politician in the tradition of the Florentine Medicis from whom she is descended, marries the French dauphin; during the minority of Charles IX, she acts as regent Anne Boleyn (1507–1536) secretly marries		**1533**

141

General/ Context	Daily Life/ Customs/ Practices	Humanities/ Fine Arts	Occupations	Education
1533				
1534 The Church of England is founded by Henry VIII and separates from the Roman Catholic Church				
1535				
1536		Marie Dentière (d. 1548), wife of a Swiss Protestant minister, writes *La guerre et délivrance de Genève,* in which she defends women's rights and discusses religious and theological questions		

WOMEN'S ROLES IN EARLY MODERN EUROPE

The world of European women in the era of the Reformation and Renaissance changed rapidly. Where medieval women had access to education and an outlet for religious expression through the Catholic Church, their 16th-century sisters in newly Protestant countries found themselves the subject of renewed debates about women's purpose in society. No longer offered the sanctuary of the convent, all-female communities that encouraged spiritual and intellectual achievement, early modern women found themselves under the rule of fathers. That rule was considered benign in assigning women an honorable place in the household as its religious and moral center; but it substituted a husband's or father's direction for the autonomy that characterized so many medieval women's lives. While philosophical discussions often lauded women's intelligence, wit, and virtue, practically speaking their opportunities for exercising those qualities were much more limited than they had been for their medieval forebears.

In this period, the humanist aspirations toward virtuous and noble action made education—what ought to be learned and who should learn it—a serious matter. Educating girls in the same way as boys, particularly in light of their important role in child rearing, merited at least theoretical consideration. In practice, however, girls often married so young and began to manage the household and produce heirs so soon that the question of educating them became moot. Nor did unmarried women fare much better; they could not attend universities since they were not permitted to hold the public positions for which a university education would equip them. Only upper-class women with tolerant relatives received anything like the education offered to men at universities.

Instead, most women were trained to be good wives and mothers. Their religious and moral education, through sermons and didactic treatises written and illustrated especially for women, taught them how to remain chaste, obedient, and

Performing Arts/ Entertainment/ Sports	Religion/ Philosophy	Science/ Technology/ Discovery	Statecraft/ Military	Reform	
			English King Henry VIII several months before the king's marriage to Catherine of Aragon is declared invalid; she is later tried and executed for adultery after falling out of favor with the king for having given birth to a girl (the future Queen Elizabeth I) and a stillborn boy		**1533**
	Elizabeth Barton (1506?–1534) is executed after being used as a pawn against King Henry VIII; she is known for her healing powers and prophecies delivered while in trances				**1534**
	St. Angela Merici (c. 1470–1540) founds the Ursuline Order, the first teaching order established in the Catholic Church				**1535**
			Turunku Bakwa, a Hausa queen of West Africa, is most famous as the mother of the future Queen Amina		**1536**
			Henry VIII of England marries Jane Seymour (1509?–1537), who		

capable of running a household. The role was embraced by most women, who saw in it enhanced opportunities for serving both man and God—serious ambitions in that period, and most worthy of respect.

As their access to a life of the mind diminished, so did their opportunities for gainful employment. The increasingly powerful merchant class eroded the traditional power of craft and trade guilds, many of which eliminated their female membership in the effort to remain competitive. A sharp division arose between personal and public life: the domestic realm was reserved to women and the public realm to men.

Depending upon her husband's wealth, a woman's domestic life might entail the drudgery of servitude, the organizational duties of the mistress of servants, or the leisure of the wealthy lady. For the latter, fashionable ideas about love and manners prescribed a "ladylike" inactivity. Hairstyles grew ornate, re-

quiring a great deal of time and assistance to execute; corsets of metal, wood, or bone, while allowing women's bodies to conform to an ideal, constrained them physically.

The experience of early modern middle- and lower-class women, though, was not the experience of all women. The era produced some remarkable leaders, among them the great English Renaissance Queen Elizabeth; Isabella of Castile, known as the "crusading warrior queen," who sent Columbus on his fateful voyage; Marguerite of Navarre, called the "peace queen," who lent financial and political support to the age's greatest thinkers and wrote the famous *Heptaméron;* and Catherine de Médicis, a skilled diplomat and ruthless tactician. Though they had their critics, such women were expected to act with force and intelligence in the public realm. At the highest levels, public power went to the powerful, be it woman or man.

	General/ Context	Daily Life/ Customs/ Practices	Humanities/ Fine Arts	Occupations	Education
1536					
1539					Marguerite of Navarre helps found the Collège de France; admired by Erasmus and Rabelais for her liberal views, such different men as Calvin and Étienne Dolet find refuge in her court
1540			The Dominicans preserve a manuscript of Peruvian Princess Capillana in which she painted ancient monuments with a short historical explanation in Castilian		
1542					
1543					
1545			French poet Pernette de Guillet (?1520–1545) writes *Rimes de gentille et vertueuse Dame Pernette de Guillet,* a collection of poems about love and friendship		

Performing Arts/ Entertainment/ Sports	Religion/ Philosophy	Science/ Technology/ Discovery	Statecraft/ Military	Reform
			dies 12 days after giving birth to Henry's first son, Edward VI	**1536**
				1539
			Marguerite of Navarre endows the town of Pau with a parliament and an exchequer	**1540**
			Henry VIII marries and divorces Anne of Cleves (1515–1557), his fourth wife, and marries Catherine Howard	
			Following the death of her husband, empress of Christian Ethiopia Sabla Wangel (d. 1568) is instrumental in the defense of her country in the wars against the Muslims of Adal	
			James V of Scotland dies, succeeded by his daughter, Mary, aged six days	**1542**
			Catherine Howard (1520?–1542) is convicted of and beheaded for adultery	
			Catherine Parr (1512–1548) marries Henry VIII of England, becoming his sixth and last wife; she seeks to soften religious persecution in England; remarrying after Henry's death, she dies after the birth of her only child	**1543**
	English Protestant Anne Askew (1521–1546), an accomplished religious rhetorician expelled from the Church by her husband for "offending priests," is tried for heresy and acquitted		A Scottish military heroine, Lilliard, leads the Scots at the Battle of Ancrum in one of their last military victories against the English in the border struggles; she kills the leader of the English	**1545**

General/ Context	Daily Life/ Customs/ Practices	Humanities/ Fine Arts	Occupations	Education
1545				
1546		Flemish artist Lavina Teerlinc (1520–1576) is a very successful painter of miniatures; she becomes court miniaturist to Henry VIII; her annual salary is higher than Hans Holbein's		
		Italian Renaissance painter Sofonisba Anguissola (1535?–1626) and her sister Elena begin their training as artists; they study painting, Latin, and music; Sofonisba is the first woman artist to establish an international reputation		
1550	At the time of the Reformation, women's attire in Germanic countries becomes tight in the bodice, laced in the front, high-collared, and somber-colored			
	Ceremonial dress for Boyar women in Russia is made of rich velvet and brocade; they wear high headdresses draped with fine veils			
	The wheel collar, made of starched linen crimped with an iron, becomes popular in the Netherlands			

WOMEN AND PROTESTANTISM

Protestantism came about as a religious revolution in Western Europe during the 16th century. Until then the Roman Catholic Church had wielded great power over the European countries. But as the Renaissance advanced, many kingships in northern Europe, resentful of papal authority, began to condemn some Church practices. The newly invented printing press facilitated the study of ancient texts and the communication of ideas. The invention of gunpowder made it no longer feasible for castles to be defended with bows and arrows, and small kingdoms joined together for mutual protection. The rise of a commercial middle class created an atmosphere in which people could rely on their individual consciences and question the power of the Church.

The Reformation began with Martin Luther, who nailed his *Ninety-five Theses* to the door of the church at Wittenberg in 1517. Protestantism, with its emphasis on personal freedom and responsibility, grew out of his challenge to Catholic authority. Protestant sects such as the Lutherans, Calvinists, Anglicans, Anabaptists, Huguenots, Moravians, Quakers, and Puritans, rejected various Catholic institutions, especially monasticism and clerical celibacy. While Protestantism avoided some repressive aspects of Catholicism, religious attitudes toward women did not change for the better. For example, Martin Luther, like most of his religious contemporaries, believed women to be spiritually weaker than men and properly subject to their control. As a corollary, Luther believed

Performing Arts/ Entertainment/ Sports	Religion/ Philosophy	Science/ Technology/ Discovery	Statecraft/ Military	Reform	
			forces, but loses her own life		**1545**
	Protestant martyr Anne Askew is retried for heresy; she is tortured on the rack in the Tower of London and burned				**1546**
			Irish princess Graine Ni Maille (fl. 1550– 1600) commands a great fleet of war galleys that preys upon English ships and villages		**1550**

that priests ought to marry and have children. Turning his back on monasticism for both men and women, Luther's emphasis on the nuclear family cut women off from the greatest avenue for autonomy women had enjoyed in the previous era. Likewise, Calvin taught that subjugation of woman to man was God's law and that woman's proper ministry was motherhood. The Church of England, or Anglican Church, established by Henry VIII after the pope denied Henry's petition for a divorce, held men superior in understanding and reasoning.

Not all Protestant sects took such a hard line on the inequality of the sexes, however. The Anabaptists, a small group persecuted by both Catholics and Lutherans, preached the equality of men and women as God's vessels. The Quakers emphasized that each person is ruled by his or her individual conscience; both men and women served the Friends as spiritual leaders.

Protestantism did give women an opportunity to participate in their own spiritual affairs; services could be conducted in the house by family members, including mothers and daughters who read from prayer books and the Bible. The erosion of the Catholic Church's power, however, did not greatly affect the daily lives of women. Protestantism, in elevating traditional concepts of marriage and the patriarchal family to new heights, merely circumscribed their sphere of activity further.

General/ Context	Daily Life/ Customs/ Practices	Humanities/ Fine Arts	Occupations	Education
1552		Italian painter Lavinia Fontana (1552–1602) is one of the first Italian women to have a successful career as an artist; 135 documented paintings of hers, more than 30 signed and dated, survive		
1553		Mary Tudor (1516–1558), known as Mary I or Bloody Mary, is proclaimed queen after the death of her half brother Edward VI		
1554		The sonnets of poet Gaspara Stampa (c. 1523–1554) are published as the *Rime;* they have earned her a place among the greatest poets of the period		
1555		Louise Labé publishes her *Oeuvres;* in her dedication of the work, she insists upon the importance of study for women		
1556		Flemish painter Caterina van Hemessen is a successful portraitist whose patron is Queen Mary of Hungary		

RENAISSANCE WOMEN ARTISTS

Class distinctions during the European Renaissance help focus some key differences between men and women artists. Male artists were usually commoners, a number of whom rose socially through their artistic achievement; most women artists, like the famous portraitist Sofonisba Anguissola (1535?–1626), an Italian from Cremona, came from noble families and learned their art as part of their education. Women generally could not attend universities, though, and had little exposure to the theo-

logical and intellectual debates affecting contemporary art. Further, their exclusion from life drawing classes limited their artistic training.

However, while the Renaissance continued to prize most highly works of religious art, the increasing secular spirit of the age helped portraiture and still life to develop, genres in which women artists excelled. One of the earliest women artists we know by name, the Bolognese sculptor Properzia de' Rossi (c.

Performing Arts/ Entertainment/ Sports	Religion/ Philosophy	Science/ Technology/ Discovery	Statecraft/ Military	Reform	
					1552
			Named by King Edward VI as heiress to the British throne, Lady Jane Grey (1537–1554) is proclaimed queen on July 9; after only 9 days, she loses the throne to her rival, Queen Mary I, and is executed in 1554		**1553**
					1554
			Mary Tudor, now married to Prince Philip of Spain, reinstates the heresy laws and begins persecuting Protestants; hundreds of people are burned at the stake during the last years of her reign (1554–1558)		**1555**
	Joan Waste, a blind Englishwoman who studied and memorized the Bible, is a victim of Mary Tudor's attempt to restore Catholicism to England: she is burned as a Protestant martyr				**1556**

1490–1530), became so popular that she inspired envy in some male artists.

Some of the most significant women artists of the period, born into artists' families, received their training from their fathers. Two famous Italian painters, Lavinia Fontana (1552–1614) and Artemisia Gentileschi (1590–?1642), were the daughters of artists. The Flemish painter Caterina van Hemessen (1528–after 1587) became a celebrated portraitist, and Henry VIII summoned Lavina Bening Teerlinc (c. 1520–1576), also of Flanders, to paint miniatures. Both the courts and bourgeois society offered women artists opportunities to develop their abilities and gain recognition. By the end of the 17th century, the idea of a woman training to paint or sculpt was no longer unusual.

	Daily Life/			
General/	Customs/	Humanities/		
Context	Practices	Fine Arts	Occupations	Education

1558

1559

Marguerite of Navarre publishes the *Hep-taméron*, an unfinished collection of tales based on personal experience rather than on traditional sources; she defends women against misogyny

1560

Spanish fashions popular at the French court include the conical hooped petticoat over which a woman wears one or two conical garments, a neck ruff, and a cap

German women of the middle class adopt Spanish fashions, with short shoulder capes, broad aprons, and tight bodices

1561

WOMEN IN TAOISM

The major religion indigenous to China, Taoism holds women in high esteem. Its philosophy has always attributed equal power to the female and male principles of yin and yang. Indeed, early Taoism so glorified the female principle that second-century Chinese women were able to hold important civil and military positions.

In religious practice, Taoism offers women three roles: lay believer, religious professional, and divine woman. Lay believers comprise the largest number of Taoist faithful. They are expected to exemplify devotion, charity, good works, and proper family conduct. Religious professionals—nuns and church officials—perform the liturgy, study doctrine, meditate, teach, and carry on research. Such women serve as examples of knowledge, sanctity, wisdom, and skill. Moreover, their professional status always offers a means of education and independence to women.

Performing Arts/ Entertainment/ Sports	Religion/ Philosophy	Science/ Technology/ Discovery	Statecraft/ Military	Reform	
			Elizabeth I (1533–1603) becomes queen of England; she reestablishes Protestantism and her reign is marked by peace and prosperity, by the emergence of England as a naval power, and by an astonishing flowering of literature; the term "Elizabethan" refers to the 45-year period of her reign, the English Renaissance		**1558**
					1559
					1560
			Though she was nominally ruler of Scotland from a few days after her birth, Mary Stuart (1542–1587), a.k.a. Mary Queen of Scots begins her actual reign		**1561**

Divine women—saints and Taoist goddesses—guide and teach the living, and use their powers in their behalf. Female saints, having come from the ranks of both lay and religious women, provide models of hope and power. One such saint was the 16th-century Tanyangzi, a teenage mystic who had a following of learned Confucian men. Goddesses possess special arts and powers expressing the ideals and desires of those who pray to them. Taoism's most important goddess is Queen Mother of the West, who governs immortality and communication between mortal and divine beings. Legend has it that she was also the lover and teacher of emperors. These and other female Taoist figures are described in the Taoist canon, the *Tao tsang,* which includes many works related to women and their history in China.

	General/ Context	Daily Life/ Customs/ Practices	Humanities/ Fine Arts	Occupations	Education
1562	Persecution of the Huguenots in France, the Wars of Religion 1562–1598	Witchcraft is made a capital offense in England			
1563	The Council of Trent reforms the Roman Catholic Church, initiating the Counter-Reformation				
1564	Birth of William Shakespeare (1564–1616), poet and playwright

Birth of Galileo Galilei (1564–1642), astronomer and scientist | In *Anatomical Reflections on All the Parts of the Human Body*, Italian anatomist Borgarucci says, "Nature places the female testicles internally. . . . Woman is a most arrogant and extremely intractable animal; and she would be worse if she came to realize that she is no less perfect and no less fit to wear breeches than man" | François Rabelais (1494?–1553) dedicates the third book of *Gargantua et Pantagruel* to the soul of Queen Marguerite of Navarre | Mlle. du Perron is one of the architects employed to design the Tuileries in Paris | The British scholar Anne Bacon, née Cooke (1528–1610)— mother of Sir Francis Bacon—is responsible for translating key Latin texts of her time into English, including Bishop Jewel's *Apologia Pro Ecclesia;* she is influential politically through her husband and their social connections to Queen Elizabeth I and her advisers |
1565					
1567					
1568					

Performing Arts/ Entertainment/ Sports	Religion/ Philosophy	Science/ Technology/ Discovery	Statecraft/ Military	Reform	
	St. Teresa of Avila (1515–1582) founds the Discalced Carmelites whose nuns live under an austere rule; one of the most famous events of her mystical career is the *transverberatio*, or piercing of her heart by an angel's arrow				**1562**
			Queen Elizabeth I of England calls the forced enslavement of Africans detestable; the following year, however, she invests in a profitable slave-running venture, lending one of her ships for the purpose		**1563**
					1564
			Margaret of Parma, regent of the Low Countries, is petitioned by 300 noblemen to abolish the Inquisition; she promises to forward the petition to her brother, Philip II of Spain, but instead raises an army that captures Antwerp the next year		**1565**
			Mary Queen of Scots is imprisoned at Loch Leven and forced to abdicate in favor of her son, James VI of Scotland, when her supporters rise up against her		**1567**
			Mary Queen of Scots flees to England, where she is again imprisoned; several plots		**1568**

	General/ Context	Daily Life/ Customs/ Practices	Humanities/ Fine Arts	Occupations	Education
1568					
1570			Painter Barbara Longhi (1552–1638) is trained in the tradition of Sofonisba Anguissola		
1571	Birth of Johannes Kepler (1571–1630), German astronomer				
1572		Spanish anatomist I de Valverde apologizes for including a chapter on the ovaries ("female testicles") in his *History of the Composition of the Human Body,* saying that "women might . . . become all the more arrogant by knowing that they, like men, have testicles"			
1575		In the French court, the conical shape of women's dress is abandoned for a more pronounced waistline and a low-cut neck, around which a lace collar is arranged			
1579	An efficient ribbon loom is invented in Danzig				
1584					
1586			Mary Sidney Herbert (1561–1621) edits her brother Sir William Sidney's poetry after his death; she publishes many translations of her own		
1587		Virginia Dare (1587–?) is the first child of English parents born in America; she is one of the settlers to disappear from the lost colony in Roanoke, VA			

Performing Arts/ Entertainment/ Sports	Religion/ Philosophy	Science/ Technology/ Discovery	Statecraft/ Military	Reform	
			to overthrow her cousin Elizabeth I of England and place the Catholic Mary on the throne fail and Mary is kept in semiconfinement		**1568**
					1570
					1571
			At the urging of Catherine de Médicis, Charles IX orders the St. Bartholomew's Day Massacre		**1572**
					1575
					1579
			Sir Walter Raleigh names the state of Virginia after Elizabeth I of England, the "virgin queen"		**1584**
	Margaret Clitherhoe (b. 1556) is martyred in England for practicing Roman Catholicism and using her home as a place of worship and hiding place for vestments and religious objects				**1586**
	Bill to reform the Church of England refused by Queen Elizabeth		Mary Queen of Scots is tried for conspiring against the life of Queen Elizabeth I of England and beheaded		**1587**

	General/Context	Daily Life/Customs/Practices	Humanities/Fine Arts	Occupations	Education
1589	Rev. William Lee (d. 1610) of Cambridge invents the first knitting machine, the stocking frame, capable of producing 1000 stitches a minute				Lady Frances Sidney makes possible through her will the foundation of Sidney Sussex College; she had a reputation as a woman who greatly valued education
1590		In Venice, an unmarried woman of rank appears in public hiding her head and part of her body in a large shawl that may, however, leave her low-cut dress exposed		Scottish lay healer Geillis Duncan is tried as a witch and executed after implicating others; Scottish witch trials of this time force women's healing skills to go underground	
1591		Margaret Winthrop (c. 1591–1647), wife of the first governor of the Massachussetts Bay Colony, is remembered for her so-called Puritan Letters, written during a 12-year period during which her husband sailed with the vanguard of the Massachusetts Bay Company	Penelope Devereux Rich (1562?–1607), the beloved of Sir Philip Sidney, is the "Stella" of his sonnet sequence *Astrophel and Stella*		
1592		Gabrielle d'Estrées (1573–1599) becomes the mistress of Henry IV of France; she bears him several children whom he later legitimizes; his plans to marry her after his divorce from Margaret of Valois are upset by Gabrielle's untimely death		During the Scottish witch trials, Agnes Sampson, a lay healer and wise woman, is implicated in a plot against King James VI and interrogated by the king himself; she is tried and executed as a witch after admitting to performing various rites	
1596	Birth of René Descartes (1596–1650), philosopher and mathematician		Painter Fede Galizia (1578–1630) of Milan has established an international reputation for her portraits by her late teens		
1599	Birth of Oliver Cromwell (1599–1658), soldier and statesman

Birth of Velazquez (1599–1660), Spanish artist | | | | |
| **1600** | William Shakespeare's *Hamlet* is first performed | European women's corsets are usually made of whalebone, | Giovanna Garzoni (1600–1670) is well known for her water | Madame Hon-Cho-Lo, a Chinese pirate of the 17th century, takes | |

156

Performing Arts/ Entertainment/ Sports	Religion/ Philosophy	Science/ Technology/ Discovery	Statecraft/ Military	Reform	
					1589
	Italian mystic St. Catherine dei Ricci (c. 1522–c. 1589) is known for her ecstasies and for acting out the scenes leading up to the Crucifixion; she corresponds regularly with St. Philip Neri, who vouches for the authenticity of her visions				1590
					1591
					1592
					1596
					1599
		The advice of Baile Edels, a mid-16th- or 17th-century expert in	Chinese warrior Shen Yunying, the daughter of an army captain,		1600

	General/ Context	Daily Life/ Customs/ Practices	Humanities/ Fine Arts	Occupations	Education
1600		but Marie de Médicis (1573–1642) introduces a short-lived fashion for metal corsets	color studies of plants and animals done on vellum Bologna is populated by women who pursue careers in a variety of fields; evidence shows that 23 female painters live there in the 16th and 17th centuries	command of her husband's pirate ship after his death; she becomes known as the Terror of the Yangtze	
1602					
1603					
1607		Pocahontas (a pet name meaning "playful" for Native American Princess Matoaka, 1595?–1617) is said to have rescued Captain John Smith, leader of the English colonists in Jamestown, from execution by her father, the great chief Powhatan; she later marries John Rolfe of Jamestown, bringing about peaceful relations between the Indians and the settlers for eight years			
1608					
1609			Judith Leyster (1609–1660) is known		

Performing Arts/ Entertainment/ Sports	Religion/ Philosophy	Science/ Technology/ Discovery	Statecraft/ Military	Reform	
		the Jewish *niddah* laws concerning menstruation and sexual contact, is regularly sought by local women in preference to that of their rabbi; her decision that Sabbath candles should be lighted before the blessing is said is incorporated into Jewish law	takes over her father's command upon his death; by special decree she is made a second captain so that she can legitimately succeed her father		**1600**
			Anne of Austria (1601–1666), the daughter of Philip III of Spain and wife of Louis XIII of France, acts as regent for her son Louis XIV during his minority		**1602**
Okuni (c. 1573–1614) virtually invents Kabuki drama when she and a popular comedian team up and perform combinations of lively mime and religious pantomime; famous for her black silk priest's robe and two swords in her belt, she establishes the Kabuki tradition of women playing men and vice versa			Queen Elizabeth I of England dies		**1603**
					1607
	St. Joan de Lestonnac (d. 1640) founds the Religious of Notre Dame of Bordeaux, an order that spreads rapidly throughout the region				**1608**
		Louise Bourgeois (1563–1636), midwife			**1609**

	General/ Context	Daily Life/ Customs/ Practices	Humanities/ Fine Arts	Occupations	Education
1609			equally for her personality and for her association with Frans Hals, whose paintings were often confused with hers		
1610		Nuns of the Order of the Visitation wear black pleated dresses of coarse wool with long wide sleeves turned back to expose tighter sleeves underneath, a white neck cloth, a black fillet, and a black veil			
1611			17-year-old Flemish artist Clara Peeters (1594–post 1657) of Antwerp is a pioneer of early 17th-century art; she helps to establish formal and iconographical conventions of still-life painting	The first known female professional criminal in England, the thief and highwaywoman Mary Frith (1584?–1659), better known as Moll Cutpurse, or the Queen of Misrule, dresses as a man	
1612		Italian painter Artemisia Gentileschi, the "quintessential female painter of the Baroque era," is the subject of a notorious rape trial			

WOMEN ARTISTS IN CHINA: A LIST OF NOTABLE NAMES

Mme. Wei (272–349): an early teacher of China's most celebrated calligraphy master, Wang Xizhi

Anonymous younger sister of Li Chang (1027–1090): superb copyist of paintings of classical subjects—pine, bamboo, and rocks

Anonymous third daughter of Wen Tong (1019–1079): bamboo painter who learned from her famous father and taught her famous son

Li Quingzhao (1084–c. 1151) and Zhu Shuzhen (12th c.): poets who also sketched notably well

Guan Daoshang (1262–1319): most famous female artist in Chinese history, a calligrapher and painter both; remembered most for her works in ink bamboo (Bamboo Groves in Mist and Rain, one of the best paintings now attributed to her, is in the National Palace Museum, Taipei)

Anonymous daughter of Qiu Ying (c. 1492–1552): one of the few artisan women to achieve enduring fame for painting, usually Buddhist deities and palace women

Wen Shu (1595–1634): painter, often of eroded garden rocks, flowers, and butterflies; examples of her work are in the Freer Gallery and in New York City's Metropolitan Museum of Art

Li Yin (1616–1685): concubine painter known for decorative flower-and-bird compositions brushed with ink on satin

Ma Shouzhen (1548–1604) and Xue Susu (c. 1565–1635): courtesan painters whose paintings were only some of the many entertainments they offered their clients; some of their works are in the Honolulu Academy of Arts, the Asian Art Museum in San Francisco, and the Metropolitan Museum of Art in New York City

Performing Arts/ Entertainment/ Sports	Religion/ Philosophy	Science/ Technology/ Discovery	Statecraft/ Military	Reform	
		to Marie de Médicis, queen of France (1573–1642), publishes the basic text on childbirth of her day			**1609**
	St. Jane Frances de Chantal (1572–1641) and St. Francis de Sales found the Order of the Visitation of the Virgin Mary as a haven for those debarred from other orders by age, health, or financial circumstances; she founds many Visitation convents all over France		Marie de Médicis (1573–1642), Italian-born queen of France, acts as regent for her son Louis XIII until 1617		**1610**
	Daughter of a noble Swiss house, the nun Jeanne de Jussie (d. c. 1611) writes *Histoire mémorable du commencement de l'hérésie de Genève* (*Memorable History of the Beginnings of Heresy in Geneva*), a sourcebook of enduring historical importance in spite of several errors in chronology				**1611**
			The "Third Lady" of Mongolia, Erketü Qatum (1570–1612), uses her influence in favor of peaceful relations with China		**1612**

Lin Xue (early 17th century) and Huang Yuanjie (mid-17th century): landscape painters

Dong Bai (1625–1651), Jin Yue (late-17th century), Cai Han (1647–1686), Gu Mei (1619–1664), and Liu Shi (1618–1664): famous concubine painters

Chai Jingyi and Zhenyi; Zhou Xi and Hu: sister teams, both concubines and artists of the mid-17th century

Chen Shu (1660–1736) and Wang Zheng (also Qing dynasty): self-motivated artists with similar tastes in impressionistic sketches and tightly executed, detailed nature studies. Chen Shu also painted figures and landscapes. He work is well represented in the National Palace Museum, Taipei

Yun Bing, Jiang Jixi, Ma Quan (all-18th century): painters specializing in floral subjects and whose surviving works share a realistic style, rich color, and fine detail

Fang Wanyi, Luo Qilan, and Wang Yuyan (all late-18th century): accomplished artists and poets

Miao Jiahui (19th century): painting instructor and "substitute brush" for the painter Empress Dowager Cixi (1835–1908)

Wu Shangxi, Yu Ling, and Ju Qing (19th century): three painters and/or collectors whose work laid the foundation for modern Chinese painting

Wu Shujuan (1853–1930): Shanghai painter considered one of two leading floral painters in her city

Ren Xia (1876–1920): painter known for works of the figure, birds, and animals whose labors were frankly commercial

	General/ Context	Daily Life/ Customs/ Practices	Humanities/ Fine Arts	Occupations	Education
1614		Believing that human blood baths ensure eternal youth, Hungarian Countess Nadasdy (Elizabeth Báthory, 1560–1614) kills 610 servant girls; she is nicknamed the Bloody Countess	Birth of Italian artist Lucrina Fetti (1614–1651?), Mantua court painter of considerable local fame		
1616		Pocahontas is baptized under the name Rebecca and is brought to England, where she is presented at court as a princess; she succumbs to illness and dies a year later	Artemisia Gentileschi becomes a member of the Academy of Art in Florence; her work is credited with transmitting the Caravaggesque style to Genoa, Naples, and Venice		
1618	The Thirty Years War begins				
1622			French writer Marie de Gournay, in *On the Equality of Men and Women*, argues against the "natural inferiority" of women's minds Dutch painter Judith Leyster becomes the only female member of the Haarlem painters' guild		
1624			Margaret Cavendish (1624?–1674), duchess of Newcastle, is known as one of the foremost women writers of 17th-century England		
1625		Priscilla Mullens (b. 1602) of Plymouth, MA, marries John Alden; one of the first marriages in Plymouth, theirs becomes a legendary story of romantic love			
1630	The Taj Mahal is built (1630–1648) in Agra by Mogul Emperor Shah Jahan as a mausoleum for his dead wife, Mumtaz Mahal (1592–1631)		Anne Dudley Bradstreet (c. 1612–1672) embarks for the New World at age 18; she is heralded as the first American poet		
1632	Birth of John Locke (1632–1704), philosopher				

Performing Arts/ Entertainment/ Sports	Religion/ Philosophy	Science/ Technology/ Discovery	Statecraft/ Military	Reform	
					1614
					1616
					1618
	Lucy de Freitas (b. 1542), a Japanese Franciscan tertiary, is martyred in Nagasaki				**1622**
	Ketevan, queen of Georgia, is executed for refusing to enter the harem of Sha'Abbas				**1624**
	Mme. de Gondi induces her husband to help her establish a company of missionaries to aid their tenants and the peasantry in small towns and villages

Death of Dayicing-Beyiji, a powerful Mongolian woman and devout Buddhist | | | | **1625** |
| | | | | | **1630** |
| | | | | | **1632** |

	General/ Context	Daily Life/ Customs/ Practices	Humanities/ Fine Arts	Occupations	Education
1634			Mogul Empress Nur Jahan (c. 1571–1645) gathers scholars, connoisseurs, poets, architects, and painters to her court, and commissions many monuments and gardens in cities throughout the empire		
1636	Harvard University is founded in Cambridge, MA				
1637					
1640		The hemlines of middle-class German women no longer trail on the ground; the dresses, tight in the bodice and elaborately gathered in the waist to emphasize the hips, reveal the feet	Portuguese nun Marianna Alcoforado (1640–1723) is famed as a poet and letter writer Highly regarded Spanish painter Maria de Abarca (d. 1656) works chiefly in Madrid between 1640–1653		
1641			French novelist Madeleine de Scudéry (1607–1701) publishes *Ibrahim, ou l'Illustre Bassa,* the first roman à clef; she mixes adventure and history with exotically disguised portraits of contemporary personalities, including herself; she is considered to have brought the sentimental romance to unprecedented heights of popularity		
1642	English Civil War begins		Louise Moillon (1610–1696), the		

Performing Arts/ Entertainment/ Sports	Religion/ Philosophy	Science/ Technology/ Discovery	Statecraft/ Military	Reform	
	St. Louise de Marrilac (1591–1660) and St. Vincent de Paul found the Vincentian Sisters of Charity, granted formal approbation in 1655				**1634**
					1636
	Anne Hutchinson (1591?–1643) is banished from the Massachusetts Bay Colony for "traducing the ministers and their ministry" by teaching that salvation could come only through grace, rather than through good works	Queen Christina of Sweden (1626–1689) charters the New Sweden Company to colonize the New World			**1637**
	Janet "Jennie" Geddes of Scotland denounces an Anglican priest, effectively striking "the first blow in the Great Struggle for freedom of conscience"				
	St. Hyacinth Mariscotti (1585–1640) guides a community of third-order Franciscans at Viterbo, Italy; instrumental in establishing two confraternities in the town, she is known for her care of the sick, the aged, and the poor				**1640**
	A tract disseminating the prophecies of Mother Shipton credits her with foretelling the deaths of Cardinal Wolsey, Thomas Cromwell, Lord Percy, and others				**1641**
		Imprisoned for witchcraft, Martine de	Heroine of the English Civil War, Lady Bril-		**1642**

	General/ Context	Daily Life/ Customs/ Practices	Humanities/ Fine Arts	Occupations	Education
1642			greatest French still-life painter of her century, does her major work before 1642		
1643	Louis XIV of France begins his 72-year reign				
1644	Ch'ing, or Manchu, dynasty (1644–1911)				
1648	Opening of the Royal Academy of Painting and Sculpture (Acad-émie Royale) in France; Louis XIV declares that it is to be open to all gifted art-ists, regardless of sex		French still-life painter Catherine Duchemin (1630–1698) is the first woman to be ad-mitted to the Acad-émie Royale		
1650		Ladies at the court of Louis XIV of France wear the *fontange*, a high, stiffly frilled linen cap with a veil; a laced bodice, or *planchette*, and a trailing outer garment with sleeves and linen cuffs, the manteau, that opens over a flounced skirt Dutch ladies wear masks to protect their skin while ice skating	The French literary *préciosité* movement (1650–1660) rejects brutal male attitudes in favor of feminine val-ues in manners and language		

WOMEN WRITING IN THE 17TH CENTURY

Between 1500 and 1800, the evolution of Western society from an oral into a written culture accelerated. The invention of the printing press in the mid-1400s, the spread of literacy, and the circulation of printed materials altered people's ideas of them-selves and their relationships to others.

In early modern Europe, occupation and social class often dictated who could read and write. While many girls learned to read, fewer learned to write as writing was considered an un-necessary skill for women who would not be called upon to record events in the family Bible, keep the business's ac-counts, or maintain any correspondence. Nevertheless, women who could write usually did, keeping diaries, composing po-etry, and compiling commonplace books for their personal use.

Some women wrote for a public. In the late 17th century, Aphra Behn (1640–1689) became the first Englishwoman to make a living as a professional writer. After a stint as a spy for Charles II, she worked as a journalist, playwright, poet, and novelist. She anonymously produced her first play in 1670; when she did add her name to the script, most believed that a man had written it. Even so, her bawdy humor was a success,

Performing Arts/ Entertainment/ Sports	Religion/ Philosophy	Science/ Technology/ Discovery	Statecraft/ Military	Reform	
		Beausoleil, the first French mining engineer, dies before release	liana Harley (1598–1643) defends her home, Brampton Bryan, during this troubled time		**1642**
					1643
			Queen Christina of Sweden takes the throne; she converts to Catholicism, and dies in poverty in Rome		**1644**
			Roman Catholic queen of England Henrietta Maria (1609–1669) is forced to flee to France at the outset of the English Civil War; she returns only after the Restoration		
					1648
			Scottish heroine Christianne Fletcher, the wife of a local minister, smuggles the Honors of Scotland—the crown, scepter, and sword—out of the besieged Dunnottar Castle; the Honors represent the authority of the Scottish sovereign		**1650**

and soon many other women, like Catharine Cockburn, Catherine Trotter, Mary Manley (1663?–1724), and Mary Pix, followed her example. But because works by women often met with skepticism and hostility, many, like Behn herself, published under a masculine pseudonym.

Katherine Philips, however, established herself as a respected English poet in the mid-1600s. Massachusetts poet Anne Bradstreet enjoyed similar success, advertised in England as the "Tenth Muse, Lately Sprung Up in America." Likewise, the poems of Anne Killigrew (b. 1660), a maid of honor at the English court and who died in 1685, became a sentimental favorite after her death. Alive, she made public only her paintings, an art form acceptable for women. The Dutch writer, painter, musician, and scholar Anna Marie van Schurman (1607–1678), known as the Sappho of Holland, was considered to embody the ideal of the Renaissance man. In the 18th century, when women writers were read eagerly by appreciative audiences of men and women, they had such forebears as these to thank for creating an environment friendly to their work.

General/ Context	Daily Life/ Customs/ Practices	Humanities/ Fine Arts	Occupations	Education
1651	Lady Anne Clifford establishes the alms-houses called St. Anne's Hospital; known as an inveterate builder, she rebuilds and refortifies the castle at Appleby and carries out the restoration of two churches and many estates			
1652				
1654	Parties of young Frenchwomen arrive in New France as brides for Colonists			

SOR JUANA INÉS DE LA CRUZ

Born humbly and out of wedlock in 1648, Sor Juana rose to become the leading woman of letters in Mexico in her century. When she was a child, her scholarly grandfather endowed Juana with a grand passion for books, giving her the run of his ample library when she learned to read on her own at three. While she was still very young, she begged her mother to let her go to Mexico City dressed as a boy so she could continue her studies. At eight, she was finally allowed to go, albeit in girl's clothes. She lived with relatives and studied more avidly than ever; she later claimed to have learned Latin in 20 lessons.

Juana soon created a sensation in the court of the Spanish viceroy, and his wife became devoted to the girl. To demonstrate her genius, the viceroy gathered 40 prestigious scholars from fields as diverse as mathematics, poetry, history, and reli-

gion. The 16-year-old Juana matched wits with all, and her fame grew.

Two years later, Juana took vows as a nun in the Order of St. Jerome. She remained in the center of court activities, however, and composed many love poems at the request of courtiers. She also pursued other ambitious reading and writing projects. She authored religious and secular poems, including her long masterpiece, *First Dream,* as well as religious exercises and carols, personal essays, and works of scholarship in many fields. She also wrote religious plays, such as *The Divine Narcissus,* which interwove Greek mythology with local Indian lore. Sor Juana had mastered several languages: she wrote comfortably in Spanish, Latin, the Náhuatl Indian language, and the dialects of Mexico's African slaves. Her per-

	Sor Juana Inés de la Cruz, born Juana de Asbaje y Ramírez de Santillana (1648–1695), Mexican nun, is famous for her deeply learned philosophical writings and for her defense of education for women; she is also known for her *villancicos* (carols), *autos sacrementales* (religious plays), and comedies		French beauty Anne Geneviève, duchess de Longueville (1619–1679), is one of the leaders of the Fronde of the Princes (conflict between the French Parlement and royal authority); she makes her peace with the court in 1653		**1651**
	Catherine de Bar (1614–1698), better known as Mère Mechthilde du Saint Sacrement, founds the Benedictines of the Holy Sacrament; Mère Mechthilde carries on a voluminous correspondence with the best known writers, historians, bureaucrats, and ecclesiastics of her time				**1652**
	Margaret Fell (1614–1702) is converted to the Quaker way of life; she later serves prison sentences for allowing Quaker meetings to take place in her home				
			Queen Christina of Sweden abdicates in favor of Charles X		**1654**

sonal library, numbering 4000 volumes, became famous in its own right.

Her most celebrated theological work was composed toward the end of her life. Upset over a bold sermon delivered by a prominent priest 40 years earlier, she was encouraged by a cleric to put her critique in writing. The resulting treatise came to the attention of the bishop of Puebla. He was so impressed with it that he reprinted it at his own expense, but he also wrote a public letter under the false name of Sor Filotea de la Cruz, disapproving of a woman's taking part in a theological dispute.

Sor Juana's reply to that letter, *Respuesta* (*Response*) *a Sor Filotea de la Cruz* (1691), was her proud defense of a woman's right to use her intellect. She insisted that women must be allowed to study, write, and teach, unleashing all of the sophisticated wit and fierce love of learning she had developed over her lifetime. It was one of the finest documents of its century asserting the rights of women as scholars, both in Europe and the New World.

Even though *Respuesta* was not published until after Sor Juana died, it circulated in the Mexican religious community. Her personal confessor, outraged, would no longer hear her confessions, and her archbishop criticized her harshly. For the rest of her life, discouraged and depressed, she concentrated on religious observance and wrote no more. She even sold her beloved books and gave the money to the poor. In 1695, Sor Juana died at 47 while nursing her sister nuns during an outbreak of disease.

	General/ Context	Daily Life/ Customs/ Practices	Humanities/ Fine Arts	Occupations	Education
1655		*L'École des filles (School for Young Ladies)* makes the first known reference to a contraceptive sheath made of linen to block semen from entering the uterus; by the century's end, upper-class women will prefer the intrauterine sponge to the linen condom			
1659		The Spanish infanta Maria Thérèse (1638–1683) introduces cocoa to France.			
1660	Height of the Classical Age in France, 1660–1680 The Restoration in England begins			Margaret Hardenbrook Philipse (c. 1659–1690) acts as business agent for Dutch merchants in New Netherlands; though twice married, she conducts shipping and trading activities using her maiden name	
1662	K'ang-hsi era, 1654–1722, a period of great literary and scholarly achievement in China, begins		Italian artist Margherita Caffi (1662–1700) is known for her distinctive style of flower painting Marie Madeleine Pioche de La Vergne, comtesse de La Fayette (1634–1693), is said to have originated the French novel of character		
1663	New France, in modern Canada, is established as a French colony				
1664	Foundation of the Royal Society's journal, *Philosophical Transactions,* the oldest existing scientific journal, published by the oldest scientific society in continuous existence since its founding; its first secretary calls science a "masculine philosophy"	London men flock to brothels when the rumor spreads that contracting syphillis will ward off the Black Death that is ravaging the city	Bolognese painter Elisabetta Sirani (1638–1665) is famed for the speed at which she paints portraits, allegories, and religious subjects; to dispel the suspicion that someone else has helped her, she invites her accusers to watch her paint a portrait in one sitting		

Performing Arts/ Entertainment/ Sports	Religion/ Philosophy	Science/ Technology/ Discovery	Statecraft/ Military	Reform	
					1655
					1659
					1660
					1662
Anne Bracegirdle (1663?–1748), English actress and intimate friend of the playwright Sir William Congreve, scores her greatest successes in his plays			Princess Nzinga Mbande Ngola (1582– 1663) of Ndongo, rules the country after the death of her brother the king; she is renowned for her diplomatic and military skills in dealing with the Dutch and Portuguese colonizers		**1663**
					1664

	General/ Context	Daily Life/ Customs/ Practices	Humanities/ Fine Arts	Occupations	Education
1665	London is ravaged by plague; more than 100,000 die				
1666	London is ravaged by the great fire, which destroys nearly the entire city				
1667	*Paradise Lost* by English poet John Milton (1608–1674) is published		English author Lucy Hutchinson (1620–?1680) writes a biography of her husband, John; the book is a unique portrait of the life of a Puritan family A collection of poems, by "the matchless Orinda," British poet Katherine Philips (1631–1664), is published posthumously		
1669			French artists, the sisters Geneviève (1645–1708) and Madeleine de Boulogne (1646–1710) are admitted to the Académie Royale Dutch still-life artist Maria van Oosterwyck (1630–1693) attracts important international patrons such as the kings of England, France, and Poland		
1670			Prominent portraitist Mary Beale (1632–1697) is considered the first British professional woman artist; she works in watercolors, oils, and pastels French still-life painter Charlotte Vignon (b. 1639) is at the height of her creative powers in the 1670s		
1671		In a letter to her daughter, the comtesse de Grignan, Marie de Rabutin-Chantal, Mme. de Sévigné (1626–1696), objects to condoms as "an armor against enjoyment and a spider web against danger"			
1677			Aphra Behn, probably the first professional woman playwright in England, publishes the		

Performing Arts/ Entertainment/ Sports	Religion/ Philosophy	Science/ Technology/ Discovery	Statecraft/ Military	Reform	
					1665
					1666
The most popular plays written by English actress Susanna Centlivre (1667?–1723) are such comedies of intrigue as *The Busy Body* (1709), *The Wonder! a Woman Keeps a Secret* (1714), and *A Bold Stroke for a Wife* (1718)		Margaret Cavendish, duchess of Newcastle, nicknamed Mad Madge because of her interest in science, writes and publishes her scientific ideas; she becomes a member of the Royal Society this year; no other woman is admitted to the Royal Society until 1945			**1667**
					1669
			Alyona, a former nun, leads a troop of rebels who help take the town of Temnikov in Russia; she is subsequently captured by government soldiers and burned alive		**1670**
	St. Rose of Lima (1586–1617) is the first canonized saint of the New World				**1671**
	The Convent of Santa Clara do Dêsterro is founded in Salvador, Bahia, Brazil, for			Mother Shipton, the 16th-century English prophetess whose predictions made their	**1677**

173

	General/ Context	Daily Life/ Customs/ Practices	Humanities/ Fine Arts	Occupations	Education
1677			play *The Rover, or The Banished Cavaliers, Part I;* she publishes part II in 1680		
1678			The Marquise Magdeleine de Sablé (c. 1599–1678) publishes her *Maximes et pensés diverse* (*Maxims and Various Thoughts*)		
1679			Distinguished Dutch still-life painter Rachel Ruysch (1664–1750) begins her professional apprenticeship at age 15; within three years she produces independent signed works; she becomes court painter to the Elector Palatine in Düsseldorf from 1708 to 1716; she continues painting well into her eighties		
1680	The Hapsburgs drive the Turks from Hungary during this decade			Aphra Behn acts as a spy for Charles II of England in Holland	
1682			Catherine Perrot, author and illustrator of two books of instruction on painting flower and bird miniatures, is admitted to the Académie Royale British Nonconformist and Whig supporter Celia Fiennes (b. 1662) records her travels; her writings are an important source of information about 18th-century economics and landscape		

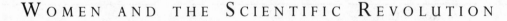

WOMEN AND THE SCIENTIFIC REVOLUTION

From classical times through the Renaissance, women practiced as herbalists, alchemists, midwives, and physicians. But the scientific revolution, beginning with the new astronomy of Copernicus, forever altered the way people viewed their relationship to the natural world. The new scientific method replaced such traditional practices with theory and experimentation. As with other branches of knowledge that required formal training, science was initially considered an exclusively male province. Women were thought intellectually incapable of grasping abstractions, of making accurate observations, or drawing well-founded conclusions. Nevertheless, many educated European women wished to pursue scientific studies.

Lady Mary Wortley Montagu (1689–1762) introduced smallpox immunization to Western Europe and began the formulation of the germ theory of disease. Like the women who followed in her footsteps, Montagu found Italy more tolerant of women scientists than England and so in Venice she began a famous salon for the discussion of scientific ideas.

In France, Marie Lavoisier (1758–1836) collaborated with

Performing Arts/ Entertainment/ Sports	Religion/ Philosophy	Science/ Technology/ Discovery	Statecraft/ Military	Reform	
	wealthy unmarried women and widows			first appearance in a 1641 tract, resurfaces in a political pamphlet entitled "The Life and Death of Mother Shipton"	**1677**
					1678
		German engraver Maria Sibylla Merian (1647–1717), one of the first observers to record the metamorphosis of insects, begins publication of *Erucarum Ortus,* engravings that help to lay the foundations for Linnaeus's classification of plant and animal species	In the Meal Tub Plot, a conspiracy against Protestants, Mrs. Cellier, a Roman Catholic, is accused of concealing documents in her house; she is tried for high treason and acquitted while the fabricator of the plot is convicted of libel, whipped, and pilloried		**1679**
					1680
		Nell Gwyn (1650–1687), the most popular mistress of Charles II of England, is instrumental in the founding of the Chelsea Royal Hospital in London			**1682**

her husband, Antoine, the founder of modern chemistry. Marie Louise Lachapelle (1769–1821) and Marie Anne Victorine Boivin (1733–1847), the most important women medical researchers in 19th-century France, made original anatomical discoveries, invented the vaginal speculum, and did groundbreaking work on the diseases of the uterus.

Natural history also attracted women. Maria Sibylle Merian of Germany and Holland was one of the first entomologists, a superb botanical artist, and a founder of biological classifications. Many women illustrated botanical texts, and as botany became more popular, women such as Priscilla Bell Wakefield (1751–1832) published books for both children and adults on the subject.

Despite their contemporaries' beliefs that women were intellectually and morally unfit for science, women of conviction pursued scientific careers. They came to contribute to every aspect of scientific endeavor including astronomy, mathematics, and the philosophy of science. It was not until the late 20th century, though, that women began to enter scientific disciplines in large numbers.

	General/ Context	Daily Life/ Customs/ Practices	Humanities/ Fine Arts	Occupations	Education
1687					French ecclesiastic and writer François de Salignac de la Mothe-Fénelon publishes *On the Education of Daughters*, a tract suggesting a limited program of study for young ladies
1688	Genroku period (1688–1703), the great flowering of Japanese literature and culture, begins The Glorious Revolution takes place in England; King James II is deposed and William and Mary of Holland become king and queen				
1690					
1691		Margaret Brent (1600–1671) is the first woman to own land in the colony of Maryland	Luisa Ignacia Roldán (1656–1704) of Seville is the first female sculptor recorded in Spain; in the early 1690s she is named Sculptor of the Chamber; she is best known for her permanent polychrome terra-cotta groups, a form she virtually invented		
1693				The mercantile enterprises of American businesswoman Mary Spratt Provoost Alexander (1693–1760) range from importing goods to be sold in her own store to supplying an American military expedition	
1694		The debate on the nature of women continues with the publication of Nicolas Boileau-Despréaux's *Satire X: Les femmes* (*Against Women*) and Charles Perrault's response, *Apologie des femmes* (*The Vindication of Wives*)			British advocate of higher education for women, Mary Astell (1668–1731) proposes the establishment of a women's college or residential academy dedicated to Queen Anne
1696			British feminist author Mary Astell publishes		

Performing Arts/ Entertainment/ Sports	Religion/ Philosophy	Science/ Technology/ Discovery	Statecraft/ Military	Reform	
					1687
					1688
			Chinese warrior Chin Liang-Yu fights at her husband's side; after his death, she leads her army to many victories in civil war		**1690**
					1691
					1693
					1694
	Jacqueline de Blémur is a renowned Bene-				**1696**

	General/ Context	Daily Life/ Customs/ Practices	Humanities/ Fine Arts	Occupations	Education
1696			"In Defense of the Female Sex" The imaginative and witty letters of Mme. de Sévigné to her daughter offer a valuable portrait of both her time and herself		
1698					
1700		A Lady of Devotion of the Order of St. John wears a black garment with a black mantle, a tight linen cap over her shaven head in memory of Christ's shroud, covered by a stiff veil, a symbol of betrothal to Christ	Annie Laurie (1682–1764) is the subject of the famous Scottish ballad written by her rejected lover, William Douglas; the song is set to new music by Lady John Scott in 1855; its heroine marries someone else who has her parents' approval		
1701	War of the Spanish Succession, 1701–1714				
1702					
1705					

Performing Arts/ Entertainment/ Sports	Religion/ Philosophy	Science/ Technology/ Discovery	Statecraft/ Military	Reform	
	dictine hagiographer at the Abbey of the Blessed Sacrament, Châtillon, France				**1696**
Francesca Margerita de l'Épine is an extremely popular singer and harpsichordist in London from 1698 to 1718; her sister, Maria Gallia, also sings in London from 1703 to 1748					**1698**
	The cult of Sitala, Indian goddess of smallpox, becomes especially important in Bengal villages; in the 19th century, the villages rally round the goddess in an effort to reunify after a time of disorder				**1700**
	American Quaker minister Mary Coffyn Starbuck (c. 1644– 1717) becomes the first recognized minister on Nantucket, MA Marie Marguerite d'Youville (1701– 1771) is the founder of the Sisters of Charity of the Hôpital Général de Montréal (Grey Nuns)		An Act of Settlement makes Sophia, wife of the elector of Hannover, and her Protestant descendants heirs to the throne of England	British writer Lady Mary Chudleigh offers her views on the status of women in her book, *The Ladies' Defense*	**1701**
			Coronation of Anne (1665–1714), queen of Great Britain and Ireland; she immediately applies £100,000 of the country's allowance to public service		**1702**
	The cult of St. Teresa (d. 1250) and St. Sanchia (d. 1229), daughters of Sancho I of Portugal, is approved by the Roman Catholic Church; both women built and supported Cistercian communities				**1705**

	General/ Context	Daily Life/ Customs/ Practices	Humanities/ Fine Arts	Occupations	Education
1706			The Académie Royale declares that no more women can be admitted; however, Anne Vallayer-Coster, Marie Suzanne Giroust, and Anna Dorothea Lisiewska-Therbusch are admitted, bringing the number of female members to four; the Académie then establishes a limit of four women members		
1709			Playwright and political pamphleteer Mary de la Rivière Manley (1663?–1724) is remembered for her scandalous chronicles of contemporary British politics and society; in 1711 she succeeds Jonathan Swift as editor of the Tory periodical *The Examiner*		Susanna Wesley (1669–1742), mother of John Wesley, founder of the Methodist Church, teaches all 19 of her children as well as the other local boys and girls at the Old Rectory; she writes religious textbooks for her classes and holds services for her students, thereby offending the local clergy
1710		The tobacco shop of well-known Boston merchant Mary Singleton Copley Pelham (1710–1789) supports the training and career of her son, mezzotint artist John Singleton Copley			
1716			Lady Mary Wortley Montague, traveler, free thinker, letter writer, and feminist, accompanies her husband to Turkey, where she writes the first of her *Turkish Letters*		
1718				Hannah Penn (1671–1726), widow of William Penn, handles the business of the province during his illness, becoming his sole executrix	
1720		Molly Mog (1699–1766), an innkeeper's daughter, becomes the most celebrated beauty in London; John Gay writes a ballad to her, "Fair Maid of the Inn"	Rosalba Carriera (1675–1757), skilled in lace making, decorating snuff box lids, and painting miniature portraits on ivory, popularizes the pastel portrait, a new type of painting; she becomes	Mary Reade (c. 1690) initially disguises herself as a male in order to serve in both Britain's army and navy; she joins a group of pirates en route to the West Indies, where she meets Irish pirate	

Performing Arts/ Entertainment/ Sports	Religion/ Philosophy	Science/ Technology/ Discovery	Statecraft/ Military	Reform	
	Vita Kimba, a prophetess in the kingdom of the Congo, originally a priestess in an African temple, preaches an African version of Christianity and claims to have been reincarnated as St. Anthony; she is denounced by a Catholic priest and burned at the stake				**1706**
			The verdict that condemned the Salem "witches" to death in 1692 is reversed

Barbara Villiers (b. 1641), the mistress of Charles II of England, dies; well established in the court, she held great influence over the king and his policy making for which she was unpopular with the politicians. | | **1709** |
					1710
					1716
		Lady Mary Wortley Montague introduces the practice of vaccination into Britain having seen it in Turkey	Charles XII of Sweden, killed at Frederickshald, is succeeded by his sister, Ulrika Eleanora		**1718**
					1720

	General/ Context	Daily Life/ Customs/ Practices	Humanities/ Fine Arts	Occupations	Education
1720			a member of the Académie Royale, despite the 1706 ruling against admitting female students	Ann Bonney (b. 1700), who has joined the group also disguised as a man; they plague the West Indies until they are captured in 1720 and sentenced to the gallows; the two escape hanging by claiming they are pregnant	
1721		Anna Magdalena Wülken marries Johann Sebastian Bach, with whom she bears 13 children; known for her fine voice and musical taste, she wrote out many of the parts for her husband's cantatas; he wrote two books of music for her, the famous *Anna Magdalena Notebooks*			
1722					
1723			Dutch painter Margareta Haverman, is expelled from the Académie Royale when members decide that the painting she submitted as a new member must have been done by her teacher as it was too good to have been done by a woman		
1724			A German-Jewish housewife, Glückel of Hameln (1645–1724), leaves behind her *Memoiren*, seven volumes that give a vivid picture of Jewish life in an 18th-century German town; considered the first work of modern Yiddish literature		
1725					

Performing Arts/ Entertainment/ Sports	Religion/ Philosophy	Science/ Technology/ Discovery	Statecraft/ Military	Reform	
					1720
					1721
	The last of Sutherland County's witch burning is held in Dornoch, England		Mentewab (d. 1769) becomes empress of Ethiopia; she is a co-ruler during the reigns of her sons		**1722**
					1723
	Foundation of the Mexican convent of Corpus Christi; the first convent for Native American women, those admitted are of the nobility, not necessarily wealthy, but "free from idolatry and racially pure"; this *monasterio*, which lasts until 1821, demonstrates (to the doubtful) that Indian women can pursue a religious life				**1724**
			Catherine I (1684?– 1727) begins a two-year reign as czarina of Russia		**1725**

	General/ Context	Daily Life/ Customs/ Practices	Humanities/ Fine Arts	Occupations	Education
1727				Elizabeth Timothy (d. 1757) takes over the publication of the first permanent newspaper in the colony of South Carolina, *South Carolina Gazette*	
1730		Around this time, whalebone panniers (hoop skirts that extend sideways instead of in a circle to exaggerate the breadth of feminine hips) become popular in England			
1731			Alison Rutherford sets up a Parisian-style literary salon in Scotland for the figures of the Scottish Enlightenment; she writes satirical and serious poetry and is an artist as well		Welsh education pioneer Bridget Vaughan (1698–1779) founds several schools and becomes the patron of the Welsh Circulating Schools
1732					
1733	"Flying shuttle" for weaving looms is developed				
1735			Parisian Claudine Alexandrine Guérin de Tencin (1685–1749) publishes the romance *Les mémoires du comte de Comminges;* though her conduct is considered immoral, her salons are populated by some of the most brilliant minds of her day		
1736				During the 18th century in England, Sarah Mapp, the "Bonesetter of Epsom," gains a wide reputation for her orthopedic skills	

Performing Arts/ Entertainment/ Sports	Religion/ Philosophy	Science/ Technology/ Discovery	Statecraft/ Military	Reform	
					1727
The greatest French tragedienne of her day, Adrienne Lecouvreur (1692–1730) employs a naturalistic style of acting in a time when a declamatory style is popular			Czarina Anna Ivanovna (1693–1740) begins her 10-year rule of Russia		**1730**
	Swiss theologian and philosopher Marie Huber (1694–1753) publishes *The Foolish World Preferred to the Wise;* her *Letters on Religion Essential to Man* appears in 1738				**1731**
		Italian physicist Laura Bassi Verati (1711–1778) begins to lecture as a professsor at the University of Bologna			**1732**
		Gabrielle Émilie Le Tonnelier de Breteuil, marquise de Châtelet (1706–1749), a renowned mathematician and physicist, helps spread the ideas of Newton and Leibniz in France			**1733**
A pupil of Giuseppe Tartini, Maddalena Lombardini de Sirmen (1735–c. 1799) is trained as a professional violinist; she later becomes both a noted singer and composer					**1735**
				British duchess of Marlborough, Sarah Churchill (1660–1744), builds the Marlborough Almshouses	**1736**

	General/ Context	Daily Life/ Customs/ Practices	Humanities/ Fine Arts	Occupations	Education
1738					
1740	War of the Austrian Succession (1740–1748)	18th-century European and Englishwomen wear long tight-fitting bodices with low square necklines; a kerchief is sometimes tucked in for modesty	Swiss author and musician Isabelle-Agnès-Elisabeth Charrière (1740–1805) is best known for her compositions for harpsichord	England's greatest pickpocket, Jenny Diver (1700–1740), is immortalized in John Gay's *Beggar's Opera*	
1741			Angelica Kauffmann (1741–1807) forges an artistic path for herself, devoting herself to historical paintings		
1742			Cornelia Smith Bradford (1719–1755) takes over the management of the *American Weekly Mercury*		
1743			Hannah Cowley (1743–1809) is one of the earliest of Englishwomen dramatists	Daughter of Benjamin Franklin, Sarah Franklin Bache (1743–1808) is best known as a relief worker during the Revolutionary War, serving food to soldiers and organizing clothing drives	
1746		Lady Grizel Baillie's *Household Book* becomes an important source for Scottish social historians			
1748					

Performing Arts/ Entertainment/ Sports	Religion/ Philosophy	Science/ Technology/ Discovery	Statecraft/ Military	Reform	
	Selina Hastings, countess of Huntingdon (1707–1791), adopts the cause of religious reformists; she establishes many chapels and safe houses, known collectively as the Countess of Huntingdon's Connection; she also establishes a training college for Methodist ministers at Trefecca House	The marquise de Châtelet and Voltaire write Eléments de la philosophie de Newton			**1738**
		The marquise de Châtelet publishes Institutions de physique, an account of Leibnizian physics that rejects Newton's concept of action at a distance	Maria Theresa, archduchess of Austria (1717–1780), becomes queen of Hungary and Bohemia; she is the mother of Marie Antoinette and Joseph II; both the Seven Years' War and the War of the Austrian Succession are fought over dominions she inherited		**1740**
		American astronomer Elizabeth Pinckney sights a comet whose appearance was predicted by Sir Isaac Newton	Czarina Elizabeth Petrovna (1709–1762) begins her 21-year rule of Russia		**1741**
					1742
	Barbara Heck (1734–1804) is known as the Mother of American Methodism				**1743**
			Scottish heroine Flora MacDonald (1772–1790) risks her life to help Bonnie Prince Charlie escape after his defeat at Culloden, the end of his effort to gain the British crown		**1746**
		Italian mathematician Maria Gaetana Agnesi (1718–1799) publishes Instituzioni analitichi ad uso della gioventù italiana (Foundations of Analysis) upon which			**1748**

	General/ Context	Daily Life/ Customs/ Practices	Humanities/ Fine Arts	Occupations	Education
1748					
1749			Suzanne Curchod Necker (1739–1794), popular political and literary saloniste at the time of the French Revolution, publishes Reflections on Divorce		
1750			The word "bluestocking," signifying a female pedant with pretentious intellectual interests, refers to Benjamin Stillingfleet, who wore blue rather than the customary white stockings		
1752			British novelist and diarist Fanny Burney, a.k.a. Madame d'Arblay (1752–1840), is one of the first novelists to deal with the experiences of young girls entering society		
1754		Julie Jeanne Eléonore de Lespinasse (1732–1776), companion and protégée of Mme. du Deffand, conducts a brilliant literary salon between 1754 and 1763; later on her own salon becomes the meeting place for the encyclopedists, such as Diderot and d'Alembert; she is remembered for her love letters, *Lettres de Mlle. de Lespinasse* (1809)	French artist Marie Victoire Lemoine (1754–1820) exhibits in the Salon de la Correspondance and the official salon of the Académie Royale British poet and author Anna Seward (1742–1809) holds literary gatherings and becomes known as the Swan of Lichfield		
1755	The first Russian institution of higher education, Moscow State University, is founded		French painter Marie Anne Elisabeth Vigée-Lebrun (1755–1842), portraitist of the Parisian aristocracy, is one of the most celebrated women artists of her time		
1756	Seven Years' War, 1756–1763 Birth of Wolfgang Amadeus Mozart (1756–1791), Austrian composer		French comedienne and novelist Marie Jeanne Riccoboni (1714–1792) publishes sentimental romances		

Performing Arts/ Entertainment/ Sports	Religion/ Philosophy	Science/ Technology/ Discovery	Statecraft/ Military	Reform	
		her fame rests; the so-called Witch (or Curve) of Agnesi is named for her			**1748**
					1749
		Known for her work in analytic geometry, Maria Gaetana Agnesi is named honorary professor of mathematics at the University of Bologna, where, however, she never lectures	Awura Pokou ends her approximately 20-year reign as queen and ruler of the Baule tribe in Africa (c. 1730–1750); while in power, she breaks away from the Asante Confederacy of Peoples and leads her tribe to a new land on the Ivory Coast		**1750**
		Publication of Mme. de Châtelet's *Dissertation sur la nature et la propagation de feu (Dissertation on the Nature and Propagation of Fire)*			**1752**
		Dorothea Christine Erxleben graduates from the University of Halle, the first woman to obtain a medical degree from a German university			**1754**
					1755
					1756

	General/ Context	Daily Life/ Customs/ Practices	Humanities/ Fine Arts	Occupations	Education
1758	Hose-knitting machine is invented		Self-taught British scholar Elizabeth Carter (1717–1806) publishes her translation of the Greek philosopher Epictetus		
1759			The *Rime* (sonnets on love and contemporary political events) and *Lettere* (*Letters*) written by Italian poet Veronica Gambara (1485–1550) are published		
1760		Abigail Stoneman (1760–1777), publican of colonial Rhode Island, MA, and New York, is the first Newport woman to marry an Englishman with a title	Swiss sculptor Madame Tussaud (1760–1850), née Marie Gresholtz, is the creator of the famous London Wax Museum		
1762			Pioneer Margaret Catchpole (1762–1869) is sent to Australia after escaping from a jail in England, where she was imprisoned for having stolen a horse and riding to London to see her lover; in Australia she runs a business and practices as a midwife		
1764	Invention of the spinning jenny in England	American society leader Anne Willing Bingham (1764–1801) establishes well-attended French-style literary/political salons in her Philadelphia home	Italian soprano Lucrezia Agujari (1743–1783, known as La Bastardella), makes her debut in Florence; noted for her very high vocal range Austrian artist Barbara Krafft (1764–1825), member of the Vienna Academy and a popular portraitist in Salzburg, receives commissions from the Church of Prague, eventually becoming official painter to the city of Bamberg, Germany		

Performing Arts/ Entertainment/ Sports	Religion/ Philosophy	Science/ Technology/ Discovery	Statecraft/ Military	Reform	
					1758
	Gauribai (1759–1809) of Gujarat, India, is known for her poetry on themes of Hindu mysticism	The marquise de Châtelet's translation of Newton's *Philosophiae naturalis principia mathematica* is published posthumously; it remains the only French translation			**1759**
					1760
	In *Émile*, philosopher Jean-Jacques Rousseau supports the notion of a "natural hierarchy" dictating women's submission to men and the precedence of motherhood over other duties		Ekaterina Alexeyevna, or Catherine the Great (1729–1796), begins her 34-year reign as empress of Russia; the beginning of her reign is characterized by liberal ideas and lively intellectual life, but after the French Revolution, she becomes repressive; her chief political accomplishments are the acquisition of Polish-held lands in Ukraine and the expansion of Russia's frontiers on the Black Sea; her intended reform of the legal code was never completely implemented		**1762**
	Maria Theresa, queen of Hungary and Bohemia, founds the Knights of the Order of St. Stephen				**1764**

	General/ Context	Daily Life/ Customs/ Practices	Humanities/ Fine Arts	Occupations	Education
1765					
1766			English-born Frances Brooke (1724–1789), considered Canada's first novelist, writes *The History of Emily Montegu* while she and her husband are stationed in Quebec		
1768		Marie Jeanne Bécu, comtesse Du Barry, better known as Mme. Du Barry (1743–1793), becomes mistress of Louis XV until his death in 1774; she wields great influence over the king and his court	British letter writer and flower artist Mary Granville Delaney is granted a royal pension and cottage by Queen Charlotte		
1769					
1770	Birth of Ludwig van Beethoven (1770–1827), German composer		The first Negro poet in America, Phillis Wheatley (c. 1753?–1784), is bought as a young child off a Boston slave ship; she quickly learns English and composes extraordinary religious poetry French still-life artist Anne Vallayer-Coster (1744–1818), is elected unanimously to the Académie Royale	Mary Beilby of England forms a working partnership with her brother, producing decorated drinking glasses and decanters	
1771			Susanna Wright (1697–1784), pioneer settler in colonial Pennsylvania, acts as a legal counselor, unofficial magistrate, and physician for her neighbors		
1772			American poet Mercy Otis Warren (1728–1814) publishes *The Adulateur*, a satiric play meant to be read rather than performed		

Performing Arts/ Entertainment/ Sports	Religion/ Philosophy	Science/ Technology/ Discovery	Statecraft/ Military	Reform	
Popular British actress and singer Sophia Snow Baddeley (1745–1786) makes her stirring London appearance as Ophelia in *Hamlet*	Doña María Clemencia Caycedo of Bogotá, Colombia, founds a convent with the mission of teaching girls				**1765**
			American frontier heroine Betty Zane (1766?–1831?) saves a besieged fort in one of the final Indian attacks during the Revolutionary War by carrying gunpowder to replenish the defenders' depleted supply		**1766**
English-born Susanna Haswell Rowson (c. 1762–1824) emigrates to the American colonies, where she writes novels and becomes an actress	Marie-Anne Rivier (1768–1838) is the founder of the Sisters of the Presentation of Mary				**1768**
	Catherine the Great secularizes Russian church property				
	Philippine Duchesne (1769–1852) is the French founder of the Society of the Sacred Heart in the US				**1769**
		Mrs. Eleanor Coade and her daughter develop a formula for reconstituted stone, known as Coade stone; they operate a successful business to produce it in England	Marie Antoinette (1755–1793) marries King Louis XVI of France; unpopular with her subjects, she is known contemptuously as Mme. Déficit, Mme. Veto, and L'Autrichienne		**1770**
					1771
British actress, novelist, and playwright Elizabeth Inchbald (1753–1821) makes her debut as Cordelia in *King Lear* in Bristol at age	Hannah Jenkins Barnard (1754?–1825) becomes a Friend; her widely debated beliefs come to be regarded by some as heretical	Caroline Herschel (1750–1848) works with her brother, astronomer William Herschel; her contributions include the			**1772**

	General/ Context	Daily Life/ Customs/ Practices	Humanities/ Fine Arts	Occupations	Education
1772			American artist Patience Lovell Wright (1725–1786), specializing in wax sculpture, models her creations on well-known living people; she dabbles in politics, even passing secret information concealed in wax figures to American forces in Philadelphia		
1773				Printer and newspaper editor Clementina Rind (c. 1740–1774) takes over the production of the *Virginia Gazette* at her husband's death	
1774			Anna Laetitia Aikin Barbauld (1734–1825) publishes her first work, entitled *Miscellaneous Pieces of Prose*	English silversmith Hester Bateman (c. 1709–1793) registers her hallmark in London's guildhall	Leonhard Usteri founds the first school for girls in Zürich, Switzerland Anna Barbauld opens a Nonconformist boarding school in England
1775		Charlotte von Stein (1742–1827) meets Johann Wolfgang von Goethe; their relationship, chiefly spiritual, lasts until Goethe leaves for Italy; the theme of renunciation that informs many of his works is derived from her teachings			
1776	American Declaration of Independence signed	Cherokee leader Nancy (or Nanye'hi) Ward (c. 1738–1822) takes her fallen husband's place in a battle between the Creeks and the Cherokees; she heads the Woman's Council and sits as a member of the Council of Chiefs	Lady Christian Henrietta Caroline Acland (1750–1815), a.k.a. Lady Harriet, accompanies her husband from England to the American Colonies; her narrative of her experiences is considered "one of the brightest episodes in the war"		
1777	Rétif de la Bretonne publishes "Les Gynographes," one of the most rabidly antifeminist pamphlets of the 18th century	Legend holds that Betsy Griscom Ross (1752–1836), creator of the first American flag of stars and stripes, is approached by a secret committee of the Continental Con-	English writer and reformer Hannah More (1745–1833) publishes the tragedy *Percy* The British writer Clara Reeves is the author of various criti-		

Performing Arts/ Entertainment/ Sports	Religion/ Philosophy	Science/ Technology/ Discovery	Statecraft/ Military	Reform	
18; she later becomes a playwright and novelist		first sightings of eight comets and 14 nebulae, and together they build telescopes and report their sightings to the Royal Astronomical Society, which names her a fellow in 1828			**1772**
					1773
	Ann Lee (1736–1784) leaves England for America, where she founds the American Shakers at Waterford, NY		Through her marriage to the duke of Devonshire, Georgiana Cavendish plays as full a role in politics as a woman can at this time		**1774**
Swiss musician Anna Barbara Fischer is active as a concert pianist in Schaffhausen			Catherine Van Rensselaer Schuyler (1734–1803), wife of American Revolutionary War General Philip Schuyler, burns the extensive wheat fields around Albany, NY, to prevent British forces from harvesting them; her courage inspires other Colonists to similar acts of resistance	In an article for *Pennsylvania Magazine,* American political philosopher Thomas Paine proposes women's rights	**1775**
					1776
			Queen Maria I (1734–1816) becomes joint ruler of Portugal when she marries her uncle, Peter III; after his death in 1787 she rules alone until she becomes insane in 1792	A strong supporter of the rights of women and racial minorities, Abigail Smith Adams (1744–1818) writes that women "will not hold ourselves bound by any laws in which	**1777**

	General/ Context	Daily Life/ Customs/ Practices	Humanities/ Fine Arts	Occupations	Education
1777		gress headed by George Washington in 1776 or 1777 to design a flag for the nascent nation	cal works as well as several gothic novels		
1778		Child of English Quaker settlers who survived the Wyoming, PA, massacres of 1778, the five-year-old Frances Slocum (1773–1847) is captured by Delawares; she is discovered by a fur trader in 1835 and meets briefly with her brother's family in 1837, but refuses to return east with them, preferring to die where "the Great Spirit will find me" Lady Eleanor Butler and the Honorable Sarah Ponsonby elope from Ireland and set up home together in Scotland, becoming known as the Ladies of Llangollen	Artist Marie Eléonore Godefroid (1778–1849), drawing teacher at an exclusive girls' school, is an early French advocate of women's rights Scottish-born writer and intellectual Joanna Baillie (1762–1851) begins writing in order to support her mother and siblings following her father's death		
1780		French rococo hairstyles change from flat graceful arrangements to towering headdresses; the friseur (the one who curls the hair) is superseded by the coiffeur, who works the coiffe, or cap, into the hair in the form of ribbons and other decorations	The marquise du Deffand, Marie de Vichy-Chamrond (1697–1780), a leader in Parisian social and intellectual circles, conducts one of the most important salons of 18th-century France	Esther de Berdt Reed (1746–1780) organizes the fundraising, purchase of materials, and production of shirts in Philadelphia for the American Continental Army; during her effort to spread the work to other Colonies, she dies suddenly	
1782		Austrian singer Constanze Weber (1763–1842) marries Wolfgang Amadeus Mozart			
1783			Author of *Les liaisons dangereuses,* Choderlos de Laclos publishes *De l'éducation des femmes* (*On the Education of Women*), suggesting a course of study designed to make women more graceful in spirit while not		

Performing Arts/ Entertainment/ Sports	Religion/ Philosophy	Science/ Technology/ Discovery	Statecraft/ Military	Reform	
			and her son rules as regent	we have no voice"; she is the wife of the second president of the US, John Adams, and mother of the sixth, John Quincy Adams	**1777**
	Catherine McAuley (1778–1841) is the Irish founder of the Sisters of Mercy		American Revolutionary heroine Mary Mc-Cauley (1754–1832), known as Molly Pitcher for carrying water to American soldiers during the Battle of Monmouth; she mans her husband's cannon when he falls in battle		**1778**
			Elizabeth Freeman, the first slave to be emancipated in the American Colonies, is given her freedom in Great Barrington, MA		**1780**
			American Revolutionary War soldier Deborah Sampson (1760–1827) dresses in men's clothing and enlists as a soldier in the Continental forces under the name of Robert Shurtleff		**1782**
An actress at 15, then a very popular Portuguese mezzo-soprano and court singer in Berlin, Luiza Rosa de Aguiar Todi (1753–1833) provokes a famous rivalry with soprano Gertrud Elisabeth Mara			The Diamond Necklace Affair (1783–1785), one of the most famous scandals in French history: the Cardinal de Rohan is tricked into buying a necklace made of 500 diamonds for Queen Marie Antoinette; the		**1783**

	General/ Context	Daily Life/ Customs/ Practices	Humanities/ Fine Arts	Occupations	Education
1783			overburdening them with knowledge Painters Marie-Louise-Elisabeth Vigée-Lebrun and Adélaïde Labille-Guiard are admitted to the Académie Royale on the same day		
1784			Hannah Adams (1755–1831), the first American woman to support herself by the pen, publishes *An Alphabetical Compendium of the Various Sects*		Countess Henrietta Benigna Justine Zinzendorf von Watteville (1725–1789) opens the Bethlehem Female Seminary, originally a Moravian girls' school now open to pupils outside the Moravian Church
1785	Invention of chlorine bleach and the steam-powered loom		British sculptor Anne Seymour Damer (1748–1828), carves the heads of Isis and Thames on the bridge that crosses the Thames in Henley, England	Ann Timothy holds the post Printer to the State of South Carolina until her death; at least 15 imprints are issued under her name	Sophie and Harriet Lee set up a school in Bath, England, with the proceeds of Sophie's play, *A Chapter of Accidents*
1786			Hester Lynch Thrale (1741–1821), hostess of intellectual gatherings, publishes *Anecdotes of the Late Samuel Johnson*		A government boarding school for girls in Vienna for the education of teachers and governesses is founded under the auspices of Emperor Joseph II
1787	US Constitution is signed at the Constitutional Convention in Philadelphia, PA; it goes into effect in 1789 The Abolition Society is formed by British Quakers to prevent the importation of African slaves to British colonies and America				Dorothea Schlözer of Germany becomes an instructor on the philosophy faculty of the University of Göttingen
1788			Specialist in portraits and genre scenes, Constance Charpentier (1767–1849) receives a Prix d'Encouragement British writer Charlotte Smith (d. 1806) publishes *Emmeline* and *The Manor House* (1793)		Hannah More opens a school in Cheddar, England, for illiterates and suffers much opposition for educating laborers; she writes moral tales for them

Performing Arts/ Entertainment/ Sports	Religion/ Philosophy	Science/ Technology/ Discovery	Statecraft/ Military	Reform	
			Comtesse Jeanne de la Motte hires a prostitute to impersonate the queen and steals the jewels herself; when all is revealed, the cardinal is exiled, the queen's name is cleared, and Mme. de la Motte is sentenced to life imprisonment— from which she later escapes to England to write her memoirs		**1783**
					1784
					1785
Famous coloratura soprano Anna Selina Storace (1766–1817) creates the role of Susanna in Mozart's *Le Nozze di Figaro* (*The Marriage of Figaro*)					**1786**
	Successor to founder Ann Lee, Lucy Wright (1760–1821) dominates the period of the Shaker society's greatest growth	Caroline Herschel's work as an astronomer is recognized by the king of England, who grants her an annual stipend of 50 pounds to continue her work		Marie Jean Antoine Nicolas Caritat, marquis de Condorcet, publishes *Letters from a Bourgeois of Newhaven to a Citizen of Virginia*, in which he issues the first French demand for political rights for women	**1787**
					1788

	General/ Context	Daily Life/ Customs/ Practices	Humanities/ Fine Arts	Occupations	Education
1789	The Third Estate declares itself to the French General Assembly The Declaration of the Rights of Man and of the Citizen is approved by the French National Assembly and proclaimed in France		Elizabeth Montagu publishes a sensational defense of Shakespeare against Voltaire, *Essay on the Writings and Genius of Shakespeare*	Japan cracks down on prostitution, banning streetwalkers and confining prostitutes to the Yoshiwara section of Edo; mixed bathing is also banned	
1790		French hairstyles become extravagant, rising straight up from the forehead, taking such shapes as the *coiffure en bandeau d'amour* (love bands) or the *chien couchant avec un pouf* (a reclining dog on a pad of hair), and incorporating artificial ships' prows, flowers, fruit baskets, and cornfields	The writings of American author Ann Eliza Bleecker (1752–1783) offer accounts of wartime conditions on the American frontier Poet Sarah Wentworth Morton (1759–1846) publishes *Ouabi, or the Virtues of Nature* Catherine Macaulay's contribution to feminism, *Letters on Education,* influences Mary Wollstonecraft's writing of *A Vindication of the Rights of Women*		
1791	The US Bill of Rights is ratified as the first 10 amendments to the Constitution	Camembert is invented by French farmer Marie Fontaine Harrel of Orne	Adélaïde Labille-Guiard (1749–1803) is official painter to French King Louis XVI's great-aunts; she is an active		

OLYMPE DE GOUGES AND MADAME ROLAND:
FRENCH REVOLUTIONARIES

Women played a prominent role in the French Revolution: they marched en masse to Versailles and returned with the king; they fought in the army; they made their grievances known in petitions for change and in the streets. But when in 1789 the groundbreaking "Declaration of the Rights of Man and of the Citizen" was written, it seemed to leave women out. Based on the American Declaration of Independence, the Declaration of the Rights of Man demanded freedom of expression, representative government, and legal equality for all citizens, but it ignored many of the additional demands that women would have sought.

A bold feminist, Olympe de Gouges stepped in to right the wrong. Her Declaration of the Rights of Woman and of Citizenesses (1791) cleverly paraphrased its namesake, substituting words applicable to women wherever appropriate. She insisted that women, too, were born free and entitled to the same inalienable rights as men, and that women deserved legal equal-

ity. She added that men should be required to recognize their illegitimate children, that both married and single women should have the right to control their property, and that women must be allowed to speak out on policital matters since they could certainly be punished by the state. Scorned at the time, her declaration aptly pointed out where women's rights were overlooked in the famous 1789 manifesto.

Olympe de Gouges had taken up the pen around 1789, when she moved to Paris after her husband's death. She found her voice in political pamphleteering and turned out more than two dozen tracts between 1790 and 1793, advocating such reforms as education for women and aid to the poor. An actress as well as a writer, she started a woman's journal and a woman's theater. In spite of her radical feminist critique of the Declaration of the Rights of Man, Olympe de Gouges was a moderate in certain ways. When King Louis XVI stood trial during the revolution, Olympe offered to defend him be-

| | | | | Women of the French Third Estate address petitions to King Louis XVI containing specific women's grievances | **1789** |

Led by market women, 4000 French women march on the National Assembly at Versailles demanding bread

Portrait of Madame Roland found on her lover's body after his execution
Photograph courtesy Archives Nationales, Paris

Viennese singer Katherina Cavalieri (1761–1801) is praised by Mozart for her voice; he composes several songs for her

French philosopher and mathematician Condorcet follows his 1787 call for women's rights with *On the Admission of Women to Citizens' Rights* — **1790**

Constitution of women's political clubs in France, countering their exclusion from men's revolutionary organization

Mozart composes the role of the Queen of the Night in his opera *Die Zauberflöte* (*The Magic Flute*) for soprano Josepha Weber

The religious leader Elspeth Buchan (1738–1791), the center of a millenarian cult, dies, disappointing her followers, the

Marie Antoinette counsels her husband, Louis XVI, to flee the French Revolution; regarded as traitors,

French feminist Olympe de Gouges (Marie Gouze) issues the *Declaration of the Rights of Woman and of the Citizen*, dedicated — **1791**

---

cause she thought the revolution, for all its potential, had targeted a victim rather than a tyrant. (He refused her help.) She also sharply criticized revolutionary leader Maximilien Robespierre, for which she was executed in November 1793—proving the truth of her statement that women could be punished for their politics.

A revolutionary woman of a very different background was Manon Philipon Roland (1754–1793). As a child she was dedicated to books, weeping over Rousseau's romantic novels, carrying Plutarch with her to church. She married Jean-Marie Roland in 1780 and, when they moved to Paris in 1791, instituted salon gatherings in their Paris suite, where artists, thinkers, and writers would converse upon lofty Enlightenment subjects. A group of salon friends developed who shared their moderate political views.

When the revolution broke out, Madame Roland's group, known as the Girondists, found itself at odds with the more radical Jacobin faction. Meanwhile, Monsieur Roland was appointed the king's minister of the interior in March 1792, and Manon directed his career behind the scenes. She drafted his letter of protest to the king criticizing Louis XVI's policies, for which the king fired him. But by August of 1792 the king had been overthrown anyway. Tensions mounted between the Jacobins and Girondists, and in June of 1793 the Jacobins expelled the Girondists from the assembly. Madame Roland was arrested in the insurrection. While in prison awaiting her trial, she wrote an important chronicle of the revolution, her *Appeal to Impartial Posterity*. She was executed on November 8, 1793, within days of Olympe de Gouges. (When her husband heard the news, he killed himself by falling on his sword.) Madame Roland's last political act was to cry on the scaffold, "O liberty! O liberty! What crimes are committed in thy name!"

	General/ Context	Daily Life/ Customs/ Practices	Humanities/ Fine Arts	Occupations	Education
1791			promoter of rights for women artists		
			Maria Ellenrieder (1791–1863) becomes the foremost woman painter in early 19th-century Germany and is admitted to the Munich Academy		
			Publication of France's first feminist magazine, *Etrennes nationales des dames,* founded on the principle that "women are equal to men in rights and in pleasure"		
1792	Height of the French Revolution, 1792–1795; the French Revolutionary Convention abolishes the monarchy, condemns the king to death, and supports the Reign of Terror	A French Revolutionary Convention decree forbids the use of the titles *Monsieur* and *Madame,* replacing them with *citoyen* and *citoyenne*			
1793	Invention of the cotton gin		French painter Nanine Vallain exhibits her portraits and paintings in the Académie Royale's salons; she is also known for her paintings of the French Revolution		Business schools for girls are founded in Germany by education reformers Suarez and Meierotto
			British poet Felicia Dorothea Hemans (1793–1835) is remembered chiefly for her narrative poems *The Landing of the Pilgrim Fathers* and *Casabianca*		Katy Ferguson, an ex-slave who purchased her freedom, establishes her school in New York, known as the Katy Ferguson School for the Poor; the students are recruited from the poorhouses and include 28 black children and 20 white children
			Swiss architect Anne Charlotte Adélaide Eynard-Lullin (1793–1868) and her husband plan, design, and oversee the construction of Palais Eynard in Geneva, Switzerland		
1794			Mrs. Ann Ward Radcliffe (1764–1823) publishes her enormously popular and influential gothic novel, *The Mysteries of Udolpho*		

Performing Arts/ Entertainment/ Sports	Religion/ Philosophy	Science/ Technology/ Discovery	Statecraft/ Military	Reform	
(d. 1820), sister of Aloysia and Constanza Weber, both singers as well	Buchanites, who believed her to be the woman mentioned in the Book of Revelation and who expected her to live forever—or at least be resurrected		they are captured and imprisoned	to Queen Marie Antoinette Etta Palm d'Aelders speaks before the National Assembly, asking for equal education for girls and equal rights for women	**1791**
			British political thinker Mary Wollstonecraft (1759–1797) writes the first major feminist tract in English, *A Vindication of the Rights of Women* French feminist Théroigne de Méricourt (Anne Tervague) tries to organize units of French "Amazons" to fight against the Austrians		**1792**
	American plantation manager Elizabeth Lucas Pinckney (1722?–1793) is distinguished for her successful cultivation of indigo		French patriot remembered for stabbing Jean Paul Marat to death in his bath, Charlotte Corday (1768–1793) is guillotined during the Reign of Terror France bars women from participating in political activity Queen Marie Antoinette is guillotined as a traitor The French Revolutionary Convention declares that women, minors, the insane, and criminals are not citizens	Supression of women's political clubs by the French Revolutionary Convention Théroigne de Méricourt is beaten up by Jacobin women for asserting the rights of women to education, politics, law, and employment; she is then confined to a lunatic asylum, where she dies African-born ex-slave Lucy Terry Prince demands an audience before the Williams College board of trustees in response to their rejection of her son based on his race, eloquently defending African-American people's desire for education	**1793**
				Theodor von Hippel of Germany publishes *On the Civil Improvement of Women;* he argues that women's abilities are the same as men's, but that they are "not simply neglected, they are deliberately suppressed"	**1794**

English feminist author Mary Wollstonecraft Illustration (1792) courtesy Sophia Smith Collection, Smith College

	General/ Context	Daily Life/ Customs/ Practices	Humanities/ Fine Arts	Occupations	Education
1795	Bread riots in Paris Establishment of the Directory in France, 1795–1799 Napoleon Bonaparte comes into power in France	Napoleon Bonaparte's attempt to revive the style of the Roman Empire lends European women's fashions greater comfort and freedom			
1796	White Lotus Rebellion against the Ch'ing dynasty in China		Married to August Schlegel, Caroline Michaelis Schlegel is responsible for many of the ideas in her husband's essays and translations of Shakespeare; she divorces Schlegel and marries the philosopher Friedrik Wilhelm Joseph von Schelling British writer Maria Edgeworth (1768–1849) publishes *The Parent's Assistant* (1796–1800) and *Moral Tales* (1801)		

Revolutionary War soldier Deborah Sampson
Illustration (c. 1797) courtesy Sophia Smith Collection, Smith College

DEBORAH SAMPSON.
Published by H. Mann. 1797.

	General/ Context	Daily Life/ Customs/ Practices	Humanities/ Fine Arts	Occupations	Education
1797			A romanticized biography of Revolutionary War soldier Deborah Sampson, *The Female Review* by Herman Mann, is published	Mrs. Keiller of Dundee, Scotland, invents her famous recipe and starts her flourishing business selling jams and conserves	
1798	French War of the Second Coalition, 1798–1799	While at the court of Naples with her husband, Sir William Hamilton, Lady Emma Hamilton (née Lyon 1761?–1815) becomes Horatio Nelson's mistress; she had earlier been the mistress of Nelson's nephew, who gave her to Hamilton in exchange for payment of his debts; the birth of their daughter Horatia causes a scandal and at Nelson's death, she is imprisoned for debt and later dies in poverty	Mary Jane Clara Clairmont (1798–1879) is the mother of Lord Byron's daughter Allegra American writer Hanna Webster Foster (1759–1840) publishes *The Boarding School,* a series of lessons of female deportment		Hannah More is forced to close her school as the result of the Blagdon controversy, in which the local squirearchy and clergy accuse her school of being an unregistered meeting place for Dissenters, a concocted charge stemming from their fear of More's educating working-class children

Performing Arts/ Entertainment/ Sports	Religion/ Philosophy	Science/ Technology/ Discovery	Statecraft/ Military	Reform	
		British architects Jane and Mary Parminter design their famous octagonal-centered 16-sided house in England	By government decree, Frenchwomen are ordered to return to their homes and forbidden to attend political meetings or to gather in the streets in groups larger than five		**1795**
Elizabeth Arnold Hopkins Poe (1787?–1811), mother of Edgar Allan Poe, makes her first stage appearance at the age of nine; most of her early roles are boys; later roles include maidens and young gentlewomen in romances and light farce Catterina Gabrielli (1730–1796), known as La Cochetta or Cochettina because she is the daughter of Prince Gabrielli's cook, is considered one of the most brilliant and beautiful singers of her time; her sister Francesca Gabrielli (1755–1795), known as La Gabriellina or La Ferrarese, is a celebrated prima donna buffa			Joséphine de Beauharnais (1763–1814) marries Napoleon Bonaparte; she is crowned empress of France in 1804 and, because she bears him no heir, Napoleon divorces her in 1809; nevertheless, her daughter by an earlier marriage later becomes queen of Holland and mother of Napoleon III		**1796**
	Ann Griffiths joins the Methodists, composing hymns for the group in her native Welsh, which are written down for her by a literate farm servant		British heroine Jemima Nicholas gathers a small band of women and frightens off the French forces by dressing as the Welsh military and preparing to defend their town; she takes French prisoners brandishing her pitchfork		**1797**
	Omiki-san Nakayama of Japan founds Tenri Kyo, one of the major sects of Shinto, and her writings become the sect's scriptures; Tenri Kyo holds that "the root of suffering and sickness is in the mind" and that those who succeed in dispelling the "eight dusts" live to a ripe old age				**1798**

	General/ Context	Daily Life/ Customs/ Practices	Humanities/ Fine Arts	Occupations	Education
1800		In order to ensure its respectability, French-women are forbidden to wear the patriotic tricolor *cocarde* From the earliest origins to the 19th century, kinship relations among the African Kongo tribe are ruled by the ideology of the *kanda*, a matriarchal descent group that bases its power on the land; this tradition is interrupted from the 15th through 17th centuries by the slave trade, but is later resumed	Novelist Sally Keating Wood (1750–1855) publishes four novels anonymously, all of them characterized by moralizing spiced up with elements of gothic horror and seduction English artist Lady Diana Beauclerk (1734–1808) exhibits the pastels and "soot-water" drawings for which she is acclaimed English writer Dorothy Wordsworth (1771–1855), younger sister of poet William Wordsworth, begins writing her *Grasmere Journals* which are a source of inspiration and often of direct quotes for her brother's writings Chinese poet Wang Tuan is said to have begun reading in her infancy and started writing verse at age seven Portrait of a Negress by Marie-Guillemine Benoist (1768–1826) establishes the artist's reputation as a painter of historical scenes when it is exhibited in Paris	Margaret Bayard Smith (1778–1844), author and early chronicler of Washington society, establishes a newspaper in Washington, *The National Intelligencer;* in 1815 she helps to establish the Washington Female Orphan Asylum	Boston businesswoman and philanthropist Elizabeth Peck Perkins (1735?–1807) cofounds the Boston Female Asylum, the first charitable institution for women in Boston In Belize, Governor Sir Alfred Moloney proposes the professional training of nurses; Marian Edith Beresford of England begins training at Belize Hospital; the experiment is officially declared successful by the medical department of British Honduras
1801			American satirical novelist Tabitha Gilman Tenney (1762–1837) publishes *Female Quixotism: Exhibited in the Romantic Opinions and Extravagant Adventures of Dorcasina Sheldon* The British Quaker Amelia Opie is the author of many poems and novels		
1802			Swiss-French belletrist Mme. de Staël (1766–1817) publishes *Delphine*, one of the first feminist psychological novels Maria Edgeworth (1767–1849) publishes her best known novel, *Castle Rackrent*		German feminist Amalie Holst publishes a tract entitled "On the Capacity of Women for Higher Education" (*Über die Bestimmung des Weibes zur höheren Geistesbildung*)

Performing Arts/ Entertainment/ Sports	Religion/ Philosophy	Science/ Technology/ Discovery	Statecraft/ Military	Reform	
			Nyirayuhi IV Nyira-tunga, queen mother of the kingdom of Rwanda, is regent for her son Yuhi IV Ga-hindiro		**1800**
French organist and harpsichordist Élisabeth Antoinette Blanchet Couperin performs in public at the age of 81					**1801**
British pianist Lucy Anderson (1790–1878), first female pianist to appear in philharmonic concerts, performs publicly between 1802 and 1862; she introduces works by Beethoven, Hummel, and others to English audiences					**1802**

	General/ Context	Daily Life/ Customs/ Practices	Humanities/ Fine Arts	Occupations	Education
1803	Birth of Ralph Waldo Emerson (1803–1882), American transcendentalist poet and writer	The English Parliament adopts a statute that makes abortion before "quickening" (when the pregnant woman first feels fetal movement) illegal; before this time, women are not considered pregnant before quickening	British writer Anne Grant publishes a collection of poems, as well as *Letters from the Mountains*	Jane Aitkin (1764–1832), American printer, bookseller, and bookbinder, publishes the constitution of the Philadelphia Female Association	Sunday high schools for both sexes are made legal in Bavaria
1804	Napoleon creates the French Empire and proclaims himself emperor; he institutes the Napoleonic code, a compilation of civil laws that forms the basis of modern civil law in France Development of a method for canning food	The Napoleonic civil code reinforces women's political inferiority and mandates their complete submission to their husbands' authority	Birth of George Sand (pen name of Amandine Lucie Aurore Dupin) Pauline Auzou (1775–1835), Mme. Haudebort-Lescot (1784–1845), and Marie-Guillemine Benoist (1768–1826) paint official portraits of women and children for the Empire Galleries at Versailles Ann and Jane Taylor of England write stories, nursery rhymes, and hymns, their best known being "Twinkle Twinkle Little Star"		
1805			Marguerite Gérard (1761–1837) becomes the first Frenchwoman genre painter to achieve professional success		
1806			British poet Elizabeth Barrett Browning (1806–1861) employs as her themes humanitarian interests, affection for her adopted Italy, religious feeling, and her love for her husband German Jewish salonist Rahel Levin Varnhagen von Ense (1771–1833), known for her brilliant conversation and progressive thought, attracts some of the most outstanding intellectuals of Germany	Italian soprano Angelica Catalani (1780–1849) earns more than $80,000 (£16,000) in one year in London	Johann Heinrich Pestalozzi starts an institute for girls in Yverdon, Switzerland

Performing Arts/ Entertainment/ Sports	Religion/ Philosophy	Science/ Technology/ Discovery	Statecraft/ Military	Reform	
				Poet, essayist, and spiritualist Sarah Helen Power Whitman (1803–1878) is acclaimed by Rhode Island women suffrage leaders as the first woman of literary reputation to endorse their cause	**1803**
	The Sisters of Notre Dame are entrusted with the teaching of women at the Institute of Notre Dame of Namur, France, co-founded by St. Julia Billiart (1751–1816)	The Lewis and Clark Expedition to explore the region between the Mississippi River and Pacific Ocean is joined by a French-Canadian trader and his Shoshoni Indian wife, Sacajawea (1787–1812), who guides the explorers through the region Sophie Germain (1776–1831), French mathematician, carries on a correspondence with Joseph Louis Lagrange and Carl Friedrich Gauss under the pseudonym "M. LeBlanc"; her work in number theory and the theory of elasticity has had enduring value in this century	Marie-Claire Dessalines (d. 1858), empress of Haiti at the time the country is liberated from France, exerts a calming influence in the strife that follows independence		**1804**
Ludwig van Beethoven writes the role of Fidelio for Constantinople-born soprano Pauline Anna Milder-Hauptmann	Hannah Rachel Werbemacher (1805–1892) is one of the few women in history to be recognized as a learned Hasidic teacher				**1805**
Originally a chanteuse in a Paris café, Italian singer Brigida Banti-Giorgi (1759–1806) is later engaged by the Grand Opera and tours Europe with great success					**1806**

	General/ Context	Daily Life/ Customs/ Practices	Humanities/ Fine Arts	Occupations	Education
1808	Import of slaves into the US forbidden			Jane Aitken publishes the only Bible ever printed by a woman in America up to this time	Elizabeth Seton establishes a school for girls in Baltimore, MD
1809	Birth of Charles Darwin (1809–1882), British explorer, naturalist, and scientist	British murderer Mary Bateman (b. 1768), whose method is to dispense magical charms in order to defraud and kill her victims, is hanged	American artist Eunice Griswold Pinney (1770–1849), known for her primitive watercolors, first begins painting		
1810			British novelist Jane Porter (1776–1850) publishes *The Scottish Chiefs,* a forerunner of the Romantic novels of Sir Walter Scott, her childhood friend Margaret Fuller (1810–1850) exercises powerful influence over intellectual life in the large east coast cities of the US; she translates and popularizes Goethe, and writes critical articles for the New York *Tribune;* she works in Italian hospitals during the war of liberation, perishing on her way back to the US when her ship is wrecked off Fire Island		German feminist and educator Betty Gleim publishes *Über Erziehung und Unterricht des weiblichen Geschlechts* (*On the Upbringing and Instruction of the Female Sex*)
1811	In Prussia *Gewerbefreiheit* (liberty to choose and exercise a trade) is instituted Birth of Charles Dickens (1811–1870), British novelist	The reformed Austrian Civil Law Code stipulates that women obey their husbands' directions; they have, however, legal power over their own property and its products	Jane Austen (1775–1817), whose works detail ordinary domestic life with satirical wit and subtle understanding, publishes *Sense and Sensibility* The British author Mary Brunton (d. 1819) writes well-received novels steeped in Christian values	Jane Aitken publishes the Philadelphia Census Directory of 1811	American educator Sarah Pierce (1767–1852) publishes *Sketches of Universal History Compiled from Several Authors: For the Use of Schools,* in an effort to make English, arithmetic, geography, and history more interesting to students
1812		David Ramsey publishes a *Memoir and Life of Martha Lauren Ramsey,* his bluestocking wife (1759–1811), which represents her as a dutiful daughter, wife, and mother who, though learned, "yield[ed] all pretensions to equality with men"	Frances Flora Bond "Fanny" Palmer (1812–1876) becomes staff artist for Currier and Ives The anonymous poem "Call to Women to Fight for Independence," found in the National Archive of Mexico, calls women to fight the Spaniards		

Performing Arts/ Entertainment/ Sports	Religion/ Philosophy	Science/ Technology/ Discovery	Statecraft/ Military	Reform	
				Charles Fourier's *Theory of the Four Movements* relates social progress to the progress of women toward freedom	**1808**
					1809
		A legend in her own time, Lady Hester Lucy Stanhope (1776–1839) leaves England forever to travel through the Middle East, camping with Bedouin tribes and eventually settling among the Druses on Mt. Lebanon, where she adopts Eastern dress and a mystical religion of her own concoction; her prophecies persuade the tribes among whom she lives that she is divinely inspired, a view shared by some English mystics of her time			**1810**
		British geologist Mary Anning (1799–1847) is involved in the finding of the first identifiable icthyosaurus and later of a plesiosaur; many significant finds of hers can be found in major British paleontological museums	Marie-Louise Christophe (1778–1851) becomes queen of Haiti as her husband, Haitian independence leader Henri Christophe, takes the throne		**1811**
	A convert to Catholicism, Elizabeth Bayley Seton (1774–1821) founds the Daughters of Charity of St. Joseph; she composes music, hymns, and spiritual discourses				**1812**

	General/ Context	Daily Life/ Customs/ Practices	Humanities/ Fine Arts	Occupations	Education
1813			Jane Austen publishes *Pride and Prejudice* Fernán Caballero, pen name of Cecilia Böhl de Faber (1796–1877), emigrates to Spain from Switzerland, where *The Seagull* (1849) marks the beginning of the regional school in Spanish literature		
1814		Abortion was made a criminal offense in France in 1810; now a new law that remains in force for 162 years permits it only to preserve the life of the mother			
1815	Defeat of Napoleon at Waterloo Abdication of Napoleon	The 1815 edition of the Brockhaus *Conversations-Lexikon* maps out the division of the sexes: "Man obtains, woman sustains . . . man resists fate itself and defies force, even in defeat. Woman, however, submits willingly and finds comfort and succor, even in her tears"			
1816		Divorce is abolished in France	Jane Austen publishes *Emma* Lady Caroline Lamb (1785–1828) anonymously publishes the novel *Glenarvon;* in it, she caricatures Lord Byron, with whom she had a brief affair		

Performing Arts/ Entertainment/ Sports	Religion/ Philosophy	Science/ Technology/ Discovery	Statecraft/ Military	Reform	
	American Roman Catholic nun Mother Mary Rhodes (1782?–1853) founds the Sisters of Loretto in Kentucky after establishing two other communities for women west of the Alleghenies			British prison reformer Elizabeth Fry (1780–1845) visits London's Newgate Prison and, inspired by the horrific conditions there, begins her lifetime commitment to prison reform; in 1819 she founds an industrial school for female prisoners	**1813**
	British religious enthusiast Joanna Scott (1750–1814) claims she is to give birth to the new messiah; in spite of her failure to make good on her claim, her cult continues after her death		Dolley Payne Todd Madison (1768–1849) is best known for having rescued official papers and a portrait of Washington when the British burned the White House

The Lovedu queens— Mujaji I, Mujaji II (d. 1894), and Mujaji III—rule Northeastern Transvaal | | **1814** |
| | | Sophie Germain wins the gold medal of the first class of the Institute of France, a section of the French Academy of Science, for her essay on elasticity | | Birth of Elizabeth Cady Stanton (1815–1902), American women's rights leader | **1815** |
| | The rule for the new religious order Daughters of the Cross, founded by St. Elizabeth Bicher des Ages (1773–1838) and St. Andrew Fournet at Maille in France, is given official approval

St. Emily de Rodat (1787–1852) founds the free school for children at Villefranche, France, that later becomes the Congregation of the Holy Family

Mary Aikenhead (1787–1858) founds the Irish Sisters of Charity, eight convents, an asylum for penitents, and the first hospital staffed by nuns | | | Elizabeth Parsons Ware Packard (1816–1897), advocate for married women's rights and protection for the insane in the US, is responsible for the passage of laws regarding jury trials for mental patients in four states | **1816** |

	General/ Context	Daily Life/ Customs/ Practices	Humanities/ Fine Arts	Occupations	Education
1817	Establishment of the New York Stock and Exchange Board, renamed New York Stock Exchange in 1863	Princess Charlotte of England, wife of future King George IV, dies in childbirth; hers is the first royal confinement attended to by physicians rather than midwives	Death of Mme. de Staël Death of Jane Austen	Known as Mother Bickerdyke, American Civil War hospital worker Mary Anne Ball Bickerdyke (1817–1901) is famous for scouring battlefields for the wounded and nursing, cleaning, and laundering under terrible conditions	In Malaysia, the first girls' school is opened in Penang
1818			Lucy Aikin (1781–1864), known for her Epistles on Women (1810), publishes *Memoirs of the Court of Queen Elizabeth* British feminist and novelist Mary Wollstonecraft Shelley (1797–1851) publishes *Frankenstein, or the Modern Prometheus* British author of young people's classics, Mary Martha Sherwood, writes her moral tale, *The History of the Fairchild Family*		
1819	Children under the age of 9 are forbidden to labor in mills in England; other young workers are limited to 12-hour days	The Washington "etiquette war," a debate over whether Cabinet wives or congressmen's wives should pay first calls on each other, reaches the level of Cabinet discussion	Birth of George Eliot (pen name of Mary Ann Evans, 1819–1880), first-rank Victorian novelist and woman of letters		Emma Hart Willard (1787–1870) writes the classic appeal *An Address to the Public; Particularly to the Members of the Legislature of New York, Proposing a Plan for Improving Female Education;* though unsuccessful, it defines the issue of women's education for its time
1820		Proponents of the "cult of true womanhood" in the US and England claim that women are the moral guardians of humanity, who should not be permitted to involve themselves in the sordid world of business, like men	The sisters Anna Claypoole (1791–1878), Margaretta Angelica (1795–1882), and Sarah Miriam Peale (1800–1885) become the earliest successful female artists in the US Karoline Gering is a popular composer of lieder in Berne, Switzerland		American educator Sarah Abbott endows the Abbott Academy in Andover, MA, with more than $10,000
1821		Jewish law imposes the obligations of pro-	Scottish born Frances Wright (1795–1852)	Birth of Clarissa Harlowe Barton, a.k.a.	Emma Hart Willard opens the Troy Fe-

Performing Arts/ Entertainment/ Sports	Religion/ Philosophy	Science/ Technology/ Discovery	Statecraft/ Military	Reform	

1817

1818

American actress with a repertoire of more than 400 roles, Mary Ann Farlow Vincent (1818–1887) wins national acclaim for her performance in Shakepearean roles and Restoration comedy

British novelist George Eliot (Mary Ann Evans)
Photograph (c. 1860) courtesy Sophia Smith Collection, Smith College

1819

1820

French philosopher and social reformer Comte Claude Henri de Rouvroy de St. Simon supports the emancipation of women as part of his system of St. Simonism

Birth of American woman suffrage leader Susan Brownell Anthony (1820–1906)

1821

Sophie Germain publishes *Recherches sur la*

British heroine Phoebe Hassall makes

| | Daily Life/ | | | |
General/ Context	Customs/ Practices	Humanities/ Fine Arts	Occupations	Education
1821	creation and sexual pleasure upon married couples; Rabbi Moses Schreiber writes that a woman may choose to use contraception, even in the face of her husband's objections	publishes *Views of Society and Manners in America;* the first woman in the US to speak publicly to an audience of men and women	Clara Barton (1821–1912), founder of the American Red Cross	male Seminary in Troy, NY, which turns out 200 teachers before the founding of the first teacher's school for women in the US
1822		American author Catherine Maria Sedgwick (1789–1867) publishes *A New England Tale*		French novelist and critic Marie Henri Beyle Stendhal demonstrates how women can both study and remain feminine in *On the Education of Women* and *On Love*
1823	The Antislavery Society is founded in England		Catherine Fitzgibbon (1823–1896) is the founder of the New York Foundling Hospital	Phoebe Yates Levy Pember (1823–1913), Confederate hospital administrator, writes *A Southern Woman's Story*

WOMEN'S EDUCATION IN 19TH-CENTURY AMERICA

Nineteenth-century America saw dramatic changes in women's educational opportunities. Brought about in part by the definition of womanhood as the moral gatekeeper of society, basic education enabled women to become better homemakers and teach their children more proficiently, thereby exercising a sounder moral influence. Consequently, the teaching profession became the quintessential work outside the home for educated women.

A movement to establish common schools in the 1820s quickly raised the literacy rate and began to close the gap that had existed between men and women. Previously, only upper-class girls had gone to school, where they acquired "accomplishments" in dance, embroidery, music, and art. But by 1850, at least half of American women could read and write. Within a generation, women had replaced men as teachers of boys as well as girls. One argument for training

them as teachers had been that they would teach at half of a man's salary or less.

The movement to educate women and prepare them for teaching resulted from pioneering efforts by individual women. In 1818, Rosa Philippine Duchesne, a French nun, arrived in New Orleans with four colleagues. She opened three boarding schools for girls in frontier towns and founded several day schools, including ones for Native American and African-American girls.

In 1821, Emma Willard opened Troy Female Seminary, the first endowed girls' school to offer a wide range of subjects, including mathematics, history, and languages. Mary Lyon founded Mount Holyoke Seminary in 1837, offering curriculum and high academic standards similar to those of men's colleges. Mount Holyoke produced a whole corps of teachers. The combination of piety and the desire for adven-

Performing Arts/ Entertainment/ Sports	Religion/ Philosophy	Science/ Technology/ Discovery	Statecraft/ Military	Reform	
		théorie des surfaces élastiques (*Inquiries into the Theory of Elastic Surfaces*)	her name serving with the Fifth Foot (Royal Northumberland Fusiliers) throughout Europe		**1821**
		Between 1809 and 1822, British vegetable physiologist Agnes Ibbetson (1757–1823) contributes more than 50 papers to *Nicholson's Journal* and *The Philosophical Magazine* on the microscopic structure and physiology of plants			**1822**
Marietta Alboni (1823–1894), Italian contralto, student of Giaccomo Rossini, makes her debut in Puccini's *Saffo* at Bologna; she makes her Paris debut in 1847 in Rossini's *Semiramide* Famous coloratura soprano Henriette Gertrude Walpurgis Sontag (1806–1854) creates the role of Von Weber's "Euryanthe"					**1823**

ture attracted numerous teachers to missionary work. Although many institutions failed for lack of funds, enough survived so that by midcentury every state had women's schools for advanced study.

In the 1840s, Catharine Beecher launched a national crusade to create a distinguished profession of women teachers, a calling, as she claimed, as noble as motherhood. She argued that enlarging the sphere of female influence would create homogeneous national institutions based on a common morality. In 1847, Beecher sent 70 newly trained teachers to the west; 400 more soon followed. Through her training schools, she persuaded the nation that women were the best and cheapest guardians of young minds.

Many other women deserve mention, among them Prudence Crandall, who admitted African-American girls to her Connecticut boarding school in 1831. Forced by a hostile community to close the school, she reopened it as an all-black institution. Frances Wright, who emigrated from Scotland, founded a settlement in Tennessee where slaves worked to purchase their freedom; Charlotte Forten followed the Union Army to teach freed slaves to read and write. Margaret Fuller, one of the foremost intellectuals of her day, held "conversations" for women in a Boston bookstore. The 19th century saw the establishment of the colleges that became known as the Seven Sisters, four of them founded by women.

The feminization of the teaching profession in the 19th century had many ramifications, not the least of which was the increased respect women gained for their intellectual abilities. By 1970, more than 85% of America's elementary schoolteachers were women, and it had long been axiomatic that women would teach American children, carrying the values of the home into the classroom.

	General/ Context	Daily Life/ Customs/ Practices	Humanities/ Fine Arts	Occupations	Education
1824		Southern cookbook author Mary Randolph (1762–1828) publishes *The Virginia Housewife,* intended to be "sufficiently clear and concise to impart knowledge [of housekeeping] to a Tyro"	Anna and Sarah Miriam Peale are elected to the Pennsylvania Academy of Fine Arts		American teacher and church worker Sophia B. Packard (1824–1891) establishes a Negro college in Georgia
1825		French saloniste Mme. Jeanne Françoise Julie Adélaïde Bernard Récamier (1777–1849), close friend of Mme. de Staël, fills her salon with the most important artists and politicians of her time, including Chateaubriand, for whom Mme. Récamier entertains a special regard	The *Journal* of Madam Knight (Sarah Kemble Knight, 1666–1727) is published; its account of a winter journey on horseback from Boston to New York in 1704–5 provides valuable information about 18th-century New England		
1826	Smithsonian Institution is founded in Washington, DC, endowed by James Smithson		The work of Norwegian painter Marie Helene Aarestrup (b. 1826) is exhibited all over Europe English novelist and playwright Mary Russell Mitford (1787–1855) publishes *Foscari*	Anne Newport Royall (1769–1854) travels through the American countryside, publishing accounts of her impressions	The first public high schools for girls open in New York and Boston
1827		Maria Martin becomes the victim in one of Britain's most famous murder cases, and her murderer, William Corder, is caught and hanged; the story is later made into a melodrama, *The Red Barn Murder,* which depicts the way women were abused by the rough justice system of the period	*The Wide, Wide World* by Susan Bogert Warner (1819–1855) is the first book by an American to achieve sales of 1 million *Freedom's Journal* publishes a letter from a black woman, "Matilda," demanding education for black women at a time when education for any woman was an unpopular issue		
1828	University of London opens		French genre painter Françoise Duparc (1726–1778) chooses		

Performing Arts/ Entertainment/ Sports	Religion/ Philosophy	Science/ Technology/ Discovery	Statecraft/ Military	Reform	
Daughter of an imperial councillor, Austrian pianist and organist Maria Theresia von Paradis (1759–1824) is a skillful blind performer for whom Mozart writes a concerto; she herself composed an opera	Angela Gillespie (1824–1887) is known as the founder of the American Sisters of the Holy Ghost				**1824**
				William Thompson publishes "An Appeal of One Half of the Human Race, the Women, Against the Pretensions of the Other Half" in London After observing slavery firsthand in the American South, Frances Wright urges the US Congress to place slaves on large tracts of land, where the profits from their work would reimburse their owners and pay for their emancipation; she makes the experiment herself but the project fails, becoming a national scandal	**1825**
	The Society of the Sacred Heart, founded by St. Madeleine Sophie Barat (1779–1865), receives the formal approbation of Pope Leo XII; daughter houses spread to 15 countries on two continents		Death of Imperatriz Leopoldina of Brazil, the consort of Pedro I, first emperor of Brazil; much beloved by her subjects, she is credited with playing a significant role in the events that led to Brazilian independence in 1825		**1826**
	Emma Hale Smith (1804–1879) marries Joseph Smith; in 1842 she becomes president of the Female Relief Society, the leading organization of the Mormon Church St. Teresa Couderc (1805–1885) runs a hostel for women pilgrims at La Louvesc, France		Death of Zulu Queen Nandi (c. 1760–1827), mother of the great warrior chief Shaka, founder of the Zulu Kingdom of Southeast Africa; she was a powerful queen mother during his rule; upon her death, Shaka carries out mass executions as a memorial		**1827**
			Queen Ranavalona I (?–1861) begins her 33-year iron-fisted rule	American social critic Elizabeth Sanders (1762–1851) anony-	**1828**

| | Daily Life/ | | | |
| General/ | Customs/ | Humanities/ | | |
Context	Practices	Fine Arts	Occupations	Education
1828 		everyday working-class people as her subjects Widowed in 1826, Scottish poet Margaret Maxwell Inglis (1774–1843) begins writing for money		
1829		Felicia Hemans publishes a collection of poetry; she also records and popularizes versions of romantic Welsh legends and translations of Portuguese and Spanish poetry		
1830	French July Monarchy, 1830–1848	The US Congress makes abortion a statutory crime	Birth of Emily Dickinson (1830–1886); only two of her poems are published during her lifetime American fashion magazine *Godey's Lady's Book,* famous for its fashion plates and art reproductions, is founded by Louis A. Godey		

American abolitionist and women's rights speaker Sojourner Truth Photograph (c. 1864) courtesy Sophia Smith Collection, Smith College

19TH-CENTURY AMERICAN WOMEN IN JOURNALISM

The era of professional female journalists in America was ushered in by a 40-year-old widow, Sarah Josepha Hale (1788–1879), with the 1828 publication of *The Ladies Magazine,* the first magazine compiled by and for women. Hale, a noted advocate of women's rights, sold *The Ladies Magazine* in 1836 to Louis A. Godey, the editor of *Godey's Lady's Book,* a journal famous for its hand-colored fashion plates. She and Godey edited it for many years, seeing its circulation rise to more than 40,000. *Godey's* continued publication through the century until 1898.

In 1834, Ann Oddbody started a paper called *Woman,* which expired so quickly that no copies remain; two years later William Newell issued the *Ladies Morning Star* out of New

York, appealing to women's moral and literary interests, but it folded within a year. Horace Greeley hired Margaret Fuller to contribute to a newspaper (though not one for women). She became America's first woman foreign correspondent, covering the Italian revolution. In the 1850s, Jane Swisshelm, Grace Greenwood, and Gail Hamilton followed suit by becoming political reporters.

The 1850s was a remarkable decade for women in journalism. Mary Ann Shadd Cary, the first black newspaper editor in North America, founded the *Provincial Freeman* in Canada. Jenny June and Fanny Fern began a new school of journalism, courting women readers by printing items of particular interest to them: fashion, recipes, and women's problems. Women be-

Performing Arts/ Entertainment/ Sports	Religion/ Philosophy	Science/ Technology/ Discovery	Statecraft/ Military	Reform	
			of Madagascar; she is able to maintain independence Queen Maria II of Portugal is deposed by her uncle, Dom Miguel, to whom she is betrothed	mously publishes a booklet praising Indian culture and condemning its destruction by General Andrew Jackson Former slave, preacher and abolitionist Isabella van Wagener (c. 1797–1883) is freed and takes the name Sojourner Truth; she preaches against slavery throughout New York and New England Mill women in Dover, NH, walk off the job to protest newly instituted restrictions	**1828**
Sister and accompanist of Mozart, Nannerl (Maria Anna) Mozart (1751–1829) is also a composer, especially of pieces for the organ	Laura Bell (1829–1894), a reformed courtesan, becomes a Christian missionary to London prostitutes				**1829**
Elizabeth Inverarity (1813–1846), Scottish vocalist and actress, makes her debut at Covent Garden in *Cinderella;* in 1832 she sings at Covent Garden and appears in concerts with the Philharmonic Society; in 1839 she debuts in New York in *Fidelio*	Foundation of the Kaiserwerther Mother House for Deaconesses by Theodor Fliedner, Germany Zoe Labouré (later St. Catherine, 1806–1876) takes the name Catherine; her visions of the Virgin Mary prompt her to have a devotional medal made	The Scottish astronomer, geologist, and mathematician Mary Somerville (d. 1879) publishes *The Mechanisms of the Heavens,* a translation and popularization of Laplace's *Méchanique céleste;* Laplace declares Somerville the only woman to have understood his work	Queen Adelaide becomes England's regent; though unpopular for her interference in politics during reform agitation of the 1830s, she subscribes £20,000 yearly to public institutions, making private donations as well	Irish immigrant "Mother (Mary) Jones" (1830–1930) has a long career as an itinerant radical organizer, particularly for the United Mine Workers	**1830**

came correspondents, sending in articles and news items about their impressions of travel and daily life.

Nellie Bly (the pen name of Elizabeth Cochrane) made America take notice of the woman reporter. Known for her "stunt" journalism—risky undercover stories for which she posed as a lunatic, beggar, or shop girl, or going up in a hot-air balloon and traveling around the world in 72 days—she provided young women a whole new idea of career and adventure. In the English press Elizabeth Banks created a similar stir. But most women journalists were society reporters, which often meant little more than traveling from one wealthy house to another to find out what gown would be worn by whom to the next party.

By the late 19th century, though, some women were earning reputations as serious journalists. Margaret Sullivan and Mary Abbott wrote for the *Chicago Tribune;* Winifred Black worked as a first string reporter for Randolph Hearst; Fanny B. Ward was one of the first reporters to go to Cuba in 1898 to cover the mysterious sinking of the American battleship *Maine* in Havana Harbor. Ella Wheeler Wilcox was a syndicated columnist writing about women's interests.

The 19th century brought women's points of view to the press. By the end of the century, journalism was a viable career for women. As the suffrage and reform movements caught fire, women found themselves making news as well as reporting it.

	General/ Context	Daily Life/ Customs/ Practices	Humanities/ Fine Arts	Occupations	Education
1830			Sarah Josepha Hale, women's rights advocate and leader of the movement to establish Thanksgiving Day, writes "Mary Had a Little Lamb"		
1831	The term "underground railroad," describing the network for helping slaves escape to the North, becomes current in the US			Amalie Sieveking heads a hospital in Hamburg (Germany) during the cholera epidemic that devastates the city Anne Newport Royall publishes *Paul Pry,* notable for its sharp editorials and local gossip; at its demise, she edits *The Huntress,* a paper taking powerful stands against political corruption, hypocrisy, and conspiracy In New England the new Industrial Revolution focuses on the textile mills; over two thirds of their workers are "mill girls"	
1832			Goethe develops the concept of the eternal feminine *(Das ewige Weibliche)* in his *Faust;* it represents the goal of all humanity's upward striving—to improve the self or the world		British scholar Hannah Kilham (1774–1832) is among the first to make a serious study of West African languages

WOMEN AND MORMONISM

The Mormon religion, or Church of Jesus Christ of the Latter-day Saints, was founded in upstate New York by Joseph Smith in 1830. After Smith was murdered, Brigham Young became the church's leader and led its members westward. They eventually founded Salt Lake City and settled throughout Utah. Mormonism's early years were marked by internal and external conflict.

The practice that engendered the greatest hostility toward the controversial new religion was polygyny, the custom of having more than one wife. In the latter half of the 19th century, social purity crusaders launched a national antipolygyny campaign. Many people advocated suffrage for Mormon women in the hope they would reform the Mormon institution of marriage. However, Mormon men, confident of

women's approval of polygyny, voted for the enfranchisement of Utah women. The territory was only the second in the country to give women the vote. Utah women, who did not agitate for the vote, nevertheless supported the franchise and joined the national suffrage movement. In 1873, Mormon women began publishing *Woman's Exponent.*

The issue of polygyny came to a crisis in the 1880s when federal legislation criminalized plural marriages and disenfranchised the women of Utah. The issue kept Utah from being admitted to the Union. In 1890, the Mormon fathers issued the Woodruff manifesto, declaring the church no longer sanctioned polygynous marriages. When Utah became a state in 1895, women's suffrage was restored.

Although outsiders had denounced the practice in the

Performing Arts/ Entertainment/ Sports	Religion/ Philosophy	Science/ Technology/ Discovery	Statecraft/ Military	Reform	
	that was considered to have miraculous properties The Church of Jesus Christ of the Latter-day Saints, or Mormonism, is founded by Joseph Smith				**1830**
British actress Sarah Kemble Siddons (1755–1831) is recognized as the greatest Shakespearean actress of her time	Shaker eldress and reformer Anna White (1831–1910) becomes the vice president of the National Council of Women of the US	Birth of English traveler Isabella Bird, who journeys through the Rocky Mountains, Japan, Korea, the Sandwich Islands, and Hawaii alone and publishes accounts of her travels	Princess Akyaawa Yikwan of Ghana (c. 1774–?) serves as one of the chief representatives of the Asante in negotiations with the British (an unheard-of position for a woman) and is credited with being responsible for the successful resolution of the talks in a peace treaty of 1831	African-American orator Maria W. Miller Stewart (1803–1879) is known for her address "Religion and the Pure Principles of Morality, the Sure Foundation on Which We Must Build," one of four famous speeches she delivered exhorting African Americans to become educated and obtain their rights; they are delivered in Boston at a time when very few women, none of them black, were able to speak from a public platform	**1831**
Polish pianist Maria Wolowska Szymanowska (1790–1832) is court pianist at St. Petersburg, where she dies of cholera; a composer of 24 mazurkas among other works, she was for a while the				*La tribune des femmes* (*Women's Tribune*), a French feminist periodical, is founded by Suzanne Voilquin; run by proletarian women, it is profoundly class conscious	**1832**

name of women's rights, Mormon women defended polygyny in the name of women's rights. The Mormons argued that plural marriages assured women their right to marry and bear children, that it controlled male licentiousness, and that it institutionalized the double standard. In the right circumstances, polygyny could and did offer women greater freedom; Mormon women were active in a wide range of activities outside the home. However, though the church elite practiced plural marriages, required for advancement in the church hierarchy, most Mormons were monogamous.

The Woodruff manifesto did not end the polygyny controversy. It took some time for the actual practice to die out; social purity reformers continued to push for a constitutional amendment outlawing it. In 1898, a Utah polygynist was elected to Congress, but with the help of several women's groups, the antipolygynists were successful in unseating him. They were less successful with a Utah senator who served from 1903 to 1907. This time, though, the church reiterated its antipolygyny stance and eventually the hostility faded.

During the 20th century, the Church of Jesus Christ of Latter-day Saints grew into a widely respected conservative religion whose support for women diminished. The church has opposed the federal equal rights amendment and excommunicated Mormon feminist Sonia Johnson, who publicly denounced the church's stand on women's rights and fought for the amendment's passage until its defeat in 1982.

	General/Context	Daily Life/Customs/Practices	Humanities/Fine Arts	Occupations	Education
1832			British author Fanny (Frances) Trollope (1780–1863) begins her literary career with the publication of *Domestic Manners of the Americans* following her trip to the US Marie Catherine Sophie de Flavigny, comtesse d'Agoult (1805–1876), French historian and feminist, writes romances and essays under the name of Daniel Stern		
1833	The American Antislavery Society is founded		British writer and translator Sarah Austin (1793–1867) publishes *Selections from the Old Testament* and *Characteristics of Goethe from the German of Falk, von Müller, and Others;* other works include urging the establishment of a national system of education and an 1859 article in the *Athenaeum* on the training of working women	Lucy Beaman Hobbs Taylor (1833–1910) is the first American woman to earn a dental degree Lady Charlotte Guest (1812–1895) of England is works manager at her husband's Dowlais Ironworks; upon his death in 1852, she becomes full manager; new ironworking techniques are developed under her management	Foundation of Oberlin College in Ohio, the first coeducational college in the US American educator Prudence Crandell defies white townspeople in Connecticut by accepting a black girl into her school; she recruits more black students, soon opening an all-black school; the town boycotts all services to her and the students, the school is vandalized, and Crandell is eventually arrested for failing to close her school The first girls' school opens in Johore Bahru, Malaysia; by 1895 it has six girls' schools

HARRIET MARTINEAU

Harriet Martineau (1802–1876) began her career as a social critic in her native England, writing articles about workers' issues such as wages and the violent antimachine riots. Deaf since childhood and raised in a strict religious household, her earliest works, like *Devotional Exercises for the Use of Young Persons* (1823), reflect a stern piety. Her fame rests on a more secular foundation, a series of stories illustrating the economic theories of Thomas Malthus, John Stuart Mill, and other contemporary thinkers.

Her analysis of social problems grabbed the attention of a wide and influential public. Her *Illustration of Political Economy* (1832, 1833, 1844) explained controversial issues of industrial society in England. Its sensitive and accurate descriptions of working conditions made her popular with workers; her anal-

Performing Arts/ Entertainment/ Sports	Religion/ Philosophy	Science/ Technology/ Discovery	Statecraft/ Military	Reform	
object of Goethe's intense infatuation				The first female anti-slavery society is established by African-American women in Salem, MA	**1832**
		 *British author Harriet Martineau* Photograph (c. 1870) courtesy Sophia Smith Collection, Smith College		British political thinker, feminist, and author Harriet Martineau publishes works combining social theory and fiction, including *Illustrations of Political Economy* (1832–34), *Poor Laws and Paupers Illustrated* (1833), and *Autobiography* (1877)	
13-year-old Clara Josephine Wieck (1819–1896) performs the first movement of Robert Schumann's First Symphony in public; the symphony is unsuccessful, though the event is not: Schumann falls in love with the young girl			3-year-old Isabella II of Spain (1830–1904) begins a reign that lasts until 1868	American abolitionist Lydia Maria Francis Child (1802–1880) publishes *An Appeal in Favor of That Class of Americans Called Africans,* a work that helps attract important support for the abolitionist movement; a journalist and reformer, she edited the *National Anti-Slavery Reformer* from 1841 to 1843 and published such pamphlets as "The Duty of Disobedience to the Fugitive Slave Act" and "The Patriarchal Institution" (1860)	**1833**
Italian violinist Teresa Savigliano (1827–1904) begins playing in public at the age of six, afterward touring Europe with great success					
Gertrud Elisabeth Schmeling Mara (1749–1833), a German soprano known for her phenomenal range, encounters serious obstacles on her way to artistic eminence, including surviving childhood rickets and the Moscow fire				French feminist Claire Démar's *Ma loi d'avenir* (*My Law for the Future*) advocates abolition of the family, collective raising of children, and complete sexual freedom for women and men alike; soon after its publication, she commits suicide	

yses were so highly regarded that they were quoted in Parliament. In order to write *Society in America* (1868), still regarded as a major European critique of American society, Martineau toured the US and recorded her observations. While in America she spoke out in support of the abolition of slavery, which she perceptively compared with the position of women.

Writing in a broad range of genres, from autobiography to children's fiction, philosophy to travel memoirs, Martineau focused consistently on issues of human rights. She can claim the distinction of being the first major woman social scientist of the 19th century.

	General/ Context	Daily Life/ Customs/ Practices	Humanities/ Fine Arts	Occupations	Education
1833					
1834	Algeria is declared a French possession		Marguerite Power, countess of Blessington (1789–1849), writes *Conversations with Lord Byron* Russian noblewoman Princess Dorothea Lievan maintains a famous salon in Paris; her wit is reflected in *The Private Letters of Princess Lieven* (1834)	Birth of Henriette Tageldsen Tiburtius, one of the first women dentists in Germany and a notable feminist reformer Hetty Howland Robinson Green (1834–1916), probably the wealthiest woman of her time, amasses over $100 million investing in stocks and real estate	Legalization of adult education for both sexes in Baden, Germany
1835			English author Grace Aguilar (1816–1847) publishes *The Magic Wreath* Bettina (Elisabeth) von Arnim (1785–1859) of *Goethe's Correspondence with a Child*, the correspondence between her and Goethe is part of Rahel Varnhagen's literary circle; she publishes other epistolary memoirs and political tracts on radical social causes		In Panama, education for girls is established
1836	Gas stoves are manufactured for home use	The first meeting of the philosophical discussion group the Trancendentalist Club is held at the home of Sophia Willard Dana Ripley (1803–1861) Establishment of Ladies' American Home Education Society and Temperance Union	Famous under the name Marcello, Adèle d'Affry (1836–1879) is one of Switzerland's first female sculptors The *Gazette des femmes* (*Women's Gazette*) begins publication; it focuses chiefly on Frenchwomen's right to petition the government Catharine Esther Beecher (1800–1878), American author and reformer, writes *Letters on the Difficulties of Religion*		Laura Wright (1809–1886) and her husband, missionaries to the Seneca Indians in western New York, devise a system of orthography for the Seneca language, producing readers and religious books in that tongue Laura Bridgman (1829–1889), stricken deaf and blind by scarlet fever, is taken to the Perkins Institute for the Blind in Boston; she is the first deaf-mute taught to communicate

Laura Bridgman at age 52, the first blind deaf-mute to be successfully educated
Photograph courtesy Sophia Smith Collection, Smith College

Performing Arts/ Entertainment/ Sports	Religion/ Philosophy	Science/ Technology/ Discovery	Statecraft/ Military	Reform	
				The Philadelphia Female Anti-Slavery Society is founded by Lucretia Mott (1793–1880) as an auxiliary to the exclusively male Antislavery Society; soon afterward the Boston Female Anti-Slavery Society is founded	**1833**
	Maria Magdalena Bentivoglio (1834–1905) is the Italian founder of the Poor Clares (Second Order of the Franciscans) in the US		Queen Maria II of Portugal regains the throne after the overthrow of her uncle by the combined forces of her father and his British allies; her reign is marked by revolution after revolution	Publication of *La tribune des femmes* (*Women's Tribune*) is banned in France	**1834**
	A leader in the movement of practical phrenology, which teaches that physiological, especially cranial, features determine character, Charlotte Fowler Wells (1814–1901) and her brothers become the most important popularizers of the pseudoscience in the 19th century Olympia Brown (1835–1926) is one of the first female Universalist ministers in the US		Muranthatisi of the Sotho (c. 1781–1835), a queen of southern Africa, acts as regent for her 13-year-old son, guiding her people through the migrations of displaced groups known as the Mfecane		**1835**
Pianist Clara Wieck is given the title of Imperial Chamber-Virtuoso in Vienna Called by some the greatest of all women vocalists, María Felicitá García Malibrán is known for her onstage improvisations, for her compositions, and for her compelling personality	Eliza Roxey Snow Smith (1804–1887), the "Mother of Mormonism," contributes to the building of the Mormon Temple in Kirtland, UT St. Mary di Rose (1813–1855) begins a career of nursing and teaching by working in a hospital in Brescia, Italy, at the height of the cholera epidemic; before the age of 30, she establishes a school for deaf-and-dumb girls and a lodging house for penniless and abandoned girls			Caroline Elizabeth Sarah Norton (1808–1877) is an ardent and influential proponent of better treatment for married women Mill women in Lowell, MA, strike, comparing their oppression as exploited workers with that of slaves At age 11, mill worker Harriet Jane Hanson Robinson (1825–1911) leads her young coworkers out in support of older workers striking in protest over wage cuts	**1836**

	General/ Context	Daily Life/ Customs/ Practices	Humanities/ Fine Arts	Occupations	Education
1837	Queen Victoria of England (1819–1901), who bestowed her name upon the Victorian age, begins her 64-year reign	Abigail Goodrich Whittelsey (1788–1858) edits *Mother's Magazine,* which sets forth principles of "proper government" and care of children	Mary Elizabeth Braddon (1837–1915), writing under the name Babington White, is best known for her 1862 *Lady Audley's Secret*		
1838	 *Queen Victoria of England* Photograph (1866) courtesy Sophia Smith Collection, Smith College		Lady Charlotte Guest publishes the first of her translations from the ancient collection of Welsh myth, the *Mabinogion* As a widow in her native Scotland, Mrs. Anne Grant (1755–1838) wrote in order to support her children	Grace Darling (b. 1815), who mans lighthouses along the Northumberland coast of England with her father, ferries a boat through the stormy sea to rescue people off the wrecked ship *Forfarshire* Known as a devoted friend of Ludwig van Beethoven, Maria Anna (Nanette Streicher) Stein (1769–1838) is the manager of her family's pianoforte factory	Mount Holyoke College, the first seminary for female teachers in the US, is founded in South Hadley, MA, by Mary Lyon (1797–1849); it opens the following year with 87 students
1839			Between 1839 and 1845, the mill girls of Lowell, MA, publish *The Lowell Offering,* a monthly magazine of poetry, fiction, and essays that gains an international reputation		
1840	The sensational trial of French poisoner Marie Lafarge (Marie Fortunée Capelle, 1816–1852) marks the first time that evidence provided by forensic medicine determines a verdict	In the mid-19th century, European and American women wear flannel knickers and knee-length dresses for bathing; women and men bathe separately American feminist, dress reformer, and editor of the feminist journal *The New Northwest,* Amelia Jenks Bloomer (1818–1894) omits the word "obey" from her marriage vows Mahbuba, a young Oromo or Galla slave,	Publication of Abigail Adams's selected letters on political, social, and personal matters to her husband and others British historian Agnes Strickland (d. 1878) is a pioneer researcher into women's history	British-born Ann Trow Lohman (1812–1878), a.k.a. Mme. Restell, begins her successful but notorious career as a New York City abortionist; she is arrested and tried for aborting quickened fetuses in 1841 and for performing an abortion in which the mother dies in 1845, but in spite of convictions, she is treated leniently and continues to practice; in 1876 she is arrested for selling contraceptive pills to an antiobscenity	Transcendentalist, and educational reformer, Elizabeth Peabody (1804–1894) becomes the first woman publisher in Boston and in the US

Performing Arts/ Entertainment/ Sports	Religion/ Philosophy	Science/ Technology/ Discovery	Statecraft/ Military	Reform	
Mezzo-soprano Rosine Stoltz (née Victorine Nöb, 1815–1903) stars at the Grand Opéra of Paris		Lady Jane Franklin, wife of the governor of Van Damien's Land (now Tasmania), becomes the first woman to climb 4000-foot Mount Wellington in New Zealand	Maria Anne Weld (1756–1837) is the unacknowledged wife of England's prince regent, later George IV	Angelina and Sarah Grimké found the National Female Anti-Slavery Society, one of the few such societies to include women of color from the start	**1837**
Italian soprano Maria Theresa Romanzini Bland (1769–1838) has a career as a popular singer in England The "Swedish Nightingale," Johanna Maria Lind, a.k.a. Jenny Lind or Mme. Jenny Lind-Goldschmidt (1820–1887), a coloratura soprano, makes her debut in *Der Freischütz;* she is introduced to the US by P. T. Barnum and spends her last years as a professor of singing at the Royal College of Music in England				When the Anti-Slavery Convention of American Women, meeting in Philadelphia, PA, is attacked by an antiabolitionist mob, Lucretia Mott calms the conference participants; the mob heads toward Mott's house, from which it is, fortunately, diverted	**1838**
As a young piano student at the Royal Academy of Music in London, Kate Fanny Loder (Lady Thompson, 1825–1904) wins the king's scholarship twice, in 1839 and 1841; she becomes a professor there in 1844, playing successful concerts and composing an opera, an overture, a violin sonata, and other works	Hélène de Chappotin (1839–1904) founds the Franciscan Missionaries of Mary in India				**1839**
Clara Wieck, a distinguished concert pianist, plays Schumann's works in her concerts	Alodia Virginia Paradis (1840–1912) is the founder of the Little Sisters of the Holy Family in Canada St. Mary di Rose founds a nursing order, the Handmaids of Charity, who work both in military hospitals and on the battlefield to succor victims and prisoners of war		Menen Leben Amede (?–c. 1853) becomes empress of Ethiopia; commanding her own army and acting as regent for her son Ali Alulas, she is wounded and captured in the battle of 1847 in the struggle for control of the country, but is ransomed by her son	Lucretia Mott is chosen one of several women delegates to the World's Anti-Slavery Convention in London; because the organizations holding the convention are opposed to public activity by women, the American women are refused participation and must sit in the balcony behind a curtain	**1840**

Jenny Lind, the "Swedish Nightingale," with her husband, Otto Goldschmidt
Photograph (c. 1850) courtesy Sophia Smith Collection, Smith College

	General/ Context	Daily Life/ Customs/ Practices	Humanities/ Fine Arts	Occupations	Education
1840		is purchased in Cairo by a Silesian aristocrat; he takes her up the Nile and to Syria		crusader, but commits suicide before she comes to trial; she leaves an estate of over $1 million	
1841			Anne Charlotte Lynch Botta (1815–1891) begins to hold the evening literary receptions for which she becomes famous Berthe Morisot (1841–1895) becomes a well-known French Impressionist English poet Sarah Flower Adams (1805–1848) is best known for her dramatic poem "Vivia Perpetua"		Lucy Cavendish (1841–1926), British philanthropist and social reformer, fights for women's educational needs and for oppressed minorities abroad
1842		Mary Todd (1818–1882) marries Abraham Lincoln; in spite of rumors that she was insane during Lincoln's lifetime, it is his assassination in 1865 together with the loss of three of her four sons that sends her into her decline, culminating in a declaration of insanity in 1875	American author, lecturer, and reformer Elizabeth Oakes Prince Smith (1806–1893) writes *Old New York,* a historical drama that appears on Broadway in 1853	American journalist Cornelia Wells Walter (1813?–1898) follows her brother as editor of the *Boston Transcript;* her improvement of the newspaper's quality wins praise from many who had been hostile to the idea of a female editor	
1843	Gambia and Natal in southern Africa become British colonies	Englishwoman Jane Webb Loudon, designer of gardens and author of gardening books, turns to writing handbooks for genteel women	Bettina von Arnim writes *Dies Buch gehört dem König* (*The Book Belongs to the King,* 1843), a plea to the king on behalf of the weavers of Silesia	An accomplished artist and translator, known as Fatima, Princess Alice Maud Mary (1843–1878), daughter of Queen Victoria, works as a nurse in the Franco-Prussian War and founds the Women's Union for Nursing the Sick and Wounded in War	A school for female watchmakers is founded in Switzerland

Performing Arts/ Entertainment/ Sports	Religion/ Philosophy	Science/ Technology/ Discovery	Statecraft/ Military	Reform	
					1840
Austrian dancer Fanny Elssler (1810–1884) tours the US, introducing folk dances, especially the tarantella				Sophie Willard Dana Ripley is one of the founding members of the Brook Farm Institute of Agriculture and Education, an experiment in cooperative labor and living	**1841**
				Pioneer Australian feminist Caroline Chisholm (1808–1877) founds a home for prostitutes and destitute girls in Sydney	
French coloratura soprano of remarkable range and flexibility, Mme. Anna Caroline de La Grange (1825–1905) makes her professional debut in Varese, Italy					**1842**
Eminent German soprano Wilhelmine Schröder-Devrient (1804–1860) creates the role of Adriano Colonna in *Rienzi* by Richard Wagner, on whose style she is said to have had an important effect					
Eminent Italian dramatic contralto Marietta Alboni (1823–1894) makes her debut at La Scala in Milan		Daughter of Lord Byron and Anna Isabella Millbanke, Augusta Ada Lovelace (1815–1852) is trained in mathematics at home; she works together with mathematician Charles Babbage on the development of his analytical engine, an early program-controlled computer, and publishes "Sketch of the Analytical Engine Invented by Charles Babbage, Esq., by L. F. Menabrea of Turin, Officer of the Military Engineers," which contains the first set of programs designed to instruct a computing machine to solve mathematical problems	In Colombia, María Martínez de Nisser publishes her diary describing her experiences as a soldier during the revolution in Antioquia; she returns to obscurity and to the role of a 19th-century Columbian woman after the war	Often considered the first French feminist, Flora Tristan publishes *Worker's Union,* analyzing oppression of workers, particularly the double oppression of working women

The Lowell Female Labor Reform Association presents petitions for the 10-hour day to the Massachusetts State Legislature in 1843 and 1844 and, after being granted public hearings, win the very first investigation of labor conditions by a governing body in the history of the US | **1843** |

	General/ Context	Daily Life/ Customs/ Practices	Humanities/ Fine Arts	Occupations	Education
1844			Birth of Mary Stevenson Cassatt (1844–1926), an American painter who will become one of the most famous members of the French Impressionist movement Finnish playwright and novelist Minna Canth (1844–1897) pioneers the new naturalism in plays		German feminist and reformer Louise Otto-Peters (1819–1895) publishes the *Frauen-Zeitung für höhere Weibliche Interessen* (*Women's Journal for Higher Feminine Interests*) In Portugal, elementary schools for girls are legalized
1845		Women in Sweden are granted equal inheritance rights	Irish poet and novelist Emily Lawless is best known for her novels *Hurrish* (1886) and *Grania* (1892) and her 1902 volume of poetry, *With the Wild Geese* The British artist Mary Linwood (1755–1845) is honored with exhibitions in London British author Geraldine Jewsbury publishes a variety of novels By the age of 89, British author Catherine Hutton (1756–1846) has written 12 volumes and contributed 60 papers to various periodicals		An official statute on Russian secondary schools for girls states that "woman, as a lower creation appointed by nature to be dependent on others, must know that she is not fated to rule but to submit herself to her husband and that only through strict fulfilment of her responsibilities to her family can she assure happiness and gain love and respect both within the family circle and without" British educational pioneer Frances Buss opens a girls' school in London
1846	The sewing machine is patented in the US		*Poems by Currer, Ellis, and Acton Bell* is published; these are the male pseudonyms of Charlotte Brontë (Currer) and her sisters Emily (Ellis) and Anne (Acton)	Royal statute admits women to registrations as merchants and artisans in Stockholm, Sweden	Recognizing the inequities in access to education, British reformer Mary Carpenter opens a "ragged school" for working-class children; she begins to publish her ideas on education the following year

CLARA SCHUMANN AND FANNY MENDELSSOHN

In *A Room of One's Own,* Virginia Woolf asks the famous question "What if Shakespeare had had a brilliant sister?" Woolf concludes that she would have been intellectually frustrated, sexually abused, depressed, and finally suicidal. The question is more positively answered by the lives of two female composers, both of whom were related to famous male composers.

Clara Josephine Wieck was born in 1819, married the composer Robert Schumann in 1840, and died in 1896. In the course of her lifetime, music, family, and close personal relationships were thoroughly intertwined. Known professionally as Clara Schumann, she had a well-established reputation as a pianist long before she even met her husband. Her father encouraged her to study piano very early, from the age of five, and she was known as a child prodigy throughout Europe. In 1838, she was honored by the Austrian court and was elected to the music society in Vienna, the prestigious Gesellschaft der Musikfreunde.

Between 1841 and 1854, Clara bore eight children, taught at the Leipzig Conservatory, composed, and toured frequently. Her compositions include works for piano, orchestra, chamber music, and many songs. She edited the collected edition of her husband's works, published between 1881 and 1893. After his

Performing Arts/ Entertainment/ Sports	Religion/ Philosophy	Science/ Technology/ Discovery	Statecraft/ Military	Reform	
Daniel Auber's opera *Crown Diamonds* is written for the immensely successful British soprano Anna Hunt Thillon (1819–1903)				Labor leader Sarah G. Bagley (fl. 1835–1847) founds and becomes the first president of the Lowell Female Labor Reform Association; she extends the movement by organizing branches of the association in many New England mill towns	**1844**
American painter and sculptor Emma Stebbins (1815–1882) exhibits her Portrait of a Lady at the Philadelphia Academy of Fine Arts Elizabeth Taylor-Greenfield (1809–1876), noted African-American singer, gives a command performance for Queen Victoria of England				American author and educator Catharine Esther Beecher publishes *An Essay on Slavery and Abolitionism with Reference to the Duty of American Women to Their Country,* addressed to Angelina Grimké; in it she asserts that "woman's sphere" does not comprehend activities that "throw [her] into the attitude of a combatant, either for herself or for others"; she is, nevertheless, a vocal supporter of women's education, by which she hopes to raise the status of "woman's sphere"	**1845**
Noted violinist Wilma Maria Frances Norman-Neruda (Lady Hallé, 1839–1911), age seven, plays a public concert with her pianist sister Amalie	Elisabeth Förster-Nietzsche (1846–1935) edits her brother Friedrich's works when he becomes insane			Catharine Esther Beecher publishes *The Evils Suffered by American Women and American Children*	**1846**

death in 1856, she was closely associated personally and professionally with the composer Johannes Brahms.

Fanny Mendelssohn (1805–1847) was as active as Clara Schumann. A pianist and composer, she was the eldest sister and confidante of the composer Felix Mendelssohn. Although in adult life Felix was far better known than his sister, they were originally taught by the same teachers. Her brother admitted that Fanny played the piano better than he did, and she remained his chief musical adviser until he left home. Afterward, she remained very close to him until their deaths, which occurred within six months of each other.

In 1829, Fanny married the Prussian court painter Wilhelm Hensel. In 1842, she took over the management of the Mendelssohn family household in Berlin, where she organized concerts and occasionally appeared as a pianist. Throughout her career, Fanny wrote about 500 musical compositions: approximately 120 pieces for piano, many lieder, chamber music, cantatas, and oratorios. Most of her work remains unpublished. However, six of her songs were published in Felix's name and several collections of piano pieces, some lieder, and a piano trio were published in her own name.

	General/ Context	Daily Life/ Customs/ Practices	Humanities/ Fine Arts	Occupations	Education
1847			Agnes Dean Abbatt (1847–1917), is an award-winning illustrator of history of Westchester, NY		
1848	The revolutions of 1848, liberal uprisings against conservative monarchies, result in the establishment of the Second French Republic, new constitutions for Prussia and other states, and a tremendous number of revolutionaries in exile or hiding in Britain, Switzerland, and the US Karl Marx and Friedrich Engels publish the *Communist Manifesto* Slavery is abolished in France's West Indies colonies	Emily Brontë catches cold at her brother's funeral and dies a few months later	Anne Brontë publishes *The Tenant of Wildfell Hall* The first French feminist daily, *La voix des femmes (Women's Voice)*, advocates women's suffrage Annette von Droste-Hülshoff (1797–1848) writes with great psychological depth and power	Birth of Dr. Susan McKinney (1848–1918), first African-American woman physician in the US Sarah Anne Worthington King Peter (1800–1877), a leader in charitable and church work in Cincinnati and Philadelphia, founds the Philadelphia School of Design	Catherine Maria Sedgwick becomes the first president of the Women's Prison Association in New York Despite her formal acceptance into a girl's seminary in Rochester, NY, the daughter of black abolitionist Fredrick Douglass is denied access to classes with the white students, an order issued by the principal, an abolitionist woman; the order holds in spite of a school vote in which only one girl votes against her participation in classes

THE FIRST WAVE OF AMERICAN FEMINISM

The American women's movement grew out of decades of increasing public involvement in social issues. By the mid-19th century, women who had been active in the abolition and temperance causes had joined forces to campaign for women's rights. Led by such figures as Lucy Stone, Abby Kelley, Anna Dickinson, Sojourner Truth, Frances Harper, Sarah Remond, and Susan B. Anthony, American women demanded equal education, control over their wages, and the vote.

In 1848, the abolitionist leader Lucretia Mott and her younger colleague Elizabeth Cady Stanton called the first Women's Rights Convention in Seneca Falls, NY. There Stanton read her Declaration of Sentiments, a manifesto declaring that "all men and women are created equal." It listed 18 legal grievances and called for major reform in suffrage, marriage, and inheritance laws. The well-attended convention was galvanized by Stanton's proposal of a resolution advocating women's suffrage. Defended by black abolitionist Frederick Douglass, the proposal was adopted: the first public demand by women for the vote.

Soon afterward, Stanton and Susan B. Anthony met, beginning the 50-year friendship and political partnership that would provide leadership for the women's movement into the next century. Stanton, considered by some a dangerous radical because of her belief in equality for women in every aspect of American society, was one of the movement's most eloquent spokeswomen. A philosopher, brilliant writer, and orator, she served as the lightning rod for women's reform by articulating the issues and gaining the public's attention. Often preoccupied in the early days by the care of her six children, Stanton was dependent upon Anthony's help and organizational skills. Anthony—an incomparable organizer and a tireless worker—kept Stanton and the movement on track.

In 1851, Stanton, Anthony, Amelia Bloomer, and other feminists took on the issue of dress reform, adapting split skirts, known as bloomers, as a practical healthful mode of dress. Bloomers did not require the tight lacing to which women of the period customarily subjected themselves; they allowed the legs far greater freedom of movement than the

Performing Arts/ Entertainment/ Sports	Religion/ Philosophy	Science/ Technology/ Discovery	Statecraft/ Military	Reform	
Fanny Cäcilia Mendelssohn Hensel (1805–1847) publishes six songs under her brother Felix's name		Maria Mitchell (1818–1889) discovers a new comet, which is named after her		British prison reformer Elizabeth Fry publishes *Memoirs*	**1847**
The intense rivalry between Julia Anna Turnbull (1822–1887), one of the earliest American ballerinas to dance such classic roles as Giselle and Esmeralda, and the brilliant young Italian dancer Giovanna Ciocca precipitates a violent riot at the Bowery Theater, New York City; though Turnbull emerges victorious, the uproar eventually causes her to leave the company		Lady Jane Franklin finances ships to rescue her lost husband; though they do not find him, they contribute substantially to knowledge of Arctic geography American astronomer Maria Mitchell is elected to the American Association for the Advancement of Science	Ellen Craft (c. 1826–1897), a southern slave, takes part in one of the boldest escapes to freedom in African-American history French feminist Jeanne Deroin's attempt to run for a seat in the legislative assembly is considered unconstitutional and she is prevented from speaking Anna Hugaard, a free black woman, influences her consort, Peter von Scholter, last governor of the Danish West Indies	American reformer Jane Swisshelm (1815–1884) energetically supports women's rights and condemns slavery and drunkenness The final resolution of the Seneca Falls Women's Rights Convention calls for "the securing to women an equal participation with men in the various trades, professions and commerce"; at the Convention not a single woman of color is present The National Convention of Colored Freedmen held in Cleveland, OH, passes a resolution saying that women should be elected delegates on an equal basis with men	**1848**

American women's rights leader Elizabeth Cady Stanton Photograph (c. 1900) courtesy Sophia Smith Collection, Smith College

narrow hobble skirts then in fashion. But as the style met with so much public derision, the activists feared that such issues as suffrage and property laws would be hurt. They gave up the bloomers.

In 1866, Stanton ran for Congress—the first woman to do so—despite the fact that women could not yet vote. In 1869, she and Anthony founded the National Woman Suffrage Association (NWSA), with Stanton as president for its entire 21-year existence. When NWSA merged with the rival American Woman Suffrage Association (AWSA) in 1890, Stanton became president of the National American Woman Suffrage Association (NAWSA); Anthony succeeded her three years later.

The suffrage activists traveled under the most strenuous conditions all over the US, Canada, and Europe, giving speeches, holding rallies, and stumping for women's rights. They took their campaign into print as well: in 1868, Anthony became the publisher and Stanton an editor of *The Revolution,* a weekly forum for women's rights. Abigail Scott Duniway published

The New Northwest, Amelia Bloomer *The Lily,* and Paulina Wright Davis *Una,* all feminist journals. With Matilda Joslyn Gage and others, Anthony and Stanton compiled the six-volume *History of Women's Suffrage,* documenting the movement all over the world, from New York to Singapore, Siberia to Australia. No sacred cow was too sacred for the reformers' reasoned criticism. To the outrage of the public and even of many feminists, the 80-year-old Stanton published *The Woman's Bible,* a commentary on and reinterpretation of the Bible's derogatory passages on women.

The combined intelligence, energy, and abilities of Elizabeth Cady Stanton, Susan B. Anthony, and the other giants of the first wave of American feminism were largely responsible for the legal, educational, and social reforms that benefited women by the end of the century. Though neither Stanton nor Anthony lived to see American women get the vote, their efforts brought the issue into the 20th century, paving the way for women's political participation on a scale of which they could only dream.

	General/ Context	Daily Life/ Customs/ Practices	Humanities/ Fine Arts	Occupations	Education
1849		Following the 1848 revolution, property franchise explicitly including women is established in many parts of the Hapsburg Empire; in some areas of Austria, professional women are enfranchised whether or not they hold property	Scottish novelist Margaret Oliphant (1828–1897) writes to support two families upon the deaths of her husband and brother	Elizabeth Blackwell (1821–1910) graduates from Geneva College in New York, becoming the first woman to receive a medical degree in the US Female doctors are permitted for the first time to practice medicine legally in the US	Swedish feminist Ellen Key (1849–1926) becomes prominent in pacifist, feminist, and humanitarian movements in her own country
1850	Taiping Rebellion (1850–1864) against the Ch'ing dynasty in China results in a Christian communal society	About this time, crinolines become popular in the US and Europe; they are superseded by hoop skirts A doctor in Georgia notices that abortions and miscarriages are much more common among his slave patients than among the white women he treats Women are granted the right to own land in Oregon According to some estimates, abortion is a common practice among middle-class Americans in the 1850s and 1860s—at a rate perhaps as high as one abortion per every five or six live births	*Narrative of Sojourner Truth* by Olive Gilbert is published Octave Thanet (pen name of Alice French, 1850–1934) advocates cooperatives over unions in her writing American artist Jennie Augusta Brownscombe (1850–1936) is best known for her genre paintings and historical scenes British writer Margaret Gatty (1807–1873) is the author of children's stories and the editor of *Aunt Judy's Magazine*, begun in 1866	Women have gained wide acceptance as teachers in the US by this date Yoruba women traders from the Creole communities of Sierra Leone dominate the internal commerce of 19th-century West Africa	Clara Barton founds one of New Jersey's first "free," or public, schools The first Danish school for girls is founded by Natalie Zahle (b. 1827) The Female (later Women's) Medical College of Pennsylvania is founded Abigail Powers Fillmore (1798–1853) sets up the first White House library Frances Buss founds the North London Collegiate School for Girls The Falloux Law in France for the first time establishes primary schools for girls, placing them under the authority of the Church
1851	The Combination Law of 1851 makes it illegal for women in the German Empire to participate in political meetings or join political associations	Amelia Jenks Bloomer (1818–1894) gives her name to "bloomers," a split skirt designed by Elizabeth Smith Miller (1822–1911) for bicycle riding US inventor Isaac Singer develops and markets the sewing machine for use in the home	Metta Victoria Fuller Victor (1831–1885) is a popular author of reform novels Elizabeth Wooster Stuart Phelps (1815–1852) is known for *The Sunny Side; or, The Country Minister's Wife*		White American education pioneer Myrtilla Miner opens a teaching college for black women in Washington, DC, the Miner Normal School, amid threats, arson attempts, and stone-throwing mobs

1849

Pauline Viardot-Garcia (1821–1910) creates the role of Fides in *Le Prophete* and Gounod's *Sapho* in Paris

As a professor of singing at the Paris Conservatory, French soprano Laure Cinthie Damoreau (née Montalant, first known as Mlle. Cinti, 1801–1863) is the author of *Méthode de chant*

1850

Italian soprano Josephina Grassini (1773–1850) is famous for her remarkable talent and beauty

British soprano Anna Hunt Thillon (1819–1903) spends 1850 to 1854 in San Francisco, where she is the first to produce opera

"Fanny Fern" (Sara Payson Willis Parton), the first American woman newspaper columnist
Photograph (c. 1850) courtesy Sophia Smith Collection, Smith College

Lucy Stone (1818–1893) leads the call for the first national women's rights convention; she also helps to found and finance the women's journal *Voice of the Women's Movement*

Between 1850 and 1870, feminist reformer Ernestine Louise Siismondi Potowski Rose (1810–1892) lectures across the US on women's rights, anti-slavery, temperance, and free thought agendas

British activist Frances Power Cobbe (1822–1904) works for women's suffrage, social reform, and against vivisection

Brazilian feminism originates in the mid-19th century with a small group of pioneer feminists

Harriet Tubman (1820?–1913) begins to lead slaves to freedom in the Underground Railroad

---

1851

Sojourner Truth, as the only woman of color present at a women's convention in Akron, OH, single-handedly saves the meeting from the jeers of hostile men, answering each of their criticisms and delivering her famous "Ain't I a Woman" speech

	General/ Context	Daily Life/ Customs/ Practices	Humanities/ Fine Arts	Occupations	Education
1852	The Second Empire in France, 1852–1870, begins	The US Congress adjourns to attend the funeral of Louisa Catherine Adams (1775–1852), wife of President John Quincy Adams, the first time this honor is conferred upon a woman In Britain, an act of Parliament removes a husband's right to enforce cohabitation on his wife by issuing a writ of habeas corpus against anyone sheltering her	Mary Russell Mitford (1787–1855) publishes *Recollections of a Literary Life* Susanna Stickland Moodie (1803–1885) describes pioneer life in the Canadian wilderness in *Roughing It in the Bush, or Life in Canada* Harriet Beecher Stowe (1811–1896) publishes her antislavery novel, *Uncle Tom's Cabin*	Calamity Jane, nickname of Martha Jane Burke (1852?–1903), is known as a Pony Express rider and scout; she was used as a heroine in a dime novel by Edward L. Wheeler	US educator Anna Peck Sill (1816–1889) founds the Rockford Female Seminary, modeled on Mary Lyon's Mount Holyoke Seminary British educator Mary Carpenter (1807–1877) opens a new style reformatory for boys; she follows it with one for girls in 1854
1853	Foundation of the Photographic Society in London		Victorian novelist Charlotte Mary Yonge (1823–1901) publishes *The Heir of Redcliffe* British novelist Elizabeth Stevenson Cleghorn Gaskell (1810–1865) is known for her depictions of country life		American educator Mary Easton Sibley (1800–1878) founds the Lindenwood Female College in Missouri Admission of women to teaching in Sweden is followed by the establishment of secondary schools and teacher training colleges for girls
1854	Société Française de Photographie founded in Paris *Bareback rider Mrs. Sherwood at the Howard Athenaeum, Boston* Illustration (c. 1854) courtesy Sophia Smith Collection, Smith College	Norwegian women are granted equal inheritance rights 	Abolitionist author Mary Hayden Green Pike (1824–1908), pen name Mary Langdon, publishes her immensely popular first novel, *Ida May* Leading black activist for the WCTU, Frances Ellen Watkins Harper (1826–1911) lectures for antislavery societies	Clara Barton assumes a clerkship in a Washington, DC, patent office, becoming perhaps the first regularly appointed woman civil servant in the US	
1855	Government vernacular schools are created in the straits settlements of Malaysia; these schools are mainly for Europeans but later instruct Eurasians, Chinese, and Indians	The composer and pianist Marie Leopoldine Pachler-Koschak (1792–1855) is best known as a close friend of Ludwig van Beethoven	Harriet Martineau (1802–1876) writes her autobiography and *A Complete Guide to the Lakes* *The Journal for Ladies*, gives impetus to the growing feminist movement in Brazil		American educator Mary Atkins (1819–1882) becomes principal and proprietor of Benicia, a girls' seminary in California, making a success out of the failing institution

Performing Arts/ Entertainment/ Sports	Religion/ Philosophy	Science/ Technology/ Discovery	Statecraft/ Military	Reform	
Italian mezzo-soprano Maria Piccolomini (1836–1899) makes a very successful debut in Florence French-born violin virtuosa Camilla Urso (1842–1902) tours America with great success at the age of 10	German-born nun Mother Benedicta Riepp (1825–1862) establishes the first Benedictine monastery in the US in St. Vincent, Westmoreland County, PA	Elizabeth Blackwell publishes *The Laws of Life, with Special Reference to the Physical Education of Girls*		Susan B. Anthony forms the Woman's NY Temperance Society with Elizabeth Cady Stanton	1852
	Suffragist and reformer Antoinette Louisa Brown Blackwell (1825–1921) becomes the first woman ordained minister of a recognized denomination, the Congregationalists, in the US		Eugénie Marie de Montijo de Gúzman, comtesse de Téba (1826–1920), wife of Napoleon III, becomes empress of the French (1853–1871)	Susan B. Anthony helps organize the Whole World's Temperance Convention American Alva Erskine Belmont (1853–1933) writes many articles and contributes large sums in support of women's rights	1853
German contralto Jeanne Sophie Charlotte Cruvelli (Crüwell, 1826–1907) enjoys tremendous success at the Paris Grand Opéra at a salary of 100,000 francs		British nursing pioneer Florence Nightingale (1820–1910) is the first to put forth basic principles of modern nursing in her *Notes on Nursing*		American Methodist and Quaker preacher Amanda M. Way (1828–1914) organizes the Women's Temperance Army to close Indiana saloons Susan B. Anthony collects 6000 signatures for a petition demanding control by women over their own earnings, possession of their children upon divorce, and the vote	1854
	Mother Mary Baptist Russell (1829–1898), helps establish the House of Mary, a shelter for unemployed women			Fugitive slave Ann Wood leads a wagonload of armed boys and girls in a shootout with slave catchers; two are killed and the rest escape to the North	1855

Harriet Beecher Stowe, author of Uncle Tom's Cabin
Photograph (c. 1880) courtesy Sophia Smith Collection, Smith College

Clara Barton, founder of the American Red Cross
Photograph (c. 1875) courtesy Sophia Smith Collection, Smith College

	General/ Context	Daily Life/ Customs/ Practices	Humanities/ Fine Arts	Occupations	Education
1856		Remarriage of Hindu widows in India is permitted by law	Elizabeth Chase Allen (1832–1911) publishes *Forest Buds, from the Woods of Maine* Frances Whitcher (1811–1852) is the first American woman to write a series of humorous sketches in Yankee dialect British novelist Dinah Maria Craik (1826–1887) publishes *John Halifax, Gentleman*	Catherine Walters (1839–1920) goes to London at the age of 17, gaining a reputation as the "last Victorian courtesan"	
1857	Indian mutiny (1857–1858) against British colonial rule in India	A British divorce act allows husbands to divorce their wives on the grounds of adultery; women must prove their husbands guilty of rape, sodomy, bestiality, or adultery in conjunction with incest, bigamy, cruelty, or desertion Danish women are granted equal inheritance rights Danish women are granted occupational freedom—that is, they may legitimately try to get employment in trades, crafts, and professions formerly closed to women	American Delia Salter Bacon (1811–1859), originates the theory that Shakespeare's plays are really the works of Francis Bacon; she publishes *The Philosophy of the Plays of Shakespeare Unfolded* Jamaican healer Mary Seacole (1805–1881) publishes her autobiography, describing her greater success with traditional methods than that of formally trained British army staff, and her service as a nurse for the British Army in the Crimean War from 1854 to 1856	Elizabeth Blackwell and her sister, Emily, (1826–1910) establish the New York Infirmary for Women and Children, staffed entirely by women A formal study of the economic origins of prostitution demonstrates that almost all prostitutes in Paris are former factory workers Emily Faithfull (1835–1895) sets up a women's printing press in Scotland, inspired by her research on women printers of the 15th century	
1858		Princess Victoria (1840–1901), daughter of Queen Victoria of England, starts an enduring fashion in wedding music when she chooses Richard Wagner's "Bridal Chorus" from *Lohengrin* and Felix Mendelssohn's "Wedding March" from *A Midsummer Night's Dream* Unmarried women are permitted to attain legal majority in Sweden at age 25 Danish women are granted the right to attain legal majority if unmarried	American poet Sarah Tittle Barrett Bolton (1814–1893) publishes "Two Graves"; her most famous poem is "Paddle Your Own Canoe" (1851) British feminists Barbara Bodichon (1827–1891), Bessie Rayner Parkes (1829–1925), Jessie Amelia Boucherett (1825–1905), Adelaide Anne Proctor (1825–1864), and others publish the *English Woman's Journal*		High schools for girls are introduced in Russia Marion Talbot (1858–1948) publishes *The Education of Women,* an exploration of the changing roles of women in a technological society Author and composer Lina Ramann (1833–1912) founds a music seminary for female teachers in Leipzig, Germany British educational reformer Dorothea Beale (1831–1906) establishes Cheltenham Ladies' College

Performing Arts/ Entertainment/ Sports	Religion/ Philosophy	Science/ Technology/ Discovery	Statecraft/ Military	Reform	
	Chinese Christian Agnes Tsao Kuo is murdered for adhering to her religious beliefs at Kwangsi during the Taiping Rebellion	The most important research of biologist Nettie Maria Stevens (1861–1912) deals with the relationship of chromosomes to heredity; she and Edmund Beecher Wilson, working independently, are the first to demonstrate that sex is determined by X and Y chromosomes	Emma Rooke (1836–1885) marries King Kamehameha IV, becoming queen of Hawaii		**1856**
One of the most acclaimed interpreters of Shakespeare of her day, American actress Charlotte Saunders Cushman (1816–1876) begins almost 20 years of "farewell performances"			One of the great heroines of modern India, Lakshmi Bai, rani of Jhansi (1835–1857), joins the Indian mutiny against the British, riding amid her own troops, wearing a soldier's uniform, and holding the reins of her horse in her mouth while wielding her sword with both hands; she is finally cut down by a British hussar	Elizabeth Oakes Prince Smith (1806–1893) publishes *A Woman and Her Needs* and begins touring as a lecturer, speaking on "The Woman Question"	**1857**
American actress Agnes Booth (1846–1910) debuts in *The Corsair* and *Popping the Question* Playing in public for the first time at the age of eight, Marie Wieck (1832–1916), sister of Clara Wieck Schumann (1819–1896), is made court pianist to the prince of Hohenzollern	Bernadette Soubirous (Bernadette of Lourdes, 1844–1879) experiences a series of 18 visions and apparitions of the Virgin Mary at the grotto of Massabielle, Lourdes, and reveals the miraculous healing properties of a nearby spring, which becomes a famous place of pilgrimage and healing for many believers				**1858**

	General/ Context	Daily Life/ Customs/ Practices	Humanities/ Fine Arts	Occupations	Education
1859		Swimming lessons are given to Parisian women for the first time Leonore Evelina Simonds Piper (1859–1950), famed as a medium, is investigated by the American Society of Psychical Research	American translator and author Mary Louise Booth (1831–1889) publishes *History of the City of New York* American Carrie Bell Adams (1859–1940) writes more than 100 anthems as well as an opera Publication of the first novel by an African-American woman, Harriet Wilson's *Our Nig* Emma Dorothy Eliza Nevitte Southworth, a.k.a. Mrs. E.D.E.N. Southworth (1819–1899), publishes her most popular work, *The Hidden Hand*	American physician Elizabeth Blackwell becomes the first woman to have her name entered on the medical register of the United Kingdom	British artist and philanthropist Louisa, marchioness of Waterford (1818–1891) founds the Old Schoolhouse
1860	The American Civil War (1860–1863) begins New York State passes a law allowing women to collect their own wages, mount lawsuits, and inherit their husbands' property; married women are granted guardianship of their children The first Married Women's Property Act is passed in New Zealand; the second is passsed in 1870	Bustles begin to replace hoop skirts in European and American women's fashions European and American women begin to wear blouse-and-skirt combinations instead of one-piece dresses Anna Isabella Milbanke (1792–1860) marries Lord Byron; they separate a year later amid rumors that she has discovered an incestuous relationship between Byron and his sister	American author Harriet Elizabeth Prescott Spofford (1835–1921) publishes her first novel, *Sir Rohan's Ghost,* anonymously Kentucky poet Sarah Morgan Bryan Piatt (1836–1919) gains a nationwide reputation as one of the South's finest poets George Eliot publishes two novels, *The Mill on the Floss* and *Silas Marner*	Emily Faithfull establishes the Victoria Press in London, where she employs and trains women as printers, acting upon the aims of the Society for the Promotion of Women's Employment	Women's Library opens in New York City

WOMEN AND DOCTORS IN THE 19TH CENTURY

During the 19th century, the medical profession aspired to a higher degree of scientific rigor in training physicians, carrying out research, and healing the sick. Legitimized by its appearance of objective benevolence, the profession exerted powerful social control, complementing organized religion as an enforcer of sex roles. In the latter half of the century, a period of ambivalent attitudes toward women, gynecology developed as a specialty. Reflected in its practice were commonly held beliefs and pseudoscientific observations about female biology that reinforced notions of women's physical and intellectual inferiority.

Doctors agreed with ancient tradition in assuming reproduction to be the most important function of the female organism. The body's energy, therefore, was thought to concentrate in the womb. Observers concluded that intense physical or intellectual activity must injure the body and atrophy the uterus. Most physicians accepted that illness in women was caused by malfunctions of the reproductive organs.

As a result, middle- and upper-class women were taught to refrain from serious study and other activities that were not domestic or social. Medical doctors warned adolescent girls that they could damage themselves by pursuing intellectual interests; at the onset of menstruation, viewed as a chronic disorder, girls were advised to take up a passive life. Bed rest was frequently prescribed for pregnancy and menopause, as if they were illnesses. Eventually, female hypochondria, invalidism, and neurasthenia became fashionable, giving rise to a prospering

Performing Arts/ Entertainment/ Sports	Religion/ Philosophy	Science/ Technology/ Discovery	Statecraft/ Military	Reform	
Marie Constance Sass (1838–1907) begins a successful career in opera with her debut at the Théâtre Lyrique		The Floating Quarantine Hospital in New York is named in honor of Florence Nightingale	19-year-old Canadian Sarah Emma Edmonds (1842–1898) enlists in the Union Army as a man; she deserts in 1863 to avoid detection, abandons her male guise, and returns to the battlefront as a nurse	Sarah Parker Remond (1826–post 1887?), noted African-American, delivers successful antislavery lectures in England, Ireland, and Scotland	**1859**
Italian soprano Adelina Juana Maria Patti (1843–1919), a child prodigy who performed for the first time in public at the age of eight, makes her debut in New York in *Lucia di Lammermoor*		A noted botanist, Almira Hart Lincoln Phelps becomes only the second woman elected to the American Association for the Advancement of Science			
Famous Viennese soprano Pauline Lucca (1841–1908) creates Selika in Meyerbeer's *L'Africaine* in Berlin					
British actress Louisa Lane Drew (1820–1897) becomes manager of Philadelphia's Arch Street Theatre	Ellen Gould Harmon White (1827–1915) and her husband, James, found the Seventh-Day Adventist Church in Battle Creek, MI; as a teenager in 1844, Harmon had the first of some 2000 visions of the City of God			Birth of Jane Addams (1860–1935)	**1860**
Viennese soprano Marie Gabrielle Krauss (1842–1906) becomes a member of the Vienna court opera				Mariya Trubnikova (1835–1897), Anna Filosofova (1837–1912), and Nadezhda Stasova (1832–1895) found philanthropic organizations with feminist goals: find cheap housing, meals, and jobs for working-class women, and start sewing workshops	
British concert pianist Mary J. A. Wurm (1860–1938) is a well-known composer					

community of specialists in women's medical complaints and a spate of books on the subject of women's health. Doctors grew rich treating mysterious ailments in patients who never got well.

Women's psychology, like their physiology, was believed to be connected to their reproductive organs. The "psychology of the ovary," the idea that a woman's mind was controlled by her ovaries, led to the promotion of gynecological surgery as the logical solution to any psychological problem, from irritability to insanity. Thousands of ovariotomies, or "female castrations," took place in the last half of the 19th century, as husbands brought their unruly wives to the surgeon to be "cured."

Poor women, however, were regarded as less delicately constituted. In contrast to their more well-to-do sisters, they were expected to work hard, often with no time off during pregnancy or after childbirth. Frequent pregnancies drained their strength. Furthermore, the unsanitary conditions in which they lived, especially in urban areas, bred infectious and fatal diseases like typhoid, yellow fever, tuberculosis, cholera, and diphtheria. Women who worked as many as 14 hours a day in unhealthy factory conditions easily fell victim to fatal or disfiguring accidents. Little or no medical care was available to them or their families. If their capacity for independent action, for survival under difficult circumstances escaped the notice of the medical theorists, their courage inspired reformers who saw in them a common humanity denied by the evidence of the doctors.

	General/Context	Daily Life/Customs/Practices	Humanities/Fine Arts	Occupations	Education
1861	Britain establishes a colony in what will become modern Nigeria	Isabella Beeton (1836–1865) influences many generations of Britons with *Mrs. Beeton's Book of Household Management* Women in Bohemia are granted equal, direct, active, and passive voting rights for the Landestag and equal proxy vote for municipal elections	Lillie Devereux Blake (1833–1913) writes for the *New York Evening Post* and *The World* (in Washington, DC) In response to Pierre Joseph Proudhon's caustic 1858 *Justice in the Revolution and in the Church*, Juliette Lamber publishes *Anti-Proudhonian Ideas*	American espionage agent Belle Boyd (1844–1900) is a courier for Generals Beauregard and Jackson Pioneering women's physician Marie Zakrzewska (1829–1902) establishes the New England Hospital for Women and Children	In Lyons, France, women are admitted for the first time to advanced study
1862	American President Abraham Lincoln delivers the Emancipation Proclamation, which declares slaves in the Confederacy free	Death of Elizabeth Siddal, wife, model, and inspiration of British poet Dante Gabriel Rossetti; he buries her with the only copy of a manuscript of his poems eulogizing their love and marriage; this is recovered in 1869 and published Tax-paying women in Sweden are given municipal franchise; by the mid-1880s, however, fewer than 7% have exercised their rights	Julia Ward Howe (1819–1910) publishes *The Battle Hymn of the Republic* British watercolorist Helen Paterson Allingham (1848–1926) makes her reputation painting England's charming cottages and gardens British author Mary Braddon (1837–1915) publishes *Lady Audley's Secret* (1862) and *Aurora Floyd* (1863) Christina Georgina Rossetti (1830–1894), sister of Dante Gabriel and William Michael Rossetti, publishes *The Goblin Market and Other Poems* and *The Convent Threshold*	Civil War nurse Amy Bradley (1823–1904) is sent as relief agent to Camp Misery, a filthy and neglected convalescent camp that she restores to cleanliness and efficiency Fredericka Mandelbaum (1818–1889) begins her career as New York City's most successful fence, handling over $12 million worth of goods from 1862 to 1884 Emily Faithfull is awarded the title Printer and Publisher in Ordinary to Her Royal Majesty by royal warrant for her establishment of the Victoria Press	The Female Middle Class Emigration Society for Governesses is founded in England Russian women are expelled from university lectures by government order after student riots for which they are held—without evidence—partly responsible Laura Matilda Towne (1825–1901) founds the Penn School on St. Helena Island, SC, one of the earliest, most long-lived freedmen's schools
1863	The first workers' party is founded in Germany	Unmarried Norwegian women are granted legal majority Finnish women are granted the communal vote in rural areas	American Amélie Louise Rives (1863–1945) publishes *Shadows of the Flames,* a realistic account of drug addiction based on her own experiences with morphine American novelist Gene[va] Stratton Porter (1863–1924) publishes sentimental novels set in the Indiana wilderness The Calcutta-born British photographer Julia Margaret Cameron (1815–1879)		Mary Ellen Pleasant, a.k.a. Mammy Pleasant (1814?–1904), is sometimes called the "mother of civil rights in California"; possibly a former slave, she assists escaped and illegally held slaves and is instrumental in securing blacks the right of testimony in California courts

Performing Arts/ Entertainment/ Sports	Religion/ Philosophy	Science/ Technology/ Discovery	Statecraft/ Military	Reform	
American Marie Bonfanti (1847–1921) becomes *prima ballerina italiana* at the Teatro della Scala in Milan, Italy Coloratura soprano Adelina Patti becomes the queen of London opera for the next 25 years	The Handmaidens of Mary Serving the Sick, founded by St. Mary Soledad (1826–1887) in Madrid, Spain, receives official approval	Hungarian explorer Florence von Sass Baker (1841–1916) explores the source of the Nile and other parts of East Africa	Military strategist Anna Carroll (1815–1893) publishes "The War Powers of the General Government," justifying Lincoln's military action against the Confederacy; her report offering a Tennessee River plan paves the way for General Sherman's march to the sea		**1861**
Mercy Lavinia Warren Bumpus Stratton (1841–1919) is signed on by P. T. Barnum for an appearance in his American Museum in New York; in 1863 she meets Charles Sherwood Stratton, a.k.a. General Tom Thumb, who falls in love with her at first sight; the two have a fashionable wedding at Grace Church in New York, attended by members of Congress, governors, and other prominent people	The prophecies of 16th-century English Mother Shipton are reissued and include her predictions of such modern technologies as the steam engine and telegraph, as well as the end of the world in 1881	American geologist Florence Bascom (1862–1945) is the first woman to receive a Ph.D. from Johns Hopkins University; later, as a professor at Bryn Mawr she forms strong graduate and undergraduate programs in geology	Belle Boyd rushes information on the location of the opposing armies to General Jackson, enabling him to recapture a Union-held city Dowager Empress Tz'u Hsi (1835–1908) reigns over China from 1862 to 1908 (1862–1873, 1875–1889, 1898–1908); she had entered the palace as an 18-year-old concubine, and six years later she became regent for her son, then for her nephew, until she finally becomes empress in 1861; she is known as a stern tyrant who has homicidal rages and smokes opium; nicknamed Old Buddha		**1862**
British pianist Agnes Zimmermann (1847–1925) makes her debut at the Crystal Palace; a successful concert pianist, she edits scores and composes works for the piano as well Mme. Marie Félicie Clémence de Reiset, vicomtesse de Grandval (1830–1907) produces the opera *Les Fiances des Rosa* at the Théâtre Lyrique			Elizabeth L. Van Lew (1818–1900), Virginia Unionist and federal agent during the Civil War, secures admission to Libby Prison, where she gathers military information to transmit to Union forces	Elizabeth Cady Stanton and Susan B. Anthony found the Women's Loyal National League collecting thousands of signatures for the abolition of slavery Mary Ann Shadd Cary (1823–1893), the first African American newspaperwoman in North America, establishes the weekly publication *The Provincial Freeman* to inform African Americans of the possibilities for living in Canada	**1863**

	General/ Context	Daily Life/ Customs/ Practices	Humanities/ Fine Arts	Occupations	Education
1863			becomes known for her portraits British actress Fanny Kemble (1809–1893) publishes *Journal of a Residence in a Georgia Plantation,* describing the horrific slave conditions she found in America		
1864		Swedish women are granted the freedom to engage in trade and other occupations from which they had formerly been barred	Civil War nurse Amy Morris Bradley begins editing *Soldiers' Journal* Frances Power Cobbe (1822–1904) publishes a variety of books, from travel literature, *Cities in the Past* (1864), to moral discussions, *Darwinism and Morals* (1872)	Dr. Mary Edwards Walker (1832–1919), appointed assistant surgeon in the Union Army despite protests from the medical director and the men of the regiment she serves, wears the same uniform as her fellow officers	
1865	Lewis Carroll publishes *Alice's Adventures in Wonderland* and *Through the Looking Glass* (1872), composed for his friend's daughter, Alice Liddell The 13th Amendment to the US Constitution is ratified; it prohibits slavery and any other denial of liberty without due process of law The American Civil War ends	Mary Eugenia Jenkins Surratt (1820–1865) is convicted as a conspirator in the assassination of President Abraham Lincoln and executed	After being captured by the Union, Belle Boyd writes *Belle Boyd, in Camp and Prison* French artist Rosa Bonheur (1822–1899) is the first woman artist to receive the Cross of the French Legion of Honor French painter Marie-Clémentine Valadon's (1865–1938) works are admired by Degas Emma Stebbins's (1815–1882) bronze statue of Horace Mann is installed in front of the State House, Boston A fictionalized account of Civil War soldier Sarah Emma Edmonds (a.k.a. Franklin Thompson, 1841–1898), *Nurse and Spy in the Union Army,* is published and sells over 175,000 copies	Dr. James Miranda Barry (1799–1865), inspector general of the British Army Medical Department, is revealed to be a woman at her death; for 50 years, she passes as a man Sister Dora of Walsall (Dorothy Wyndlow Pattinson, 1832–1878) begins her career in nursing, during which she improves standards of hygiene and patient care, copes with the casualties of large-scale industrial disasters, and stems the spread of disease Belle Starr (née Myra Belle Shirley, 1848–1889), legendary American "Bandit Queen," takes up with the notorious Younger Brothers and Jesse and Frank James	The University of Zurich in Switzerland opens its doors to women

Performing Arts/ Entertainment/ Sports	Religion/ Philosophy	Science/ Technology/ Discovery	Statecraft/ Military	Reform	
				American abolitionist and "conductor" on the Underground Railroad, Harriet Tubman leads a raid that frees 750 slaves; during the American Civil War she becomes the first woman in the US to lead troops into battle	**1863**
Swedish soprano Christine Nilsson (1843–1921) is remarkable for her vocal range, compassing 2½ octaves; she debuts at Théâtre Lyrique, Paris, where she remains for three years before touring Europe and America

Violinist Camilla Urso organizes her own concert company with which she tours Canada | Elizabeth Parsons Ware Packard (1816–1897), advocate for married women's rights and protection for the insane in the US, is responsible for the passage of laws regarding jury trials for mental patients in four states; works include *Christianity and Calvinism Compared* and *Great Disclosure to Wickedness* (1865) | | The first of the Contagious Disease Prevention acts is passed in England followed by two more acts in 1866 and 1869; they are designed to regulate female prostitution through police supervision and compulsory gynecological examinations; acts repealed in 1886 | | **1864** |
| | | American physician Mary Harris Thompson (1829–1895) helps to establish the Chicago Hospital for Women and Children; the best known woman surgeon of her time, she is the first, and for many years the only, woman to perform major surgery in Chicago | The first women's conference in Leipzig leads to the founding of the Allgemeine Deutsche Frauenverein (General German Women's Association)

Virginia Unionist Elizabeth L. Van Lew engineers the disinterment of the body of a Union officer who has been framed and dishonorably buried; she has his body removed secretly and given decent burial

Dr. Mary Edwards is the first woman to be awarded the US Medal of Honor for her service to the Union Army | | **1865** |

Performing Arts/ Entertainment/ Sports	Religion/ Philosophy	Science/ Technology/ Discovery	Statecraft/ Military	Reform

	General/ Context	Daily Life/ Customs/ Practices	Humanities/ Fine Arts	Occupations	Education
1866	Norwegian women obtain occupational freedom	The Republican party, though a longtime supporter of the American women's rights movement, introduces the 14th Amendment to the Constitution, specifically denying the vote to women	Amanda Ira Aldridge (1866–1956), black English composer, pianist, and teacher, writes under the name of Montague Ring Augusta Jane Evans Wilson (1835–1909) publishes *St. Elmo,* a novel whose popularity in 19th-century America is surpassed only by that of *Uncle Tom's Cabin* and *Ben Hur* Elizabeth Chase Allen (1832–1911) publishes *Poems*	American journalist Mary E. Clemmer Ames (1831–1884) writes a weekly column, "Woman's Letter from Washington," for the New York City *Independent* Dr. Ann Preston (1813–1872) is the first woman dean of the Female (Women's) Medical College of Pennsylvania The London and National Society for Women's Service is founded	German feminist and reformer Anna Schepeler-Lette (b. 1829) and her husband, Adolf, found the Lette-Verein, a progressive association for the advancement of women, in Berlin Dr. Lucy Beaman Hobbs Taylor (1833–1910) becomes the first woman to obtain a doctor of dentistry degree in the US

WOMEN IN MEDICINE

In many cultures, the care of the sick has traditionally fallen to women. From earliest times, women have sought out healing roots, herbs, and medicaments, experimenting with materials and techniques to ease suffering. Their ability to bestow comfort and health upon victims of disease and injury has been accepted at times with reverence and gratitude, at other times with suspicion, hostility, and contempt. Women's access to professional medical training has always reflected the attitudes of their era.

In the Roman Empire, women as well as men practiced general medicine and surgery. Like their Roman predecessors, medieval women physicians' practice was not limited to obstetrics or female patients. In fact, 24 women have been identified as surgeons in Naples between 1273 and 1410; in Frankfurt between 1387 and 1497, we find references to 15 female practitioners, most of them Jewish, none of them midwives. Some of the most important medical treatises of the Middle Ages were written by women, such as the 11th-century Salerno physician Trotula or the abbess Hildegard of Bingen. Salerno emerged in the 10th and 11th centuries as a center for medical learning, where a famous group of women wrote learned Latin medical texts based on the most respected Greco-Islamic sources.

University medical faculties established in the 13th century began to exclude women from advanced medical education and thence from the most prestigious kinds of practice. At the same time, less formally trained healers organized guilds, of which women became members, enabling them to draw a salary and "licensing" them to practice within their cities. Though women continued to practice medicine at all levels until the 15th century, formally trained female physicians were never numerous.

As professional medicine replaced medicine as a craft, women were excluded more and more from technical training. By the 18th century, shut out from guilds, universities, patronage, and licensing, women practiced only the profession of midwifery for which they were duly licensed, usually by a bishop. Competition between midwives and male physicians was occasionally fierce, each denouncing the other as greedy on the one hand and ignorant on the other. The appearance of "man-

Performing Arts/ Entertainment/ Sports	Religion/ Philosophy	Science/ Technology/ Discovery	Statecraft/ Military	Reform	
French mezzo-soprano Celéstine Galli-Marié (Marié de l'Isle, 1840–1905) creates the role of Thomas's Mignon at the Paris Opéra-Comique

Dancer Maria Bonfanti (1847–1921) debuts in the US in the first musical comedy, the lavishly produced *The Black Crook*

Agnes Booth begins the first of seven seasons as leading lady for the Boston Theatre | Angela Hughes (c. 1806–1866) is the founder of the first Catholic hospital in New York City

Legal journalist Catharine Van Valkenburg Waite (1829–1913) publishes *The Mormon Prophet and His Harem,* intended to inflame popular sentiment against the "dangerous character" of the "religious monarchy . . . growing up in the midst of the Republic" | | Death of cavalry officer Nadezhada Durova (b. 1783), a Russian woman who left her husband, disguised herself as a man, and soldiered in a Cossack regiment for eight years, eventually becoming an officer

Empress Carlota of Mexico (1840–1927), daughter of King Leopold of Belgium and wife of Maximilian, goes to France to persuade Napoleon III to leave his troops in Mexico; she loses her sanity while visiting the Vatican, never recovering it again | German feminist reformers Louise Otto-Peters (1819–1895) and Auguste Schmidt (1833–1902) publish *New Highways,* a feminist newspaper

The American Equal Rights Association, seeking both black and women's suffrage, is founded by Elizabeth Cady Stanton, Susan B. Anthony, Martha Coffin Pelham Wright, and Ernestine Rose

Dr. Mary Edwards Walker (1832–1919) becomes president of the National Dress Reform Association, but alienates her fellow reformers by adopting as her regular attire a completely masculine outfit

Establishment of the Vienna Women's Employment Association, which campaigns for women's admission to jobs as postal and telegraph workers | **1866** |

midwives" in England in the 18th century in fact aroused ridicule and distrust among both women and men for several decades.

Not until the last half of the 19th century did university medical facilities open their doors to women, and then only under duress. In France the first woman intern was burned in effigy by classmates. In 1882 three women who completed the medical course and passed the examinations at a Spanish university were denied degrees; instead, they were given certificates that did not allow them to practice. In the US, such women as Elizabeth and Emily Blackwell established their own Women's Hospital and Medical College to train women when American universities refused to admit them. British women could train at the University of Edinburgh, but were not necessarily permitted to practice. Russian faculties admitted women only when the annexation of Central Asian territories created a demand by Muslim women for female physicians. The University of Zurich early accepted women as students of both medicine and law; foreign women flocked into these programs.

Objections to women entering the profession were many: the belief that women could not take the mental and physical strain of the work; that menstruation and childbirth would interrupt their work; that they would unsuit themselves for their proper domestic sphere; that treating male patients would render them indelicate—in short, the "inevitable" loss of femininity. Political objections, too, were raised: Czar Nicholas II reluctantly permitted the University of St. Petersburg to accept women when the secret police informed him that Russian women studying medicine abroad were becoming "subversive."

Today, some of the same prejudices and hostile attitudes prevent women from advancing in the field. In the 1970s, many medical schools still blocked admission to female candidates; graduates found it difficult to procure internship and residency positions. Though the situation has improved over the past 15 years, few women occupy the more prestigious jobs in medicine, often taking the salaried positions in hospitals, industry, and government that men eschew. In many ways women who enter medicine today are still pioneers.

	Daily Life/	Humanities/		
General/ Context	Customs/ Practices	Fine Arts	Occupations	Education

1866

1867

In New Zealand women taxpayers are permitted to vote in local elections

Austrian women are banned by law from joining or forming political associations

Mary Louise Booth is named editor of the brand-new *Harper's Bazaar* magazine

English musician Sarah Ann Glover (1785–1867) invents the tonic sol-fa system of notation

Danish novelist Marie Bregendahl (1867–1840) is known for her sympathetic portrayal of Jutland peasant life

British-born Anglican sisters Emma Caroline Taylor (Eldress Phoebe, 1821–1890), Elizabeth Ann Rogers (Sister Beatrice, 1829–1921), and Ellen Albertina Polyblank (Sister Albertina, 1840–1930) establish St. Andrew's Priory, a school for girls, in Honolulu

Due to the efforts of Harriet Burbank Rogers (1834–1919), the Clarke Institute for Deaf Mutes receives its charter and is the first school in the US to teach the deaf using German principles of articulation and lipreading

British social reformer Josephine Butler (1828–1906) becomes the president of the North of England Council for Promoting Higher Education of Women

British women's rights leader Josephine E. Butler
Photograph (1873) courtesy Sophia Smith Collection, Smith College

1868

A monument is erected in Wyoming to honor Eliza Hart Spalding (1807–1851), pioneer missionary to Oregon and one of the first women of US citizenship to cross the Rocky Mountains

French composer Mme. Marie Clémence de Reiset produces the opera *Piccolini* at the Paris Opéra Comique

Elizabeth Stuart Phelps Ward (1844–1911) publishes *The Gates Ajar*

Countess Teresa Guiccioli (1801?–1873) writes *My Recollections of Lord Byron,* a memoir dealing with their lifelong relationship

Myra Colby Bradwell (1831–1894) undertakes the management and publication of the *Chicago Legal News*

Augusta Lewis Troup (c. 1848–1920) becomes a reporter for the New York *Sun;* she later learns typesetting

New York City's Pioneer Woman's Club, Sorosis, is founded by newspaper columnist and women's rights activist Sara Payson Willis Parton (1811–1872)

Established by Emily and Elizabeth Blackwell, the Women's Medical College in New York raises the standards of women's medical training

Performing Arts/ Entertainment/ Sports	Religion/ Philosophy	Science/ Technology/ Discovery	Statecraft/ Military	Reform	
				Later exiled from France, French communard Louise Michel (1830–1895) founds France's first feminist organization; the group's moderate goals include improvement of women's education, the prevention of prostitution, and higher pay for working women	**1866**
British soprano Mary Anne Wilson Welsh (1802–1867) is such a successful performer that she earns £10,000 the very first year of her short career Vesta Tilley (1864–1952) makes her stage debut at the age of three in England; later she is known for her specialty—male impersonation				British suffragist Lydia Becker (1827–1890) is a founding member of the Manchester National Society for Women's Suffrage; as a result of Parliament's failure to grant women suffrage, she, Dame Millicent Garrett Fawcett (1847–1929), and other British feminists form the National Society for Women's Suffrage Hungary's achievement of self-government engenders a feminist movement dedicated to the improvement of girls' education	**1867**
American soprano Minnie Hauck (1852–1929) becomes a member of the Vienna Court Opera; successful both in Europe and the US, she is also court singer in Prussia, Officier de l'Académie, Paris, and a member of the Roman Music Academy German soprano Mathilde Lichtenegger Mallinger (1847–1920) creates the role of Eva in Wagner's *Die Meis-*	Formation of the Chicago Association of the Kingdom of Woman, a religious institution governed by women and headed by Sophronia Kilbourn			A general meeting of the Allgemeine deutsche Frauenverein deals for the first time with the question of the participation of German women in law making and government British-born activist Kate Sheppard (1848–1934) emigrates to New Zealand in the late 1860s where she campaigns for dress reform, married women's rights and	**1868**

	General/ Context	Daily Life/ Customs/ Practices	Humanities/ Fine Arts	Occupations	Education
1868			American author Louisa May Alcott (1832–1888) publishes her best known novel, *Little Women*		
1869		After resisting his advances for many years, Ann Eliza Webb Young (1844–post-1908) marries Brigham Young, becoming his 19th—and, according to her, his last—plural wife (he had at least 70); feeling neglected, she sues for divorce in 1873, causing a sensation in the press; a woman of considerable dignity, she survives the slurs cast on her character, becoming a popular lecturer against polygyny and a moving force in the passage of federal antipolygyny legislation A Criminal Diseases Act regulating prostitution easily passes in the New Zealand legislature	Lilly Martin Spencer (1822–1902), known for her genre paintings and portraits, completes her most famous work, Truth Unveiling Falsehood Harriet Beecher Stowe publishes "The True Story of Lady Byron's Life" in *Atlantic Monthly* in an effort to defend her deceased friend against calumny	In her final year writing for the *Brooklyn Daily Union,* Mary E. Clemmer Ames earns a salary of $5000, the largest ever paid to an American newswoman at that time Myra Colby Bradwell passes the Illinois bar examination but is denied admission on the basis of sex; she takes her case to the Supreme Court, which in 1873 upholds the judgment of the lower court, giving all persons, regardless of sex, freedom in selecting an occupation Arabella Mansfield (1846–1911) of Iowa becomes the first woman regularly admitted to the practice of law in the US Elizabeth Garrett Anderson (1836–1917) qualifies to practice medicine in England by passing the apothecaries' exam; her success creates panic in the apothecaries' guild, which changes its rules to exclude women, though it had had no such regulations before	The Chicago Medical College admits three women Female lawyers are licensed in the US General enforcement of freedom of trade and lifting of guilds' exclusion of women in Germany results in an influx of women into hitherto closed trades Norwegian women are admitted to the teaching profession Austrian women are first admitted as primary school teachers Sophia Jex-Blake (1840–1912) and four other female medical students begin their studies at a university in Scotland, but are prevented from graduating by the hostility of the male students British teacher Emily Davies (1830–1921) opens her "college" in Hitchin, England, where she prepares students for the Cambridge University examinations Higher education courses and public lectures are approved for Russian women

Performing Arts/ Entertainment/ Sports	Religion/ Philosophy	Science/ Technology/ Discovery	Statecraft/ Military	Reform	
tersinger; she becomes a singing teacher at the Prague Conservatory in 1890				status, and women's suffrage Lydia Becker makes the first public speech by a woman on the subject of votes for women in Great Britain at the Manchester National Society for Women's Suffrage	**1868**
Austrian soprano Amalie Materna (1845–1918) begins her career in opera as a soubrette, but becomes prima donna of the Vienna Court Opera	Caroline Augusta White Soule (1824–1903), American author, church worker, and Universalist minister, coorganizes the Woman's Centenary Aid Association; she becomes a minister of St. Paul's Universalist Church in Glasgow, Scotland, in 1879	Alexandrine Tinne (1839–1869), a Dutch heiress who made several expeditions in East Africa and the Sahara, including a search for the sources of the White Nile, is killed by Tuareg tribesmen who apparently coveted her wealth Though she has been invited to attend Prof. Benjamin Peirce's lectures on quarternions, astronomer Mary Watson Whitney (1847–1921) must wait outside the college gates for him to escort her to the classroom since Harvard is not officially open to women	Wyoming Territory is the first American political body that allows women to vote; when it becomes a state in 1890, it also becomes the first US state to do so Frances Ellen Watkins Harper stands with Frederick Douglass against the leadership of the American Equal Rights Association when Elizabeth Cady Stanton and Susan B. Anthony withdraw their support for black suffrage	The careers of Russian-born American immigrant Emma Goldman (1869–1940) include public speaker, writer, publisher, agitator for free speech, feminist, pioneer advocate of birth control, popularizer of the arts, and anarchist; she is deported to the Soviet Union, where she soon clashes with the government and leaves the country in disillusionment A bill giving married women a right to their own earnings, drafted by Myra Colby Bradwell, is lobbied through the Illinois legislature by Bradwell, her husband, Elizabeth Cady Stanton, Catharine Waite, and others Union of German Women's Educational and Occupational Associations, founded under the auspices of the Lette-Verein, holds its first conference American feminists Susan B. Anthony, Elizabeth Cady Stanton, and Martha Coffin Pelham Wright (1806–1875) found the National Woman Suffrage Association (NWSA) Foundation of the American Woman Suffrage Association by feminist reformers Lucy Stone, Julia Ward Howe, and others	**1869**

	General/ Context	Daily Life/ Customs/ Practices	Humanities/ Fine Arts	Occupations	Education
1869					
1870	The French Third Republic, 1870–1940, begins	Married British women who are employed are granted the right to spend their own earnings	English watercolorist Helen Paterson Allingham becomes an illustrator and engraver for *The Graphic;* she also produces wood engravings for *Once a Week* and *Cornhill Magazine*	The British government begins to employ women as clerical workers	Cornelia Ann Phillips Spencer (1825–1908), North Carolina educational crusader, cofounds the Women's College of the University of North Carolina at Greensboro
		The Spanish penal code in the Philippines enacts a law against abortion; the law was still in effect as of 1989	American southern writer Frances Christine Fisher Tiernan, pen name Christian Reid (1846–1920), publishes *Valerie Aylmer*	Paiute Indian leader Sarah (Thoc-me-tony) Winnemucca (c. 1844–1891), fluent in Spanish and English as well as three Indian languages, serves as an interpreter at Camp McDermitt in Nevada; she later acts as a representative of her people before Secretary of the Interior Carl Schurz and President Rutherford B. Hayes	Clara A. Swain (1834–1910), pioneering female medical missionary, teaches classes in anatomy, physiology, and medicine to orphan girls and young married women in Bareilly, India
		Abortion of any kind is declared an excommunicable offense by Pope Pius IX	Popular American poet Rose Alnora Hartwick Thorpe (1850–1939) publishes one of her best-known poems, "The Curfew Must Not Ring Tonight"		Susan Smith McKinney Steward becomes the first black woman to receive a New York Medical College degree
				Dorothy Dix, pen name of Elizabeth Meriwether Gilmer (1870–1951) writes advice on domestic problems	Ellen Henrietta Swallow Richards (1842–1911) becomes the first woman admitted to the Massachusetts Institute of Technology
				Sisters Victoria Claflin Woodhull (1838–1927) and Tennessee Celeste Claflin (1846–1923) open the brokerage firm of Woodhull, Claflin & Company	In response to closing the Chicago Medical College to women, Dr. William Byford and Dr. Mary Harris

1869

Maria Deraismes (1828–1894) and Léon Richer publish the journal *Women's Rights*, which promotes women's rights activism; the League for Women's Rights is founded in France

British liberal theorist John Stuart Mill publishes the enormously influential essay *The Subjection of Women;* the "feminist bible," its appearance coincides with the foundation of feminist movements in several European countries

Women are active participants at the founding convention of the National Colored Labor Union

---

1870

Mme. (Marie Louise Cecily) Emma Lajeunesse Albani (1852–1930), Canadian dramatic soprano, makes her debut as Amina in *La Sonnambula* in Messina; she makes her US debut in the same role at the New York Academy of Music in 1874

Noted German pianist Adèle Aus der Ohe (1864–1937), composer of two piano suites and a concert etude, among other works, tours widely with great success

American editor, reformer, and presidential candidate Victoria C. Woodhull
Photograph (1872) courtesy Sophia Smith Collection, Smith College

Marie Goegg's International Association of Women is revived under the name of "Solidarité"

Victoria Woodhull and her sister, Tennessee Claflin, found *Woodhull and Claflin's Weekly,* a newspaper in which they expound their views favoring woman suffrage, free love, short skirts, and legalized prostitution

British reformer Josephine Butler founds the Ladies' National Association for Repeal to fight against the Contagious Disease Prevention acts

During the 1870s, British feminists call for "voluntary motherhood," the idea being that women can refuse to submit to their husbands' sexual demands

Austrian feminist leader Marianne Hainisch (1839–1936) presses the Vienna Women's Employment

	General/Context	Daily Life/Customs/Practices	Humanities/Fine Arts	Occupations	Education
1870					Thompson (1829–1895) begin the Women's Hospital Medical College Oxford University first admits women to the examinations Sophia Smith (1796–1870) leaves $393,105 toward the establishment of a women's college—the future Smith College—in Northampton, MA
1871	Paris Commune, March–May 1871	Victoria Woodhull attacks popular preacher Henry Ward Beecher (1813–1887) for conducting an illicit affair with Elizabeth Tilton, wife of editor Theodore Tilton During the Paris Commune, rumors of *pétroleuses*, or women incendiaries, supposed to have set fire to Paris are rampant; the myth influences subsequent Republican governments to repress feminist activity Under the new German Empire's criminal code, abortion is punishable by up to five years in prison	The letters of Caroline Schelling (1763–1809), published this year offer insights into the German Romantic movement American art historian Clara Waters (1834–1916) publishes three art handbooks reissued for 20 years: *A Handbook of Legendary and Mythological Art* (1871); *Painters, Sculptors, Architects, Engravers, and Their Works* (1874); and *Artists of the Nineteenth Century and Their Works* (1879) George Eliot begins serial publication of *Middlemarch*, considered by many to be her finest work		Louise Michel, French anarchist-socialist, writer, and teacher, defends the famous Paris Commune, where she takes charge of social and educational policies British educator Anne Jemima Clough begins teaching female students in Cambridge, where she hopes to improve female education by producing better teachers rather than women with college degrees Danish reformer Fredrik Bajer (1837–1922) establishes the Women's Reading Society to offer unmarried middle-class women access to advanced education
1872	Buddhist priests are permitted by the Japanese government to marry and to eat meat	Finnish townswomen gain the communal vote The US Comstock Law makes it a criminal offense to import, mail, or transport in interstate commerce	American novelist Eleanor Hallowell Abbott (1872–1958) publishes in her lifetime an autobiography, 14 books, and 75 magazine stories English novelist Marie Louise de la Ramée	The German Woman's Association promotes the idea of training women as lawyers to handle divorce cases for women and to defend female criminals	Amy Morris Bradley (1823–1904) opens the Tileston Normal School in Wilmington, DE, to train local women as teachers Maria Parloa (1843–1909), American pioneer in teaching home

Performing Arts/ Entertainment/ Sports	Religion/ Philosophy	Science/ Technology/ Discovery	Statecraft/ Military	Reform	
				Association to demand admission of girls to grammar schools in order to fit them for jobs; the association instead asks for a Höhere Mädchen-schule (high school for girls), to train girls for motherhood	**1870**
				Foundation of the (Austrian) Association of Women Teachers and Educators	
Swedish-American operatic soprano Olive Fremstad (1871–1951), after whom the heroine of Willa Cather's novel *The Song of the Lark* (1915) is modeled, is the foremost interpreter of soprano roles in German and Italian opera of her day	Hindu seer and teacher Sri Sarada Devi (1853–1920) marries at the age of 18, but she and her husband lead a celibate life; at his death, she makes her way to Calcutta, where she gives spiritual instruction and becomes known as the Holy Mother			Upon paying her taxes, New Hampshire lawyer Marilla Marks Young Ricker (1840–1920) demands the right to vote as an "elector"; though her ballot is refused, she does vote, probably the first woman in the US to do so on this basis	**1871**
				The Communist Manifesto appears for the first time in English in the US in the pages of *Woodhull and Claflin's Weekly*	
				French activist Elisabeth Dimitrieff forms the Women's Union, which organizes women into syndicates	
				Foundation of the Danish Women's Association by Fredrik and Mathilde (1840–1934) Bajer	
				One of the 19th-century's greatest suffragists, Abigail Jane Scott Duniway (1834–1915) founds the women's rights journal *The New Northwest*	
An intimate friend of Giuseppe Verdi, mezzo-soprano Teresa Stolz (1834–1902) creates the role of Aïda in Italy			Swiss feminist Marie Goegg founds the Association for the Defense of the Rights of Women	Committee of the Women's Suffrage Association argues before the judiciary committee of the New York State legislature	**1872**
			Having broken with suffragist leaders, Victoria Woodhull holds her own convention,	Susan B. Anthony and eight other women are arrested for voting in	

General/Context	Daily Life/Customs/Practices	Humanities/Fine Arts	Occupations	Education
1872	any contraceptive or abortifacient Illinois women's rights bill "[securing] to all persons freedom in the selection of an occupation, profession, or employment" becomes law In response to lobbying by feminist lawyer Belva Ann Lockwood (1830–1917), the US Congress passes a law guaranteeing equal pay for equal work in federal jobs	(1839–1908), writing under the name "Ouida," publishes her best-known work, the children's book *A Dog of Flanders* Popular novelist Anna Bartlett Warner (1827–1915) publishes *Gardening by Myself,* the first book by an American woman urging women to garden with their own hands	Emily Warren Radelisky supervises the construction of the Brooklyn Bridge for her invalid husband Charlotte E. Ray (1850–1911) becomes the first black woman lawyer in the US Austrian women are admitted to the postal and telegraphic service	economics, publishes *The Appledore Cook Book* The Danish Women's Association establishes a women's trade school in Copenhagen At her death, Scottish astronomer, geologist, and mathematician Mary Somerville (1780–1872) leaves money specifically for the purpose of establishing educational opportunities for women unlike those she herself had received; in 1879, Somerville College at Oxford is established in her name
1873	Because of their unequal social positions, the marriage of Hannah Cullick (1833–1909) and Arthur Munby is kept secret while she acts as his servant; her diaries are published, at her request, long after their deaths, as *The Diaries of Hannah Cullick: Victorian Maidservant* (1984)	Irish-born composer Augusta Mary Anne Holmès (1847–1903) publishes the psalm *In Exitu Israel* French novelist Colette (1873–1954) writes her first novels in collaboration with her husband under the pseudonym Willy	The Vienna World Exhibition includes a pavilion showcasing women's work The Illinois State legislature passes a law stipulating that "no person shall be precluded or debarred from any occupation, profession or employment (except military) on account of sex"	Dr. Mary Jane Safford (1834–1891) joins the faculty of the newly opened Boston University School of Medicine as a professor of women's diseases Author Sarah Chauncey Woolsey, a.k.a. Susan Coolidge (1835–1905), revolutionizes school story books by blending imaginary and real-life episodes

AMERICAN WOMEN TAKE TO THE LAW

The first woman lawyer may have been a Babylonian who, according to a clay tablet in the British Museum, brought a suit against her brother-in-law. She pleaded her own case and won. Between 1239 and 1249, Bettisia Gozzadini occupied the juridical chair at the University of Bologna. The first woman lawyer in Colonial America, Margaret Brent (c. 1601–1671) was involved in more lawsuits than any other citizen between 1642 and 1650.

The legal field, however, has been particularly difficult for women to break into. The first American woman admitted to the bar, Arabella Mansfield, was in Iowa in 1869; but the same year Myra Bradwell was denied admission to the bar in Illinois on the ground that she was a woman. When she took her case to the US Supreme Court, it backed the state of Illinois and declared the female sex "unfit for many of the occupations of civil life." Though Illinois passed an act in 1872 giving all persons, regardless of sex, freedom to choose their occupation, Bradwell did not reapply to the Illinois bar until 1890, when she was finally admitted.

One popular rationale for keeping women out of the legal system was their inevitable encounter, professional though it may be, with the seamier side of life. Women's natural timidity and delicacy, it was thought, made them unfit for such an occupation. By taking on men's work, women would upset the natural functions of the sexes. Women who nevertheless pursued legal careers were regarded as misfits, sometimes not even respectable.

Although women began to be admitted to law schools in small numbers in the late 1800s (by 1890 there were 200 women lawyers in the US), once licensed, they were almost

Performing Arts/ Entertainment/ Sports	Religion/ Philosophy	Science/ Technology/ Discovery	Statecraft/ Military	Reform	
			which declares her the presidential nominee of the Equal Rights Party; African-American leader Frederick Douglass is named her running mate, an honor he ignores	Rochester, NY; they are freed on bail, but are tried and fined in 1873 Mrs. Steven Pitts, editor of *Pioneer*, a suffragist paper, draws a pistol on the Hon. David Meeker as he quiets a crowd of suffragists jeering an antisuffragist speaker Lucy Stone and her husband, Henry Brown Blackwell, edit *Woman's Journal* (1872–1893)	**1872**
American actress Blanche Lyon Bates (1873–1941) enjoys great success in such plays as *The Musketeers, Children of the Ghetto,* and *Madame Butterfly* Canadian-born comedian Marie Dressler (1873–1934) plays broad comic roles onstage and on screen		The attainments in botany and natural history of botanist Lydia White Shattuck (1822–1889) were "remarkable for the time [when] there were very few women in the country who could be ranked with her in that respect"; her collections form the basis of the notable Mount Holyoke College botanical garden		American temperance reformer Eliza Jane Trimble Thompson (1816–1905) marches with a group of women on liquor-selling druggists of Hillsboro, OH An eloquent and persuasive advocate of women's rights, Abba Louisa Goold Woolson (1838–1921) publishes *Woman in American Society* Astronomer Maria Mitchell founds the	**1873**

uniformly excluded from courtroom practice and limited to office work. Unable to establish their own practices, some women lawyers took jobs in government agencies, edited law journals, became teachers of law, or gave up the profession.

Alarmed by the legal and economic discrimination against women in American society, a few, like Belva Lockwood, chose to fight. She wrote and lobbied for an equal pay for equal work bill for women in government employment, passed by Congress in 1872. In 1876, Lockwood was denied admission to the Supreme Court; she lobbied Congress, spurring the "Lockwood bill" into legislation: it gave women the right to practice in federal courts and Lockwood became the first woman admitted to practice before the court. Still, by 1920 only 3% of American lawyers were women.

Although in the 20th century women have made great strides in the legal system—both by changing laws and by making careers as lawyers—discrimination still abounds. In 1972 in Title IX of the education amendments, Congress banned financial aid to educational institutions that discriminate on the basis of sex, and in 1975 the Equal Credit Opportunity Act ended discrimination against women by financial institutions. Similar laws have made great headway in granting women legal equality. The high number of equity suits, class-action complaints, and sex discrimination charges are forcing society to further reduce the legal disparities between men and women. An Equal Rights Amendment has yet to be passed in the US.

By 1980 there were more than 45,000 women practicing law in the US, about 10% of all US lawyers. Between 1971 and 1981, the proportion of women lawyers and judges rose from 4% to 14%.

	General/ Context	Daily Life/ Customs/ Practices	Humanities/ Fine Arts	Occupations	Education
1873			Mary Mapes Dodge (1831–1905) edits the popular children's periodical *St. Nicholas Magazine* from 1873 to 1905		
			Emma Stebbins's most famous work, the Angel of the Waters, part of the Bethesda fountain in Central Park, New York City, is unveiled		
1874	Ghana (Gold Coast) in West Africa becomes a British colony		Composer Augusta Mary Anne Holmès writes the one-act stage work *Hero et Leandre* American portraitist Romaine Brooks's (1874–1970) most interesting works are her portraits of lesbians	Bethenia Angelina Owens-Adair (1840–1926), pioneer American physician, earns two medical degrees, with specialties in women and children's medicine and eye and ear; a vocal supporter of eugenical sterilization for criminals, epileptics, and the insane and agitator for temperance and women's suffrage, she is a frequent contributor to the feminist newspaper *The New Northwest* American missionary Clara A. Swain opens the first hospital for women in India	Emily Davies, determined that female students follow the same course of study as men, establishes a college for women on the outskirts of Cambridge, at Girton
1875		Lydia Estes Pinkham (1819–1883) patents and sells her family's home remedies as Lydia E. Pinkham's Vegetable Compound	May Alcott, a.k.a. Mme. Neriker (1840–1879), American painter, opens an art center in Concord, MA; the sister of Louisa May Alcott, she is the model for Amy March in *Little Women* The Paris Salon accepts *La Pièce de Conviction*, a painting by American artist Emily Sartain (1841–1927) American sculptor Anne Whitney (1821–1915) wins first place in an anonymous competition; when the committee learns she is a woman, the commission is withdrawn Russian-born occultist Helena Petrovna Bla-	Elizabeth Blackwell accepts the chair of gynecology in the New Hospital and London School of Medicine for Women The board of midwifery examiners in Edinburgh resigns in protest when Sophia Jex-Blake tries to have women placed on the medical register through the midwifery license Franziska Tiburtius and Emilie Lehmus graduate from the University of Zurich with degrees in medicine, the first German women to become certified physicians Emma Paterson of London becomes the	The British Royal College of Surgeons admits women for the first time Newnham Hall is established to train female teachers with Anne Jemima Clough as principal; it gains status as a Cambridge University college in 1880 Between 1864 and 1875, the number of girls in Russian grammar schools increases from 4335 to 27,470

Performing Arts/ Entertainment/ Sports	Religion/ Philosophy	Science/ Technology/ Discovery	Statecraft/ Military	Reform	
				(US) Association for the Advancement of Women	**1873**
				The Association for Married Women's Property Rights is founded in Sweden	
	Woman's Parent Mite Missionary Society of the African Methodist Episcopal Church is founded and becomes one of many women's groups supporting missionary women during the late 19th century	Russian mathematician Sofia Vasilevna Kovalevskaia (1850–1891) becomes the first woman to receive a doctorate from a German university, awarded in absentia and without examinations	Rhode Island legislature passes a women's suffrage amendment to its constitution

The widowed Queen Emma of Hawaii becomes a candidate for the throne when King Lunalilo (1832–1874) dies without naming a successor; the legislature votes for a king of the rival royal line | Abba Woolson lectures throughout the US to emphasize the "physical discomfort and disease" promoted by constricting fashionable garb

Establishment of the (American) National Women's Christian Temperance Union | **1874** |
| American actress Mary Antoinette Anderson (1859–1940) makes her debut as Juliet at Macauley's Theatre in Louisville, KY

21-year-old pianist Julie Rivé-King (1854–1937) debuts with the New York Philharmonic Society

Célestine Galli-Marié creates the role of Carmen at the Paris Opéra Comique | *Science and Health,* the official statement of Mary Baker Eddy's Christian Science doctrine, is first published | Ellen Henrietta Swallow Richards is credited as the founder of home economics as both a science and profession; she becomes a world-renowned sanitary chemist; at her urging, MIT establishes a women's laboratory

Harriet Chalmers Adams (1875–1937), American explorer, traveler, writer, and lecturer on Latin America and Hispanic culture, writes for *National Geographic* for 28 years | Supreme Court hands down the *Miner* v. *Hoppersatt* decision that states that women are considered "persons" within the boundaries of the 14th Amendment, but are not entitled to vote | Antoinette Louisa Brown Blackwell argues that Darwin's theory of evolution supports women's emancipation

The French monarchist government bans Maria Deraismes and Léon Richer's organization, the Society for the Improvement of Women's Lot

Feminist reformer Eliza L. Sproat Randolph Turner (1826–1903) publishes the suffrage tract *Four Quite New Reasons Why You Should Wish Your Wife to Vote* | **1875** |

	General/ Context	Daily Life/ Customs/ Practices	Humanities/ Fine Arts	Occupations	Education
1875			vatsky (1831–1891) founds the Theosophical Society in New York; her books on occult matters include *Isis Unveiled* (1877) and *The Secret Doctrine* (1888)	first woman to attend the Trades Union Congress's national meeting as a full delegate	
1876	The telephone is patented by Alexander Graham Bell (1847–1922)			The Second Reich places no restriction on who may practice the "healing arts," the first German women to become physicians, Emilie Lehmus and Franziska Tiburtius, establish a clinic in Berlin Women gain the right to register as physicians in Great Britain Austrian women working as postal and telegraph operators form a union	The Russian government regularizes higher education courses for Russian women; special medical courses are established to train women doctors to treat Muslim women in Central Asian tribes who will not consent to be treated by a male doctor Russian women graduates are refused permission to teach in elementary schools or to enter professions for which degrees are required
1877	By this year, the courses of the great African rivers Congo, Niger, Nile, and Zambesi have been explored and determined Invention of the phonograph by Ameri-	Known as Lemonade Lucy, Lucy Webb Hayes (1831–1889), wife of President Rutherford B. Hayes, bans the serving of alcoholic beverages in the White House	British composer Mary Ann Virginia Gabriel (1825–1877) is known for her cantatas and operas Anna Sewell (1820–1878) publishes her beloved novel *Black*	Female physicians are granted legal permission to practice in England Elizabeth Garrett Anderson, one of the first women to qualify as a doctor in Britain, founds the Elizabeth	Helen Magill White (1853–1944) earns a Ph.D. in Greek from Boston University, the first woman to receive a Ph.D. from an American university Foundation of International Federation of

EXPLORERS AND TRAVELERS

Depending on how you define them, either a mere handful of extraordinary 19th-century women broke with tradition and ventured into the unknown or thousands of surprisingly ordinary ones did. We know a fair amount about the first group, many of whom published lively books about their adventures, but we are only beginning to learn about the others.

In the case of the first group of aristocratic and middle-class women adventurers, better education, a greater awareness of the world around them, and an increasing frustration with everyday life drove some women into the wilderness. While other middle-class women tried to engage the world outside their drawing room through social activism, a few decided to go the full distance, escaping not only their domestic and community roles but the community itself. What one expert has called "wayward women" becomes a phenomenon in the 19th century: women setting off on their own to the remotest parts of the globe to risk, challenge, and defy.

Among the wayward middle-class European women who sought adventure, freedom from convention, or intellectual stimulus were writers, scientists, missionaries—and women like Isabella Bird (1832–1904) who, however dutiful and retiring at home, reported a great sense of freedom in the "congenial barbarism of the desert." Bird traveled in and wrote about Hawaii, Japan, Persia, Kurdistan, Tibet, and China.

Mme. Hommaire de Hell, a Belgian, traveled in Russia and Turkey, where she discovered numbers of other European women already living in exile. Frederika Bremer (1801–1865), the Swedish novelist and peace activist, traveled around the world seeking backgrounds for her novels. Alexandra Tinne of the Netherlands explored Africa. Lady Hester Stanhope (1776–1839) left English society to establish a "petty Kingdom" in Lebanon. Lady Anna Brassey (1839–1887) sailed around the world in the yacht *Sunbeam* in 1876.

Performing Arts/ Entertainment/ Sports	Religion/ Philosophy	Science/ Technology/ Discovery	Statecraft/ Military	Reform	
					1875
Emma Cecilia Thursby (1845–1931), American concert singer, appears with Mark Twain in a series of four programs	British religious philanthropist Agnes Weston establishes the first of her Sailors' Rest homes, providing Christian support for seamen in difficult circumstances	Shih Mai-Yu (Dr. Mary Stone) graduates from University of Michigan's medical school, becoming the first Chinese woman to earn an American M.D.		Ann Eliza Webb Young publishes her exposé of Mormon women's lives, *Wife No. 19, or The Story of a Life in Bondage*	**1876**
Amalie Materna creates the role of Brünnhilde at Bayreuth				Literary feminist Hedwig Dohm (1833–1919) calls for the establishment of a German female suffrage society; her call is rejected	
Cissie Loftus is the stage name of Scottish actress Marie Cecilia McCarthy (1876–1943), a star of stage and early film noted for impersonating other stars					
American actress Maude Adams (Maude Kiskadden, 1872–1953), begins her career billed as "La Petite Maude" in *Fritz*			Fanny Baker Ames (1840–1931) becomes a founding member and, in 1887, president of Philadelphia's New Century Club	The Allgemeine deutsche Frauenverein petitions the Reichstag for consideration of women's rights in the new civil code	**1877**
Venezuelan pianist Teresa Carreño (1853–1917) begins			A bill to amend the Constitution to allow women to vote where	Catherine Mumford Booth (1829–1890) and her husband found	

The other, much larger group of women explorers does not come down to us as the story of individuals. Thousands of women, many of them not privileged, educated, or intentionally wayward, were driven by desperation, ambition, or sheer determination from the familiarity of home to pioneer some of the earth's most daunting territories, from Africa to Australia to the Wild West of the US.

Organizers of British women's migration societies explored and traveled extensively before arranging passage for countless other women who settled new territory in Canada, New Zealand, Nigeria, Kenya, and Jamaica, among other places. In the US, pioneer women not only trekked west with their families and settled new homesteads but some also built claim shacks to dig for gold or took land and developed it alone. By 1885, for example, Mary Meegher owned the largest ranch on the Pacific slope. Pioneer women did well in the face of hardship, often showing more optimism than their male counterparts, more flexibility, more physical and psychological endurance. On some journeys, only women survived. All types of women made the trip: college girls, fancy women, middle-aged ladies, bloomer girls, teachers, missionaries, tough army women, ordinary middle-class wives.

The 19th century, the golden age of missionary activity, saw legions of women, descendants of the intrepid pilgrims of the Middle Ages, undertake extraordinary travels and live to tell uplifting if hair-raising tales. Mary Bird, sent out alone to Persia by the Christian Missionary Society as its first female worker, traveled 500 miles on camelback to get there. Lucy Broad covered over 100,000 miles in her 10 years as an evangelist for the Women's Christian Temperance Union, often traveling by bicycle over parts of South Africa, Mauritius, Madagascar, Australia, Tasmania, New Zealand, Samoa, and Fiji.

	General/ Context	Daily Life/ Customs/ Practices	Humanities/ Fine Arts	Occupations	Education
1877	can Thomas Alva Edison		*Beauty: The Autobiography of a Horse* Nadezhda Filaretovna von Meck (1831–1894) grants Tchaikovsky an allowance that permits him to concentrate on his music Writing as "Josiah Allen's Wife," Marietta Holley (1836–1926) advocates temperance and women's rights	Garrett Anderson Hospital, specializing in the treatment of women and children, later becomes dean of the London Medical School for Women, she becomes the first woman mayor in England	Friends of Girls in Geneva, Switzerland; the organization offers protection, aid, and shelter to young girls the world over
1878		Elizabeth Rowell Thompson (1821–1899) gives the US government financial aid to establish the Yellow Fever Commission and other charities	American Rachel Crothers (1878–1958) writes about the place of women in the modern world Anna Katharine Green (1846–1935) writes *The Leavenworth Case,* reputedly the first detective fiction written by an American woman Irish novelist Margaret Wolfe Hungerford (1855?–1897) publishes the best known of her more than 30 novels, *Molly Bawn*	Emma Abbott (1850–1891), American opera singer forms the Emma Abbott Opera Company	Noted coloratura soprano Selma Nicklass-Kemptner (1849–1928) becomes a teacher at the Vienna Conservatory Oxford founds the Association for the Education of Women the same year that its first two women's colleges are established
1879		Josephine Cochrane of Illinois invents the first mechanical dishwasher	Ada Rehan (1860–1916) becomes the leading lady in Daly's Theatre, New York City, for 20 years Louise Pauline Marie Heritte-Viardot (1841–1918) composes the opera *Lindora* Canadian novelist Mazo de la Roche (1879–1961) writes chiefly about an Ontario family, the Whiteoaks *A Doll's House* by Henrik Ibsen is published; its conclusion, in which Nora leaves her husband, shocked audiences Dorothy Canfield Fisher; (1879–1958) chronicles New England life in her books	British physician Matilda Chaplin Ayrton (1846–1883) acquires a certificate in midwifery from the London Obstetrics Society, opens a midwife's school in Japan, and is awarded her M.D. in Paris in 1879	The Harvard Annex, a program of higher education for women, opens its doors Zilpha Drew Smith (1852–1926), social worker, establishes training classes for district social work agents and study classes for volunteers American educator Anna Hallowell (1831–1905) establishes free kindergartens in poor neighborhoods in Philadelphia Women are admitted to Brazil's institutions of higher learning

PLAIN FACTS
ABOUT
WORKING WOMEN;
BY
REV. T. DE WITT TALMAGE,   REV. S. D. BURCHARD,
HON. DAVID DUDLEY FIELD,   HON. JOHN R. BRADY.
WITH
MUSICAL AID
BY
Mrs. FLORENCE RICE KNOX,   Miss HENRIETTA BEEBE,
HENRY EYRE BROWNE,   CARYL FLORIO.

THE FIFTEENTH ANNIVERSARY
OF THE
Working Women's Protective Union,
At Chickering Hall, Nov. 19th, 1878.

NEW YORK:
WORKING WOMEN'S PROTECTIVE UNION, 38 BLEECKER STREET.
1879.

Title page of 1878 brochure, Plain Facts About Working Women, *put out by Working Women's Protective Union, New York*
Photograph courtesy Sophia Smith Collection, Smith College

Performing Arts/ Entertainment/ Sports	Religion/ Philosophy	Science/ Technology/ Discovery	Statecraft/ Military	Reform	
playing in public at the age of 12; a composer as well, she is known for her salon pieces for piano Austrian operetta soprano Georgine von Januschowsky (1859–1924) becomes a soubrette at the Theater an der Wien (Vienna); until she becomes prima donna at the Imperial Opera in 1893			they are taxed is defeated in the US House of Representatives Queen Victoria becomes empress of India	the British Salvation Army Formation of the American Committee for the Prevention of Legalizing Prostitution African-American reformer Lucy Parsons (1853–1942) begins her long career as an activist by joining the Labor party	**1877**
Wagnerian soprano Rosa Hasselbeck Sucher (1849–1927) becomes prima donna at the Royal Opera in Berlin Sophie Menter-Popper (1846–1914) becomes court pianist to the emperor of Austria	Anna Howard Shaw (1847–1919) graduates in 1878 as the only woman in her class in Boston University's divinity school; when she applies for ordination, her application is denied and her license to preach repealed	Physicist Sarah Frances Whiting (1847–1927) opens the second undergraduate teaching laboratory in the US at Wellesley College *Emmeline Pankhurst, British suffragist* Photograph (c. 1903) courtesy Sophia Smith Collection, Smith College		President of the (US) WCTU, Annie Turner Wittenmeir, writes *History of the Women's Temperance Crusade* Emmeline Pankhurst (1858–1928) advocates for Britain's proposed Married Women's Property Act International Women's Rights Congress takes place in Paris	**1878**
Once a ballet dancer with the Imperial Opera in Berlin, Katharina Senger-Bettaque (b. 1862) becomes a soprano and sings on the same stage Eugénie Émilie Juliette Folville (b. 1870) makes her debut in Liège as a concert violinist; she frequently directs her own orchestral pieces and conducts an ancient music concert annually at the Liège Conservatory	Mary Baker Eddy (1821–1910) founds the Church of Christ, Scientist in Boston, MA	Mary Mahoney (1845–1926) becomes the US's first black professional nurse Publication of mathematician Sophie Germain's *Oeuvres philosophiques* (*Philosophical Works*)	For the first time, a US constitutional amendment to grant full suffrage to women is introduced in Congress; it is introduced every year until its passage in 1920	Going by her Native American name, Inshta Theumba ("Bright Eyes"), Susette La Flesche Tibbles (1854–1903) agitates for reform that results in the allotment of reservation land with citizenship rights to individual Native Americans Frances Elizabeth Caroline Willard (1839–1898) becomes president of the WCTU; she also works for reforms in narcotics and prostitution laws and suffrage	**1879**

	General/ Context	Daily Life/ Customs/ Practices	Humanities/ Fine Arts	Occupations	Education
1880	This decade sees the expansion of French colonial power in Africa and Indochina Canned fruits and meats first appear in American markets	Danish law grants married women economic independence Women are denied admission to the bar by the Kentucky legislature The Camille Sée Law permits French girls to receive a secondary school (*lycée*) education	Musicologist Lina Ramann (1833–1912) publishes a life of Franz Liszt (1811–1886) in three volumes (1880–1894) Death of English novelist George Eliot *Helen Keller, American blind and deaf lecturer* Photograph (c. 1900) courtesy Sophia Smith Collection, Smith College	Emily Stowe (1831–1903) becomes the first woman authorized to practice medicine in Canada British journalist Lady Florence Dixie (1857–1905) becomes the first woman war correspondent to cover the Boer War Maria Longworth Nichols Storer (1849–1932) opens Rookwood Pottery, the first art pottery in Ohio German seamstress Margarete Steiff founds Steiff Co., a firm that makes quality stuffed toys	Four women are admitted informally to the Cambridge University examinations; all four win firsts, including Charlotte Angas Scott (1858–1931), who attains eighth place in mathematics, an unprecedented field for women in England Helen Keller (1880–1968), stricken deaf and blind at the age of 19 months, learns to speak through signs at the age of 10 The first French teachers' training school for women is founded at Fontenay-aux-Roses Australian schools for girls provide serious education based on standards equal to those for boys
1881			Matilda Serao's (1856–1927) works, including *Il Ventre di Napoli* (*The Womb of Naples,* 1884) and *Il Paese di Cuccagna* (*The Land of Cockaigne,* 1891), realistically depict Neapolitan life British suffragist Frances Power Cobbe publishes *The Duties of Women*	French female factory workers are permitted to open bank accounts without the consent of their husbands Reputedly the first woman to join the Knights of Labor, Elizabeth Flynn Rodgers (1847–1939) heads the all-woman local assembly no. 1789 in Chicago	The American Association of the Red Cross is organized by Clara Barton, who is chosen its president Formal admission to third-year exam (tripos) at Cambridge University is granted to women, though not their right to receive Cambridge degrees The University of Melbourne is the first Australian university to admit women
1882	Two US judges decide that women may sue their husbands for assault and battery French feminist leader Maria Deraismes becomes the first woman freemason	Sigrid Undset (1882–1949), Norwegian novelist, is famous for are *Kristin Lavransdatter* (1920–1922) Virginia Adeline Woolf (1882–1941) will become a central figure in the Bloomsbury Group		San Francisco lawyer Marion Marsh Todd (1841–post 1913), member of the Greenback Labor party in California, is nominated for state attorney general	Women are denied admission to Harvard Medical School The Harvard Annex is incorporated under the name "The Society for the Collegiate Instruction of Women," with Elizabeth Agassiz (1822–1907) as president; although all classes are taught by Harvard faculty, Harvard does not agree to an official institutional link; only in 1893, when the annex

Performing Arts/ Entertainment/ Sports	Religion/ Philosophy	Science/ Technology/ Discovery	Statecraft/ Military	Reform	
French pianist Arabella Davison Goddard (1836–1922) begins playing in public at the age of six; at eight, she plays before Queen Victoria; by age 12 she has published six waltzes and played at the grand national concerts; at 17, she plays at the Leipzig Gewandhaus, retiring at age 44 Italian violinist Teresina Tua (b. 1866) takes first prize at the Paris Conservatory Emma Cons (1837–1912) opens the Royal Victorian Coffee Music Hall, later known as the Old Vic, where she organizes lectures and concerts and serves coffee rather than alcoholic beverages	Methodist preacher Anna Howard Shaw is ordained by the Methodist Protestant Church, the first woman minister of that denomination; later, recognized as a talented orator, Shaw becomes a leader in the American woman suffrage movement	Alice Bennett, American physician and hospital superintendent, receives a Ph.D. from the University of Pennsylvania, the first ever awarded by that institution to a woman Sarah Ann Hackett Stevenson (1841–1909), American physician and author of science textbooks, writes *The Physiology of Woman*		Alice Bennett (1851–1925) is appointed the first woman superintendent of the women's section of the State Hospital for the Insane in Norristown, PA, where she abolishes use of straitjackets and chains, setting a widely imitated example for the reform of mental institutions Feminists in Copenhagen establish a branch of Josephine Butler's International Abolitionist Federation for the elimination of prostitution	**1880**
Josephine Cohan (1876–1916) performs with her brother George M. Cohan in family vaudeville acts		The Harvard Observatory produces several world-class female astronomers, among them Williamina Paton Fleming (1857–1911), Antonia Maury (1866–1952), Henrietta Leavitt (1868–1921), and Margaret Harwood (1885–)	Czar Alexander II (b. 1818) is assassinated by a woman revolutionary	Susan B. Anthony finances and publishes *The History of Women's Suffrage,* which eventually totals six volumes Harriet Jane Hanson Robinson, former Lowell, MA, millworker, writes *Massachusetts in the Woman Suffrage Movement*	**1881**
Sarah Bernhardt (1844–1923) appears in the title role of *Fédora* wearing a soft felt hat with a center crease American actress Viola Emily Allen (1867–1948) makes her debut in *Esmerelda*, becoming an instant success German dramatic contralto Marianne Brant (Marie Bischof, 1842–1921) creates the role of Kundry in Wagner's *Parsifal*		Ellen Henrietta Swallow Richards writes *The Chemistry of Cooking and Cleaning*  *French actress Sarah Bernhardt (Rosina Bernard)* Photograph (c. 1891) courtesy Sophia Smith Collection, Smith College	Death of Muganzirwazza of Buganda (c. 1817–1882), one of the last of the powerful queen mothers of East Africa; regent for her son Mutesa I, she continued to be a powerful political force even after his coming of age	American suffragist Rachel Foster Avery (1858–1919) directs the campaign for a suffrage amendment in Nebraska Foundation of the World's Women's Christian Temperance Union French suffragist Hubertine Auclert founds the suffragist newspaper	**1882**

	General/ Context	Daily Life/ Customs/ Practices	Humanities/ Fine Arts	Occupations	Education
1882			Clara Barton persuades the US to join the International Red Cross British writer Ellen Ada Bayly (1857–1903) sympathizes with the movements for Irish home rule and greater opportunities for women American poet Emma Lazarus's (1849–1887) sonnet "The New Colossus" is inscribed on the pedestal of the Statue of Liberty		adopts the name "Radcliffe College" in honor of Harvard's first female benefactor, does the link become official Alice Elvira Freeman Palmer (1855–1902) founds the American Association of University Women
1883	First meeting of the Fabian Society of Great Britain	Convicted of murdering her daughter, Emmeline Meaker becomes the first woman ever hanged in Vermont	American author and feminist Lillie Devereux Blake publishes *Woman's Place To-day* Constance Fenimore Woolson (1840–1894), realist author and novelist, publishes *For the Major* Augusta Mary Anne Holmès writes two symphonies, *Lutece* and *Les Argonautes* South African novelist Olive Schreiner (1855–1920), writing under the name Ralph Iron, publishes her *The Story of an African Farm* British author Rhoda Broughton (1840–1920) publishes a variety of novels, including *Belinda* (1883)	Josephine St. Pierre Ruffin (1842–1924) becomes Boston's first black woman municipal judge Textile designer Candace Thurber Wheeler (1827–1923) founds Associated Artists, a New York textile firm entirely made up of women	Augusta Stowe-Gullen (1856–1943) is the first woman to receive a medical degree in Canada Sarah Tyson Heston Rorer (1849–1937) opens the Philadelphia School of Domestic Science Women's medical courses in Russia are closed down; by the mid-1880s most higher education courses for women have been abolished and the role of the feminist Society to Finance Higher Courses for Women is greatly reduced
1884	Manufacture of viscose rayon, the first synthetic fiber, in France	Author of etiquette books and novels of manners, Mary Elizabeth Wilson Sherwood (1826–1903) publishes her most influential and successful work, *Manners and Social Usages* Divorce is reinstituted in France, though the law still favors men	Quirina Alippi-Fabretti (1849–1919), Italian painter, exhibits her work in Turin American author and art critic Elizabeth Robins Pennell (1855–1936) writes her first book, *The Life of Mary Wollstonecraft* Poet and novelist Eunice Tietjens (1884–	Katharine Isabel Hayes Chapin Barrows (1845–1913) is the first woman to work as a stenographer for congressional committees as well as official reporter and editor of the National Conference of Charities and Correction until 1904; she later serves in a similar position for the	A professional nurse, Sophia French Palmer (1853–1920) founds a nurse's training school in New Bedford, MA; she founds and superintends others, and serves as editor in chief of the *American Journal of Nursing*

Engraving of American Jewish poet Emma Lazarus Illustration (c. 1869) courtesy Sophia Smith Collection, Smith College

Performing Arts/ Entertainment/ Sports	Religion/ Philosophy	Science/ Technology/ Discovery	Statecraft/ Military	Reform	
Prussian soprano Therese Malten (1855–1930), creates the role of Kundry in Wagner's *Parsifal* at Bayreuth Italian mezzo-soprano Alice Barbi (b. 1862) makes her debut in Milan				Huda Sh'arawi (1882–1947) forms the first women's association in Egypt in 1910 and establishes the Women's Union in 1924 England passes the Married Women's Property Act	**1882**
Wagner's widow, Cosima Liszt Wagner (1837–1930), creates and manages the Bayreuth Festival "Swedish Nightingale" Jenny Lind is appointed professor of singing at the Royal College of Music in London; cofounder of the London Bach Choir	Hannah Whitall Smith (1832–1911) cofounds the Women's Christian Temperance Union and becomes the first superintendent of its national evangelistic department	With the publication of *Myths of the Iroquois,* Erminnie Adelle Platt Smith (1836–1886) becomes the first woman ever to engage in the field of ethnology American ethnologist Matilda Coxe Evans Stevenson (1849–1915), the first American ethnologist to turn serious attention to children, publishes "Religious Life of the Zuñi Child"		British campaigner Margaret Llewelyn Davies (1861–1943) is the founding secretary of the Women's Cooperative Guild Kageyama Hideko (1865–1927) devotes her life to the plight of women in near-feudal Japan; in 1883 she opens a school for women with her mother, which is later closed because of its liberal policies The Danish Women's Association is torn by controversy between Elisabeth Grundtvig (1856–1945) and Georg Brandes; while Brandes calls for women to enjoy the same sexual freedom as men, Grundtvig argues for the abolition of state control of prostitution and, in the absence of reliable forms of contraception, stricter codes of sexual morality for men	**1883**
Musical comedy star Lillian Russell (Helen Louise Leonard, 1861–1922) makes a hit in London starring in *Polly, or, the Pet of the Regiment;* over the course of her stage career, she becomes particularly well known for her roles in Offenbach and Gilbert and Sullivan operettas,	American reformer and peace advocate Hannah Clark Johnston Bailey (1839–1923) publishes *Reminiscences of a Christian Life*	American physician Elizabeth Blackwell publishes *The Human Element in Sex* Mme. Delong-Tuyssusian invents a device for cutting metal plates Ellen Henrietta Swallow Richards establishes the world's first	The end of Afua Koba's reign; the queen mother of the Asante Empire of West Africa beginning c. 1834, she is in power during a turbulent period of Asante history; she plays an important role in negotiations with the British and in her state's internal political life	Women's suffrage legislation is introduced in Sweden by Frederick Borg, whose bill is rejected with laughter Foundation of the Norwegian Association for the Promotion of Women's Interests Foundation of the Finnish Women's Association led by Baron-	**1884**

	General/ Context	Daily Life/ Customs/ Practices	Humanities/ Fine Arts	Occupations	Education
1884		A reform in the German civil law code establishes a legal majority for German women	1944) publishes *Profiles from China* (1917)	National Prison Association and the Lake Mohonk Conferences on the Indian, the Negro, and International Arbitration	
			British composer Alice Mary Smith Meadows White (1839–1884) is noted for her symphonies and cantatas		
			American author Helen Hunt Jackson (1830–1885) publishes *Ramona*		
			English essayist Violet Paget (1856–1935), writing under the name Vernon Lee, publishes *Euphorion*		
			British playwrights Edith Cooper (1862–1913) and her aunt Katherine Bradley (1846–1914) jointly write and publish plays under the pseudonym Michael Field		
			Civil War diarist Mary Chesnut (1823–1886) revises her journals, which relate the life among the Confederacy elite in Richmond, VA		
1885	Belgium becomes a major colonial power in Africa Madagascar becomes a French protectorate	British colonial rule in Central Africa shifts the balance of labor; men flock to the cities while women and children remain in rural areas, performing the work that used to be done by men as well as their own All women are permitted to vote in local elections in New Zealand	American portrait painter Cecilia Beaux (1863–1942) exhibits her first full-length portrait at the Pennsylvania Academy of Fine Arts Italian artist and author Francesca Alexander (1837–1917), keeps elements of Tuscan and north Italian folk culture alive in her works Eliza Allen Starr (1824–1901), American lecturer on art and religion, publishes *Pilgrims and Shrines* Jeanette Meyers Thurber (1850–1946) secures a charter to develop the American School of Opera and the American Opera Company	Elizabeth Cochrane Seaman, writing as Nellie Bly (1867–1922), becomes a reporter for the *Pittsburgh Dispatch,* reporting on poor working conditions in factories, problems of working girls, slums, divorce, and political corruption	Sophia Jex-Blake establishes the Medical School for Women in her Edinburgh dispensary after a falling-out with colleague Elizabeth Garrett Anderson Throughout the 1880s, Australian universities open their doors to women

Performing Arts/ Entertainment/ Sports	Religion/ Philosophy	Science/ Technology/ Discovery	Statecraft/ Military	Reform	
as well as musical revues A string quintet by prolific British composer Ethel Smyth (1858–1944) is first performed		sanitary chemistry laboratory and travels around the world to teach engineers to set up similar labs	Queen Yaa Akyaa (?–1917), known as the Mother of the Asante, is famous for ruling Ghana through her sons; a trader of great wealth, she is captured by the British and exiled in 1896	ess Alexandra Gripenberg (1859–1913); its demands include equal rights to higher and professional education, suffrage, equal pay for equal work, and "the same moral restrictions in law and custom for men as those that now prevail for women"	**1884**
American violinist Maud Powell (1868–1920) debuts with both the Berlin and New York philharmonics Russian pianist Annette Essipova (1851–1914) is pianist to the Russian imperial court Noted as a gifted actress and singer of *chansons*, Yvette Guilbert (1867–1944) makes her debut first as an actress in 1885, then as a singer in 1890 Polish pianist Natalia Janotha (1856–1932) becomes court pianist to the German emperor British concert soprano Liza Lehmann (1862–1918) makes her debut in England		Florence Augusta Merriam Bailey (1863–1948) becomes the first woman associate member of the American Ornithologists' Union Philanthropist Elizabeth Rowell Thompson contributes $25,000 toward the establishment of one of the first endowments in the US for "the advancement and prosecution of science in its broadest sense" American ethnologist Matilda Coxe Evans Stevenson founds the Women's Anthropological Society of America		British labor activist Alice Sophia Cunninham Acland (1849–1935) founds the Women's Cooperative Guild; its motto is "Of the whole heart cometh hope" and its aim, "Caring and sharing" American Mary Clement Leavitt (1830–1912) founds the New Zealand Women's Christian Temperance Union The Fredrika Bremer Society is founded to "procure and allot endowments to women" and to "better the salaries paid to women" The Danish Women's Association founds the magazine *Women and Society*, edited by Elisabeth Grundtvig	**1885**

	General/ Context	Daily Life/ Customs/ Practices	Humanities/ Fine Arts	Occupations	Education
1885			English accompanist Mary Grant Carmichael (1851–1935) composes popular songs, suites for piano, and the operetta *The Snow Queen* French artist Marie Laurencin (1885–1956) a Cubist, specializes in portraits, lithographs, etchings, and woodcuts Lucy Lane Clifford (?–1929) publishes *Mrs. Keith's Crime* French artist-designer Sonia Delaunay-Terk (1885–1979) uses bright colors and bold geometric patterns Augusta Mary Anne Holmès composes the symphony *Irlande*		
1886	The Vermont legislature passes a bill granting women suffrage British become colonial rulers in the region of modern Kenya Tokyo's Imperial University is established International Workers Day begins as 180,000 workers strike in the US	American philanthropist Ellin Leslie Prince Lowery Speyer (1849–1921) helps establish the New York Skin and Cancer Hospital Sarah Tyson Heston Rorer publishes her renowned *Philadelphia Cookbook* Through the efforts of British abolitionist Josephine Butler and others, the Contagious Disease Prevention acts are repealed	Rose Alnora Hartwick Thorpe (1850–1939) publishes her famous poem "Remember the Alamo" Emilia de Quiroga Pardo Bazán (1852–1921) introduces French naturalism into Spanish literature Noted American art critic, and historian Mariana Alley Griswold Van Rensselaer (1851–1934) publishes *Book of American Figure Painters* British needlewoman Rachel Kay Shuttleworth (1886–1967) devotes her life to the practice, teaching, and appreciation of the art and craft of needlework; becomes well known for her lace and embroidery Frances Eliza Hodgson Burnett (1849–1924), English-born American author, publishes the popular children's book *Little Lord*	Lucretia Blankenburg (1845–1937) helps secure the appointments of Philadelphia's first police matron Anandibai Joshee becomes the first Hindu woman and first Indian woman to become a medical doctor Harriet Hubbard Ayer (1849–1903) founds a large cosmetics company, the first American woman to do so Journalist Nellie Bly is expelled from Mexico for her scathing exposés of the country's poverty and corruption	American nurse Linda Richards (1841–1930) opens Japan's first training school for nurses Russian mathematician Sofia Vasilevna Kovalevskaia (1850–1891) is admitted to the Paris Academy of Science Galician coloratura Anna Maria Aglaia Orgeni (1843–1926) becomes a voice teacher at the Dresden Conservatory The Royal Holloway College is established in England for the higher education of women

Performing Arts/ Entertainment/ Sports	Religion/ Philosophy	Science/ Technology/ Discovery	Statecraft/ Military	Reform	
				Norwegian feminist Gina Krog (1847–1916) founds the Women's Suffrage Society	**1885**
				Physician Martha George Rogers Ripley (1843–1912) establishes a home for unmarried mothers in Minneapolis; in 1887, it is chartered as the Maternity Hospital, offering care to rich and poor, married and unmarried women	**1886**
				Foundation of the Danish Women's Progress Association	
				British labor activist Emma Paterson dies, leaving a legacy that includes the unionizing of women workers in a wide variety of trades—among them upholstery, bookbinding, millinery, dress making, printing—and establishing the Trades Union Congress's Women's Committee	

	General/ Context	Daily Life/ Customs/ Practices	Humanities/ Fine Arts	Occupations	Education
1886			*Fauntleroy* (1886); other works include *Sara Crewe* (1888) and *The Secret Garden* (1911)		
1887	Women's Christian Temperance Union is founded in Victoria, Australia, by American Mary Clement Leavitt (1830–1912)		A famous singing teacher at the Vienna Conservatory, Mathilde Graumann Marchesi (1826–1913) publishes *Marchesi and Music* American author Edna Ferber (1887–1968) counts among her many achievements a Pulitzer Prize, a seat at the famous Algonquin Round Table, and plays and novels that became popular films	Nellie Bly is hired by the *New York World,* where, in disguise, she allows herself to become a victim of exploitation, then reveals herself and writes an exposé; her techniques pave the way for the socially responsible muckrakers and lead to reforms Rita Lobato de Freitas Velho Lopez becomes the first licensed female physician in Brazil; Eloiza Inunza Diaz and Ernestine Barahona Pérez become the first licensed female physicians in Chile Matilde Montoya becomes the first licensed physician in Mexico	Emilie Kempin is the first woman to earn a degree from the University of Zurich, Switzerland Louise Héritte-Viardot (1841–1918) establishes a music school in Berlin after leaving the Hoch Conservatory of Frankfurt, where she had been a singing teacher Nadia Juliette Boulanger (1887–1979) is the first female instructor at the Paris Conservatory; her pupils include Aaron Copland, Virgil Thompson, and Walter Piston
1888	Invention of the gramophone		Louise Blanchard Bethune (1856–1913) is the first female elected to the American Institute of Architects Mme. Marie Félicite Clémence de Reiset produces her opera *Atala* in Paris	German concert singer and teacher Jenny Meyer becomes the proprietor of the Stern Conservatory of Berlin Mathilde Weber publishes *Female Physicians for Women's Diseases,* a	A women's annex to Columbia College (NY) is sanctioned by the trustees Historian Lucy Maynard Salmon (1853–1927) becomes the first history teacher at Vassar College

WOMEN'S RIGHTS IN AUSTRALIA

Australian women are unique in two significant ways: most who originally emigrated to Australia were criminals, shipped there on prison boats from England's overcrowded jails; they remained a scarce resource, outnumbered by almost a third until the 1980s. They have, nonetheless, encountered most of the same social inequalities and deprivations faced by women in the rest of the world. Australians have emphasized traditional women's roles as homemakers at the expense of their education, employment, and political power.

As Sydney and Adelaide industrialized in the second half of the 19th century, emigration to Australia became increasingly middle class and the country started to outgrow its origins as a penal colony. Feminism developed first in the cities, before it moved to the frontier. Reformers like Caroline Chisholm (1808–1877) and the female philanthropists who followed her worked to improve the conditions and status of women. They were supported by numbers of middle-class men, radical liberals who had emigrated to Australia to realize social goals England resisted. In the 1870s, more and more girls began to attend secondary school, and by the 1880s women were entering the university.

Many women's issues soon came under the wing of the Women's Christian Temperance Union, started in 1885 with help from American Mary Clements. A major WCTU focus

Performing Arts/ Entertainment/ Sports	Religion/ Philosophy	Science/ Technology/ Discovery	Statecraft/ Military	Reform	
					1886
British-American actress Lynn Fontanne (1887–1983) enjoys enormous popularity as a stage actress together with her husband, Alfred Lunt; the two, considered America's first couple of the stage, star chiefly in light comedies Austrian violinist Marie Soldat (b. 1864) forms a popular women's string quartette that tours widely	Dr. Meta Howard, Methodist missionary, opens the first hospital for women in Korea, known as the House Where Sick Women Are Cured			Daughter of prominent American suffragist Lucy Stone, Alice Stone Blackwell (1857–1950), feminist and humanitarian radical, graduates from Boston College in 1881, one of only two women, and president of her class; she edits *The Woman's Column,* a collection of items on women's rights circulated free to newspapers In an effort to prevent the repeal of woman suffrage in Utah, Mormon women's rights activist Emmeline Wells (1828–1921) publishes suffrage articles, letters, and editorials and lobbies both in Washington and Utah; despite her efforts, woman suffrage is repealed	**1887**
Lotte Lehmann (1888–1976), German-born American soprano, is famous for her interpretations of German lieder Dame Edith Mary Booth Evans (1888–				Lillie Devereux Blake secures laws providing for the presence of women doctors in mental institutions and women matrons in police stations The Italian parliament rejects a bill granting	**1888**

was women's suffrage—but always with the primary goal of eradicating the evils of alcohol. "Self-reliant" women, they claimed, would lend "a higher tone of social purity" to their country. Australian women gained full voting rights by 1908, earlier than women in Europe and the US, but their primary goal was to use their vote to civilize "the rough masculinity of Australian society," not wield conventional political power.

Australia's emphasis on the special moral status of women resulted in a social conservatism that upheld the nuclear family, which depended on women remaining in traditional roles as a force for social stability. Women's enfranchisement ensured that social control would remain in the hands of the middle class.

One sign of that social control was the long-standing government policy that legally kept women's wages lower than men's until 1967. But as the need to "civilize" Australia became less acute, some of the early social conservatism with regard to women's rights began to erode. Since the 1970s, beginning with the Whitlaw Labor government, some feminist social legislation has been passed, including an equal employment opportunity act, the Family Law Act (which established no-fault divorce), and federal funding for child-care centers and nursing homes. By the 1980s more women than men were enrolled in higher education, though women remained underrepresented in engineering, the sciences, business, and agriculture.

	General/ Context	Daily Life/ Customs/ Practices	Humanities/ Fine Arts	Occupations	Education
1888			American Agnes Repplier (1855–1950) is known for her graceful, witty, and well-informed essays Noted French pianist Cécile Louise Stéphanie Chaminade (1861–1944) composes the successful "ballet symphonie" *Callirhoë* and the "symphonie lyrique" *Les Amazones* Elizabeth Robins Pennell writes a series of travel books, illustrated by her husband, artist Joseph Pennell, beginning with *Our Sentimental Journey Through France and Italy*	work that calls for the admission of women to the medical profession	Establishment of the National Council of Women of the US American pacifist and activist Jane Addams (1860–1935) visits Toynbee Hall in London, the inspiration for Hull House in Chicago

Jane Addams, founder of Hull House
Photograph (c. 1910) courtesy
Sophia Smith Collection, Smith
College

	General/ Context	Daily Life/ Customs/ Practices	Humanities/ Fine Arts	Occupations	Education
1889	British colonize Rhodesia (modern Zambia and Zimbabwe) The first premixed self-rising pancake mix is marketed in the US	The minimum marriage age for Swedish girls is raised from 15 to 17	Active in the Dadaist movement, Swiss painter Sophie Tauber-Arp (1889–1943) will be one of the first artists to take abstraction as a point of departure	Druggist licenses granted to women in Connecticut Born on an Omaha reservation, Susan La Flesche Picotte (1865–1915) becomes a medical missionary for the Women's National Indian Association As a publicity stunt, Nellie Bly is sent	Educator Maria Louise Baldwin (1856–1922) becomes the first African-American woman school principal in Massachusetts; she supervises 12 white teachers and more than 500 children, 98% of them white Rev. John Franklin Goucher offers an endowment to the

Performing Arts/ Entertainment/ Sports	Religion/ Philosophy	Science/ Technology/ Discovery	Statecraft/ Military	Reform	
1976), English actress, will be nominated for Oscars for *The Chalk Garden* (1964), *Tom Jones* (1963), and *The Whisperers* (1967) Mrs. Patrick Campbell (née Beatrice Stella Tanner, 1867–1940), a.k.a. Mrs. Pat, making her stage debut out of financial necessity, begins a successful career in the theater				equal suffrage to women The International Council of Women and the National Council of Women meet at an international congress held in Washington, DC Foundation of the International Council of Women in Zurich; it serves as the umbrella for all women's organizations The Order of the Precious Crown is established by Emperor Meiji (1852–1912) of Japan to recognize Japanese or foreign women for distinguished service; the order is awarded twice a year and is divided into eight classes The Women's Suffrage League is formed in Adelaide, Australia, under the auspices of the WCTU Foundation of the Danish Women's Suffrage Society (Dansk Kvindelig Valgretsforening) The conservative General German Women's Association refuses to send official representatives to the founding meeting of the International Council of Women, because "in Germany, we have to work with great tact and by conservative methods"	**1888**
Viennese-born soprano Emma Juch (1863–1939) founds her own opera company Croatian soprano Ilma di Murska (1836–1889) is famous for her remarkable range of nearly 3 octaves Soprano Emma Eames (1865–1952) debuts at the Grande Opéra de		Sofia Vasilevna Kovalevskaia assumes the chair in mathematics at the University of Stockholm, Sweden, becoming the first woman since Laura Bassi and Maria Gaetana Agnesi in the 18th century to hold a chair at a European university	Taytu Betul (1850–1918) becomes empress of Ethiopia; during her 14-year reign she administers large holdings of land, leads her own army, and helps found and name Addis Ababa, the modern capital; she retires from political life after the death of her husband, Emperor Menilek II, in 1913	Jane Addams and Ellen Gates Starr (1860–1940) found the landmark Chicago settlement house, Hull House, dedicated to community service German reformer Hanna Bieber-Böhm founds the Verein Jugendschutz (Association for the Protection of the Young) in Berlin	**1889**

	General/ Context	Daily Life/ Customs/ Practices	Humanities/ Fine Arts	Occupations	Education
1889				around the world in commercial transportation to challenge the 80-day record of Jules Verne's fictional Phineas Fogg; she completes the trip in 72 days 6 hours and 11 minutes	Woman's College of Baltimore, later Goucher College
				The Women's Catholic Order of Foresters, a fraternal life insurance society, is formed in Illinois	Dr. Emilie Kempin establishes the Women's Law School in New York City
				Elsie Inglis (1864–1917) of Scotland qualifies as a doctor and gains the right to study surgery; she undertakes a career as a military medical officer	American philologist Martha Carey Thomas leads the group of feminists who secure admission of women students to the Johns Hopkins Medical School as a condition of a large gift to its endowment
				Laura Martinez de Carvajales y Camino becomes Cuba's first licensed woman physician; Cecilia Grierson becomes Argentina's first licensed woman physician	
1890	Pans made out of aluminum (lighter and more easily cared for than traditional iron) are invented in Ohio	American and European women begin to wear knickerbockers instead of skirts for bicycle riding	The first woman to report a prize fight, Winifred Sweet Black (1863–1936) becomes a reporter for the San Francisco Examiner	Russian-born Rosa Ginzberg Ginossar (b. 1890) will become the first woman admitted to the Israeli bar and the first woman attorney to practice in that country	Ann Sullivan Macy (1866–1936) teaches the deaf and blind Helen Keller to speak
	The Austrian government withdraws the right of property franchise from women; a public protest is organized by Auguste Fickert (1855–1910)	Clubwomen Ellen Hardin Walworth (1832–1915), Flora Adams Darling (1840–1910), and others found the Daughters of the American Revolution	Death of Mary Edmonia Lewis (1845–past 1909?), the first African-American woman sculptor to receive acclaim in the US	There are 2.7 million African-American girls and women over the age of 10; over one million of them work for wages in the dirtiest and lowest paid work; work conditions are essentially the same as those under slavery	Philippa Garrett Fawcett (1868–1948) attains top mathematical success at Cambridge, but does not receive a degree as the university does not grant women full degrees until 1948
		By 1890, the average white woman born in the US bears no more than four children	British pianist Dora Estella Bright (b. 1863) is best known as a composer of piano concertos and orchestral variations		A teacher-training college for women is established in Egypt
			British artist Marlow Moss (Marjorie Jewell, 1890–1958) will become one of the founding members of the Abstraction-Creation School	In the late 19th and early 20th centuries, Chinese and Japanese prostitutes are brought into the US and indentured on average four or five years without wages	Mrs. Humphrey Ward (1851–1920) establishes University Hall in London, intended as a meeting place for working men and women
			Victoria Woodhull edits The Humanitarian in Britain during the 1890s	Amy Leslie (née Lillie West, 1855–1939) becomes the first female drama critic of the Chicago Daily News	

Performing Arts/ Entertainment/ Sports	Religion/ Philosophy	Science/ Technology/ Discovery	Statecraft/ Military	Reform	
Paris as Juliette in Gounod's *Roméo et Juliette* Swedish soprano Ellen Gulbranson (b. 1863) makes her operatic debut as Brünnhilde in Bayreuth Having debuted under the name of Ada Palmerson in the title role of Massenet's *Manon,* soprano Sibyl Swift Sanderson (1865–1903) debuts in Paris at the Opéra-Comique in his *Esclarmonde,* written especially to feature her upper register; she is praised for her high cadenzas, known as her "Eiffel Tower notes"					**1889**
American stage actress Georgiana Emma Drew Barrymore (1856–1893) achieves her greatest success in *The Senator* Milka Ternina (1863–1940), Croatian dramatic soprano, is named court singer in Munich	American Christian Science leader Augusta Emma Simmons Stetson (1842–1928) becomes the first preacher of the First Church of Christ, Scientist in New York City; in 1891 she organizes the New York City Christian Science Institute American missionary Mary Mills Patrick (1850–1940) becomes the first president of the American College for Girls in Istanbul, Turkey, known as Istanbul Woman's College until 1924 Teresa Martin (1873–1897), author of *Story of a Soul*, becomes a Carmelite nun in Lisieux, France; canonized in 1925, St. Teresa is the patron of foreign missions and of all works for Russia	Upon receiving her DDS from the University of Michigan Dental School, Dr. Ida Gray (1867–1953) becomes the first African-American woman dentist in the US British artist Marianne North (1830–1890), a botanical artist of exceptional skill, traveled alone to remote parts of the world to record plant life	Elizabeth Cady Stanton becomes the president of the National Woman Suffrage Association	Janie Porter Barrett (1865–1948), African-American social welfare leader, founds the Locust Street Social Settlement, one of the first for African Americans in the US Alice Stone Blackwell helps reconcile the American Woman Suffrage Association and the National Woman Suffrage Association; they merge as the National American Woman Suffrage Association Mrs. Humphrey Ward establishes the Anti-Suffrage League, believing that women's interests are already represented under the 1884 reform bill, which enfranchised a broader base of men The (US) National Federation of Women's Clubs is established	**1890**

	General/ Context	Daily Life/ Customs/ Practices	Humanities/ Fine Arts	Occupations	Education
1890					
1891		According to British law, husbands are no longer allowed to kidnap and imprison their wives	Sophia Hayden (1869–1953) is the first woman to earn an MIT degree in architecture; she is the designer of the Women's Building for the Columbian Exposition in Chicago American photographer and author Laura Gilpin (1891–1979) is known for her studies of Navajo Indians	British nurse and traveler Kate Marsden (1859–1931) establishes a leper hospital in Siberia The Philadelphia New Century Club's president, Lucretia Longshore Blankenburg, assists in the selection of two women as factory inspectors	Emilie Kempin-Spyri becomes the first female university lecturer in Zurich Jane Eliza Lathrop Stanford (1828–1905) and her husband, Leland, found Stanford University in California Mary Emma Woolley (1863–1947) becomes the first woman to enter Brown University; she attends classes with men as a guest until separate women's classes open later in the year

Poet Edna St. Vincent Millay
Photograph (c. 1942?) courtesy
Skidmore College Rare Books
and Special Collections

	General/ Context	Daily Life/ Customs/ Practices	Humanities/ Fine Arts	Occupations	Education
1892	Melba toast is named after Australian opera singer Nellie Melba	Mary Elizabeth Wilson Sherwood publishes *The Art of Entertaining* California horticulturist Kate Olivia Sessions (1857–1940) founds Balboa Park in San Diego Lizzie Andrew Borden (1860–1927) is charged with the ax murder of her father and stepmother in Fall River, MA	American composer Amy Marcy Cheney Beach (1867–1944) writes a work for dedication to the Woman's Building at the World's Columbian Exposition in Chicago Publication of *Iola Leroy; or Shadows Uplifted,* by Frances Ellen Watkins Harper, a major work of the black women's renaissance of the 1890s Emilia de Quiroga Pardo Bazán publishes *Cuentos de Marineda* Edna St. Vincent Millay (1892–1950) publishes her first collection, *Renascence and Other Poems,* in 1917 English novelist Ivy Compton-Burnett (1892–1969) writes about power struggles in English country houses		American actress Kate Josephine Bateman (1843–1917) opens her own acting school Women are admitted to Scottish universities on equal terms with men Hassidic scholar Hannah Rachel Werbemacher (1805–1892) holds classes in Jewish law for her followers every Sabbath afternoon

Performing Arts/ Entertainment/ Sports	Religion/ Philosophy	Science/ Technology/ Discovery	Statecraft/ Military	Reform	
				British suffragist Charlotte Despard (1844–1939) is elected a poor law guardian for Kingston upon Thames; this type of office is among the first open to women in England	**1890**
American actress Julia Arthur (1869–1950) becomes famous playing Queen Fortunetta in *The Black Masque of the Red Death;* she plays opposite Maurice Barrymore in *Lady Windemere's Fan* in 1893, and retires in 1924 after forming her own company

The Creole Show is the first black production to feature singing females, Boston, MA | Anna Carpenter Garlin Spencer (1851–1931), American minister, lecturer, and writer on ethics and social problems, becomes minister of the Bell Street Chapel in Providence, RI | | Fanny Baker Ames becomes the first woman factory inspector in Massachusetts

Lydia Kamekeha Liliuokalani (1838–1917) becomes queen of the Hawaiian Islands; deposed in 1893, she is a staunch opponent of annexation | Esther Roper (1870–1938) becomes secretary of the North of England Society for Women's Suffrage, holding the position until 1905

The Australian Women's Christian Temperance Union supports women's suffrage; but the Women's Suffrage League, formed in Sydney, breaks with the WCTU

Josephine Shaw Lowell (1843–1905) cofounds with Maud Nathan the New York Consumers League, the first in the US | **1891** |
| Eminent English contralto Dame Clara Butt (1873–1936) makes her London debut; works written especially for her include Elgar's *Sea Pictures*

Mme. Marie Félicie Clémence de Reiset produces her opera *Mazappa* in Bordeaux

Oscar Wilde (1854–1900) writes the title role of *Lady Windermere's Fan* for English actress Lillie Langtry (1852–1929), known as the Jersey Lily; she often dresses as a man and adopts the name "Mr. Jersey" in order to race horses | | Dr. Anna Broomall (1847–1931) is among the first female members of the Philadelphia Obstetrical Society

Mathematician Christine Ladd-Franklin (1847–1930) introduces her seminal theory of color vision; her work is recognized during her lifetime, but gets little attention in histories of color theory

British Egyptologist and writer Amelia Blanford Edwards (1831–1892) writes and lectures about her studies in Egypt, raises money for the Egyptian Exploration Society, and leaves funds in her will to establish the first chair of Egyptology in Britain | | Publication of *A Voice from the South* by Anna Julia Cooper, an attack on the racism of white women's organizations

African-American journalist and part owner of the *Memphis Free Speech,* Ida Bell Wells-Barnett, a.k.a. "Iola" (1862–1931), writes an impassioned defense of three Memphis men lynched by a white mob; founds antilynching societies, black women's clubs, and a society to combat racial segregation in New York, Boston, Great Britain, and elsewhere, 1892–1895

Led by Finnish teacher Lucina Hagman (1853–1946), the newly founded Union of Women's Societies (Kvinnosaksförbunds | **1892** |

	General/ Context	Daily Life/ Customs/ Practices	Humanities/ Fine Arts	Occupations	Education
1892			A major figure of the Irish renaissance, Lady Isabella Augusta Persse Gregory (1859–1932) meets William Butler Yeats, to whose literary movement she lends financial, social, and artistic support		
			Charlotte Perkins Gilman (1860–1935) publishes her famous short story "The Yellow Wallpaper"		
			British artist Paule Vézelay (Margary Watson-Williams, b. 1892) spends her life painting in Paris and England, where she records the country as it lives through the Second World War		
1893		New Zealand becomes the first nation to grant women's suffrage	Birth of Dorothy Parker (1893–1967), author and critic known for her sharp wit; member of the Algonquin Round Table and an active campaigner for civil rights	Adelaide Sophia (Hunter) Hoodless helps found Canada's National Council for Women and becomes its first treasurer	Dorothea Beale (1831–1906) establishes St. Hilda's Hall in Oxford as a branch of St. Hilda's College for Women Teachers, which she founded in Cheltenham in 1885; it joins Oxford University in 1901
			German reformers Helene Lange (1848–1930) and Gertrud Bäumer (1873–1954) found the influential feminist journal *Die Frau*	Bertha Honoré Palmer (1849–1918) organizes Chicago millinery workers and becomes vice president of the Chicago Civic Federation	By this date, over half of all students in New Zealand universities are women
			Kentuckian Mildred Hill publishes her song "Good Morning to All"; Robert H. Coleman adds a second verse beginning "Happy birthday to you"	Medical adviser to Queen Min of Korea, Lillias Stirling Horton Underwood (1851–1921) is a close friend and confidante to the royal consort; *Fifteen Years Among the Top-knots* appears in 1904	
			British composer Clara Kathleen Barnett Rogers (1844–1931) publishes *The Philosophy of Singing*	Brazilian-born midwife and author Marie Josefina Mathilda Durocher (1809–1893) becomes a leader in her profession in Brazil	
			Birth of Dorothy Sayers (1893–1957), best known for her detective novels featuring Lord Peter Wimsey;		

Quaker Oats packing room
Photograph (1893) courtesy Sophia Smith Collection, Smith College

Performing Arts/ Entertainment/ Sports	Religion/ Philosophy	Science/ Technology/ Discovery	Statecraft/ Military	Reform	

Eleanora Duse, Italian actress
Photograph (1902) courtesy Sophia
Smith Collection. Smith College

1892

Unionen) concentrates its energies on suffrage

Victoria Matthews (1861–1907) and Maritcha Lyons create in Brooklyn and Manhattan the first clubs led exclusively by black women, the Woman's Loyal Union

---

1893

The first cross-country skiing competition for women takes place in Sweden

Actress Mary G. Shaw (1854–1929), an ardent feminist, appears in an all-woman production of Shakespeare's *As You Like It* in New York City

Italian tragedian Eleanora Duse (1859–1924), one of Europe's great thespians whose reputation rivals Sarah Bernhardt's, makes her New York City debut

American violinist Maud Powell (1868–1920) is invited to perform at the Chicago World's Fair and to read a paper on "Women and Music" at one of the fair's musical congresses

Psychologist Milicent Washburn Shinn (1858–1940) publishes *Notes on the Development of a Child*

The British explorer and anthropologist Mary Henrietta Kingsley (1862–1900) sails to West Africa to collect and research new species of freshwater fish

Queen Liliuokalani of Hawaii is deposed; she formally renounces her royal claims two years later

Fannie Barrier Williams (1855–1944) is responsible for the formation of the National League of Colored Women

May Eliza Wright Sewall heads the World's Congress of Representative Women, held in conjunction with the Columbian Exposition in Chicago; at the exposition six African–American women accuse the congress of indifference to the history of African–American women

Auguste Fickert founds the General Austrian Women's Association

Ida Wells helps organize a women's committee to produce a brochure entitled "The Reason Why the Colored American Is Not in the World's Columbian Exposition," to be distributed at the World's Fair in Chicago

	General/ Context	Daily Life/ Customs/ Practices	Humanities/ Fine Arts	Occupations	Education
1893			she also produces works of theology and scholarship Feminist Sarah Grand (pseudonym of Frances Elizabeth McFall, 1862–1943) publishes *The Heavenly Twins,* exposing many sensitive aspects of married life, sexuality, and moral hypocrisy		
1894			British feminist Violet Hunt (1866–1942) publishes a number of novels including *The Maiden's Progress* Kate O'Flaherty Chopin (1851–1904), is best known for *The Awakening* (1899), a classic of American feminist fiction Harriet Hosmer's last major work, a statue of Queen Isabella, is unveiled in San Francisco		Bryn Mawr elects Martha Carey Thomas its first woman president Mary Woolley and Anne Tillinghast Weeden receive the first A.B. degrees ever awarded to women by Brown University The Russian chief of police reports that 42% of the 114 Russian women studying abroad are "disloyal"
1895		Ex-slave Lucy Terry Prince becomes the first woman to address the Supreme Court of the US, successfully defending a land claim Australian women's entry into universities and professions is limited by a judicial decision declaring that women are not "persons"; any piece of legislation that does not specifically name them, bars them	Ida Minerva Tarbell (1857–1944) publishes *A Short Life of Napoleon Bonaparte* that sells 100,000 copies Publication of *America the Beautiful* by Katharine Lee Bates (1859–1929) American poet Babette Deutsch's (b. 1895) works include such collections as *Poetry in Our Time* (1952)	Lillian D. Wald (1867–1940) founds a nurses' settlement on Henry Street in New York City; by 1913 the Henry Street Visiting Nurses' Service employs 92 nurses divided into specialized staffs, who make over 200,000 visits annually in Manhattan and the Bronx	The General German Women's Association grants Hildegard Ziegler a fellowship, enabling her to become the first German woman to pass the gymnasium *Abitur* (final exam) Through the efforts of Hungarian feminists, Hungarian universities open their doors to women Czar Nicholas II increases quotas for the

Performing Arts/ Entertainment/ Sports	Religion/ Philosophy	Science/ Technology/ Discovery	Statecraft/ Military	Reform	
				British pioneer of workhouse reform, Louisa Twining (1820–1912) "retires" after years of active campaigning for social reform	**1893**
Paris-born pianist Clotilde Kleeberg (1866–1909) is made Officier de l'Académie, a rare professional honor Jules Massenet writes *Thais* for American soprano Sibyl Sanderson Maud Powell forms the Maud Powell String Quartet, which tours the US widely for four years Scottish composer Helen Hopekirk (b. 1856) writes a number of orchestral pieces	Rose Hawthorne Lathrop, a.k.a. Mother Mary Alphonsa (1851–1926), and her husband, George Parsons Lathrop, Roman Catholic convert, publish a history of the Sisters of the Visitation, *A Story of Courage*	Florence Bascom becomes the first woman elected as a fellow of the Geological Society of America Charlotte Angas Scott publishes *An Introductory Account of Certain Modern Ideas in Plane Analytical Geometry*		The Federation of German Women's Associations is founded Ellen Gates Starr, cofounder of Hull House, founds the Chicago Public School Art Society in an effort to keep great art before the eyes of slum dwellers World's Young Women's Christian Association (WYWCA) is established in Geneva The Australian Women's Suffrage League gathers 11,000 signatures on a suffrage petition The Icelandic Women's Association gathers support for the foundation of an Icelandic university	**1894**
Birth of Kirsten Flagstad (1895–1962), Norwegian opera singer, considered the greatest Wagnerian soprano of her day American soprano Suzanne Adams (1872–1953) makes her professional debut at the Paris Opera as Juliette; in 1898, she sings at Covent Garden in London, and in 1899 makes her US debut at the Metropolitan		Grace Chisolm Young earns a doctoral degree in mathematics at the University of Göttingen, the first doctoral degree in any subject awarded in the normal way by a German university to a woman Nature writer and bird protectionist Mabel Osgood Wright (1859–1934) publishes *Birdcraft; A Field Book of Two Hundred Song, Game, and Water Birds*	Queen Min of Korea is assassinated by Japanese soldiers	Octavia Hill (1838–1912) founds the preservation society the National Trust for Places of Historical Interest and National Beauty Norwegian feminist Gina Krog's (1847–1916) National Women's Suffrage Association takes root in Norway, moving away from economics and education toward political and moral concerns	**1895**

	General/ Context	Daily Life/ Customs/ Practices	Humanities/ Fine Arts	Occupations	Education
1895		Foundation of the National Federation of Afro-American Women; Margaret Washington is its first president	Candace Thurber Wheeler (1827–1923) publishes the essay "Interior Decoration as a Profession for Women"		St. Petersburg course and establishes the Medical Institute for Women that leads to full medical qualification
		Establishment of the Russian Women's Mutual Benefit Society; fosters a feminist consciousness among its members, but does not actively fight for women's rights	Welsh artist Gwendolyn Mary John (1876–1939) is famous for her austere portraits of women		
1896	The first modern Olympics are held in Athens The earliest trading stamps, issued by S&L, become available in the US	Fannie Merritt Farmer (1857–1915) publishes the influential *Boston Cooking School Cook Book,* an innovative work in which all measurements are precise and all recipes have been carefully tested to produce identical results every time	Julia Hänel von Cronenthal (1839–1896) composes four symphonies and 22 piano sonatas Amy Marcy Cheney Beach's (1867–1944) Gaelic Symphony is performed by the Boston Symphony Orchestra The world's first woman director, Frenchwoman Alice Guy-Blanché (1873–1968), makes her first film, *The Fairy in the Cabbage Patch* American novelist Sarah Orne Jewett (1849–1909) publishes her masterpiece, *The Country of the Pointed Firs*	The New York City health board enforces a law regulating women in mercantile establishments After a 20-year absence, German soprano Karoline Wichern (1836–1906) returns to choral direction in prisons British artist, designer, and architect Mary Watts (1850–1937) runs a craft school and a business, Terracotta Arts, in Compton, England	Oxford University admits women but refuses to grant them degrees The University of Edinburgh accepts women students

HARRIET HOSMER

"She emancipates the eccentric life of a perfectly 'emancipated female' from all shadow of blame by the purity of hers," wrote Elizabeth Barrett Browning about her friend, the American-born sculptor Harriet Goodhue Hosmer (1830–1908). A friendly, witty, and enormously talented artist, Hosmer numbered British aristocrats, famous authors, and even Continental royalty among her friends and patrons. Accustomed to working in mannish trousers, shirt, and jacket, her clipped hair under a beret to keep out the marble dust, Hosmer's "eccentricity" had its roots in her early education. As a rough-and-tumble child,

she was sent to a school run by liberal women who encouraged her to turn her interest in mechanics and talent for clay modeling into the serious profession of sculpting. Hosmer set up a studio and learned anatomy from her physician father. She then traveled to St. Louis to study privately, since women could not attend medical school at that time.

In 1852, her father sent her to Rome under the care of actress Charlotte Cushman (1816–1876), a family friend, to work with the English sculptor John Gibson. Gibson's tutelage and the sculptural wealth of Rome helped her develop her technique.

Performing Arts/ Entertainment/ Sports	Religion/ Philosophy	Science/ Technology/ Discovery	Statecraft/ Military	Reform	
After her appearance at the Théâtre de la Monnaie, Brussels, French soprano Georgette Leblanc (d. 1941) tours the Continent giving affecting song recitals in costume Augusta Mary Anne Holmès writes *La Montagne Noir,* an opera unsuccessfully mounted by the Grand Opera of Paris				African-American women organize the Women's Era Club, a response to the lynchings and sexual abuse of black women of this period	**1895**
				German feminist leaders Lida Heymann and Anita Augsburg Photograph (c. 1916) courtesy Sophia Smith Collection, Smith College	
Lilli Lehmann (1848–1929) makes her debut in Prague, Danzig, and Leipzig, and in the same year receives a life appointment at the Royal Opera in Berlin American silent screen actress Lillian Diana Gish (1896–1993) will make her name in such classic films as *Birth of a Nation* Maude Adams (1872–1953) forms a partnership with playwright James Barrie		Florence Bascom is the first woman to be appointed assistant geologist with the US Geological Survey; she is later promoted to geologist and assigned the Midatlantic Piedmont area Astronomer Mary Watson Whitney's (1847–1970) observation of Nova Aurigae paves the way for the study of other variable stars	Yaa Asantewaa (c. 1850–1921), queen mother of one of the Asante states of Ghana, and her forces fight the British troops until her capture After the proclamation of the protectorate in 1896, the colonial government in Sierra Leone popularizes the practice of allowing women to hold the office of paramount chief	German feminists Anita Augsburg (1857–1943), Lida Gustava Heymann (1868–1943), Minna Cauer (1841–1922), and Marie Stritt (1856–1928) mount a campaign against the legislature's cavalier disregard of women's rights The National League of Colored Women elects Mary Church Terrell its first president Salvation army leader Maud Charlesworth Booth (1865–1948) launches the Volunteers of America	**1896**

A friend in St. Louis secured her a commission from the St. Louis Mercantile Library for the life-size statue Beatrice Cenci. Her next work, Puck, became a great success when the prince of Wales bought a replica; she eventually sold 50 copies for $1000 each.

Public recognition followed when she won a commission from the state of Missouri to create a huge statue of Sen. Thomas Hart Benton. As her successes made her financially independent, she lived more and more in England, with occa-

sional forays to Rome. Her last major work, a statue of Queen Isabella commissioned by the city of San Francisco, was unveiled in 1894. In 1900, she returned to Watertown, MA, devoting much of her time to perfecting a perpetual-motion device. Hosmer was the first and probably the most successful of the mid-19th-century American women to become sculptors; her statues were much admired by contemporaries, one of whom credited her with creating "some of the purest modern examples of Greek art."

	General/ Context	Daily Life/ Customs/ Practices	Humanities/ Fine Arts	Occupations	Education
1897	Radio transmission over long distances is achieved by Guglielmo Marconi		Jessie Willcox Smith (1863–1935), illustrates Longfellow's *Evangeline* Charlotte Porter (1857–1942) helps found the American Music Society, the American Drama Society, and the Drama League of America American political radical Josephine Frey Herbst (1897–1969) explores the decay of capitalism in such novels as *Pity Is Not Enough* (1933) American novelist Willa Cather (1873–1947) begins her career as a newspaperwoman in Pittsburgh Mother Mary Alphonsa publishes a memoir of her father, *Memories of Hawthorne*	Sophonisba Preston Breckenridge (1866–1948) is the first woman to be admitted to the Kentucky bar Sophie Levy Lyons (1848–1924) abandons a successful career as a famous international swindler and bank robber to become the first society columnist in the US	Maria Louise Baldwin is invited to be the first woman to deliver the annual Washington's birthday memorial address before the Brooklyn Institute The University of Vienna allows women to matriculate Alice McLellan Birney (1858–1907) becomes the first president of the National Congress of Mothers, designed to teach the importance of child-care education Foundation of the International Catholic Association of Homes for the Protection of Girls in Fribourg, Switzerland
1898	Spanish-American War begins Foundation of Peking University Foundation of the American National Institute of Arts and Letters Extension of the rights of Russian women doctors	George Bernard Shaw's 1898 play *Mrs. Warren's Profession*, which concerns a former prostitute whose earnings allow her to have her daughter raised in middle-class refinement, opens to a storm of public protest in New York and closes soon after; it is not produced in Britain until 1925 Union soldier Sarah Emma Edmonds is buried with full military honors in the Grand Army of the Republic Cemetery in Houston, TX, the only woman there	Photographer Berenice Abbott (b. 1898) is known for her photographs of famous people and for her studies of New York City and the Atlantic coast Ethel Smyth composes the opera *Fantasio* with her own libretto American writer Gertrude Franklin Horn Atherton (1857–1948) publishes *The Californians* Queen Liliuokalani of Hawaii writes the song "Aloha Oe" Australian novelist Elizabeth von Arnim (1866–1941) writes about her life married to a Pomeranian count in *Elizabeth and Her German Garden* The memoirs of the Scottish writer Elizabeth Grant are published posthumously as *Memoirs of a Highland Lady*	Birth of Amelia Earhart, "Lady Lindy, First Lady of the Air"; she founds the "Ninety-Nines," an international organization of licensed women pilots, and garners many honors, including the French Legion of Honor, the Distinguished Flying Cross, and the National Geographic Gold Medal	The Women's Medical College of the New York Infirmary hands over its function to Cornell University Medical College when it admits women on equal terms Milicent Washburn Shinn receives a Ph.D. from the University of California; she is the first woman and only the 11th person to receive that degree from the university French pianist, violinist, teacher, conductor, and composer Juliette Folville becomes professor of pianoforte at the Liège Conservatory

Performing Arts/ Entertainment/ Sports	Religion/ Philosophy	Science/ Technology/ Discovery	Statecraft/ Military	Reform	
Finnish dramatic soprano Aïno Ackté-Jalander (1876–1944) makes her debut in Paris as Marguerite; she later makes her US debut in the same role at the Metropolitan in New York City; other roles include Juliet, Ophelia, Gilda, Nedda, Elsa, Elisabeth, Sieglinde			The French Socialist Congress demands equal political and economic rights for women; the first political party to do so, it does not succeed	Marguerite Durand founds the feminist paper *La fronde,* the first daily entirely produced by women	**1897**
American suffragist Annie Smith Peck (1850–1935), following her sensational ascent of the Matterhorn in 1895, becomes the first woman to climb Mount Orizaba; a pioneer in women's mountaineering, she is one of the founders of the Alpine Club in 1902				Formation of the National Union of Women's Suffrage Societies (NUWSS) under the leadership of British feminist Millicent Garrett Fawcett

Because of low recruitment levels, the Danish Women's Suffrage Society and the Women's Progress Association are absorbed into the Danish Women's Association | |
| Dorothy Gish (1898–1968) plays in the famous *Orphans of the Storm,* in which she stars with her sister, Lillian

Comic actress Clara Fisher's (1811–1898) career encompasses 72 years of male and female roles | Nehanda of Zimbabwe (c. 1863–1898), priestess and prophetess, one of a long line of Zimbabwean religious leaders, leads the Shona in a revolt against the white colonizers of Cecil Rhodes, but is captured; before her execution, she is pressured to convert to Christianity, but she refuses | Canadian cardiologist Maude Elizabeth Seymour Abbott (1869–1940) is appointed curator of the medical museum at McGill University; she founds and edits *The Bulletin of the International Association of Medical Museums*

Mabel Osgood Wright helps found the Connecticut Audubon Society

Polish-French chemist Marie Skłodowska Curie (1867–1934) and Pierre Curie discover polonium and radium; they also discover that thorium gives off radioactivity, a term coined by Marie | Anita Newcomb McGee (1864–1940) is the first woman appointed surgeon in the US Army; she later founds the Army Nurse Corps as a permanent part of the army

Austrian Empress Elizabeth (1837–1898) is assassinated by Italian anarchist Luigi Luccheni

China's Dowager Empress Tz'u Hsi exiles the emperor when he attempts to institute Westernizing reforms, throws his favorite concubine down a well, and arrests his associates, having them cut in half at the waist | In *Women and Economics,* pioneering American feminist economic theorist Charlotte Perkins Gilman (1860–1935) argues for female economic independence; she is among the first to propose centralized nurseries and cooperative kitchens to free women from domestic drudgery

Foundation of the moderate Danish Women's Associations' Suffrage Federation (Danske Kvindeforeningers Valgrets Forbund)

Death of Eleanor Marx (1855–1898), a leading figure in the British Socialist movement | **1898** |

Polish scientist Marie Curie
Photograph (1903) courtesy Culver Pictures, Inc.

	General/ Context	Daily Life/ Customs/ Practices	Humanities/ Fine Arts	Occupations	Education
1898			Elizabeth Cady Stanton publishes her autobiography, *Eighty Years and More*		
1899	Boer War (1899–1902) begins	Passage of Iceland's Married Women's Property Act	Mary Antin (1881–1949) publishes *From Polotzk to Boston* American Alice Barber Stephens (1858–1932) wins a gold medal at a London exhibition of women's work for her drawings for George Eliot's *Middlemarch* Lizette Woodworth Reese's (1856–1935) "Tears" is published in *Scribner's Magazine* Elizabeth Dorothea Cole Bowen (1899–1973) is famed for her explorations of the lives of upper-middle-class characters Eliza Allen Starr publishes *The Three Archangels and the Guardian Angel in Art* for which she is awarded a medallion by Pope Leo XIII Irish novelist Edith Oenone Somerville (1861–1949) and her cousin Violet Martin (1862–1915, writing as Martin Ross) collaborate on many novels	Medical certification is open to women in Prussia and elsewhere in the German Reich The last bandit to rob a stagecoach in the US is Pearl Hart (1878–1925) Isabel Eaton publishes an essay on domestic service in W.E.B. Dubois's study *The Philadelphia Negro*, revealing that 91% of black women workers in Pennsylvania were employed as domestic servants The experiences of Abby (1828–1893), Georgeanna (1833–1906), and Jane Stuart Woolsey (1830–1891) as relief workers during the American Civil War are chronicled in *Letters of a Family During the War for the Union*	The International Council of Nurses is founded in London; its mission is to raise internationally the professional standing of nurses
1900	Boxer Rebellion against foreign influence in China, supported by the empress dowager		Portraitist Ellen Gertrude Emmet Rand (1875–1941) establishes her studio in New York City Lady John Douglas Scott (née Alicia Ann Spottiswoode, 1811–1900) is best known for composing "Annie Laurie" Welsh artist Gwendolyn Mary John (1876–1939), known for her portraits of women, exhibits her work with the New English Art Club in London	The National Women's Business Association opens its first office in New York City Disguised as a boy, Winifred Sweet Black is the first outside journalist and only woman to enter Galveston, TX, after the tidal wave and storm of 1900 that killed 7000 people After a highly successful career, Galician coloratura soprano Marcella Sembrich manages her own op-	Dr. Yayoi Yoshoika establishes Japan's first medical school for women, the Tokyo Women's Medical College Katharine Lucinda Sharp (1865–1914) establishes the Illinois State Library Adah B. Samuels Thoms (1863?–1943) graduates from the Woman's Infirmary and School of Therapeutic Massage, the only African American in a class of 30

American sculptor and feminist Alice Morgan Wright Photograph (c. 1900) courtesy Sophia Smith Collection, Smith College

Performing Arts/ Entertainment/ Sports	Religion/ Philosophy	Science/ Technology/ Discovery	Statecraft/ Military	Reform	
					1898

Pianist Katherine Ruth Heyman (d. 1944) makes her debut in Boston; she acquires an international reputation as an interpreter of Scriabin

As a pupil at the Paris Conservatory, soprano Marguerite Jeanne Frère (b. 1879) wins two opera prizes and debuts at the Paris Opera

American soprano Ellen Beach Yaw (1868–1947) is sometimes known as Lark Ellen

Margaret Anne Cusack (1829–1899), an Irish Poor Clare, is a champion of human rights and defender of the poor

Annie Wood Besant (1847–1933), member of the Fabian Society, works among the poor in England; upon meeting Mme. Blavatsky, she becomes a theosophist, founding Central Hindu College in Benares, India

Fanny Bullock Workman (1859–1925) and her husband make the first of seven expeditions into the northwest Himalayas to explore the Karakorum range; they map and photograph the area, and keep records of altitude, ice, snow, and glacier movement, temperatures, and the effects of high altitude living on the human body

German revolutionary socialist Rosa Luxemburg (1870–1919) becomes the leader of the German Socialist party

Egyptian lawyer and judge Qasim Amin writes *The Emancipation of Women*, an influential argument for women's rights

Temperance reformer Carry Nation (1846–1911), armed with bricks, hatchets, and hymns, enters a saloon, sings, shouts imprecations and biblical passages, and smashes bottles, furniture, and decorations

Marie Stritt (1856–1928) becomes president of the Federation of German Women's Associations, leading the movement distinctly to the left

African-American suffragist Lottie Wilson Jackson proposes a resolution at NAWSA that addresses the segregation on trains that forces black women to ride in the smoking cars; her proposal is defeated

"Mrs. Greenleaf, the girls are in!" Susan B. Anthony with Jean B. Greenleaf on the day coeducation is approved for the University of Rochester, 1900 Photograph courtesy Sophia Smith Collection, Smith College

| | | | | | **1900** |

London-born cellist May Henrietta Mukle (b. 1880), child prodigy, plays in a trio with violinist Maud Powell and Anna Mukle

Italian soprano Lina Cavalieri (1874–1944) debuts in *Pagliacci*, becoming an internationally popular performer

At age 40, Mary Morris Vaux Walcott (1860–1940) is the first woman to climb Mt. Stephen in British Columbia

Katherine Augusta Westcott Tingley (1847–1929) founds the famous Utopian community at Point Loma, CA; originally intended as a Theosophical school and community, it soon expands in scope, becoming a cultural mecca for artists, poets, writers, horticulturalists, and others

Ethnologist Mary Kingsley (1862–1900) dies of typhoid fever in South Africa while nursing soldiers during the Boer War

Dr. Florence Keller becomes the first female physician in New Zealand; she is subsequently appointed physician to the Maoris and their royal family

Death of Natélégé (c. 1855–c. 1900), queen of the Nzakara of the Central African Republic, the first woman of her people to be acclaimed a chieftain in her own right

Irish-born Sarah Grand (Francis Elizabeth Bellenden McFall, 1845–1943), suffragist, writer, and feminist, is mayor of Bath for six terms

Susan B. Anthony chooses Carrie Chapman Catt (1859–1947) as her successor as president of NWSA; Catt is mainly responsible for the passage of the 19th Amendment

Dr. Elsie Inglis sets up the first maternity center in Scotland run by two women, the Elsie Inglis Hospital

International Ladies Garment Workers Union (ILGWU) is founded

	General/ Context	Daily Life/ Customs/ Practices	Humanities/ Fine Arts	Occupations	Education
1900			British writer and il-lustrator Beatrix Potter (1866–1943) privately publishes *The Tale of Peter Rabbit* Birth of best-selling novelist Taylor (Jane Miriam Taylor) Cald-well (1900–1985) Photographer Imogen Cunningham (1883–1976) begins her 75-year career	era company in Ger-many Zurich University graduate Agnes Hacker becomes the first fe-male physician hired by the Berlin police force Laura Esther Rodriguez-Dulauto becomes Peru's first licensed woman physi-cian Minna (1878–1948) and Ada (1875–1960) Everleigh open the Everleigh Club, a lav-ish 50-room brothel in Chicago's Levee	Norwegian violinist Maia Bang (1877–1940) founds a music school in Oslo, where she made her debut; she is the author of several methods for violin A pupil of Kullak, Tausig, and Liszt, pia-nist Martha Remmert founds the Liszt Acad-emy for Piano in Ber-lin Full matriculation in the University of Freiburg, Germany, opens to women
1901	 *Susie King Taylor, former slave, Civil War nurse, and memoirist* Photograph (1902) courtesy Sophia Smith Collection, Smith College		American composer Carrie Jacobs Bond (1862–1946) publishes *Seven Songs as Un-pretentious as the Wild Rose* Myrtle Reed (1874–1911) publishes *The Spinster Book,* which puts forward the com-pletely helpless female as a model Alice Cadwell Hegan Rice (1870–1942) is best known for *Mrs. Wiggs of the Cabbage Patch* Magda Portal (b. 1901) is the foremost poet of Peru	Carrie Jacobs Bond sets up her Bond Shop in which she does her own publishing and selling E. Cora Hind (1861–1942) becomes the agricultural journalist for the Winnipeg *Free Press* May (Beatrice Des-mond) Churchill, a.k.a. May Lambert, "Chicago May," and "Queen of the Bad-gers," plans the great robbery of the Parisian American Express	Mary Emma Woolley becomes president of Mount Holyoke Col-lege; she improves the famous women's col-lege's financial, intel-lectual, and academic credentials with re-markable efficiency Mother Mary Al-phonsa founds the Rosary Hill Home, tended by the Servants of Relief for Incurable Cancer, in West-chester, NY
1902			Susie King Taylor, a former slave, publishes her memoirs, *Reminis-cences of My Life in Camp with the 33rd*	Polish-born cosmeti-cian Helena Rubin-stein (1872–1965) starts her skin-care business in Melbourne,	Southern educator Martha McChesney Berry (1866–1942) opens the Boy's Indus-trial School, later

---

HOW BEAUTIFUL ARE THE FEET

Foot binding, the tradition of maiming the feet of Chinese women, endured from about 1100 to 1900—surely one of history's most dramatic examples of male dominance. Aristo-cratic women manifested their quality by being unable to walk without assistance. Confined to their chambers, entirely dependent on their families and servants, women with tiny feet embodied a complex of social, economic, and sexual ideas that signified more than masculine control of female bodies.

A young girl between the ages of four and eight would have all four little toes bent under each foot and pulled toward the heel by tight bands of cotton or silk. The big toe of each foot was left alone. Often toes putrefied and dropped off. Blood poisoning and other infections threatened the child whose cir-

Performing Arts/ Entertainment/ Sports	Religion/ Philosophy	Science/ Technology/ Discovery	Statecraft/ Military	Reform	
	 *Hattie Tom, Apache* Photograph (1899) courtesy Sophia Smith Collection, Smith College			Radical feminists break away from the Danish Women's Association and form the National League for Women's Suffrage American "Mother" Ella Reeve Bloor (1862–1951) joins the Socialist party; she later helps to organize the Communist Labor party Bertha Lutz organizes the Brazilian Federation for the Advancement of Women and is instrumental in achieving the franchise for women in 1932	**1900**
Hungarian contralto Margarete Matzenauer (b. 1881) makes her debut in Strasbourg; her career extends to solo appearances with orchestras, recitals, films, and teaching	Methodist preacher Alma Bridwell White (1862–1946) claims never to prepare a sermon, but to choose a text and "wait for the heavenly dynamite to explode"; she organizes an independent fundamentalist sect, the Methodist Pentacostal Church, which becomes the Pillar of Fire Church in 1917; the sect stresses primitive Methodist tenets, including the ordination of both men and women; she becomes the church's senior bishop, the first female bishop of any Christian church	Matilda Stevenson publishes her major work, *The Zuñi Indians: Their Mythology, Esoteric Fraternities, and Ceremonies* While in Havana, Claire Louise Maass (1876–1901), a nurse in Florida, Cuba, and the Philippines during the Spanish-American War, volunteers to undergo experiments in yellow fever research; she submits to the bite of a culex mosquito and dies	Hannah Kent Schoff (1853–1940), pioneer for juvenile justice, is the first woman asked to speak before the Canadian Parliament	Feminist and organizer of Indian reform Amelia Stone Quinton (1833–1926) becomes one of the founders of the National Indian Association Foundation of the Women's Club of Prague, the first recorded manifestation of Czech feminism German feminist Gertrud Bäumer begins publication of her great history of the international women's rights movement, *Handbuch der Frauenbewegung* (*Handbook of the Women's Movement*), 1901–1906	**1901**
Self-taught Spanish contralto Maria Gay (1879–1943) debuts in Brussels as Carmen on only five days' notice;	A pioneer in economical foreign missions programs, Lucy Whitehead McGill Waterbury Peabody	Kate Olivia Sessions (1857–1948) introduces new varieties of plants for cultivation in the San Diego area,	International Woman's Conference in Washington, DC, creates a committee for suffrage	Jane Addams publishes *Democracy and Social Ethics*	**1902**

culation was so hampered. As the foot, its arch permanently destroyed, became a withered stump, the excruciating pain intensified even if the bindings were loosened. Walking unaided became impossible. After several years, the feet no longer hurt quite so much, but they never again functioned normally.

Feet perfectly maimed according to prescribed custom, feet perpetually painful, provided Chinese culture with a potent erotic symbol. These deformities signified beauty, elegance, feminine dependence, wealth, high social status, virtue, refinement, and physical allure. Sexual activities in which women with bound feet participated seem inevitably to have included men's unwrapping and fondling the feet—their very smell was said to be a sexual stimulant; considering the pain, the stimulus was also sadistic. The practice was banned in 1934.

	General/ Context	Daily Life/ Customs/ Practices	Humanities/ Fine Arts	Occupations	Education
1902			*United States Colored Troop* American painter Isabel Bishop (1902–1988) is known for her paintings and drawings of women in everyday settings British children's author Edith Nesbit (1858–1924) publishes *The Five Children and It*	Australia; by 1917 she has salons in London, Paris, Philadelphia, San Francisco, and Boston Because the Society of Swiss Painters, Sculptors, and Architects accepts women only as nonparticipating members, female artists in Switzerland form the Gesellschaft Schweizevischer Malerinnen, Bildhauerinnen u. Kunstgewerblerinnen (Society of Swiss Women Painters, Sculptors, and Arts and Crafts Workers)	called the Mount Berry School for Boys Katherine Pettit (1868–1936) and May Stone open the Hindman Settlement School in Kentucky, which teaches household skills and handicrafts to the mountain families
1903	The Prix Goncourt, the most sought-after and respected French literary prize, is established The Wright Brothers make the first successful flight in an airplane at Kitty Hawk, NC  American author Gertrude Stein, taken while she was a medical student at Johns Hopkins c. 1900 Photograph courtesy Sophia Smith Collection, Smith College	An outbreak of typhoid fever in New York City is traced to "Typhoid Mary" Mallon (1870?–1938), a carrier of the disease who takes jobs handling food, often under an assumed name; she refuses to stop and in 1915 is placed under detention until her death in 1938	Mary Hunter Austin (1868–1934), publishes *The Land of Little Rain,* a sympathetic treatment of Native Americans Kate Douglas Smith Wiggin (1856–1923) publishes *Rebecca of Sunnybrook Farm* Gertrude Stein (1874–1946) studied psychology at Radcliffe College and medicine at Johns Hopkins University; she settles in Paris this year with Alice B. Toklas and becomes a controversial expatriate literary figure as well as a patron and critic French-born American writer Anaïs Nin (1903–1977) is best known for her erotic diaries and novels as well as for her love affair with novelist Henry Miller Renowned British garden designer Gertrude Jekyll (1843–1932) designs the gardens at Hestercomb, England	Maggie Lena Walker (1867–1934), an African American from Virginia and daughter of former slaves, becomes the first woman bank president in the US, heading the St. Luke Penny Savings Bank in Baltimore, MD Marie Louise Van Vorst (1867–1936) and her sister-in-law Bessie McGinnis Van Vorst (1873–1928) infiltrate factories and mills, acquainting themselves with the problems of child labor and other abuses; they publish their findings in *The Woman Who Toils: Being the Experience of Two Ladies as Factory Girls*	American educator Celestia Susannah Parrish (1853–1918) founds and becomes first president of the Southern Association of College Women American educator and children's rights advocate Julia Richman (1855–1912) opens many schools in New York City for delinquents, chronic absentees, and overage students, as well as encouraging special classes for the mentally and physically handicapped

Performing Arts/ Entertainment/ Sports	Religion/ Philosophy	Science/ Technology/ Discovery	Statecraft/ Military	Reform	
she subsequently makes successful concert tours in Europe and the US, performing at Covent Garden in London, the Metropolitan Opera House in New York, and the Chicago Opera Scottish operatic soprano Mary Garden (1877–1967), distinguished by her acting ability, is chosen by Debussy over Maeterlinck's mistress for the premiere performance of *Pelias et Melisande,* causing a rift between composer and librettist	(1861–1949) helps to produce a widely distributed series of textbooks designed for women's study groups between 1902 and 1929 Eleven-year-old Maria Goretti of Corinaldo, Italy, is sexually assaulted and stabbed repeatedly by an 18-year-old neighbor; she dies a day later, forgiving her murderer; she is declared blessed by Pope Pius XII in 1947 and canonized in 1950 in the piazza of St. Peter's before the largest crowd ever assembled for a canonization	such as the queen palm (*Arecastrum romanzoffianum*), the bunyabunya tree (*Araucaria bidwilii*), and the camphor tree (*Cinnamomum camphora*), as well as many acacias, bougainvilleas, succulents, and other now common plants		Foundation of the Landsföreningen för Kvinnans Politiska Rösträtt (Swedish Women's Suffrage Association) Anita Augsburg and Lida Gustava Heymann found the German Union for Women's Suffrage (Deutscher Verband für Frauenstimmrecht) in the city of Hamburg, where the German ban on women's participation in political activity does not apply Death of American women's rights leader Elizabeth Cady Stanton	**1902**
British soprano Florence Gertrude Easton (1884–1955) debuts with the Moody-Manners Opera Company in London American actress Mary G. Shaw, one of the first performers to introduce American audiences to the works of Ibsen, tours the US in his *Ghosts,* and later in *Hedda Gabler* American actress Viola Emily Allen forms her own acting company		Geographer Ellen Churchill Semple (1863–1932) publishes *American History and Its Geographic Conditions,* a work that attracts much attention among scientists and the general public Marie and Pierre Curie receive the Nobel Prize for Physics for their study of radioactivity Ellen Browning Scripps (1836–1932) establishes the Marine Biological Association of San Diego, which becomes the Scripps Institution of Oceanography in 1925 On a scientific expedition to northern Baltistan, Fanny Bullock Workman climbs the 21,000-foot Mt. Koser Gunga, setting an altitude record for women climbers	A women's suffrage bill passes in Arizona	Polish-Jewish immigrant Rose Schneiderman (1882–1972) speaks on behalf of women's suffrage; she serves from 1907 to 1950 as an organizer of the American National Women's Trade Union League Emmeline Pankhurst and her two daughters, Christabel (1880–1958) and Sylvia (1882–1960), found Britain's Women's Social and Political Union; they use militant tactics to disrupt public meetings and engage in acts of civil disobedience The (American) National Women's Trade Union League is founded by middle-class and working women to foster women's education, lobby for protective legislation, and help women organize unions	**1903**

French diarist Anaïs Nin
Photograph (c. 1928) courtesy Skidmore College Rare Books and Special Collections

	General/ Context	Daily Life/ Customs/ Practices	Humanities/ Fine Arts	Occupations	Education
1904		Pioneering feminist Frances Power Cobbe dies and is buried next to her companion and lover, sculptress Mary Lloyd	Gene Stratton-Porter (Geneva Grace, 1863–1924) achieves popularity with *Freckles* A founder of the Poetry Society of America, Jessie Belle Rittenhouse (1869–1948) publishes her important anthology, *The Younger American Poets* Lady Isabella Augusta Persse Gregory founds the Irish National Theatre, later the Abbey Theatre Japanese political activist Kageyama Hideko publishes her autobiography, *Half a Life as a Common-Law Wife* British feminist novelist May Sinclair (1865–1946) publishes *The Divine Fire;* she is noted for her use of Freudian psychology	British-born Evangeline Cory Booth (1865–1950), fourth-generation member of the Salvation Army, begins a 33-year career as leader of the US Salvation Army	Mary McLeod Bethune (1875–1955) founds a school for black girls in Daytona Beach, FL, which eventually becomes Bethune-Cookman College The International Alliance of Women—Equal Rights, Equal Responsibilities is founded in Copenhagen to eliminate discrimination against women and work for equal opportunity, including suffrage Helen Keller graduates cum laude from Radcliffe College In Russia, the Women's Medical Institute is incorported into the state education system

American financier Hetty Green
Photograph (1904) courtesy Sophia Smith
Collection, Smith College

	General/ Context	Daily Life/ Customs/ Practices	Humanities/ Fine Arts	Occupations	Education
1905		US President Grover Cleveland writes in the *Ladies' Home Journal* that women of sense do not want to vote: "The relative positions to be assumed by men and women in the working out of our civilization were assigned long ago by a higher intelligence than ours"	American novelist Edith Wharton (1862–1937) publishes *The House of Mirth* George Bernard Shaw bases his play *Major Barbara* on the life of American actress and philanthropist Eleanor Robson Belmont (1879–1979)	Women's Business League of New York is incorporated Winifred Holt (1870–1945) and her sister, Edith, start the New York Association for the Blind; she founds the first Lighthouse for the employment, education, and recre-	Girls are admitted to Iceland's newly founded high school

Performing Arts/ Entertainment/ Sports	Religion/ Philosophy	Science/ Technology/ Discovery	Statecraft/ Military	Reform	
Frances Davis Alda (1883–1952), New Zealand lyric soprano, debuts as Manon at the Paris Opéra-Comique

Noted Australian mezzo-soprano Ada Crossley (1874–1929), a popular performer at English festivals, makes an important concert tour of Australia

Isadora Duncan (1878–1927) introduces nontraditional dance to the world; she is the first dancer to go without tights, shoes, and the constricting costume of ballet | | | To compel Namibian men to fight, women of Namibia protest German colonial rule by refusing to bear children or have sexual relations | International Congress of Women in Berlin, June 6–20

Susan B. Anthony cofounds the International Woman Suffrage Alliance and is made president of the International Leadership Conference in Berlin; the organization is chaired by Carrie Chapman Catt until 1923

Ida Minerva Tarbell publishes the powerful *The History of Standard Oil,* an indictment of that company's practice; it creates a sensation upon which her reputation rests

Bertha Pappenheim founds the German Organization of Jewish Women

Led by Rosika Schwimmer (1877–1948), the Hungarian radical feminist Union for Women's Rights is founded in connection with the International Woman Suffrage Alliance

Moderate Hungarian feminists found the National Council of Women, campaigning against alcohol, pornography, "white slavery," and dueling

Adjeng Kartini (1879–1904) is the first to claim the right of education for women in her aristocratic class and for the people of Java | **1904** |
| American actress and director Antoinette Perry (1888–1946) makes her New York stage debut in *Mrs. Temple's Telegram*

Having begun as a concert pianist, Melanie Kurt (1880–1941) turns to singing, performing with great success | American Hannah Greenbaum Solomon (1858–1942) founds the National Council of Jewish Women

Maria Longworth Nichols Storer seeks through personal influence to get Archbishop John Ireland appointed to the cardinalate; President | As a graduate student at Cornell Medical College, Martha Tracy (1876–1942) works as an assistant to Dr. William B. Coley; she is credited with helping him develop Coley's fluid, used in the treatment of sarcoma | Oklahoma welfare leader and political reformer Kate Barnard (1875–1930) is appointed matron in charge of the Provident Association of Oklahoma City; she wins recognition for her role in the Shawnee Convention, where she takes part in bargaining for | Austrian Baroness Bertha von Suttner (1843–1914) wins the Nobel Peace Prize

British suffragists Christabel Pankhurst and Annie Kenney are arrested for heckling at a Liberal party meeting in Manchester, becoming the first of many suffragists to | **1905** |

General/Context	Daily Life/Customs/Practices	Humanities/Fine Arts	Occupations	Education
1905		American poet Anna Hempstead Branch publishes "The Monk in the Kitchen" Indian poet Sarojini Naidu (1879–1949), the "nightingale of India," publishes *The Golden Threshold,* a collection of poems written in English Baroness Orczy of England writes *The Scarlet Pimpernel*	ation work for the blind in 1923	
1906	Alice Lakey (1857–1935) helps secure passage of the Pure Food and Drug Act In the US, the backlash against upper- and middle-class white women's use of birth control combined with growing racial prejudice prompts Theodore Roosevelt to admonish well-born white women for participating in willful sterilization, a practice becoming known as racial suicide The last municipal voting rights remaining to Austrian women are removed by civil law reform, causing feminists to demand repeal of the law prohibiting them from joining political	French artist Louise Abbéma (1858–1927) is named a Chevalier German author Ricarda Huch (1864–1947) is best known for her essays on German Romanticism and for her historical novels Swedish artist Hilma af Klint (1862–1944) produces images she claims are dictated by spiritual guides	Rheta Childe Dorr (1866–1948) becomes the first editor of *The Suffragist* Birth of Margaret Bourke-White (d. 1971), American photographer known for her studies of industries, social and economic conditions, news personalities Marie Curie becomes the Sorbonne's first female professor when she takes over her husband's position Christabel Pankhurst graduates in law from Victoria University but is not permitted to practice because of her sex	Isabel Bevier and Susannah Usher publish *The Home Economics Movement,* enlarged under the title *Home Economics in Education* (1924) Mary Adelaide Nutting becomes the first nurse to hold a professorship at Columbia University, New York City Mary MacArthur Anderson establishes Britain's National Federation of Women Workers Grace Hoodley Dodge helps to establish the Young Women's Christian Association (YWCA) and is the first woman ever to serve on the New York Board of Education

INDIA'S WOMEN WRITERS: A LIST OF NOTABLE NAMES

These Indian poets and novelists write in English:

Toru Dutt (1856–1877): published her first book, *A Sheaf Gleaned in French Fields,* in Calcutta in 1876; a second posthumous volume of poems, *Ancient Ballads and Legends of Hindustan,* appeared in 1885

Sarojini Naidu (1879–1949): poet and freedom fighter with Mahatma Gandhi

Kamala Markandaya (b. 1927): novelist whose work on the subject of being a woman in modern India deals with sociological and economic problems

Anita Desai (b. 1937): novelist whose works deal with psychological complexities including the violent aspects of human relations

These widely read authors, mostly fiction writers, are well

Performing Arts/ Entertainment/ Sports	Religion/ Philosophy	Science/ Technology/ Discovery	Statecraft/ Military	Reform	
Italian singer Dame Adelina Patti makes her first recording for His Master's Voice at the small concert theater on her estate in England	Theodore Roosevelt writes her a sharp rebuke, urging her to promise to keep out of Vatican politics while her husband remains a diplomat; when she fails to reply, Roosevelt dismisses Storer; the case becomes a scandal when the Storers take it to the press		groups supporting abolition of child labor and welfare The Victoria Assembly in Australia passes a bill granting suffrage to women	be arrested in Britain for this kind of outburst The Czech Committee on Women's Suffrage is founded by F. Plamnikova Women's rights are not mentioned in Czar Nicholas II's October Manifesto calling for civil liberties; outraged feminists, led by the intellectuals, writers, and journalists Mariya Chelkhova, Olga Volkenshtein, and Zinaida Mirovich form the All-Russian Union of Equal Rights for Women	**1905**
Actress Fay Templeton (1865–1939) makes her name by doing imitations of other famous actresses Italian actress Adelaide Ristori (1821–1906) is acclaimed for her appearances in Italian and classical French drama as well as in Shakespearean roles		The University of Bonn, Germany, supports the *Habilitation* (the equivalent of postdoctoral publication that qualifies the candidate to be promoted to a professorship) of the zoologist Countess Marie von Linden; after polling the university's faculty on the question of female professors, the Ministry of Education decides to reject the proposal, but Countess von Linden nevertheless receives a raise, the title of professor, and the directorship of a parasitology laboratory Fanny Bullock Workman sets an altitude record for women climbers, scaling a 23,300-foot peak in the Nun Kun range	The Victoria (Australia) Legislative Council rejects the bill extending suffrage to women though it had been passed by the assembly the year before Oregon's suffrage amendment is rejected Finland becomes the first European nation to give women the vote	Susan B. Anthony dies Carrie Chapman Catt speaks at the opening of the Inter-Urban Political Equality Council in New York, a group founded to promote equal rights for women Not yet 16 years old, Elizabeth Gurley Flynn delivers a speech at the Harlem Socialist Club entitled "What Socialism Will Do for Women" The *London Daily Mail* coins the term "suffragette" for women who campaign for women's suffrage Anarchists Emma Goldman and Alexan-	**1906**

known for portraying the experiences and dilemmas of women in India today:
Amrita Preetam: Punjabi writer
Ashapurna Devi, Mahashweta Devi, and Anurupa Devi: Bengali writers
Kandanika Kapadika: Gujrati writer

MK Indira and Anusuya Shankar "Triveni": Kannada writers
Kausalya Devi Kodoori: Telugu writer
Ismalt Chugtai and Qurratul Ain Hyder: Urdu writers
Mahadevi Verma, Usha Devi Mitra, and Krishna Sobti: Hindi writers
Kusumavati Deshpande: Marathi writer

	General/Context	Daily Life/Customs/Practices	Humanities/Fine Arts	Occupations	Education
1906		associations and institutions of universal suffrage The permanent wave is introduced in London; it costs $1000 and takes eight to 12 hours to accomplish			
1907	The first self-contained electric clothes washer is developed in Chicago Records of book sales in America suggest that from 1895 to 1907 books by women become as popular as books by men In France, married women are given the right to dispose of their own wages	Harriot Stanton Blatch (1856–1940) is prohibited from dining alone in a restaurant; she sues with the support of the New York Equal Suffrage League	Julia Ward Howe is the first woman elected to the National Institute of Arts and Letters British author Daphne du Maurier (1907–1989) writes mysterious works such as *Rebecca* (1938) British novelist Rumer Godden (b. 1909) is known for *Black Narcissus* (1939) British author Elinor Glyn (1864–1943) writes and publishes a best-selling romantic novel entitled *Three Weeks,* and later writes film scripts for the silent pictures in Hollywood Dresden-born Paula Modersohn-Becker (1876–1907) is recog-	The first Christmas "stamps" are sold by American Emily Perkins Bissell (1861–1948) to raise money for tuberculosis research British nursing pioneer Edith Louisa Cavell (1856–1915) sets up a nursing school in Belgium From 1907 to 1967, Australian government policy mandates that women's wages be lower than men's	Italian education reformer Maria Montessori (1871–1952) opens the first Montessori school for children in Rome Hajiya Ma'daki (b. c. 1907) is a driving force behind the establishment of schools for girls in Nigeria Martha Van Rensselaer (1864–1932) and Flora Rose become cochairwomen of home economics in the college of agriculture at Cornell University

CLARA ZETKIN

Socialist and feminist Clara Zetkin was born in Saxony in 1857. When the family moved to Leipzig in 1872, Clara became acquainted with that city's bourgeois women's movement. In 1878, she met some exiled Russian Socialists and her views swung to the left. Clara worked for the underground Socialist movement in Germany and Switzerland, was fired from two positions as a governess, and suffered a break with her family for her radical views. In 1882, Clara moved in with Ossip Zetkin, a Russian Socialist she had met in Leipzig. He had moved to Paris after Germany passed its Anti-Socialist Law of 1878. Although she took his name and they had two children together, Clara and Ossip never married. When Ossip fell ill (he died in 1889), Clara stepped into his shoes, honing her skills as a writer and activist. At the Second Socialist International meeting in Paris in 1889, Clara rose to international prominence. She helped plan the conference, translated, and delivered an influential speech on women's role in the movement.

When the law banning socialism in Germany lapsed in 1890, Clara moved to Stuttgart with her two sons. As the editor of *Die Gleichheit* (*Equality*), the women's magazine of Germany's Social Democratic party, she learned firsthand the challenges faced by the working class in Germany. Over several years, this experience caused her views on women within socialism to change. She had previously believed that women's struggle against capitalism must not be separate from men's; since industrialism had given women opportunities for economic independence, their struggle was exactly the same as that of any worker. Now she recognized that women's jobs often presented unique problems demanding protective laws. She also became convinced that women needed to make a special effort to gain civil rights, such as the vote, as well as economic power; raising Socialist children, too, was valid political work. Frustrated when male Socialists took over leadership positions in the

Performing Arts/ Entertainment/ Sports	Religion/ Philosophy	Science/ Technology/ Discovery	Statecraft/ Military	Reform	
				der Berkman found the journal *Mother Earth*	**1906**
British pianist Myra Hess (1890–1965) makes her London debut	Yale University hosts the first Women's Missionary Conference, issuing a warning to male students not to disrupt the proceedings	Martha Wollstein (1868–1939) joins the first experimental analysis team of polio in the US at the Rockefeller Institute	The British House of Commons defeats an effort to extend suffrage to women	The American Society for Keeping Woman in Her Proper Sphere is formed	**1907**
Irish actress May Craig (1889–1972) stars in *Playboy of the Western World*		Gertrude Bell (1889–1926) publishes *The Desert and the Sown,* in which she records her travels through the Arabian desert and her experiences as an archeologist in the Middle East	Chinese feminist Ch'iu Chin (1875?–1907) wears men's clothes, preaches revolution and liberation of women	In *Socialisme et féminisme* Lydia Pissarjevsky casts doubt on Marx's notion that revolution will affect men's treatment of women	
Hungarian pianist Yolande Mérö (b. 1878) debuts as a soloist with the Dresden Philharmonic					
May Robson (1858–1942) makes her name as a popular comic character actress				The Icelandic Women's Association is founded by Bríet Bjarnhédinsdóttir (1856–1940)	
Australian longdistance swimmer Annette Kellerman is arrested for indecent exposure in Boston for appearing on the beach in a one-piece skirtless bathing suit					

movement, she supported the creation of separate Socialist women's groups.

By 1907, as secretary of the Second Socialist International's new women's section, she grew more committed to revolution. She adopted the radical thought of Rosa Luxemburg, who was assassinated in 1918 trying to bring Lenin-style revolution to Germany. Because a visit to Russia had revealed to her the oppression of the czarist regime, Clara also felt deeply the Russian Revolution of 1905–6. Meanwhile, she was disappointed that the German Social Democratic party, moderating its views, accepted gradual change rather than revolution. She came to believe that socialism would move forward best if women remained separate within it. This belief put her at odds with the Communist party when she joined in 1919.

Clara led Socialist efforts to stop World War I; like most Socialists she believed that the real hostilities existed between workers and capitalists, not among workers of different nations. She welcomed Russia's Bolshevik Revolution and became Lenin's friend. When the Nazis took power in Germany in 1933, she fled to Russia, where she died later that year.

Since her death she has been viewed in conflicting ways. Orthodox communists, praising her revolutionary commitment, minimize her feminism; feminists, suspicious of her opposition to bourgeois feminism, minimize her commitment to revolution. Her ideas, indeed, evolved constantly. In her heyday before World War I, she was the most influential Socialist thinker in Europe on the issue of women's role within socialism. Russian Socialist Alexandra Kollontai and France's Louise Saumoneau adopted many of her ideas. As a writer, speaker, and activist, Clara Zetkin devoted her life to progress for workers of both sexes.

	General/ Context	Daily Life/ Customs/ Practices	Humanities/ Fine Arts	Occupations	Education
1907			nized as a pioneer of modern art Alice Babette Toklas (1877–1967) meets Gertrude Stein in Paris and begins their life-long lesbian relationship		
1908	The first Mother's Day is celebrated, in Philadelphia, PA	New York City passes the Sullivan Ordinance, prohibiting women from smoking in public places Danish law grants communal suffrage to women on a property qualification, with special provisions for wives who have no income in their own right In Iceland, all women are granted full equality in municipal suffrage Liberalization of the German Empire's Combination Law of 1851 forbidding women to participate in political assemblies	Eliza Frances Andrews, pen name Elzey Hay (1840–1931) publishes *The War-Time Journal of a Georgia Girl* Marian Nevins McDowell opens an artists' retreat, the McDowell Colony, in Peterborough, NH American detective story writer Mary Roberts Rinehart (1876–1958) publishes *The Circular Staircase* Canadian novelist Lucy Maud Montgomery (1874–1942) publishes *Anne of Green Gables*	T. H. Becker opens a brokerage office only for women traders in New York City Esther Voorhees Hanson becomes the first superintendent of the newly established US Naval Nurse Corps Adah Thoms plays a leading role in the organization of the National Association of Colored Graduate Nurses American journalist Nancy Hale (1908–1988) is the *New York Times's* first female reporter	Isabel Bevier institutes the teaching of scientific home economics at the University of Illinois, establishing a house on campus as a laboratory of study—the first of its kind Women gain the right to matriculate in Prussian universities Alpha Kappa Alpha, the first sorority for black women, is founded in Washington, DC The *Journal of Home Economics* is established by Ellen Henrietta Swallow Richards
1909	The National Association for the Advancement of Colored People (NAACP) is founded by W.E.B. DuBois, Jane Addams, Mary W. Ovington, and others	Swedish women are permitted by law to stand for municipal office	Missouri artist Rose O'Neill (1874–1944) designs Kewpie dolls Swedish novelist Selma Lägerlof (1858–1940) receives the Nobel Prize for Literature Publication of the wildly successful best-seller *The Rosary* by	Margaret Dreier Robins (1868–1945), president of the National Women's Trade Union League, helps to obtain money, legal counsel, relief, and support for striking garment workers in New York, Philadelphia, and Chicago, 1909–1911	Martha Berry opens the Mount Berry School for Girls Bertha Erdmann becomes the first director of the first university school for nursing in the US at the University of Minnesota

Performing Arts/ Entertainment/ Sports	Religion/ Philosophy	Science/ Technology/ Discovery	Statecraft/ Military	Reform	
Eugenia H. Farrar becomes the first singer ever to broadcast over radio					**1907**
Queen Alexandra of England extends the distance of the marathon by 385 yards so that her family can watch the start from the windows of Windsor Castle; though in subsequent years the length of the course varies, in 1921, the International Amateur Athletic Federation fixes its official length at the queen's stipulated 26 miles 385 yards Nora Bayes (1880–1928), American comedy and vaudeville singer, is a sensation in *Follies of 1908* in which the song "Shine on Harvest Moon" (cowritten with her husband) is especially popular The first American-trained singer to perform with the Royal Opera at Covent Garden, Corinne Rider-Kelsey (1877–1947), a.k.a. Mme. Rider-Reed, debuts as Micaëla in *Carmen*	Mary Baker Eddy begins publication of the *Christian Science Monitor*	Sara Josephine Baker (1873–1945), American physician, public health administrator, and child health care pioneer, establishes the Division of Child Hygiene in the Health Department, the world's first tax-supported agency devoted exclusively to improving the health of children and the first public US health agency Psychologist Margaret Floy Washburn (1871–1939) publishes *The Animal Mind,* an important work on animal behavior	Mrs. G. Barney is elected city collector of Montgomery, MO, but is not permitted to take office because she is a woman Crystal Macmillan (1882–1937) becomes the first woman to address the British House of Lords, advocating, without success, that female graduates of the Scottish universities should be allowed to vote along with male graduates for the parliamentary seat representing these universities Death of Chinese dowager empress Cixi, for 52 years the power behind the Qing throne	In London, 500,000 American and European women demonstrate for suffrage Wealthy American reformer Maud Younger (1870–1936) founds the Waitresses' Union in San Francisco after waitressing in order to learn about the life of working women Vienna-born Lady Constance Lytton (1869–1923) becomes a very active suffragette in England and is imprisoned several times German feminist Helene Stöcker persuades the legal commission of the Federation of German Women's Associations to endorse the legalization of abortion The Congress of Russian Women is the last public demonstration of Russian feminists before the 1917 revolution Irish nationalist Constance Markiewiecz (1868–1926) founds the Irish Women's Franchise League	**1908**
Alice Huyler Ramsey becomes the first woman to drive a car from New York City to San Francisco; her trip lasts 67 days Czech contralto Ernestine Rössler Schumann-Heink (1861–1936) creates the role of Clytem-		American explorer and photographer Mary L. Jobe Akeley (1878–1966) explores British Columbia; Mount Jobe is named after her Esther Boise Van Deman (1862–1937), the first woman Roman field archeologist, identifies a means of	The Irish national covention votes down women's suffrage The Wisconsin senate passes a suffrage bill The Massachusetts legislative committee rejects a bill to grant equal suffrage to women	112 militant suffragists are arrested in London in an attempt to see Lord Asquith The International Ladies' Garment Workers Union (ILGWU) calls a strike to protest poor working conditions and low wages	**1909**

	General/ Context	Daily Life/ Customs/ Practices	Humanities/ Fine Arts	Occupations	Education
1909			English popular novelist Florence Barclay (1862–1921) By her death, Martha Finley (1828–1909) has published 26 Elsie Dinsmore books María Montoya Martínez (b. 1887), first female recipient of the US Indian Achievement Award, produces her first black-on-black pottery, for which she will become world famous		With the National Baptist Women's Convention, black educator Nannie Burroughs (1883–1961) opens the National Trade and Professional School for Women and Girls in Washington, DC; its motto is "We specialize in the wholly impossible"

Lizzie Maltesta, a child worker in a New York sweatshop, early 1900s
Photograph courtesy Sophia Smith Collection, Smith College

	General/ Context	Daily Life/ Customs/ Practices	Humanities/ Fine Arts	Occupations	Education
1910	China abolishes slavery The Kansas attorney general rules women may wear trousers Father's Day, launched by Sonora Louise Smart Dodd (1882–1978), is observed for the first time in Spokane, WA	Western women begin to wear V-neck shirts, which some condemn as immoral The Printers' Association of America mounts an effort to prevent the illustration of women's skirts on billboards Charlotte Vetter Gulick cofounds the Campfire Girls The US Congress passes the Mann White Slave Traffic Act to prohibit interstate and foreign transport of females for immoral purposes Kisaeng, Japanese guided tours to South Korea for the purpose of visiting prostitutes, begin	Carrie Jacobs Bond composes her masterpiece, "A Perfect Day" Anna Akhmatova (1889–1967), Russia's greatest woman poet, publishes her first work Jessie Bell Rittenhouse helps found the Poetry Society of America American Zionist author Jessie Ethel Sampter (1883–1938) publishes *The Seekers* American Harriet Ware (b. 1877) composes the cantata Sir Olaf Australian Henry Handel Richardson (pen name of Henrietta Richardson, 1870–1946) publishes *The Getting of Wisdom* Artist Laura Knight (1877–1970) paints Daughters of the Sun in Lamora, England	Mme. C. J. Walker (a.k.a. Sarah Breedlove, 1867–1919), the first African-American businesswoman to become a millionaire in the US, opens her corporation headquarters; her hair-care products, still marketed today, are so successful that her company rivals those of Helena Rubenstein and Elizabeth Arden	Jane Addams becomes the first woman to receive an honorary degree from Yale University Egyptian women's rights activist Huda Sh'arawi succeeds in getting girls' schools opened in Egypt
1911	Establishment of The Blue Rider, a group of expressionistic artists in Munich	March 8 is named International Women's Day	Soprano Mme. Albani, a favorite in Britain's Covent Garden, publishes *Forty Years of Song*	Harriet Quimby is the first woman to receive a pilot's license from Aero Club of America	Katherine Gibbs (1865–1934) founds the first school for secretaries, educating women in business

Performing Arts/ Entertainment/ Sports	Religion/ Philosophy	Science/ Technology/ Discovery	Statecraft/ Military	Reform	
	nestra in Strauss's *Elektra* Lyric soprano Alma Gluck (1884–1938) makes her Metropolitan Opera debut English contralto of Peruvian and French descent Marguerite D'Alvarez makes her American debut with the Boston Opera Company Actress Mary G. Shaw promotes the suffrage movement by appearing in Elizabeth Robins's play *Votes for Women*	dating buildings by examining the composition and size of mortar and bricks		Countess Andrássy, president of the Hungarian National Council of Women, claims that Hungarian women have no interest in women's suffrage American labor activist Elizabeth Gurley Flynn (d. 1964) becomes a leading organizer of the International Workers of the World Death of Peruvian feminist, author, and social reformer Clorinda Matto de Turner (b. 1852)	**1909**
Bohemian soprano Emmy Destinn (Kittl, 1878–1930) creates the role of Minnie in Puccini's *Fanciulla del West* at the New York Metropolitan Opera Billed as the "Last of the Red-Hot Mamas," Sophie Tucker (1884–1966) achieves stardom as a vaudeville performer American dancer Irene Castle (1893–1969) is credited with starting the bobbed hair fad in the US Dramatic soprano Geraldine Farrar (1882–1957) makes her Metropolitan Opera debut Blanche Stuart Scott makes the first flight by a woman, flying 12 feet off the ground in an Ely machine	The world conference of Young Women's Christian associations is held in Berlin	*Bambusa gibbsiae,* or Miss Gibbs's Bamboo, is named for English botanist Lillian Gibbs, the first woman known to scale Mount Kinabalu in Borneo; she collects over 1000 botanical specimens for the British Museum on that trip Marie Curie publishes *Traité de radioactivité* ("Treatise on Radioactivity")	The US Senate hears a resolution to abolish sex discrimination in the Constitution The state of Washington passes a constitutional amendment permitting women suffrage	Jane Addams publishes *Twenty Years at Hull-House* The Woman Suffrage party forms in New York City as a political party Luisa Capetillo (1880–1922) founds the first Puerto Rican feminist magazine, *Woman* Scottish trade union activist Mary Macarthur (1880–1921) and suffrage worker Selina Cooper (1864–1946) participate in the Cradley Heath Chainmakers' strike	**1910**

New York City sweatshop, early 1900s
Photograph courtesy Sophia Smith Collection, Smith College

Performing Arts/ Entertainment/ Sports	Religion/ Philosophy	Science/ Technology/ Discovery	Statecraft/ Military	Reform	
American actress Rosalind Russell (1911–1976) is known for her roles as a tough, self-sufficient woman	Noted Anglican mystical theologian Evelyn Underhill (1875–1941) publishes her seminal work, *Mysticism*	Dr. Christine Bonnevie is the first woman admitted to the Norwegian Academy of Science	The California senate approves a bill granting equal suffrage The Wisconsin senate rejects its suffrage bill	Jane Addams becomes the first head of the National Federation of Settlements and the first vice president of the National American	**1911**

	General/ Context	Daily Life/ Customs/ Practices	Humanities/ Fine Arts	Occupations	Education
1911	Revolution in China; Hsuan-t'ung, the last emperor of China, abdicates in February 1912 *British suffrage cartoon (1911): "Polling Booth. Companions in Disgrace"* Photograph courtesy Sophia Smith Collection, Smith College  **POLLING BOOTH.** **COMPANIONS IN DISGRACE.** Convicts and Women kindly note, / Are not allowed to have the vote; / The difference between the two / I will now indicate to you. / When once the harmful man of crime, / In Wormwood Scrubbs has done his time. / He at the poll can have his say, / The harmless woman *never* may. C. H. *Printed and Published by the Artists' Suffrage League, 259 King's Road, Chelsea.*		American novelist Anne Douglas Sedgwick (1873–1935) publishes *Tante* American sculptor Janet Scudder (1869–1940) becomes popular for her garden statuary American poet Elizabeth Bishop (1911–1979) is a Pulitzer Prize winner and consultant at the Library of Congress The novels of Italian writer Alba de Céspedes (b. 1911) concern the position of modern Italian women American-born poet Hilda Doolittle (pen name H.D., 1886–1961) joins the literary circle of Ezra Pound	In the Triangle Shirtwaist Company fire 146 workers, mostly women and children, perish; 80,000 people march down Fifth Avenue in New York City to attend the funeral The first female president of the American Library Association is Therese Hubbell West Elmendorf of Buffalo, NY Uruguayan attaché Clotilde Luisi is the first woman to enter diplomatic service in any country British suffragist Helena Swanwick (1864–1939) edits Common Cause	and liberal arts as well as secretarial skills *British suffrage cartoon (1911): "The Anti Suffragist"* Photograph courtesy Sophia Smith Collection, Smith College  THE ANTI SUFFRAGIST!
1912	Republican period in China, 1912–1949	Wife of a wealthy mine owner, Molly Brown (1867–1932) is on the *Titanic* when it goes down; she rescues fellow passengers, giving them her clothing to protect them from the cold; she is hailed as a hero upon her arrival in New York 15 women are let go from their jobs at the Curtis Publishing Company in Philadelphia after being seen dancing the turkey trot Juliette Low (1860–1927) forms the first American unit of Girl Guides (later renamed the Girl Scouts of America)	Russian Ella von Schultz-Adaievski (1846–1926) composes the opera *The Dawn of Freedom* Mary Mills Patrick publishes *Sappho and the Island of Lesbos* American Jean Webster (1876–1916) writes *Daddy-Long-Legs;* it awakens public concern for institutionalized orphans Harriet Monroe (1860–1936) founds and edits *Poetry: A Magazine of Verse* British writer Katherine Mansfield (1888–1923) begins her literary career German aristocrat Frieda von Richtofen (1897–1956), married with three children, elopes with D. H. Lawrence Sarojini Naidu publishes *The Bird of Time*	Sergeant Isabella Goodwin is the New York City Police Department's first female police detective The League of Advertising Women is founded by efficiency expert Christine Frederick in New York City Dr. Maria Paz Mendoza-Guazon is the first female medical doctor of the Philippines Fanny Harwood is the first British woman licensed in dental surgery Foundation of the National Organization of Public Health Nursing	Ida Tarbell publishes *The Business of Being a Woman,* in which she argues that "women [have] a business assigned by nature and society which [is] of more importance than public life" Evelyn Bishop (d. 1926) is the first director of Pi Beta Phi Settlement School of Gatlinburg, TN, established to educate mountain children and encourage home industries; today the Arrowmont School of Crafts draws 1000 craftspeople to its summer classes Maria Montessori publishes *The Montessori Method*

Performing Arts/ Entertainment/ Sports	Religion/ Philosophy	Science/ Technology/ Discovery	Statecraft/ Military	Reform	
Russian Ida Rubenstein (b. 1893) performs in the premiere of D'Annunzio's and Debussy's Martyr de St. Sebastien, written for her Famed American mountain climber Annie Smith Peck, aged 61, unfurls a banner inscribed "Votes for Women" at the top of Mount Coropuna in Peru The first woman to make a solo trip on horseback across the North American continent, Nan Jane Aspinwall arrives in San Francisco from New York in 301 days British actress Marie Tempest (1866–1942) becomes a theatrical manager and stars in her own productions		Kono Yasui becomes the first Japanese woman to receive a Ph.D. in science The first woman to be awarded two Nobel prizes, Marie Curie receives her second Nobel Prize for Chemistry for the discovery of radium and polonium Ellen Churchill Semple publishes her most important work, *Influences of Geographic Environment, on the Basis of Ratzel's System of Anthropo-Geography*	while the legislature passes a suffrage bill The Illinois senate passes a suffrage bill The Massachusetts house rejects its suffrage bill The Norwegian Cabinet approves admitting women to most state offices The US Supreme Court upholds women's right, recognized under civil law, to their husbands' property Radical Chinese feminists join the revolutionary groups that overthrow the Qing dynasty and establish a republic	Woman's Suffrage Association Ida Tarbell publishes *The Tariff in Our Times,* a study attacking protective tariffs about which President Woodrow Wilson remarked, "She has written more good sense, good plain common sense, about the tariff than any man I know" Flora MacDonald Denison (1867–1921) is an early leader of the Canadian women's suffrage movement and president of the Canadian Suffrage Association	**1911**
Mountain climber Dora Keen becomes the first woman to reach the summit of Mount Blackburn in Alaska Italian soprano Lucrezia Bori (née Borgia, 1887–1960) joins the Metropolitan Opera Company Moravian soprano Maria Jeritza (b. 1887) becomes a member of the Vienna State Opera American actress Laurette Taylor (1884–1946) stars in Hartley Manners's *Peg o' My Heart,* written especially for her Lilian Mary Baylis (1874–1937) takes over the management of the Old Vic Russian ballerina Anna Pavlova (1885–1931) settles in London and begins her great international career	Zionist Henrietta Szold (1860–1945) founds the Jewish welfare organization Hadassah in New York	Pioneer researcher in the scientific aspects of nutrition, Mary Davies Swartz Rose (1874–1941) publishes the widely used *A Laboratory Handboook for Dietitians* and later *The Foundations of Nutrition* (1927) Fanny Bullock Workman and her husband explore the 50-milelong Siachen (Rose) glacier, the largest in the Himalayas, making the first descent of the Kalberg glacier on their way back	The Virginia legislature rejects a bill to amend the state constitution to allow equal suffrage for women The Michigan legislature passes a suffrage bill Arizona passes a woman suffrage bill A suffrage amendment passes both Iowa houses NAWSA campaigns for a federal amendment granting equal rights to women In response to the government's intention to revoke women's suffrage in Bohemia, Czech feminists issue a "Women's Appeal to the Bohemian Nation" 76-year-old Abigail Duniway is the first woman to vote in her home state of Oregon	Grace Abbott (1878–1939) heads the Immigrants' Protective League Elizabeth Gurley Flynn leads 20,000 American women in the Bread & Roses Textile strike Czech suffragists refuse to attend a feminist conference in Vienna, objecting to the use of German for the proceedings Hungarian feminists protest the failure to include a promised property franchise for women in an electoral reform bill Emergence of the German Society for the Prevention of the Emancipation of Women	**1912**

	General/ Context	Daily Life/ Customs/ Practices	Humanities/ Fine Arts	Occupations	Education
1912					
1913	Brillo pads, made of steel wool and soap, are sold in the US A Chicago company produces the first refrigerator for domestic use	Interior decorator Elsie de Wolfe (1865–1950) sweeps away Victorian clutter and dark paneling, replacing it with pale painted walls, light fabrics, and mirrors England passes the Prisoners' Temporary Discharge for Ill-Health Act: female prisoners are released if their health fails but are rearrested when well again; the "Cat and Mouse Act" is repealed in 1914	Sculptor Janet Scudder has a one-woman show of portrait medallions in New York City Eleanor Hodgman Porter (1868–1920, writes *Pollyanna* Louisa Boyd Yeomans King (1863–1948) founds the Garden Club of America Marie Adelaide (Belloc) Lowndes (1868–1947), writing under the name Belloc Lowndes, publishes *The Lodger* Willa Cather publishes *O Pioneers!* Elizabeth Robins's *My Little Sister* deals with the white slave trade	The International Council of Nurses meets in Cologne, Germany; Adah Thoms is one of the first three African-American delegates to that body Anna Spencer becomes professor of sociology and ethics at the Meadville (PA) Theological School Italy forbids women lawyers to practice on the grounds that they are too unreliable as their husbands' consent to their activities might be withdrawn in midproceeding	Katherine Pettit founds the Pine Mountain Settlement School in Kentucky, teaching health care, ballad singing, folk dancing, and crafts to the local families Between 1913 and 1914, all German universities allow women to matriculate; 859 women are studying medicine at German universities in the winter semester of 1913
1914	World War I (1914–1918) begins Mother's Day, the second Sunday in May, is declared a national holiday by President Woodrow Wilson	Mary Phelps Jacobs of New York patents the design for the first modern bra, made of handkerchiefs, ribbon, and cord Mary Sherman lobbies for the creation of a National Park Service (1916) and national park areas in the Rockies (1915) and Grand Canyon (1919) Chilean-born Eugenia Errazuriz (1860–1954) is regarded as one of the creators of the minimalist interior design ethic	Jessie Willcox Smith illustrates *A Child's Garden of Verses* British writer May Sinclair is the author of fiction, poetry, criticism, and prose, including the novels *The Three Sisters* (1914), *The Tree of Heaven* (1917), *Mary Olivier: A Life* (1919), and *The Life and Death of Harriet Frean* (1922) Mrs. M. B. Wood is the first recorded crossword contributor	Canadian-born entrepreneur Elizabeth Arden (1878?–1966) founds a multimillion-dollar cosmetic empire Lizzie S. Sheldon is nominated to become a supreme court justice of Kansas African-American pioneer Mary Fields (1832–1914) becomes a legend in Montana as a restaurant owner, mail coach driver, and a freight hauler	Janie Porter Barrett opens the Virginia Industrial School for Colored Girls *Methods of Teaching Jewish Ethics,* by American educator Julia Richman (1855–1912), appears posthumously The University of Delaware (the last state in the Union to provide an institution of higher learning for women) establishes its Women's College

Performing Arts/ Entertainment/ Sports	Religion/ Philosophy	Science/ Technology/ Discovery	Statecraft/ Military	Reform	
Australian women enter their first Olympic competition; swimmer Fanny Durak wins a gold medal in freestyle					**1912**
English actress Vivien Leigh (1913–1967) is best known for her role as Scarlett O'Hara in the movie *Gone With the Wind* (1939) Spanish mezzo-soprano Conchita Supervia (1899–1936) debuts in Buenos Aires at the age of 14 British-born Ethel Leginska (née Liggins, b. 1890) conducts the Boston Philharmonic, the Chicago Women's Symphony, and a women's orchestra in Boston In Los Angeles, CA, Georgia Broadwick makes the first parachute jump by a woman		Women get the vote in Illinois Women are granted equal voting rights in Norway The first jury of women is drawn in California The Feminist Congressional Union is established in the US by Alice Paul (1885–1977); it becomes the National Women's Party in 1916		5,000 suffragists march down Pennsylvania Avenue in Washington, DC; they are heckled and slapped; after this incident, suffragists are allowed to present petitions in the US Capitol for a constitutional amendment Due to efforts of lawyer Hortense Ward (1872–1944), the Texas legislature passes the Hortense Ward Act, granting property rights to married women Emily Davison (1872–1913) throws herself in front of the king's horse on Derby Day shouting "Votes for Women" and dies as a result; supporters are outraged at the concern shown for the horse, not their colleague Hungarian feminists invite the International Woman Suffrage Alliance to hold its congress in Budapest, forcing authorities to moderate their hostility for the sake of international opinion	**1913**

Miriam Leslie (Mrs. Frank Leslie), American journalist
Photograph (1892) courtesy Sophia Smith-Collection, Smith College

Silent screen star Constance Talmadge (1900–1973) begins her film career Alice Brady begins her screen career in *Ye Sow;* she later appears in *Forever After* (1918) and *The Bride of the Lamb* (1926), which she produces herself American film comedian Pearl White (1889–1938) reaches stardom in *The Perils of Pauline*		The Feminist Alliance protests a law by which American women forfeit their citizenship by marrying aliens The privilege of voting is taken away from women in Geneva, Switzerland, because they do not use it The (American) National Association Opposed to Woman Suffrage issues a statement claiming that the feminist political agenda includes support of "free love"		Kate Barrett travels abroad as special representative of the labor department to investigate the treatment of deported American women The word "suffragette" is declared libelous in Germany Mrs. Frank Leslie leaves her nearly million-dollar estate to Carrie Chapman Catt, to be expended in the cause of women's suffrage	**1914**

General/ Context	Daily Life/ Customs/ Practices	Humanities/ Fine Arts	Occupations	Education
1914				

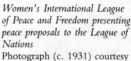

American suffrage cartoon (1915): "The Next Rung" Photograph courtesy Sophia Smith Collection, Smith College

Surgeon Elsie Inglis organizes Scottish Women's Hospitals

British social reformer Margaret Damer Dawson (1875–1920) founds the Women Police Volunteers in London, the forerunners of today's British policewomen

Women's International League of Peace and Freedom presenting peace proposals to the League of Nations Photograph (c. 1931) courtesy Sophia Smith Collection, Smith College

1915	Lipstick is sold for the first time	Russian Nathalia Goncharova (1881–1962) lead the Rayonist and neoprimitivist movements	Daisy Florence Simms (1873–1923), a leader in the Young Women's Christian Association, establishes "industrial clubs" in laundries, mills, factories, and stores across the US; there are 375 by this time, and their number continues to grow	Sarah Byrd Askew (1877–1942) introduces the idea of county libraries in New Jersey; 12 are opened under her leadership
	US Court of Appeals rules that night work for women is illegal	Jessie Willcox Smith illustrates *Little Women*		The Cambridge (MA) Law School for Women is organized
	American Justice Morchauser rules in *L. Kuenstler* v. *Kopke* that women's earnings belong to their husbands	English novelist Dorothy Richardson (1873–1957) pioneers the stream of consciousness school	Louisa Garrett Anderson (d. 1943) is Britain's chief surgeon of the Women's Hospital Corps during WWI	Hannah Kent Schoff, vice president of the National Congress of Mothers from 1898 to 1902, publishes *The Wayward Child,* based on her years of work
		Posthumous publication of *Verse* of American poet Adelaide Crapsey (1878–1914),		

THE ITALIAN WOMEN'S MOVEMENT

The commitment of women in Italy to political rights was forged in the risorgimento, Italy's struggle from 1815 to 1860 to become a unified country. After decades of dedication and sacrifice, the women who had fought for unification were keenly disappointed that the first civil code, drawn up in 1865, failed to give them the vote and placed married women under the authority of their husbands.

Beginning in 1872, women began to respond to this setback by publishing political journals. While the journals themselves often lasted only a few years, they gave the women who worked on them an opportunity to meet with other activists and compare ideas. The most important journal, *La Donna,* addressed women of all classes; it developed the concept of the "citizen mother," who, whether or not she worked outside the home, served her country by training her children in patriotism. The journals opened doors in higher education to women in the 1870s and 1880s.

The Leagues to Promote Female Interests, founded by Anna Marie Mozzoni, also strove to keep various social classes working together. Mozzoni fought especially for women textile workers whose wages were only half those of men. But in the 1890s, women of different classes parted company. Moderate feminism, affiliating with international women's organizations, aimed to secure voting rights. Professional and educational op-

Performing Arts/ Entertainment/ Sports	Religion/ Philosophy	Science/ Technology/ Discovery	Statecraft/ Military	Reform	
Sophie Tucker organizes a jazz band and bills herself as the "Queen of Jazz" After a successful stage career with the Imperial Ballet in St. Petersburg, Princess Seraphine Astafieva trains premier ballerinas Dame Alicia Markova and Dame Margot Fonteyn British actress Mrs. Patrick Campbell performs the role of Eliza Doolittle in *Pygmalion*, a role created for her by George Bernard Shaw	 *Women's Political Association of Australia marching in the International Suffrage Alliance section of a suffrage parade, 1915* Photograph courtesy Sophia Smith Collection, Smith College			The Women's Peace Parade is held in New York City to protest WWI Physician Rachelle Slobodinsky Yarros (1869–1946) combines the practice of medicine with social reform; she helps found the American Social Hygiene Association Lady Constance Lytton's *Prisons and Prisoners: Some Personal Experiences by Lady Constance Lytton and Jane Warton,* compares the genteel treatment she got when imprisoned under her own name and title with the rough treatment she got under the name Jane Warton	**1914**
Eva Tanguay (1878–1947), famous as "the I don't care girl" of the popular stage from 1904 to 1915, is one of the highest paid vaudeville performers of her time	A Scottish missionary in eastern Nigeria, Mary Slessor (1848–1915) is noted for living according to African custom Inuit shaman Higilak practices in Canada's Northwest Territories	Obstetrician and surgeon Dr. Bertha Van Hoosen (d. 1952) is founder and president of the American Women's Medical Association German-Jewish mathematician Emmy (Amalie Emmy) Noether (1882–1935) is prevented from lecturing in public by German law excluding women from obtaining the *habilitation* (permission to lecture); between 1915 and 1918,	Women are appointed as justices in southern Australia The king of Denmark signs bills granting suffrage to the women of Iceland and Denmark The Massachusetts House and Senate pass a women's suffrage amendment Governor Clark of Iowa signs an Iowa constitutional amendment for women's suffrage	Jane Addams and Carrie Chapman Catt found the Women's Peace party Rose Harriet Pastor Stokes (1879–1933) authors *The Woman Who Wouldn't,* about an emancipated woman who becomes a labor leader The International Committee of Women for Permanent Peace (later, the Women's International League for Peace and Free-	**1915**

portunity and equal legal rights were also important issues. More radical women joined the Socialist party in 1892. At the urging of male Socialist leaders, they began to put the interests of all workers in eradicating capitalism above women's issues; Socialist women also fought for protective laws and for suffrage.

When a 1913 law granted voting rights to still more groups of men but not to women, Italian women's rights activists were again dismayed. But patriotic sentiment flourished among bourgeois women in the war years of 1914–18. While Socialists argued whether to support war—they saw it as a way to divide workers—women turned to more conservative goals. After the

war, Socialist women and men faced the challenge of fascism, which gained support by viciously denouncing the Socialist party. By the time Benito Mussolini seized power in 1922, Socialists in Italy, women included, had been harassed, intimidated, and driven underground.

Under the Fascist regime, divorce became illegal; women were pressed to stay home and bear children for the state. In 1938, a law passed restricting women to only 10% of the higher-level jobs in government and business. After the fall of the Fascists, women in Italy regained the freedoms and finally won the right to vote.

General/ Context	Daily Life/ Customs/ Practices	Humanities/ Fine Arts	Occupations	Education
1915		who developed the poetic form the cinquain, derived from Japanese poetry American Susan Glaspell (1882–1948) coorganizes the Provincetown Players Sarojini Naidu publishes *The Broken Wing* (1915–1916) Edith Sitwell (1887–1964) publishes *The Mother and Other Poems*		with delinquent children

Edith Sitwell, English poet and critic
Photograph (c. 1955) by Cecil Beaton; courtesy
Sophia Smith Collection, Smith College

General/ Context	Daily Life/ Customs/ Practices	Humanities/ Fine Arts	Occupations	Education
1916	The first birth control clinic in the US opens in Brooklyn, New York Florine Stettheimer (1871–1944) is a central figure in the legendary Stettheimer family salon in New York, which attracts some of the most distinguished members of the avant-garde; known for both her paintings and poetry, she holds a one-woman show whose lack of success causes her to revise her style in the direction of the fantastic and theatrical	Marie Louise Van Vorst publishes *War Letters of an American Woman* H.D. publishes her first book of poetry, *Sea Garden* From 1909 to 1916, Charlotte Gilman publishes her own magazine, *The Forerunner,* in which her feminist utopian novel, *Herland,* appears Katrina Trask's antiwar play, *In the Vanguard,* is first presented American poet Amy Lowell (1874–1925), publishes "Patterns"		Mother Georgia Stevens (1870–1946) founds a Chair of Liturgical Music at Manhattanville College in New York Sarah Ellen Fisk (1886–1976) pioneers education for mentally retarded children with the New York Board of Education Aurelia Reinhardt (1877–1948) becomes president of the financially shaky California women's institution Mills College Clara Damrosch Mannes (1869–1948) and David Mannes found the Mannes Music School in New York City

American poet Amy Lowell
Photograph (c. 1916) courtesy Sophia
Smith Collection, Smith College

Performing Arts/ Entertainment/ Sports	Religion/ Philosophy	Science/ Technology/ Discovery	Statecraft/ Military	Reform	
		the problem is solved by a colleague, David Hilbert, who allows her lectures to be announced under his own name	British nurse Edith Cavell faces a firing squad for her work in Belgium, where she nursed the wounded of all nationalities and helped British soldiers escape from enemy territory	dom) is founded; it seeks to do away with war and to build peace through freedom A petition containing 500,000 names of coast-to-coast supporters of a woman suffrage amendment to the US Constitution is delivered to President Woodrow Wilson The World Union of Women for International Concord, founded in Geneva, supports the international peace movement	**1915**

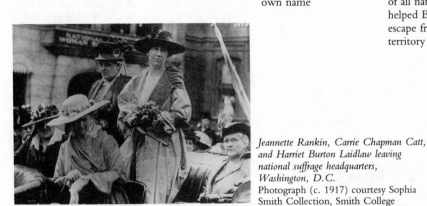

Jeannette Rankin, Carrie Chapman Catt, and Harriet Burton Laidlaw leaving national suffrage headquarters, Washington, D.C.
Photograph (c. 1917) courtesy Sophia Smith Collection, Smith College

Performing Arts/ Entertainment/ Sports	Religion/ Philosophy	Science/ Technology/ Discovery	Statecraft/ Military	Reform	
Chanteuse Edith Piaf (1916–1963) is known for her husky voice and tragic love songs, such as "La Vie en Rose" Viennese violinist Erica Morini (b. 1906) debuts in her home town at the age of 10; at 15, she tours the US, where she is recognized as a superb technician Coloratura soprano Amelita Galli-Curci (b. 1889?–1963) debuts in Chicago Lois Weber (1881–1939) directs the film *The Dumb Girl of Portici* starring Russian ballerina Anna Pavlova; the film is praised as a "testamonial of the finest female imagination in filmland" Adele Astaire (Adele Austerlitz, 1898–1981) wins fame as the dance partner of her brother, Fred, 1916–1932; she is said to have been the more talented of the two	English religious novelist Sheila Kaye-Smith (1887–1956) publishes *Sussex Gorse*		Denmark's Equal Suffrage Act goes into effect Jeanette Rankin becomes the first woman elected to the US House of Representatives, four years before the 19th Amendment gives women the right to vote Zawditu (d. 1930) rules as empress of Ethiopia from 1916 to 1928; during her rule, slavery is abolished Dr. Alexandra Chalmers-Watson (the first woman M.D. from Edinburgh University), Louisa Garrett Anderson, Flora Murray, and Helen Gwynne-Vaughan lead the new Women's Army Auxiliary Corps	British trade union activist Dame Anne Loughlin (1894–1979) leads the successful clothing workers' strike in west Yorkshire The National Women's Party is founded in America Ethel Smyth composies "March of Women," the anthem of the suffragettes	**1916**

Britishwoman manufacturing 4.5-inch cartridge cases
Photograph (c. 1916) courtesy Sophia Smith Collection, Smith College

	General/ Context	Daily Life/ Customs/ Practices	Humanities/ Fine Arts	Occupations	Education
1917	Czar Nicholas II abdicates; Russian Revolution, 1917–1922, begins Frozen food processing is invented in the US Pilot Julia Clark becomes the first female airplane fatality when her biplane crashes in Illinois	Helena Rubinstein creates the "vamp look" for silent screen actress Theda Bara Film star Betty Grable (1917–1973) is a pinup girl during WWII Foundation of Altrusa International, an international organization for professional women based in Chicago, IL; it serves general humanitarian	Laura E. Richards and Maude Howe Elliott win the Pulitzer Prize for Biography for *Julia Ward Howe* Dame Ethel Smyth composes the opera *The Boatswain's Mate* British painter Dora Carrington (1893–1932) becomes a member of the Bloomsbury group	Sara Josephine Baker is the first woman to receive a Ph.D. in public health from New York University Bellevue Hospital Medical School Foundation of Israel's Women Workers' Council by Rachel Shazar-Katznelson (b. 1888) Mary Florence Lathrop becomes the first woman to be admitted to the American Bar Association	Women are admitted to the College of Physicians and Surgeons at Columbia University Radcliffe women are admitted to Harvard Medical College Painter Irene Weir (1862–1944) founds the School of Design and Liberal Arts in New York City Annie Warburton Goodrich becomes director of the new Army School of Nursing at Walter Reed Army Hospital

Press photographer Jessie Tarbox Beals
Photograph (1918) courtesy Sophia Smith Collection, Smith College

Members of the US Women's Land Army working in a lumberyard
Photograph (1917) courtesy Sophia Smith Collection, Smith College

Female Polish soldiers on an excursion in the forest
Photograph (c. 1918?) courtesy Sophia Smith Collection, Smith College

	General/ Context	Daily Life/ Customs/ Practices	Humanities/ Fine Arts	Occupations	Education
1918	Pulitzer prizes are awarded annually for excellence in journalism and letters The Russian Imperial family is executed in July; foundation of the Russian Communist party	In Great Britain, the Representation of the People Act recognizes women's war effort by extending the vote to most women over 30 Dr. Marie Stopes (1880–1958) founds one of the world's first birth control clinics in north London	Olga Rozanova (1896–1918) illustrates booklets published by Russian futurist poets Willa Cather publishes *My Antonia* Italian book illustrator Leonor Fini (b. 1918) is noted for her surrealistic paintings of women Uruguayan poet Juana de Ibarbourou (b. 1895), known as Juana de América, publishes her quasi-narcissistic poem "Diamond Tongues"	Women take over the writing, editing, and management of *The Atlantic City Evening Union;* Mary N. Chenworth becomes editor in chief According to the Bureau of Labor Statistics, 1,426,000 women joined the American workforce since 1911 and replaced 1,413,000 men in jobs since 1914	Professor of English at Vassar, Alice D. Snyder (1887–1943) publishes *The Critical Principle of the Reconciliation of Opposites as Employed by Coleridge* Nina Karlovna Bari (1901–1961) enters the faculty of physics and mathematics at Moscow State after the revolution; she is the first woman to both enroll in and graduate from the university

Russian Imperial family
Photograph (1901) courtesy Sophia Smith Collection, Smith College

Performing Arts/ Entertainment/ Sports	Religion/ Philosophy	Science/ Technology/ Discovery	Statecraft/ Military	Reform	
American comedian Zasu (Eliza Susan) Pitts (1900–1963) begins her film career, making over 100 films

Lois Weber is for many years the only successful woman director in American films | Founder of the Pillar of Fire Church, Alma Bridwell White is its senior bishop, the first female bishop of any Christian church | Social scientists and nutritionists Frances Stern and Gertrude T. Spitz publish *Food for the Worker*, "to show the need for the unification of science, social work, income and nutrition"

Margaret Sanger establishes the Birth Control Clinical Research Bureau (renamed the Margaret Sanger Research Bureau in 1943) | Ohio passes a bill allowing women to vote in presidential elections

The Minnesota House of Representatives passes a bill granting full suffrage by a constitutional amendment

President Wilson establishes the Woman's Committee of the Council of National Defense, designed to organize and coordinate American women's war efforts

A bill for equal suffrage in Ontario is endorsed by the Canadian government

The new Soviet government of Russia gives the vote to women and declares equality between the sexes

Dutch dancer Mata Hari (Margarethe Zelle 1876–1917) is executed by the French for espionage | American Grace Abbott writes *The Immigrant and the Community*

Political activist Mollie Steiner (1897–1980) is arrested under the Sedition Act during WWI for opposing US intervention in Russia and sentenced to 20 years in prison

American social worker and opponent of public relief Mary Ellen Richmond (1861–1928) publishes *Social Diagnosis*

The Women's Indian Association is established

Colette Reynaud starts the "feminist, Socialist, pacifist and internationist" paper *Women's Voice*

Indian labor activist Anusuyaben Sarabhai organizes India's first major strike | **1917** |
| | |

Ambulance drivers passing through French village on British western front
Photograph (c. 1918) courtesy Sophia Smith Collection, Smith College | | | |
| Soprano Rosa Ponselle (Ponzillo, 1894–1981) debuts at the Metropolitan Opera

Soprano Claudia Muzio (1892–1936) debuts at the Metropolitan Opera

Australian soprano Nellie Melba (1861–1931) is made a Dame Commander of the British Empire | American evangelist Aimee Semple McPherson (1890–1944) founds the International Church of Foursquare Gospel

British religious philanthropist Agnes Weston receives a burial with full naval honors, very rare for women, for her dedication to improving the lives of sailors | Marine zoologist Mary Jane Rathbun (1860–1943) receives her Ph.D. for *The Grapsoid Crabs of America*

Dr. Martha Wollstein and her colleague Harold Amoss develop a new method for the preparation of antimeningitis serum and establish criteria for its standardization | Irish Nationalist Constance Markiewicz is the first woman elected to the British Parliament; she refuses her chair as the representative of the St. Patrick's League of Dublin, having no allegiance to the crown

Japanese feminist Fusaye Ichikawa (1893–1981) founds the New Women's Association and the Woman's Suffrage League of Japan

Hélène Brion, author of *The Feminist Way: Woman, Dare to Be!*, which attacked Socialists and trade unions for insensitivity to women's issues, is imprisoned for disseminating pacifist propaganda | Women in Hamburg, Germany, protest proposed laws for increasing population and prohibiting birth control information

Editor and scholar Kate Stephens (1853–1938) publishes *Workfellows in Social Progress*, an essay protesting the use of the word "female" in discussing women

Italian-Russian Angelica Balabanoff (1878–1965) becomes a commissioner of foreign affairs for the Communist party

Constance Agatha Cummings (née Horton, b. 1918) founds the Sierra Leone Women's Movement | **1918** |

General/Context	Daily Life/ Customs/ Practices	Humanities/ Fine Arts	Occupations	Education
1918				
1919 Weimar Republic in Germany

Foundation of the Italian Fascist party by Benito Mussolini

Foundation of the International Congress of Working Women

A Jewish matriarch and her children in Russia Photograph (c. 1918) courtesy Rita F. Greenspan | The first commercial airplane passengers, Mrs. J. A. Hodges and Miss Ethel Hodges, fly from New York City to Atlantic City, NJ

Foundation of the Medical Women's International Association in London; its members, female medical doctors, work cooperatively to improve international hygiene | Käthe Kollwitz (1867–1945) is the first woman elected full member of the Prussian Academy of the Arts

William Randolph Hearst hires architect Julia Morgan to build his mansion, Casa Grande

Sculptor Mary Evelyn Longman is the first woman elected a member of the (American) National Academy of Design

Jessie Redmon Fauset (1882–1961) edits *Crisis*

American author Fannie Hurst (1889–1968) publishes | Mlle. Marie Prodham becomes the director of the Bank of Geneva

Elisa Orsi is the first woman to plead before an Italian court

War photographer Therese (née Mabel) Bonney (1895–1978) will found the first American illustrated press service in Paris

American Lena Madeson Phillips (1881–1955) founds the National Federation of Business and Professional Women's Clubs, Inc. (BPW)

Following the 1918 strike by the Union Streetcar Conductors | New York University decides to admit women to the medical college

The rousing editorial of Nebraska-born journalist Anna Louise Strong (1885–1970) helps to launch the Seattle general strike of 1919; she spends most of her life in Moscow and Peking, covering and promoting the Russian and Chinese revolutions

Foundation of the International Federation of University Women in London, a group concerned with raising the status of academic women on an international level |

THE JAPANESE WOMEN'S MOVEMENT

Japanese organizations dedicated to the rights of and protections for women date from the late 19th century. In the 1880s, female textile workers struck for better conditions, and two wealthy women, Kishida Toshiko and Fukuda Hideko, sought equal rights from within the Liberal party. The Women's Christian Temperance Union worked against prostitution and concubinage starting in 1886; they soon added suffrage to their demands. After the turn of the century, the Commoners' Society, a social democratic group led by men, pointed to capitalism as the source of women's oppression and fought for women's political rights.

But Japanese women faced many obstacles to progress. Excluded from most higher education opportunities, unable to manage their own property if married, they were also barred from political organizations and meetings by a law of 1900. In addition, centuries of custom gave men final authority within the household.

Several prominent activists emerged in Japan starting in 1911, when the Bluestocking Society was founded by young Hiratsuka Raichō. Her journal, *Bluestocking,* featured translations of feminist writings from overseas, includng works by the American

anarchist Emma Goldman and the British psychologist Havelock Ellis. The journal succeeded far beyond expectations and opened public discussion of a broad range of women's issues. Hiratsuka went on in 1919 to form with fellow writer Fusaye Ichikawa the New Woman Society, which lobbied successfully to repeal the law banning women from going to political meetings.

Ichikawa, a potent suffrage activist, worked for the International Labor Organization and led the political wing of the powerful Tokyo Federation of Women's Organizations. This group made a name for itself by helping victims of the great Kanto earthquake in 1923; it then campaigned against prostitution, hazardous working conditions for women, educational restrictions, and limitations on political rights. Ichikawa also founded the League for Women's Suffrage in 1924: she believed a single-issue organization could achieve more in the fight for voting rights.

The 1920s saw a flurry of activism on women's issues, especially suffrage. The All-Kansai Federation of Women's Organizations was the largest group at three million members, but the League for Women's Suffrage, the National Association of

Performing Arts/ Entertainment/ Sports	Religion/ Philosophy	Science/ Technology/ Discovery	Statecraft/ Military	Reform	
			In Britain for the first time, women are eligible to vote and run for election to the House of Commons		**1918**
			Queen Salote Tubou III (1900–1965) reigns over Tonga from 1918 to 1965		
German dancer Mary Wigman (d. 1973) begins performing in her own dance recitals, exhibiting a free and forceful style that discards the conventional "prettiness" of classical ballet; the Wigman style becomes an international cult known as free dance; she establishes schools in many German cities and in the US, where she tours as a soloist and with her "girl dance group"; she characteristically performs to special percussion scores created for her

French tennis player Suzanne Langlen (1899–1938) becomes British women's sin- | The Union Mondiale des Organisations Féminines Catholiques (World Union of Catholic Women's Organizations) is founded in Paris to promote peace and Catholic ideals among women

Daughters of the nobility, Kagoshima, Japan, 1917-1921 Photograph courtesy Sophia Smith Collection, Smith College

 | | 21 states ratify the 19th Amendment, to grant American women the right to vote in federal elections

Italy grants women suffrage

Attorney General Brundage decides that women may sit as delegates in the Republican and Democratic conventions

American-born Viscountess Nancy Witcher Langhorne Astor (1879–1964) becomes the first female member of Parliament in Great Britain | Fanny Garrison Villard (1844–1928) founds the Women's Peace Society in New York City

Rosa Luxemburg and Karl Liebknecht lead the Communist uprising to oppose Germany's entrance into the world war

French feminist Nelly Roussel declares a "strike of the wombs" in protest of the postwar government's policy of forced maternity

Huda Sh'arawi leads 300 women to the British High Commission to protest the killing of civilians, including women, in | **1919** |

Women Primary School Teachers, the National Women's Christian Temperance Union, and various Buddhist and Christian women's groups also campaigned for women's right to vote. In 1931, a government-sponsored bill allowing women to vote in local elections passed the House of Commons but failed in the House of Peers.

For some time, the government had sought to check the influence of feminist groups by creating its own, more conservative women's organizations. During the 1904–5 war against Russia, the government-sponsored Patriotic Women's Society swelled to half a million members. Although it succeeded in aiding the families of soldiers and giving women a way to participate in politics, many feminists criticized it as a sell-out. The government continued this practice with such groups as the Greater Japan Federation of Women's Societies, led by hand-picked male officers, during the 1930s and 1940s. The militarism Japan experienced from 1931 to 1945, however, turned most women's attention to wartime problems, such as life under an essentially totalitarian regime, hunger, dislocation, deaths in the family, and the loss of the war.

Some activists continued to organize their own groups, though, intent on such reforms as an end to prostitution, consumer protection, birth control, and welfare legislation that would aid mothers and children. The last of these, which fit in with the government's pro-family views, resulted in welfare legislation in 1936.

Because the victorious Allies saw women's oppression as a legacy of Japan's outdated militarism, the occupation forces of 1945–1951 made a point of updating women's rights. A new constitution allowed women to vote and participate in politics, granted them rights within the family, and guaranteed equal pay for equal work: at that time Japanese women had more rights than American women.

Japanese women have voted at a higher rate than men since 1968. For the last 20 years, large and powerful women's groups have achieved success in such areas as consumer protection and environmental issues. Most groups remain committed to the idea that women are naturally domestic, an idea criticized by a small number of feminists who urge a sharper focus on women's autonomy and full participation in the public sphere.

	General/ Context	Daily Life/ Customs/ Practices	Humanities/ Fine Arts	Occupations	Education
1919			a collection of stories about New York City Jewish life British novelist May Sinclair publishes *Mary Olivier* British sculptor Dame Barbara Hepworth (1903–1975) wins a scholarship to study art in Leeds	protesting the employment of female conductors, the War Labor Board rules in favor of the continued employment of women Sylvia Beach opens the first American bookshop in Paris, Shakespeare and Co.	

English gentlewomen at work in a munitions factory just after WWI
Photograph (1919) courtesy Sophia Smith Collection, Smith College

	General/ Context	Daily Life/ Customs/ Practices	Humanities/ Fine Arts	Occupations	Education
1920	French law bans the sale of contraceptives	The American Civil Liberties Union is founded by social reformers, including Jane Addams, Helen Gurley Flynn, and Helen Keller French designer Gabrielle "Coco" Chanel (1883–1971), who left an indelible imprint on contemporary fashion, introduces the "little black dress" as a staple of women's wardrobes Marie Stopes opens her first Mother's Clinic for Birth Control in London; initially only married women are allowed access to its information and counseling services The Soviet government legalizes abortion; while physicians are not allowed to refuse abortions to women less than two and a half months pregnant, they are required to try to discourage them, especially women in their first pregnancies	American literary scholar Myra Reynolds (1853–1936) publishes *The Learned Lady in England, 1650–1760* Alexandra Exter (1882–1949) is an innovative scenic and costume designer whose work defines theatrical design in the USSR in the 1920s Artist Elaine Fried de Kooning (1920–1989) combines abstract expressionism with representational style Lauren Harris (1885–1970) is a founding member of the Canadian art movement known as the Group of Seven Composer Ethel Smyth is created Dame Commander of the British Empire American poet Genevieve Taggard (1894–1948) founds and edits *The Measure: a Journal of Verse*	American labor leader Mary Anderson (1872–1964) serves as head of the Federal Women's Bureau until 1944 The US Congress grants army nurses "relative" rank, giving them authority next after that of medical officers in military hospitals, but without the privileges and salary of commissioned rank American women are permitted to practice law in every state by this year Central African women abandon rural areas in large numbers to work in new colonial towns, where they sell domestic skills, sometimes including their bodies; regulations are enacted by African and European men to control their labor	Klavdiya Nikolaeva Artyukhina, a typesetter, and Aleksandra Vasilevna Artyukhina, a textile worker, head the Soviet Women's Organization Oxford University, which has admitted women since 1884, consents to grant them degrees

Performing Arts/ Entertainment/ Sports	Religion/ Philosophy	Science/ Technology/ Discovery	Statecraft/ Military	Reform	
gles champion from 1919 to 1923 and 1925

Amy Woodforde-Finden (d. 1919), Chilean-born composer, is known for her setting of Laurence Hope's verses in her *Indian Love Lyrics,* which enjoy international popularity | | | A proposal for women's suffrage comes before the French Senate, but is ignored

Women are granted the right to sit in New Zealand's parliament

The American Communist party is established | Egyptian anti-British demonstrations

The southern leaders of the National Association of Colored Women draw up their list of grievances; first on the list is the conditions of domestic service workers, including a protest against white male employers expecting the right to take sexual liberties with their servants

American activist for black liberation Anita Whitney (b. 1867) defies the law by speaking on lynchings to a white women's civic league; she is arrested and sentenced to a term in San Quentin Prison | **1919** |
| American choreographer Ruth St. Denis (1871–1968) brings Eastern dance to the West; together with her husband, Ted Shawn, she creates the Denishawn School in Los Angeles, America's first serious dance school

Viennese soprano Anna Bahr-von Mildenburg (b. 1872) becomes dramatic director for Wagner's works at the Munich Opera

German film star of international reputation, Lil (Marta Maria Liletta) Dagover (1897–1927) stars in the classic *The Cabinet of Dr. Caligari* | Joan of Arc is canonized by the Roman Catholic Church

Halide Hanoum, Turkish feminist leader Photograph (c. 1920) courtesy Sophia Smith Collection, Smith College | Turkish physician Safieh Ali is one of the first female medical doctors in her country | Alice Robertson of Oklahoma is elected to the House of Representatives

Harriet Taylor Upton (1853–1945) is appointed vice chairman of the Republican National Executive Committee, one of the first women in the US to hold such a high party position

Ratification of the 19th Amendment to the US Constitution confers nationwide suffrage upon women

Black women registered to vote in Savannah, GA, are denied ballots in several locations in the city

Chinese Communist leader Chen Li participates in military action while pregnant

Julia Catherine Stimson (1881–1948), superintendent of the US Army Nurse Corps, becomes the first woman major in the US Army | The Women's International Zionist Organization is established in London; its mission is to awaken national consciousness in Jewish women and to promote social work in Israel

Egyptian social activist Huda Sh'arawi becomes head of an organization of women teachers and establishes a women's union

The League of Women Voters is formed in Chicago to educate women in the use of the vote and to improve the economic, political, and social conditions of the country

Charlotte Woodward, an American working woman, is the only woman who attended the Seneca Falls convention in 1848 who lives long enough to exercise her right to vote

Beginning of the women's liberation move- | **1920** |

General/ Context	Daily Life/ Customs/ Practices	Humanities/ Fine Arts	Occupations	Education
1920	France orders severe fines and prison sentences for anyone who performs or receives an abortion; the law is widely disregarded and the rate of abortion rises to 500,000 a year within the next 50 years; botched abortions cause an estimated 500 deaths a year		*Russian woman wearing the veil and costume of a religious order* Photograph (c. 1920) courtesy Sophia Smith Collection, Smith College	
	*Officer recruits in the WRENS, 1920s* Photograph courtesy Sophia Smith Collection, Smith College			
1921	The first Miss America Pageant, won by Margaret Gorman of Washington, DC, is held in Atlantic City, NJ

Louisa Boyd Yeomans King is the first woman to receive the George White Medal of the Massachusetts Horticultural Society, the highest gardening award in America | Edith Wharton receives a Pulitzer Prize for Fiction for *The Age of Innocence*

The Woman Movement, or Suffrage Monument, by sculptor Adelaide Johnson, is dedicated in Washington, DC; it represents the portrait heads of Elizabeth Cady Stanton, Susan B. Anthony, and Lucretia Mott | Russian immigrant Clara Goldhurst is the world's first female put-and-call dealer; she later founds her own financial firm in New York

Louise Stanley is appointed head of the Bureau of Home Economics

Margaret Farrar (d. 1984) edits *The New York World's* crossword | |

LADIES SING THE BLUES

The blues, simple melodies and repetitive choruses using flatted thirds and sevenths, originated in America after the Civil War in the rhythmic shouts and calls of field hands and street vendors. The golden age of the blues, the 1920s, brought great artists like Bessie Smith and "Ma" (Gertrude Pridgett) Rainey, who between them recorded hundreds of records, to the attention of an international public. They didn't just sing: Ida Cox and Bessie Smith each composed hundreds of songs while they toured for years with road shows.

Blues songs celebrated the sadness, losses, and frustrations of difficult lives, and did so with a bitter realism foreign to most popular song. While most blues bemoaned relationships between the sexes, blues songs also dealt with other miseries and threats to well-being from natural disasters like floods and fires to prison, slavery, old age, and disease.

The persona, or voice, in women's blues underwent an evolution from early Ma Rainey lyrics about passive, suffering women to lyrics of the 1920s in which Bessie Smith or Ida Cox express more active, even aggressive responses to man's inhumanity to woman. In the later songs, though the woman may feel heartsick about her man's infidelity, she may skip town, return home to mother, or "get me a razor and a gun," as one Bessie Smith lyric proclaims.

Women's blues adopted the frank sexuality of male blues singers, departing radically from the blind unquestioning fidelity expressed in earlier songs. By challenging men to perform on demand or face public humiliation, these blues songs made

Performing Arts/ Entertainment/ Sports	Religion/ Philosophy	Science/ Technology/ Discovery	Statecraft/ Military	Reform	

Mrs. F. J. Runyon, president of First Woman's Bank in Tennessee
Photograph (c. 1920) courtesy Sophia Smith Collection, Smith College

Mary Margaret McBride, first lady of radio, interviews Eleanor Roosevelt
Photograph courtesy Sophia Smith Collection, Smith College; reprinted from the Springfield *Sunday Republican*

ment in Vietnam, brought about by French influence in the schools **1920**

Between 1910 and 1920, Hermila Galindo of Mexico is the collaborator of President Venustiano Carranzza; she combines service to the revolutionary cause with campaigning for women's rights

Madam Alimotu Pelewura (1900–1951), a leader of women in Lagos, Nigeria, influences the formation of nationalist political parties, including the Nigerian National Democratic party and the Nigerian Union of Young Democrats, during the 1920s and 1930s

American blues singer Bessie Smith (1894–1937), "Empress of the Blues," makes her first recording

Irish patriot Maud Gonne (1866–1953) becomes the first ambassador of the Irish Free State to Paris

Moravian soprano Maria Jeritza joins the Metropolitan Opera Company, where she

One of the most important women in mathematics in Russia, Pelageya Polubarinova-Kochina (b. 1899) benefits from the revolution's integration into the universities of "higher courses for women"; her main contributions are applications to hydrodynamics of the theory of complex functions and the analytic the-

Eleanor Roosevelt (1884–1962) is her husband's representative in political life when he is crippled by polio

The Louisiana legislature passes a law admitting women to public office

Women's suffrage passes in a revision of the Dutch Constitution

The International Co-operative Women's Guild, founded in London, seeks to advance the interests of housewives and works for international cooperation and peace **1921**

the startling public assertion that women experience sexual desire and expect sexual fulfillment.

From the 1920s to the 1940s prominent blues vocalists included Victoria Spivey, the "Texas Moaner," and that other famous moaner Clara Smith, "the World's Champion Moaner"; Sippie Wallace, the "Texas Nightingale"; the prolific Sara Martin, and Mamie Smith, the first black vocalist to record a blues song. Alberta Hunter—who was still performing in the 1970s—was the first black singer to record with a white band; and "Sweet Mama Stringbean," Ethel Waters, also sang popular music and carved out a career on the screen. Lil Green and Bertha "Chippie" Hill pushed the blues into the forties with the arrival of a new sound that *Billboard* in 1949 was to call rhythm and blues.

Rhythm and blues stars Julia Lee and Dinah Washington made popular a music with more complex harmonies and 16- as well as 12-bar blues, music in which electrical instruments now played an increasingly central part. In 20 years "Queen of the Blues" Dinah Washington recorded some 450 songs, revamping popular standards in the process of putting R&B in the Top 10. By the 1960s and 1970s, Janis Joplin would be inspired by "Big Mama" Willie Mae Thornton, followed by Linda Hopkins and Koko Taylor, who toured not only the country but the world.

In contrast to the choral music of the spiritual, the blues was a solo: secular music that combined anguish and humor, a music of survival well suited to the grittier side of reality experienced by black women.

| | Daily Life/ | | | |
General/ Context	Customs/ Practices	Humanities/ Fine Arts	Occupations	Education
1921			puzzle, the first woman to hold the job	

1922

Refugee woman at the YWCA, Foyer des Alliées, Lyons, France,
1920s
Photograph courtesy Sophia Smith Collection, Smith College

	Humanities/Fine Arts	Occupations	Education
	African-American Georgia Douglas Johnson (1886–1966) publishes *Bronze* Anne Nichols (1891– 1966) writes *Abie's Irish Rose* Annie Swinnerton is the first woman elected to the British Royal Academy of Art in this century *Chronicles of Chicora Wood* by Elizabeth Waties Allston Pringle (1845–1921) is pub- lished posthumously Emily Post (1873– 1960) publishes *Eti- quette*, which makes her the arbiter of American manners Sylvia Beach helps James Joyce edit and revise *Ulysses* Poet Genevieve Tag- gard publishes *For Ea- ger Lovers*	Monica Cobb becomes the first woman lawyer to plead a case in En- gland Lucile Curtis (b. 1894) is the US's first female Foreign Service officer The US Government Printing Office de- clares that male and female employees will receive equal pay for the same work Ivy Williams is the first woman to be called to the English bar; she declines, choosing to teach at Oxford rather than to practice law Helena Normanton becomes the first woman to practice as a barrister in England	Elise Richter (d. 1942) becomes Austria's first female professor

1923

General/Context	Daily Life/Customs/Practices	Humanities/Fine Arts		Education
	Dr. Rachelle Yarros establishes the second birth control clinic in the US in a heavily populated Chicago neighborhood The word "scofflaw" is coined by Kate L. Butler of Massachusetts as an entry in a contest that asked for the best word to "stigmatize those who scoff at the Prohibition law"	French pianist Ger- maine Tailleferre (b. 1892) composes the music for the ballet Le Marchand d'Oiseaux Edna St. Vincent Millay receives the Pulitzer Prize for *The Ballad of the Harp- Weaver, A Few Figs from Thistles and Other Poems* *One of Ours* by Willa Cather receives the Pulitzer Prize for Fic- tion Diane Arbus (1923– 1971), is known for photographing odd,		American library edu- cator Sarah Comly Norris Bogle (1870– 1932) conducts a li- brary course in Paris out of which the Paris Library School grows in 1924 Philanthropist Mary Louise Curtis Bok (b. 1876) founds the Cur- tis Institute of Music, Philadelphia Aurelia Reinhardt is elected national presi- dent of the American Association of Univer- sity Women Founder of the South- ern Highland Handi-

Performing Arts/ Entertainment/ Sports	Religion/ Philosophy	Science/ Technology/ Discovery	Statecraft/ Military	Reform	
creates the roles of Turandot and Helena in the US		ory of differential equations	Women vote for the first time in Belgium Mary Ellen Smith (1862–1933) is appointed minister without portfolio in 1921–1922 for British Columbia		**1921**
Soprano Elisabeth Rethberg (1894–1976) sings with the Metropolitan Opera, 1922–1942 English actress Margaret Leighton (1922–1976) is known for her Tony Award-winning roles in *Separate Tables* and *Night of the Iguana* Gracie Allen (1895–1964), American comedienne and actress, begins working with George Burns Swedish contralto Gertrud Wettergren makes her debut at the Stockholm Royal Opera The American Athletic Union establishes the National Indoor and Outdoor Track Championships for Women Canadian-born comedienne Beatrice Gladys Lillie (1898–1989) wins an international reputation for sophisticated humor in her first hit show, *Charlot's Revue*	The Protestant Episcopal Church in the US removes "obey" from the marriage ceremony At the death of Italian Sister Bertilla Boscardin (b. 1888), who worked with sick children and wounded soldiers, followers flock to her grave where miracles of healing attributed to her intercession are reported	Bessie Coleman (1893–1926) receives her pilot's license from the Federation Aéronautique Internationale (International Aeronautic Federation) in France, becoming the first African-American woman pilot	In a general strike protesting the imprisonment of Kenyan anticolonial leader Harry Thuku in Nairobi, Mary Muthoni Nyanjiru accuses the male leaders of cowardice when they try to disperse the crowd after receiving assurances from the British; she incites the crowd to follow her instead and, when she is killed in the subsequent fighting, she becomes a heroine of the Kenyan independence movement The (US) Women's National Committee for Law Enforcement, headed by Lucy Whitehead McGill Waterbury Peabody, is formed to ensure the enforcement of the Volstead Act mandating Prohibition	Foundation of the Federação Brasileira pelo Progresso Feminino (Brazilian Federation for the Advancement of Women) by biologist Bertha Lutz Birth of newspaperwoman and civil rights activist Daisy Gatson Bates, who will be instrumental in the integration of Little Rock, AR, public schools	**1922**
Adrienne Bolland, French aviator, sets a record by looping the loop 98 times within a period of 58 minutes Bertha Horchem ascends 16,300 feet, setting the aviation record for women Maria Callas (Maria Kalogerolpoulou, 1923–1977), Greek-American operatic soprano, will become one of her generation's great divas Alma Cummings and her partner set a world record, dancing non-stop for 27 hours at		Margaret Sanger organizes the first conference on birth control in the US and, in 1925, the first international conference Psychiatrist Lauretta Bender (d. 1987) develops the Bender Gestalt Visual Motor Test Microbiologist Gladys Dick and physician George Dick isolate the cause of scarlet fever; they later develop the Dick test for diagnosis, prevention, and treatment of the disease	Women are granted suffrage in the Philippines Suffragist and women's rights leader Alice Paul writes and campaigns for the ratification of the US Equal Rights Amendment (ERA)	Suffragists Nettie Rogers Shuler (1862–1939) and Carrie Chapman Catt publish *Woman Suffrage and Politics*	**1923**

	General/Context	Daily Life/Customs/Practices	Humanities/Fine Arts	Occupations	Education
1923			sometimes abnormal subjects  *American poet Marianne Moore* Photograph (c. 1951) courtesy Skidmore College Rare Books and Special Collections		craft Guild, Lucy Morgan inaugurates the Penland Weavers in North Carolina, the oldest and largest summer crafts school in the US The American Physical Education Association's National Committee on Women's Athletics resolves that year-round athletics programs should be made available to girls
1924	Benito Mussolini seizes power in Italy Joseph Stalin takes office as leader of the Communist party in the Soviet Union		Russian choreographer Bronislava Nijinska (1891–1972) founds the Theatre de Danse in Paris English author Margaret Kennedy (1896–1967) publishes her best-seller, *The Constant Nymph* Georgia O'Keeffe (1887–1986), the most famous woman artist of the 20th century, produces *Dark Corn* American poet Marianne Craig Moore (1887–1972) publishes *Observations*	Polly (Pearl) Adler (1900?–1962) opens her bawdy house in New York, patronized by notable literary wits, underworld figures, movie stars and tycoons Helen Rogers Reid (1882–1970) is vice president of the merged *New York Herald Tribune*, overseeing all departments; she becomes president in 1947	Edith Abbott (1876–1957), American social work educator and reformer, helps establish the School of Social Service Administration of the University of Chicago, the first such program in the US Mrs. Lugan Keene is appointed professor of anatomy at London University
1925	Adolf Hitler writes *Mein Kampf*	British colonial law in Trinidad and Tobago sentences women to four years' imprisonment for attempting to induce their own or another's miscarriage At about this time, Turkey bans the custom requiring women to veil their faces Twenties' silent-screen star Clara Gordon Bow (1905–1965), known as the "It Girl," becomes a symbol of the flapper	Dutch novelist Johanna van Ammers-Küller publishes *The Rebel Generation* Publication of humorist Anita Loos's (1893–1981) enormously successful *Gentlemen Prefer Blondes* Welsh novelist Hilda Vaughan (b. 1892) writes *Battle to the Weak,* set in Wales	The New York State Assembly passes the Joiner bill allowing women to work 48 hours a week The Frontier Nursing Service is established in Kentucky by Mary Breckenridge Marianne Moore becomes acting editor of the literary magazine *The Dial*	Frances Stern (1873–1947), social worker and dietitian, sets up the Nutrition Education Department to train foreign and American doctors, dentists, social workers, and nurses in dietetics A lifelong feminist who once carried a "Votes for Women" banner into the Himalayas, explorer Fanny Bullock Workman endows four American women's colleges: Radcliffe, Smith, Bryn Mawr, and Wellesley

Performing Arts/ Entertainment/ Sports	Religion/ Philosophy	Science/ Technology/ Discovery	Statecraft/ Military	Reform	

1923

the US's first dance marathon

Hooked rug with birth control message, c. 1925
Photograph courtesy Sophia Smith Collection, Smith College

Miriam "Ma" Ferguson reads her inaugural address as governor of Texas, 1925
Photograph courtesy Sophia Smith Collection, Smith College

1924

American mezzo-soprano Gladys Swarthout (1904–1969), a member of the Chicago Civic Opera Company, expands her career to include concert, radio, and film performances

Aviator Adrienne Bolland loops the loop 212 times, breaking her own 1923 record

Ora Washington is the first black woman to win the American Tennis Association singles title

Women are denied official recognition and full voting power in synods and presbyteries by the general council of the Presbyterian Church in the US

American Belle Carter Harmon becomes the first woman in the world ordained as a deacon of the Methodist Episcopal Church

Nina Bang becomes the first female government minister in Denmark

The first woman nominated for vice president of the US on the Democratic ticket is Lena Jones Springs of South Carolina, who receives 18 votes

"Ma" (Miriam A.) Ferguson wins the Democratic nomination for governor of Texas with more than 80,000 votes

Ellen Wilkinson becomes the British Labor party's first woman member of Parliament

British activist Annie Kenney publishes *Memoirs of a Militant,* a record of her longtime involvement with the Pankhursts in the Women's Social and Political Union

1925

Florence Rena Sabin, teacher, public health specialist, and medical researcher in histology and TB control
Photograph (c. 1925) courtesy Sophia Smith Collection, Smith College

Dr. Florence Sabin (1871–1953) is the first woman elected to the (US) National Academy of Sciences; she is also the only woman to become a full member of the Rockefeller Institute during its first 50 years

Foundation of the (US) Society of Women Geographers by explorer Harriet Chalmers Adams (1875–1937)

Mary Morris Vaux Walcott publishes *North American Wild Flowers*

Elected to the US Congress, Mary Teresa Norton serves until 1951; she is the first woman to chair a national party platform committee, the first to be elected a freeholder in New Jersey, the first to chair three House committees, and the first elected to Congress from the East; she is also credited with passage of the Fair Labor Standards Act of 1938

Sarojini Naidu becomes the first Indian woman president of the Indian National Congress

Mary Ellen Richmond argues for compulsory physical examinations and raising the legal age for marriage

African-American labor activist Lucy Parsons is a leading force in the newly founded International Labor Defense

In Nigeria, thousands of women protest against taxation, the British system of authority and rights of enforcement; the British blame men for the disturbance, not believing in women's ability to organize against them; educa-

	General/ Context	Daily Life/ Customs/ Practices	Humanities/ Fine Arts	Occupations	Education
1925					
1926	*The Jazz Singer,* the first talking film, makes its debut	The first federal prison in the US built exclusively for women, the Federal Industrial Institution for Women in West Virginia, has no guards and no walls surrounding it; its first superintendent is Dr. Mary B. Harris Two Japanese girls clasp hands and leap into a live volcano when they learn of Rudolph Valentino's death Count Hermann Keyserling edits *The Book of Marriage,* to which George Bernard Shaw refuses to contribute, claiming that "no man can tell the truth about marriage while his wife is alive"	British author Sylvia Townsend Warner (1893–1978) publishes *Lolly Willowes* Amy Lowell receives the Pulitzer Prize for Poetry for *What's O'Clock* Italian novelist Graziela Deledda (1875–1936) depicts peasant life in Sardinia and receives the Nobel Prize for Literature Katrina Trask's Saratoga Springs, NY, estate, Yaddo, opens as an artists' colony	Lucia Welch becomes the first woman sheriff in England Clara Senecal becomes the first woman sheriff in New York State Turkish women are admitted to the bar and the bench Mary Dillon is elected president of the Brooklyn Borough Gas Company after working there for 23 years Violet Neatly Anderson of Chicago, IL, becomes the first black woman to practice law before the US Supreme Court	Martha McChesney Berry establishes Berry College Christine Ladd-Franklin receives a Ph.D. in philosophy from Johns Hopkins University for work completed 44 years before The Women's Service Library, one of the chief repositories for women's history materials, is established by the Fawcett Society in London
1927	The wall-mounted can opener, a labor-saving device, is sold in the US The first nonstop solo Atlantic flight is made by American pilot Charles A. Lindbergh	Women's Day is observed in Moscow Women's hemlines rise from the ankle to just beneath the knee, reflecting, some believe, the economic prosperity enjoyed in the West Shortly before strangling to death with her scarf in a freak automobile accident, American dancer Isadora Duncan publishes her autobiography, *My Life*	Leonora Speyer's *Fiddler's Farewell* receives the Pulitzer Prize for Poetry German musicologist Marie Lipsius (1837–1927), writing under the pen name La Mara, is known for her works on Liszt and Beethoven British author of short stories and novels Elizabeth Bowe publishes *The Hotel* Russian Alexandra Kollontai (1872–1952) publishes *A Great Love;* she becomes the highest ranking woman in Lenin's government, despite his disagreement with her feminist views	Anna Goldfarb becomes the first Russian woman to hold the position of censor Phoebe F. Omlie receives a commercial transport license, the first pilot's license granted to a woman by the US Commerce Department	Edith Abbott and Sophonisba Breckinridge establish the *Social Service Review* and launch the University of Chicago Social Services Series Scripps College for Women in Claremont, CA, is founded by Ellen Browning Scripps

Dancer Martha Graham
Photograph (c. 1965) courtesy Skidmore College Rare Books and Special Collections

A British veterinarian at her work, 1920s
Photograph courtesy Sophia Smith Collection, Smith College

Performing Arts/ Entertainment/ Sports	Religion/ Philosophy	Science/ Technology/ Discovery	Statecraft/ Military	Reform	
				tional and economic reforms are spurred by the event, but apply only to men	**1925**
Gertrude Ederle, the first woman to swim the English Channel, does so 2 hours faster than any man Dame Marie Rambert (1888–1982) founds the Ballet Rambert, Britain's oldest ballet company English-born Eva Le-Gallienne (b. 1899) founds the Civic Repertory Theatre in New York City; she co-founds the American Repertory Theatre in 1946 Martha Graham (1912–1991), grande dame of American modern dance, founds the Martha Graham Dance Company		Dr. Lois E. Hinson becomes the first woman to graduate from the University of Georgia College of Veterinary Medicine, the first woman supervisor in the USDA Federal Meat Inspection Division, the first female chief of staff veterinarian in the US Department of Agriculture, and the first woman elected national president of the National Association of Federal Veterinarians Mary L. Jobe Akeley goes to Africa with her husband to collect specimens for the American Museum of Natural History; much of her work appears in its Great African Hall Russian mathematician Nina Karlovna Bari receives the Glavnauka Prize for her postgraduate thesis in problems from the theory of trigonometric series	Women gain the right to run for elective office in India The prophetess Nyiraburumbuke leads a revolt in Rwanda against the Belgian colonial government, 1926–1927 The Finnish government names Miina Sillanpaa as its first female Cabinet member, and Finland is the first country in the world to have female members of parliament Miriam Ma Ferguson wins the governorship of Texas	Amrit Kaur (1889–1964) founds the Indian Red Cross and the All-India Women's Conference Rosika Schwimmer founds the Hungarian Feministrak Egesulete, a feminist-pacifist organization instrumental in many of Hungary's social reforms, including suffrage The International Woman Suffrage Alliance meets in Paris 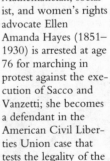 *Hungarian peace worker Rosika Schwimmer* Photograph (c. 1940) courtesy Sophia Smith Collection, Smith College	**1926**
Lena Phillipps sets the altitude record for women flyers at 11,000 feet Annie Peck Smith climbs to a higher altitude in the Himalayas than any human being before her; Huascaran Cumbre Aña Peck is named in her honor Polish harpsichordist Wanda Landowska (b. 1877) establishes her own school of music at St. Leu-La-Forêt, France; she has an international reputation as a performer of 17th- and 18th-century cembalo music German concert pianist and composer Louise		Viennese mathematician Hilda Geiringer (later von Mises, 1893–1973) is made *Privatdozent* (unsalaried lecturer) at the University of Berlin; she is proposed as an extraordinary professor in 1933, but Hitler's rise to power causes her to lose her job and leave the country  *Palestinian woman wearing heavy gold coins around her head—her dowry—Beirut, Syria* Photograph (c. 1925) courtesy Sophia Smith Collection, Smith College	Frances E. Willis (b. 1899) achieves many firsts in her 37-year-long career with the US Foreign Service, which she begins this year: first woman appointed the highest rank in the service, first woman to assume charge of a post, first woman appointed ambassador, first woman appointed career minister, and first woman appointed ambassador to more than one country	Mathematician, socialist, and women's rights advocate Ellen Amanda Hayes (1851–1930) is arrested at age 76 for marching in protest against the execution of Sacco and Vanzetti; she becomes a defendant in the American Civil Liberties Union case that tests the legality of the arrests	**1927**

	General/ Context	Daily Life/ Customs/ Practices	Humanities/ Fine Arts	Occupations	Education
1927					
1928		The Ligue Internationale des Mères et Éducatrices pour la Paix (International League of Mothers and Women Teachers for the Promotion of Peace) is founded in Paris to raise the younger generation in the spirit of international understanding The World Association of Girl Guides and Girl Scouts is founded in London	British author Radclyff Hall's *The Well of Loneliness* is judged obscene for its portrayal of lesbian love Dorothy Thompson (1894–1961) publishes *The New Russia* Genevieve Taggard publishes *Travelling Standing Still,* a collection of her poems One of the most distinctively Australian writers, Fiji-born novelist Katherine Susannah Prichard (b. 1884) publishes works reflecting her sensitivity to the plight of the working class Norwegian novelist Sigrid Undset is awarded the Nobel Prize for Literature Publication of American novelist and playwright Djuna Barnes's (1892–1982) best known work *Ryder* Janet Flanner (1892–1978) begins her 50-year stretch as Paris correspondent for *The New Yorker,* writing under the name "Genet"	Lady Mary Heath becomes the first woman pilot in passenger service Ruth B. Shipley becomes the US's first woman passport division chief The Soroptimist International Association, a union of all Soroptimist Clubs, which promote the highest ethical standards among the foremost women of all professions, forms in Antwerp, Belgium	Cambridge University in England graduates its first women British educational pioneer Louisa Lumsden (1840–1935) receives her M.A. in classics, even though she passed her Cambridge University examinations 55 years ago in 1873, when she attends the university's first graduation for women Virginia Woolf gives two lectures at Girton and Newnham colleges in Cambridge entitled "Women and Fiction," later published as *A Room of One's Own* The first Egyptian women are admitted to the Egyptian National University in Cairo

First generation of Turkish female doctors graduating from Haydos Pasha Medical School
Photograph (1928) courtesy Sophia Smith Collection, Smith College

Nurse in a Turkish birthing room, 1928
Photograph courtesy Sophia Smith Collection, Smith College

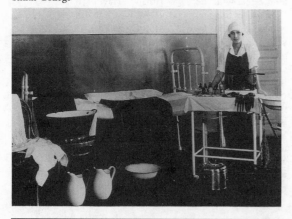

Women in an American cigar-making factory
Photograph (1929) courtesy Sophia Smith Collection, Smith College

	General/ Context	Daily Life/ Customs/ Practices	Humanities/ Fine Arts	Occupations	Education
1929	The Great Depression (1929–1933) begins with the October 24 crash of the stock market	The Nationalist party (KMT) in China promulgates a new civil code that permits women to own and inherit property, ini-	*Scarlet Sister Mary* by Julia Peterkin receives the Pulitzer Prize for Fiction	Sumati Morarjee becomes the first woman to run a large shipping company, the Indian Scindia Steam Navigation Company	An accomplished pianist, Charlotte Frances Hortense Parent (1837–1929), author of a pianoforte method, founds the

Performing Arts/ Entertainment/ Sports	Religion/ Philosophy	Science/ Technology/ Discovery	Statecraft/ Military	Reform	
Adolpha Le Beau (1850–1927) leaves a considerable oeuvre, including choral works, piano pieces, and songs					**1927**
French coloratura soprano Lily Pons (1904–1976) becomes the reigning Metropolitan Opera diva, 1928–1953

American actress and soprano Grace Moody (b. 1901) begins her singing career in New York revues and musical comedies, making her Metropolitan Opera debut in 1928; she appears with the Paris Opéra-Comique and Covent Garden (London), where she is wildly popular, in part, perhaps, because of her appearances in film musicals

Aviator Phoebe F. Omlie becomes the first woman to enter the national air tour

German soprano Elisabeth Rethburg creates the role of Helen in Strauss's *Aegyptische Helena*

German concert pianist Anna Falk Mehlig (1846–1928), having made many successful tours of Germany, England, and America, is court pianist to the king of Würtemberg | | American socialite Louise Arner Boyd (1887–1972) makes her first trip to the Arctic; during the 1930s, she organizes four scientific expeditions to the region, bringing back samples of plants and animals and taking thousands of photographs of great scientific value

Mary Lee Jobe Akeley receives Cross of the Knight, Order of the Crown from King Albert of Belgium for her work in Africa

Anthropologist Margaret Mead (1901–1978) publishes her first book, *Coming of Age in Samoa*

Members of the First Arab Women's Congress, Saudi Arabia, 1929
Photograph courtesy Sophia Smith Collection, Smith College | V. Zeltlin becomes the first woman to be appointed district attorney of the Soviet province of Tula

Great Britain grants women's suffrage

American suffragette turned politician Ruth Hanna McCormick Simms (1880–1944) seeks the Republican nomination for congressman-at-large from Illinois, leading a field of eight in the primary election; in the general election, she leads all Republicans on the ticket, including Herbert Hoover

Golda Meir (born Golda Myerson, 1898–1978) becomes secretary of the Women's Labor Council in Palestine

Women win the right to vote in Puerto Rico

Often named in polls as the world's most influential woman, Eleanor Roosevelt becomes a political leader in her own right, heading up the national women's campaign for the Democratic party

At age 24 British politician Jennie Lee becomes the youngest Member of Parliament of her time; the Independent Labor member later becomes minister of education | American writer and activist Ray (Rachel Conn) Strachey (1887–1940), active in England, publishes a history of the modern women's movement, *The Cause;* later works include the biography *Millicent Garrett Fawcett* (1931)

Prime Minister Golda Meir of Israel, late 1950s
Photograph courtesy Sophia Smith Collection, Smith College | **1928** |
| German actress Marlene Dietrich (1901–1992) appears in *The Blue Angel*, the film that establishes her screen reputation for | Between 1929 and 1930, Kenya's Church Missionary Society mounts its most vigorous opposition to clitoridectomy, a | Florence Augusta Merriam Bailey becomes the first woman fellow of the American Ornithologists' Union | Ruth Peterson and Evelyn Southworth testify before the US Senate, becoming the first women, other than members of Con- | The Aba Riots, better known as the Women's War, take place in southeastern Nigeria: tens of thousands of women in Iboland | **1929** |

	General/ Context	Daily Life/ Customs/ Practices	Humanities/ Fine Arts	Occupations	Education
1929	Philanthropists Abby Greene Aldrich Rockefeller (1874–1948), Lizzie Plummer Bliss (1864–1931), and Mary Quinn Sullivan (1877–1939) found the Museum of Modern Art in New York City	tiate divorce, and bring suit against unfaithful or polygynous husbands Janie Porter Barrett is awarded the William E. Harmon Award for Distinguished Achievement Among Negroes	Antoinette Perry directs her first success, *Strictly Dishonorable,* by Preston Sturges Champion of revolutionary China, Agnes Smedley (1892?–1950) writes *Daughter of Earth,* a novel that reflects her alliance with Indian revolutionary Virendranath Chattopadhyaya British writer Phyllis Bentley (b. 1894) publishes *Carr*	Dorothy Harrison Wood Eustis of Nashville, TN, establishes the first Seeing Eye dog class	École Préparatoire au Professorat (Preparatory School for Teaching) in Paris Open Door International for the Economic Emancipation of the Woman Worker is founded in Brussels, Belgium

Baskets for holding babies, Saudi Arabia
Photograph (c. 1929) courtesy Sophia Smith Collection, Smith College

	General/ Context	Daily Life/ Customs/ Practices	Humanities/ Fine Arts	Occupations	Education
1930	German Fascists, or National Socialists, under Adolf Hitler suppress socialism, communism, and begin to send dissidents, Jews, deviants, and foreigners to concentration camps Pop-up toasters are marketed in the US	Trousers become acceptable attire for women who play golf and ride horses Englishwoman Olave St. Clair, Lady Baden Powell (1889–1977), is appointed World Chief Guide by the World Association of Girl Guides and Girl Scouts The Pan-Pacific Women's and Southeast Asia Women's Association, founded in New York City, promotes peace and cooperation among the people of the Pacific Abortion becomes a crime "against the integrity and health of the race" in Mussolini's Italy; but illegal abortions continue at a rate of half a million a year	Katherine Anne Porter (1890–1980) publishes *Flowering Judas* Eminent American painter Cecilia Beaux publishes her autobiography, *Background with Figures* Dorothea Lange's (1895–1965) Depression photographs make the American public take notice of citizens who have fallen on disastrous hard times British novelist E. H. (Emma Hilda) Young (1880–1949) publishes her novel *Miss Mole;* other works include *William* (1925) and *The Vicar's Daughter* (1928) Elisabeth Whitworth Scott (1898–1972) is an architect in England; her work can be found in Cambridge, Stratford-upon-Avon, and Cheltenham British writer Edith Olivier (1879–1948) publishes a collection of stories, *Moonrakings* American classicist Edith Hamilton	Florence Lowe Barnes becomes the first woman to fly from Los Angeles to Mexico American journalist, novelist, and heiress Eleanor Medill Patterson (1881–1948) takes over the *Washington Herald* as editor and publisher The US Senate confirms Annabel Matthews as the first female member of the tax appeals board The Massachusetts State Police Force appoints the first female state police officers, Mary Ramsdell and Lotta Caldwell Ellen Church becomes United Airlines' first flight attendant Boeing hires eight nurses to act as flight attendants The Associated Country Women of the World, based in London, is founded to facilitate mutual aid among women farmers all over the world	Sarah Byrd Askew receives the first honorary degree ever given by the New Jersey College for Women (later Douglass College) of Rutgers University The Worldwide Federation of Young Catholic Women is founded in Ghent, Belgium; it seeks to further understanding and exchange among young Catholic girls of different nationalities Egyptian authorities Muhammad Aly and Clot Bey establish a school for midwives; the first graduates are ostracized by Egyptian society until the authorities hold annual joint celebrations for the graduates of the schools of medicine and midwifery

Suttee stone in Orcha, near Jhansi, India, marking the site where, following a long-established custom, three wives immolated themselves on the funeral pyres of their husbands
Photograph (1930) courtesy Sophia Smith Collection, Smith College

Performing Arts/ Entertainment/ Sports	Religion/ Philosophy	Science/ Technology/ Discovery	Statecraft/ Military	Reform	
sultry, impassive sexuality Canadian actress Fifi D'Orsay (1904–1983), the French Bombshell, utters her trademark " 'Ello beeg boy" in *They Had to See Paris* Gertrude Berg (1899–1966) broadcasts "The Rise of the Goldbergs," a radio program about a Jewish family in New York Considered the "mother of blues," singer Ma Rainey (Gertrude Melissa Nix Pridgett, 1886–1939) pioneers blues recording in the 20s and 30s	traditional form of female genital mutilation widely practiced among indigenous people of Kenya	Having earned the degree of Doktor-Ingenieur from the Technical University in Hannover, Germany, where she is the only woman in most of her classes, mathematician Irmgard Flügge-Lotz (1903–1974) joins a group of leading German aerodynamicists; her work in applied mathematics leads to her promotion to the head of the group in theoretical aerodynamics; she later becomes the first woman to attain the rank of full professor in Stanford University's engineering college	gress, to be permitted on the Senate floor Margaret Bondfield (1873–1953) becomes the first woman in the British Cabinet, as the minister of labor Eleanor Rathbone (1872–1946) becomes a Member of Parliament as an Independent Member for the Combined English Universities; she fights for the rights of women in England as well as in the British colonies	rebel against the British colonial authorities, protesting the decision to assess the taxable wealth of women; they harass government agents, attack European-owned property, and force local chiefs acting as representatives of British authority to give up power; more than 50 women are killed in clashes with troops before authorities regain control	**1929**
Dramatic soprano Gina Cigna (b. 1904), creator of the title role of Respighi's *La Fiamma,* joins La Scala in Milan, Italy Ruth Nichols flies from Long Island to California, the first transcontinental flight by a woman The University of Southern California polo team refuses to play against the University of California at Los Angeles until its one female member is replaced by a male British pioneer aviator Amy Johnson (1904–1941) becomes the first woman to make a solo flight to Australia, leaving from London Margaret Dumont (Margaret Baker, 1889–1965) becomes famous as Groucho Marx's straightwoman in seven Marx Brothers films, beginning with *Animal Crackers*	Sarah E. Dickson of Wisconsin becomes the first woman Presbyterian elder Informally ordained in Germany, Regina Jonas practices as a Reform rabbi; she later dies in the Theresienstadt concentration camp Pope Pius XI issues the encyclical *Casti connubi,* which mandates the use of the rhythm method of birth control *Women making a protest against Zionism in Jerusalem* Photograph (1929) courtesy Sophia Smith Collection, Smith College	The New York City Woman's Hospital installs an X-ray machine and radium for cancer patients Dr. Martha Wollstein becomes the first woman member of the American Pediatric Society	After two months in office as an Illinois congresswoman, Ruth Hanna McCormick Simms announces she will run for the Senate; she becomes embroiled in charges of political expediency and is defeated China's first female major general, Chen Li, is one of 30 women to survive the famous Long March to Shensi in 1930; she later leads Communist troops against the Nationalist forces Carmen Naranjo (b. 1930), born in Cartago, Costa Rica, begins publishing her political writings; during the 1970s she serves as ambassador and Cabinet minister in the social democratic government; all her work and writing are aimed at national liberation Mary McLeod Bethune serves as President Franklin D. Roosevelt's only black woman adviser during the 1930s; she serves Presidents Hoover and	Jane Addams publishes *The Second Twenty Years at Hull-House* In Vietnam, the Anticolonialist Women's Association involves women in the struggle for independence and reunification *A Gujarati shepherd girl of Kashmir* Photograph (1929) courtesy Sophia Smith Collection, Smith College	**1930**

	General/ Context	Daily Life/ Customs/ Practices	Humanities/ Fine Arts	Occupations	Education
1930			(1867–1963) is remembered for her accessible interpretations of ancient Greek and Roman life in *The Greek Way*	Foundation of the International Federation of Business and Professional Women in London, an organization that seeks to further the interests of professional women	
1931		Louise Waterman Wise (1847–1947), charitable worker and Zionist, creates the woman's division of the American Jewish Congress Concert pianist Olga Hickenlooper Samaroff (1882–1948) helps to found the Musicians' Emergency Fund of New York	Pearl S. Buck (1931–1973) publishes the novel *The Good Earth* Gertrude Vanderbilt Whitney founds the Whitney Museum of American Art Bernadotte E. Schmitt wins the Pulitzer Prize for History for *The Coming of War, 1914* Irma Rombauer (1877–1962) publishes *The Joy of Cooking* at her own expense	The Betsy Ross Corps, the first reserve corps of American women air pilots for noncombatant aviation duties in national emergencies, is organized Adelaide Marriott (b. 1883) incorporates the Handicrafts Association of Canada into the Canadian Handicrafts Guild and works to upgrade and expand craftwork in Canada	British writer Naomi Margaret Mitchison publishes *The Corn King and the Spring Queen*, a historical novel of ancient Greece and Rome; other works include *The Conquered* (1923), *The Rib of the Green Umbrella* (1960), and *Memoirs of a Space Woman* (1962)
1932		Foundation of the Chinese Women's Association, Inc., in New York City By 1932 at least 26 states in America have passed compulsory sterilization laws; Margaret Sanger defines the unfit that qualify for sterilization as "morons, mental defectives, epileptics, illiterates, paupers, unemployables, criminals, prostitutes and dope fiends," offering as the alternative lifelong segregation in labor camps	Comtesse Anna de Noailles (1876–1933) publishes *The Book of My Life* Laura Elizabeth Ingalls Wilder (1867–1957) publishes *Little House on the Prairie* Pearl S. Buck wins the Pulitzer Prize for Fiction for her novel *The Good Earth* Mabel Dodge Luhan (1879–1962) publishes a memoir of her relationship with D. H. Lawrence, *Lorenzo in Taos* German painter Gabriele Münter (1877–1962) is among the founders of the New Artists' Association of Munich Hebrew poet Yocheved Bat-Miriam (1901–1980) publishes *Me-Rahok* (*From Afar*)	Entrepreneur Tillie Lewis (née Myrtle Erlich) makes $12,000 a year selling securities in New York; in 1934 she introduces the Italian tomato industry to the US Amelia Earhart flies from Newfoundland to Ireland in 14 hours 56 minutes, the first solo transatlantic flight by a woman Laurette Schimmoler of Ohio becomes the first woman airport manager in the US, earning a salary of $510 a year	

Aviator Amelia Earhart and philanthropist Ethel Dreier Photograph (1928) courtesy Sophia Smith Collection, Smith College

Performing Arts/ Entertainment/ Sports	Religion/ Philosophy	Science/ Technology/ Discovery	Statecraft/ Military	Reform	
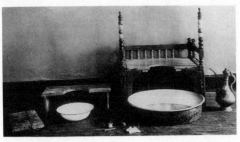 *Birthing stools, Saudi Arabia* Photograph (c. 1929) courtesy Sophia Smith Collection, Smith College			Truman in a similar capacity British Labor activist Bessie Braddock (1899–1970), dubbed "Battling Bessie" by the press, serves as Liverpool city councillor until 1961		**1930**
French soprano Lily Pons (b. 1904) debuts at the Metropolitan Opera The first major aviation competition between men and women, the National Air Race between Los Angeles, CA, and Cleveland, OH, is won by Phoebe Omlie When a permanent theater company is established at the Old Vic, Lilian Mary Baylis reestablishes the Sadler's Wells Theatre to make it the home for London's opera and ballet		Florence Augusta Merriam Bailey becomes the first woman to receive the Brewster Medal of the American Ornithologists' Union, for *Birds of New Mexico* (1928) Ellen Churchill Semple publishes *The Geography of the Mediterranean Region: Its Relation to Ancient History*	Suffrage is granted to women over 23 in Spain	Jane Addams shares the Nobel Peace Prize with Nicholas Murray Butler; she donates half her prize to the Women's International League for Peace and Freedom Jessie Daniel Ames founds the Association of Southern Women Against Lynching Promoting equal rights for women of all nations and races, the St. Joan's International Social and Political Alliance is founded in London	**1931**
Australian soprano Marjorie Lawrence debuts at Monte Carlo Stage and screen actress Helen Hayes (1900–1993) wins an Academy Award for her role in the film *The Sin of Madelon Claudet;* she is known as the First Lady of the American Theater The first concert of an orchestra composed entirely of women takes place in Vienna Florence Wolf Dreyfuss becomes chairman of the board of the Pittsburgh Pirates baseball team		Mabel Todd's Maine island becomes the National Audubon Society's Todd Wildlife Sanctuary Emmy Noether is awarded the Alfred Ackermann-Teubner Memorial Prize for the Advancement of the Mathematical Sciences, receiving for the first time in her career the recognition denied her because of her sex, religious background, and political opinions; at the International Mathematical Congress in Zurich, she becomes the only woman invited to deliver a plenary address	Brazilian women are granted suffrage Hattie Wyatt Caraway of Arkansas becomes the first woman to be elected to the US Senate (apart from Rebecca Felton, who held her seat for only one day), to chair a committee, to conduct Senate hearings, and to preside over Senate sessions President Hoover appoints Mary Woolley a delegate to the Conference on Reduction and Limitation of Armaments in Geneva, where she is the first woman to represent the US at an important diplomatic conference The French Senate rejects women's suffrage for the third time		**1932**

	General/ Context	Daily Life/ Customs/ Practices	Humanities/ Fine Arts	Occupations	Education
1933	Treaty on equal nationality rights for women is signed by 11 nations Establishment of the first German concentration camp for women at Ravenbruck near Berlin; it trains SS *Ausseherinnen* (overseers), 3500 female supervisors then sent to work at other camps	The US National Economy Act is passed, resulting in the dismissal of many women, whose husbands also hold federal positions, from government jobs	Publication of Gertrude Stein's *Autobiography of Alice B. Toklas* British anarchist writer Ethel Mannin writes on politics, pacifism, and child care British scholar Helen Waddell publishes *Peter Abelard;* a medievalist of renown, she is known for her translations of medieval Latin works	Former governor of Wyoming Nellie Tayloe Ross becomes the first female director of the US Mint Nightclub owner Texas Guinan (1889–1933) is known for her catch phrase, "Hello, Sucker!" Pearl McIver becomes the first public health nurse in the US Public Health Service The US Postal Service permits women to become postmistresses	
1934	The Congress of Industrial Organizations (CIO) is formed; unlike the American Federation of Labor (AFL), with which it later merges, the CIO promotes the acceptance of women into labor unions Invention of nylon	Bonnie Parker (1910–1934) is killed in a gun battle with police, ending a two-year crime spree with partner Clyde Barrow that includes 12 murders and many bank robberies China bans the binding of women's feet	Dame Margot Fonteyn (1919–1991) becomes the British Royal Ballet's prima ballerina, 1934–1975 Jungian psychoanalytic critic Maud Bodkin publishes the influential *Archetypal Patterns in Poetry* American playwright Lillian Hellman publishes *The Children's Hour* Isak Dinesen (pen name of Baroness Karen [Dinesen] Blixen, 1885–1962) publishes *Seven Gothic Tales* New Zealand producer and author of detective fiction Ngaio Marsh (1899–1982) publishes *A Man Lay Dead*	Florence Ellinwood Allen (1884–1966), American judge, becomes the first woman on the US Court of Appeals where she issues a landmark opinion that affects New Deal public works programs The first aerial police officer in the US is commercial transport pilot Cora Sterling of the Seattle, WA, police force The first headquarters of the American Youth Hostels, Inc., is opened in Massachusetts by Isabel Smith and her husband The first woman to fly airmail transport from Washington, DC, to Detroit is Helen Richey	
1935	The anti-Semitic Nuremberg Laws include a law forbidding the employment of German maids under the age of 45 in Jewish households	Scottish economic historian Isobel Grant establishes the Highland Folk Life Collection to record the disappearing traditional Scottish culture Hummel figurines inspired by the drawings of German artist Sister Maria Innocentia (b. Berta Hummel, 1909–1946) become a major industry	American Faith Baldwin (1893–1978) publishes *American Family* Antonia Brico founds the New York Women's Symphony Orchestra Doris Humphrey (1895–1958) founds the Juilliard Dance Theatre	Gretchen B. Schoenleber joins the New York Cocoa Exchange as the first woman stock exchange member in the US Trans World Airlines (TWA) hires the first regular "air hostesses" on passenger flights Dorothy Arzner (1900–1979), the first female director of	Lucy Diggs Slowe (1885–1937), dean of women at all-black Howard University, founds the National Council of Negro Women Dora Russell and her husband, Bertrand, set up an experimental school in England, Beacon Hill School, where they strive for a home-like family envi-

Performing Arts/ Entertainment/ Sports	Religion/ Philosophy	Science/ Technology/ Discovery	Statecraft/ Military	Reform	
The first black prima donna, Caterina Jarboro of the Chicago Opera Company, sings *Aïda* American actress Jean Harlow (Harlean Carpenter, 1911–1937), known as the Blonde Bombshell, makes one of her most popular films, *Dinner at Eight*	Dorothy Day (1897–1980) founds the Catholic Worker Movement in New York City; the *Catholic Worker* is a journal for pacifism and social reconstruction	Through the efforts of Eleanor Clarke Slagle, occupational therapy programs are instituted in state as well as private hospitals in New York State	Frances Perkins (1880–1965) is secretary of labor, the first female Cabinet member in US history American-born Asian women can regain American citizenship after ending marriages to foreigners, according to the amended Cable Act of 1922	Labor activist Rose Schneiderman becomes a member of the National Recovery Administration's Labor Advisory Board	**1933**

Indian girls at school
Photograph courtesy
Sophia Smith Collection,
Smith College

Performing Arts/ Entertainment/ Sports	Religion/ Philosophy	Science/ Technology/ Discovery	Statecraft/ Military	Reform	
Hettie Dyrenfurth breaks a mountain climbing record by climbing 24,700 feet up the Queen Mary Peak of the Himalayas Babe Didrikson, one of the first great women in baseball, pitches a full inning against the Brooklyn Dodgers for the Philadelphia Athletics Screen debut of child actress Shirley Temple in *Stand Up and Cheer* American Jeannette Piccard is the first woman to pilot a 175-foot hydrogen balloon into the stratosphere, to a record 57,559 feet		French physicists Frédéric and Irène Joliot-Curie (1897–1956) develop the first artificial radioactive element, a form of phosphorus Former actress Maude Adams works for General Electric, developing an iridescent light bulb widely used in performing arts American anthropologist Ruth Benedict (1887–1948) publishes her controversial *Patterns of Culture* Anne Morrow Lindbergh (b. 1906) receives a National Geographic Society medal; her essays *Gift from the Sea* (1955) are addressed especially to women	Florence Ellinwood Allen becomes the first woman appointed to the US Circuit Court A supporter of Communist forces in China, Agnes Smedley publishes an account of the organization and growth of the Red Army's campaign against the Kuomintang, *China's Red Army Marches*	Dora Jones founds the New York Domestic Workers Union; after five years, only 350 out of 100,000 workers have been organized—historically, domestic workers have been one of the most difficult groups to organize The World Congress of Women Against Fascism takes place in France; African-American college graduate Mabel Byrd is elected one of the conference secretaries; emerging as a leading personality is African-American Lulia Jackson, who argues for a war against fascism	**1934**
Italian-American soprano Licia Albanese (b. 1913), wins first prize for singing in the National Italian Contest and makes her official debut at Parma; her honors include the Order of Merit in Italy and the Lady Grand Cross of the Equestrian Order of the Holy Sepulchre, given by Pope Pius XI; her roles include Mimi, Mar-		American botanists Wanda K. Farr and Dr. Sophia H. Eckerson discover the double cell wall of cellulose Irène and Frédéric Joliot-Curie win a Nobel Prize for Chemistry for synthesizing new radioactive elements	The French Senate rejects another proposal for women's suffrage		**1935**

	General/ Context	Daily Life/ Customs/ Practices	Humanities/ Fine Arts	Occupations	Education
1935			Publication of Enid Bagnold's (1889–1981) *National Velvet* American sculptor Malvina Hoffmann (1887–1966) creates Races of Mankind, a group of 101 life-size statues, for Chicago's Field Museum British Elizabeth Bowen publishes *The House in Paris* Australian novelist Kylie Tennant (b. 1912) publishes her prizewinning novel, *Tiburnian* American artist Grandma Moses (1860–1961) begins her painting career	sound films, directs *Craig's Wife* The opera *Gale* is the first written and conducted by a woman, Ethel Leggins The New York State Assembly passes a bill on the 48-hour work week for women	ronment that makes children eager to learn

Women in rural Bihar returning home with pitchers full of water from a community well
Photograph (1930) courtesy Sophia Smith Collection, Smith College

	General/ Context	Daily Life/ Customs/ Practices	Humanities/ Fine Arts	Occupations	Education
1936	The Spanish Civil War, 1936–1939, begins	Selling, importing, or advertising any form of birth control device or method becomes illegal in Ireland	First publication of Margaret Mitchell's (1900–1949) *Gone With the Wind* British writer Stevie Smith publishes her *Novel on Yellow Paper*	Margaret Bourke-White becomes the first female photographer for *Life* magazine American fashion photographer Louise Dahl-Wolfe (b. 1895) begins a 23-year stint with *Harper's Bazaar* Anne McCormick (1882–1954) joins the editorial board of the *New York Times* as "freedom editor"; she is the first woman on the board	Mathematician Dorothy Bernstein (b. 1914) takes her Ph.D. qualifying exam at Brown University; her orals last eight hours and are conducted by the entire mathematics faculty; when she discovers that others' orals lasted only two and a half hours, she is told that hers were "extra long because she was a woman and because she had taken most of her courses at a midwestern university"
1937	An eight-hour work day law is passed in Illinois Polystyrene becomes commercially available in the US; used for such products as kitchen utensils and toys, it is one of a number of synthetics	Mexican women vote for the first time The Albanian parliament bans the wearing of veils New York State law now allows women to serve as jurors	British composer Maude Valérie White (1855–1937) is known chiefly for her piano pieces, a mass, and popular songs, including "Pictures from Abroad" Isak Dinesen publishes *Out of Africa*	Mae Bainton becomes the first woman to be appointed a deputy US marshal Minnie Vautrin (1886–1941) runs a refugee camp for women and children in Nanking during and	Identical educational programs are instituted at girls' and boys' *lycées* in France

Performing Arts/ Entertainment/ Sports	Religion/ Philosophy	Science/ Technology/ Discovery	Statecraft/ Military	Reform	

guerite, Violetta, Desdemona

1935

Film star Bette (Ruth Elizabeth) Davis (1908–1989) wins her first Oscar for her role in *Dangerous*

Rika "Rixi" Markus is the first woman to attain the rank of World Bridge Grandmaster by winning the first two European women's championships in 1935 and 1936

At age 27, dancer Catherine Littlefield (1908–1951) founds the Littlefield Ballet, later to become the Philadelphia Ballet

American soprano Geraldine Farrar acts as a radio commentator for the Metropolitan Opera broadcasts

Zamboanga Woman Pro-Suffrage Conference, Philippines
Photograph (1936) courtesy Sophia Smith Collection, Smith College

---

Josephine Baker (1906–1975) is the first black singer/ dancer to achieve stardom on the Paris stage

Ethiopian Women's Work Association develops the gas mask

Eleanor Roosevelt speaks out for the disadvantaged in her newspaper column, "My Day"

1936

Myra Hess is named Royal Philharmonic gold medalist for piano; in the same year she is created Dame Commander of the British Empire

In the Jarrow March, the unemployed march to London to raise awareness of their plight; they are joined by their MP, Ellen Wilkinson, known as Red Ellen

Aviator Beryl Markham is the first person to cross the Atlantic from east to west taking off from England

Hideko Maehata of Japan wins the Olympic gold in the 200-meter backstroke

---

Alice Brady wins an Academy Award for her portrayal of Mrs. O'Leary in *In Old Chicago*

Kate Olivia Sessions becomes the first woman to receive the Meyer Medal, awarded by the American Genetic Association for distinguished service in plant introduction

Julia Sims is the first woman to serve as foreman of a federal grand jury

1937

On June 1, American aviator Amelia Earhart begins her around-the-world flight; on July 2, her plane is lost near

For her pioneering work in the field of

Madam Chiang Kaishek of China shares the honor of *Time* magazine's Man of the Year Award with her husband

	General/ Context	Daily Life/ Customs/ Practices	Humanities/ Fine Arts	Occupations	Education
1937	introduced to lighten the burden of the homemaker	Famous for her literary salons, Mabel Dodge Luhan cultivates such figures as D. H. Lawrence, Gertrude Stein, and John Reed	American Clare Booth Luce publishes *The Women*	after the sack of the city by the Japanese Anne O'Hare McCormick, foreign correspondent for the *New York Times,* is the first woman to receive a Pulitzer Prize for Journalism	
1938		Married women become legal majors in France	Peggy Guggenheim is acknowledged the 20th-century's principal female patron of modern art; her multimillion-dollar art collection is preserved in her 18th-century Venetian palazzo on the Grand Canal Marya Zaturenska receives the Pulitzer Prize for Poetry for *Cold Morning Sky* American journalist Ruth McKenney (1911–1972) publishes *My Sister Eileen* Helen Rosaline Ashton (1891–1958) publishes a fictional biography, *William and Dorothy,* about the Wordsworths	Edith Head (1899–1981) is Hollywood's first female head of design Margaret Fogarty Rudkin (1897–1967) launches her baking company, Pepperidge Farm, Inc. African-American women domestic workers in New York City start their days "slave market" style: they are picked out by white housewives at designated street corners, and work 72-hour weeks at the lowest wages of all occupations	Stella Charnaud Isaacs (1894–1971) organizes Britain's Women's Voluntary Services
1939	World War II (1939–1945) begins in Europe		Judy Chicago (b. 1939) pioneers the first Women's Art Program in the US, located in Chicago German novelist Netty Reiling Radvány (1900–1983), writing under the name Anna Seghers, publishes her most famous novel, *The Seventh Cross* Russian-born French novelist Nathalie Sarraute (b. 1900) writes the experimental novel *Tropismes* Lillian Hellman publishes *The Little Foxes* Sculptor Gertrude Vanderbilt Whitney (1875–1942) designs the Spirit of Flight for the 1939–1940 New York World's Fair	Dorothy Schiff is New York City's first female newspaper publisher, publishing *The New York Post* Eleanor Medill Patterson (1881–1948) combines the *Washington Herald* and the evening *Times* into the *Times-Herald*; by 1943 it has the largest circulation in Washington and by 1945 earns over $1 million a year in profits Austrian psychologist Anna Freud, having left Austria for England in 1938, works at and later becomes head of the Hampstead Child Therapy Clinic; she was her father, Sigmund Freud's partner starting in her twenties	The first female dean of a graduate school, Dr. Freida Wünderlich, heads the graduate faculty of political and social sciences at The New School for Social Research in New York City First woman teacher at the Académie Colarassi, Paris, New Zealand modernist painter Frances (1869–1947) Hodgkins

Performing Arts/ Entertainment/ Sports	Religion/ Philosophy	Science/ Technology/ Discovery	Statecraft/ Military	Reform	
Howland Island in the Pacific Ocean		chemistry, research chemist Emma Perry Carr (d. 1972) is the first woman to receive the Francis Garvan Medal			**1937**
Dinah Shore (Fannie Rose Shore, 1917–1994) begins her career as a popular US singer

Anita Lizana of Chile is the first South American, male or female, to become one of the world's top 10 tennis players

Ella Fitzgerald (b. 1918), the First Lady of Jazz, wins both a Silver Award and the Met Poll; by 1991, she has won eight Grammy awards | | Sarah F. Whitine (d. 1941), "census taker" of the sky, is the first woman elected as an officer of the American Astronomical Society, and the first woman to hold a titled corporation appointment at Harvard | Democrat Crystal Bird Fauset (1893–1965) is the first African-American woman elected to the US House of Representatives

At the outbreak of the Sino-Japanese War, Agnes Smedley joins the Red Army, cropping her hair and wearing fatigues; she publishes her account of the experience in *China Fights Back: An American Woman with the Eighth Route Army* | | **1938** |
| Gertrude Huntley is listed as the unofficial US women's checker champion

American singer/actress Judy Garland (1923–1969) is best known for her role in *The Wizard of Oz*

English actress Joyce Irene Grenfell (1910–1979) performs her own monologues in one-woman shows

Because the DAR denies her the chance to sing at Constitution Hall on account of her race, soprano Marian Anderson (1899–1993) sings at the Lincoln Memorial in Washington, DC, before a crowd of 75,000; to protest that prohibition, Eleanor Roosevelt resigns from the DAR | | Irène and Frédéric Joliot-Curie prove that fission of the uranium atom can lead to a chain reaction | Helena Z. Benitez becomes the first Southeast Asian chairperson of the UN Commission on the Status of Women; she is credited with founding the Home Economics Association in her native Philippines | The Birth Control Federation of America begins its "Negro Project," designed to control the population of people it deems less fit to rear children, rather than as a means to allow women of color more control over their reproductive lives

African-American labor activist Lucy Parsons officially joins the Communist party after working with party members unofficially since the 1920s | **1939** |

Old women and young girls playing a game at a village group meeting in China Photograph (c. 1930) courtesy Sophia Smith Collection, Smith College

339

	General/ Context	Daily Life/ Customs/ Practices	Humanities/ Fine Arts	Occupations	Education
1939					
1940	The fall of France to Germany Nylon stockings become commercially available in the US; they prove so popular that silk stockings become obsolete overnight Wrinkle-resistant fabrics made of polyester, a synthetic fiber, become available, freeing women from some of the burden of ironing	A woman suffrage law becomes a statute in Quebec The first recipient of a US Social Security check, social reformer Ida Fuller (1875–1975), receives over $20,000 for her $22 investment in the program One hundred women are honored by the (US) Women's Centennial Congress for holding positions that were not open to women a century earlier	University of Chicago Chaucerian scholar Edith Rickert (1871–1938) and Prof. John M. Manly produce the 8-volume *The Text of the Canterbury Tales, Studied on the Basis of All Known Manuscripts* Music historian Rosa Newmarch (1857–1940) is notable for her work on modern Russian music; among her works are *The Russian Opera, The Russian Arts, Life of Tschaikowsky, Jean Sibelius,* and translations of the biographies of Brahms, Borodin, Liszt, César Franck, and Tschaikowsky into English After years of officially imposed silence, Anna Akhmatova begins publishing again; she continues when she is evacuated from Leningrad to Tashkent, 1941–1944 American novelist and short story writer Carson McCullers (1917–1967) publishes her first novel, *The Heart*	The US Department of Labor reports that less than 17% of all married women in the US are employed outside the home Dorothy Vredenburgh Bush becomes the first woman secretary of the Democratic National Committee; she subsequently oversees nine national conventions According to the 1940 US census, 59.5% of employed African-American women are domestic workers, 10.4% are in nondomestic service organizations, and 16% are still working in the fields	

WOMEN'S WORK IN THE UNITED STATES

Until late in the 19th century most American women who earned an income worked at home, taking in boarders or sewing, for example, or doing other domestic work. Domestic service outside the home, one of the oldest occupations of women, also remained common.

In 1890, two thirds of the US population lived in rural areas and nearly half of all families made a living from the land. The farm was the last stronghold of the family as an economic unit. Nevertheless, by 1890 1 million women worked in factories. Mostly unmarried, they made up three quarters of all the nation's women who worked for pay outside the home. Women schoolteachers, some 250,000 by the end of the 19th century, enjoyed the highest prestige of all female wage earners.

The 20th century brought social changes in industrialized nations. The purpose and structure of the family altered as technology advanced, economies grew, populations increased, urban areas expanded, and women gained more rights. Working- and middle-class women now had job opportunities beyond the domestic sphere. The number of women working outside the home steadily rose as the growth of industry demanded typists, stenographers, and file clerks. A widening range of manufactured products enabled women to work in retail shops. Expanding government bureaucracies used new technologies, hiring women as telephone operators, clerks, and low-level administrators. As corporations, too, found single women cheap and compliant labor, the clerical workforce became feminized.

Performing Arts/ Entertainment/ Sports	Religion/ Philosophy	Science/ Technology/ Discovery	Statecraft/ Military	Reform	
Catherine Littlefield choreographs *American Jubilee,* a dance on bicycles, for the 1939 World's Fair					**1939**
African-American singer and actress Ethel Waters (1900–1977) stars in the play *Cabin in the Sky*

Long one of the world's foremost so-pranos in opera and concert, Luisa Tet-razinni (1871–1940) tours the world, scor-ing success after suc-cess

Lucia Chase (1897–1986) becomes princi-pal dancer with the American Ballet The-atre

Screen star Irene Marie Dunne (1898–1990) makes her repu-tation in both drama and comedy, starring in such films as *My Favorite Wife* and *I Remember Mama* (1948)

Catherine Littlefield choreographs *It Hap-pens on Ice,* a ballet for skaters | | Mary E. Pennington (1872–1952), recog-nized for her pioneer-ing work on food preservation, receives the Garvan Medal and joins the American Chemical Society

Bernice M. McPher-son (1901–1976) wins a US Navy award for developing a welding process for weapons sights that greatly re-duces production costs; she later be-comes the first woman member of the Ameri-can Welding Society | Queen Wilhelmina Helena Pauline Maria (1880–1962), constitu-tional monarch of the Netherlands from 1890 to 1948, comes to symbolize Dutch resistance to the Nazis; during the war, she establishes her govern-ment in exile in En-gland; she eventually abdicates in favor of her daughter, Julianna

According to the *New York Times,* Dr. Anna Glover becomes the first British woman to be appointed to a rank corresponding to ma-jor: deputy assistant director of medical services for the Auxil-iary Territorial Service, Eastern Command | Mother Ella Reeve Bloor (1862–1951) publishes an autobiog-raphy describing her days as a labor orga-nizer from her pre-Socialist days to her work with the Com-munist party | **1940** |

Indian women police
Photograph (c. 1930) courtesy Sophia Smith Collection, Smith College

During World War II, because of their sudden access to skilled, well-paying jobs once performed by men, women made their next great advances in the work world. Many women discovered how much they liked working outside the home, earning an independent income; many also discovered the difficulties of being working mothers. While many women gave up their wartime work, most did not drop out of the workforce but took other jobs, most in the service sec-tor.

Despite gains, women still suffer inequalities in the work-place, among them underemployment and low wages. By 1990 the average American woman's earnings had risen to only 72% of the average man's. On the average, more women than men still enter lower-paying occupations, and they work fewer hours; they have, on the whole, less education, less job expe-rience, and fewer skills.

On the other hand, new educational choices are helping women enter professions largely closed to them in previous decades. Today more college women choose business than any other major. The same percentage of women as men are now professionals or managers; still, only 3% of top executives in major corporations are female. American women now account for 40% of the workforce; they will make up half of the work-force by the turn of the century.

	General/ Context	Daily Life/ Customs/ Practices	Humanities/ Fine Arts	Occupations	Education
1940			*Is a Lonely Hunter;* other important works include *Reflections in a Golden Eye* (1941), *A Member of the Wedding* (1946), and *The Ballad of the Sad Café* (1951) American sculptor Nancy Stevenson Graves (b. 1940) is known for her precise, imaginative camouflage paintings and lunar landscapes		
1941	The United States enters World War II after the bombing of Pearl Harbor on December 7 *Traditional and modern Egyptian dress* Photograph (1931) courtesy Sophia Smith Collection, Smith College		American Ruth Crawford-Seeger (1901–1953) becomes the first woman to win a Guggenheim Fellowship for musical composition Margret Elizabeth Rey (b. 1906) is best known for her *Curious George* books Mary O'Hara (1885–1980) writes *My Friend Flicka* American writer Sally Benson (1900–1972) publishes *Junior Miss* Finnish author Maria Jotuni (1880–1943) receives a Finnish drama award for her play *Klaus, Master of Lovhikko*	British pioneer aviator Amy Johnson (1903–1941) disappears when the plane she is flying crashes into the Thames estuary; the trophies she won and her pilot's log book can be seen at the Sewerby Hall Museum and Gallery, where she had performed the opening ceremonies five years earlier	
1942	Liberia and Ethiopia abolish slavery	Hanna Reitsch is the first woman to receive the Iron Cross in Germany	Ellen Glasgow (1874–1945) wins the Pulitzer Prize for Fiction for *In This Our Life*	Dr. M.H.D. Lin becomes the first woman member of the International College of Surgeons	

AMERICAN WOMEN IN WORLD WAR II

World War II brought about a radical change in attitudes about women working and altered women's role in the labor force. It also created an unprecedented opportunity for American women to live in communities of women, in both military and civilian life. American women had participated as members of the armed services since the formation of the Army Nurse Corps in 1901; unofficially they had played an active part in every war from the Revolution on. During World War I, when the armed forces officially extended service opportunities beyond the Nurse Corps, over 12,000 women enlisted. Most of them performed clerical and administrative jobs, but some became recruiters, camouflage designers, and translators.

World War II brought the newly formed Women's Army Corps, Women Marines, Women's Army Air Corps, Navy WAVES, and Coast Guard SPARS. They recruited women for noncombat positions to free more men to fight. The armed forces provided women a way to experience life outside the confines of traditional female roles.

Women civilians experienced major changes, with six million women civilians taking paying jobs during the war. They worked as riveters, stevedores, bus drivers, and drill-press oper-

All Asian Women's Conference, Lahore, India Photograph (1931) courtesy Sophia Smith Collection, Smith College

1940

Pianist Myra Hess (1890–1965) is created Dame Commander of the British Empire

Mary Astor (Lucille Vasconcellos Langhanke, 1906–1987) becomes a *film noir* star in *The Maltese Falcon;* she wins an Oscar for *The Great Lie*

The Andrews Sisters, Laverne (1913–1967), Maxine (b. 1918), and Patti (b. 1920), become popular radio performers during WWII; they entertain American troops and star in such films as *Buck Privates* (1941), *Private Buckaroo* (1942), and *Follow the Boys* (1944)

The *New York Times* reports that Elisa Rosales Ochoa becomes the first woman to hold a congressional seat in the Philippines

Women vote for the first time in Panama

Congresswoman Jeannette Rankin (1880–1973) casts the only vote in Congress against the American Declaration of World War II

1941

Aviator Beryl Markham's autobiography, entitled *West with the Night,* is set mainly in Africa; it

Edith Stein (b. 1891), Jewish Carmelite philosopher, dies in Auschwitz

Screen star Hedy Lamarr (Hedwig Eva Marie Keisler, b. 1913), before the invasion of Austria by

Annette Abbott Adams (1877–1956) is appointed the first woman appellate judge in California

1942

ators. Women accounted for 12% of shipyard workers and a remarkable 40% of the labor in aircraft plants. The sudden demand for workers boosted women's wages higher and made their working conditions better than ever before; African Americans, older women, and wives benefited the most. Three fourths of the women who took up jobs during the war were over 35; 60% were married; and over half of them had young children.

Military and civilian women found themselves in charge and with new responsibilities as heads of households, earning salaries, wearing men's work clothes, and performing men's work, all within mostly female communities. Many women, by circumstance or choice, found themselves socializing strictly with women, and some fell in love. Lesbian relationships were quietly tolerated in the armed services if the partners behaved with discretion.

During World War II women proved themselves capable of many kinds of work previously restricted to men. At the end of the war, although more than 80% of the women working wanted to keep their jobs, layoffs began in order to provide work for returning servicemen. By the end of 1946, two million women had lost their jobs in heavy industry, a clear message that their place was once more in the home.

General/ Context	Daily Life/ Customs/ Practices	Humanities/ Fine Arts	Occupations	Education
1942		Marjorie Kinnan Rawlings describes the region in Florida in which she lives in *Cross Creek* Margaret Leech (1894–1974) wins the Pulitzer Prize for History for *Reveille in Washington* American novelist Mary McCarthy (1912–1989) publishes *The Company She Keeps*	Anne A. Lenz becomes the first commissioned officer in the Marine Corps Women's Reserve, as clothing expert, outfitting the troops, before public announcement of the new Women's Reserve has been made Margaret Farrar is appointed the first editor of *The New York Times*'s Sunday crossword puzzle page	
1943		Russian-born American novelist Ayn Rand (1905–1982) publishes *The Fountainhead,* a polemical work of enduring popularity The Pulitzer Prize for History goes to Esther Forbes (1894?–1967) for *Paul Revere and the World He Lived In* Kathryn Forbes (pen name of Kathryn Anderson McLean, 1909–1966) is most famous for her short stories about her Norwegian immigrant grandmother, collected as *Mama's Bank Account,* and later drama-	Alicia Patterson (1906–1963) founds, edits, and publishes *Newsday* Aileen Osborn Webb (b. 1892) founds the American Craftsmen's Educational Council, a national clearinghouse for information; in 1964 she helps found the World Crafts Council	

Girls doing athletics at the Institute of Physical Education for Women Teachers, Cairo, Egypt
Photograph (c. 1943) courtesy Sophia Smith Collection, Smith College

MODERN WOMEN WARRIORS

Entering the arena in greater numbers and in more regimented ways than ever before, modern women have fought and died for their political beliefs in national revolutions, wars, and police actions. As soldiers, aviators, and spies, on rescue squads and on the front lines, they have performed heroically in this most threatening of all endeavors.

In Russia, Sofya Pervoskaya was publicly hanged in 1881 for her part in the assassination of Czar Alexander II. Ch'iu Chin, China's first woman revolutionary and the first to join Sun Yat-sen's party in 1904, was injured assembling a bomb. In 1906 she formed the People's Army. She was captured in 1907 and beheaded after extreme torture; she never broke her silence. By 1925 a large number of women revolutionaries ex-

isted in China, and 1.5 million were organized under the Kuomintang.

By World War I, large numbers of European women became quickly unhappy with traditional supporting roles; they chose instead dangerous front-line nursing and ambulance-driving roles. Edith Cavell, an English nurse in Belgium, was executed by the Germans in 1915 for espionage. By 1917 combat battalions of Russian women were organized and the Winter Palace was defended by a women's battalion against the Bolsheviks in October 1917.

From the Warsaw ghetto to the French Resistance, women fought against Nazi Germany, among them Hanna Szenes (1921–1944), a Hungarian Jew who became a Zionist and a

Performing Arts/ Entertainment/ Sports	Religion/ Philosophy	Science/ Technology/ Discovery	Statecraft/ Military	Reform	
describes her early flying and racehorse training in Kenya

Mexican actress Dolores Del Rio (Lolita Dolores Martinez Asunsolo Lopez Negrette, 1908–1983) makes her most famous film, *Journey into Fear* (1947) | Simone Weil (1909–1943), French philosopher and essayist committed to the cause of social justice, goes to London to work with the French Resistance

American philosopher Susanne K. Langer (b. 1895) publishes one of her most influential works on aesthetics, *Philosophy in a New Key: A Study in the Symbolism of Reason, Rite, and Art;* others include *Feeling and Form: A Theory of Art* (1953) and *Problems of Art* (1957) | the Nazis the wife of a wealthy Austrian arms dealer, collaborates with film score composer George Antheil in developing her idea for a remote-controlled radio system that produces undetectable, undecipherable, and unjammable transmission; they patent the device and offer it for use against the Nazis, but the War Department fails to adopt it | American Lt. Anne G. Fox becomes the first woman to earn a Purple Heart

American Mildred Elizabeth Gillars (1900–1988), known as Axis Sally, broadcasts Nazi propaganda to American troops during WWII; she is later captured and imprisoned by the Allies for 12 years | | **1942** |
| American dancer Agnes de Mille (1905–1993) choreographs the Broadway musical *Oklahoma!*

American actress Jean Arthur (Gladys Georgianna Greene, 1908–1991) stars in "screwball" comedies of the 1930s and 1940s, such as *The More the Merrier,* for which she is nominated for an Oscar

The All American Girls Professional Baseball League is started by the owner of the Chicago Cubs, Philip K. Wrigley; it | | Dr. Leona M. Libby becomes a prominent member of the Manhattan District Group of scientists, builders of the first nuclear reactor, from 1943 to 1947

Mexican painter Frida Kahlo Photograph (c. 1943) by Marcel Sternberger, © Ilse Sternberger | Soviet airwoman Lily Litvak, a teenage flying instructor known as the White Rose of Stalingrad, shoots down 12 German planes in aerial combat before she is shot down herself and killed

Aline Sitoe (c. 1920–1944), queen of the Diola of Senegal, is exiled by the French for her anticolonialist policies; she began her rule in 1936, turning her people against the French with her battle cry, "The white man is not invincible" | Dame Anne Loughlin (1894–1979) becomes the first woman to assume the presidential position in the Trades Union Congress in Britain | **1943** |

member of the Palestine underground army. She parachuted into Yugoslavia, but was captured, tortured, and beaten. Silent to the end, she was executed by firing squad. Among the hundreds of women in the French Resistance were Marthe Ricard, a World War I French pilot, and Marie Madeleine Fourcade, who organized and directed one of the largest resistance organizations in Europe.

World War II changed women's experience of war: starvation, rape, pillage, and mass murder once again became the tactics that communities had not experienced since the Middle Ages. In Britain and the Soviet Union, women were drafted, and thousands of Russian women saw combat, 100,000 earning military honors. The Soviets had an all-female 122nd Air Group whose most famous member was Lily Litvak, a Soviet air ace with 12 German planes to her credit before she was shot down and killed.

In the 1991 Gulf War, women soldiers fought side-by-side with the men. Though they acquitted themselves with honor, many military leaders remain uncomfortable with the sacrifice of women in combat, arguing in the teeth of contrary evidence that women's relative physical weakness makes them more vulnerable to breakdown and that their presence in male squadrons erodes soldiers' bond with one another. That a soldier might be subjected to torture or might die under fire seems to many a greater obscenity if that soldier is a woman than a man. Nevertheless, fully aware of those gruesome possibilities, women continue to enlist and to perform as heroically as men.

	Daily Life/ Customs/ Practices	Humanities/ Fine Arts	Occupations	Education
General/ Context				
1943		tized as *I Remember Mama* by John Van Druten Betty Wehner Smith (1904–1972) publishes her first and most popular novel, *A Tree Grows in Brooklyn*		
1944	Frenchwomen are given the vote Anne Frank (1929–1944), a Dutch Jewish girl famous for her diary written while in hiding from the Nazis in Amsterdam, dies in Bergen-Belsen	H.D. publishes her powerful works *The Gift* and *Trilogy*, 1944–1946 British novelist Elizabeth Goudge (1900–1984) publishes her best-known work, *Green Dolphin Street* American writer Jean Stafford (1915–1979) publishes *Boston Adventure* American social worker Lillian Smith (1897–1966) writes *Strange Fruit* Russian-born novelist Elsa Troilet (1896–1970) wins the Prix Goncourt for *Fine of 200 Francs*	American broadcast journalist noted for her hard-nosed questioning at press conferences, May Craig (1889–1975) serves as a war correspondent Helen Valentine founds *Seventeen* magazine, serving as editor in chief until 1950	

WOMEN AND THE HOLOCAUST

The Holocaust, the systematic murder of six million Jews and others by Adolf Hitler's Nazi Germany, has left the world some of its darkest images of humanity. It has also provided evidence of woman's astonishing capacity to endure even the most hideous hardships. Women in the concentration camps survived more successfully than the men: women sought and gave help to one another while men in their struggle to survive tended to become loners.

The history of women on both sides of the Holocaust has not received attention equal to that of men. At the Nuremberg Trials, for instance, only one female defendant was prosecuted, a doctor from Auschwitz. Voluminous records testify to the atrocities supervised or committed by women against both women and men. Recent commentators emphasize the gender-specific aspects of Jewish women's experiences and vulnerabilities in the Holocaust. Even in the partisan camps,

rape and sexual abuse were common. These included not only systematic sexual torture, but also sterilization, brutal medical experimentation, enforced prostitution, and even a gender-based life-or-death selection process. At Auschwitz, for example, only young childless women were spared. Naked in the selection lines, older women, women with children, and women obviously pregnant were sent directly to be gassed. To save the lives of pregnant women who did manage to survive the initial selection, an inmate doctor, Gisela Perl, terminated their pregnancies. An all-woman orchestra was forced to play even at initial selections and executions; they also played accompaniment for those on their way to the gas chambers.

Many women formed life-sustaining "camp sister" relationships and organized to counter the brutalities of camp life. Some risked their lives to produce art: French Resistance in-

Performing Arts/ Entertainment/ Sports	Religion/ Philosophy	Science/ Technology/ Discovery	Statecraft/ Military	Reform	
consists of 10 teams and lasts 10 years			American aviator Jacqueline Cochran (1910–1980) organizes the Women's Air Force Service		**1943**
British singer Kathleen Ferrier (1912–1953) begins training seriously as a professional singer, becoming one of the best-loved singers of her day			Clare Boothe Luce (b. 1903), playwright, author, war correspondent, and political activist, serves two terms in Congress (1943–1947)		
Swedish actress Ingrid Bergman (1915–1982) wins an Oscar for her role in *Gaslight*		California University reports on a painless childbirth method—a paravertebral sympathetic nerve block	Grace Ford, announces the *New York Times*, is the first woman to be appointed assistant attorney general of New Jersey	Laura Gray (1909–1958) becomes the cartoonist for *The Militant,* a Socialist Workers' Party's publication, producing a cartoon a week, 1944–1957	**1944**
German dancer Hanya Holm (b. 1898), one of the "Big Four" choreographers in the US, choreographs one of her greatest Broadway shows, *Kiss Me Kate*			Ana Rabinsohn Pauker (1894–1960) becomes Romania's first female minister of foreign affairs	Headquartered in Turkey, the International Federation of Women Lawyers seeks, through cooperation with other juridical organizations, equal rights for women	
African-American choreographer Katherine Dunham (b. 1912) mounts Rites of Passage, a dance adapted from puberty and fertility rituals of anonymous primitive peoples; its performance is banned in Boston			An Ohio Republican representative, Frances Bolton (1885–1968), is the first woman in Congress to visit the war theater	Egyptian social activist Huda Sh'arawi founds the All-Arab Federation of Women	

mate Violette Rougier from Ravensbruck and Helga Weissova-Hoskova, a teenager at Terezin, whose drawings illustrate life in the camps; Charlotte Delbo, author of plays like *Who Will Carry the Word,* at Ravensbruck and Auschwitz. Others supported storytelling, religious observances, theatrical performances, and education for younger inmates.

Women also participated in the active resistance to the Holocaust. They organized major ghetto uprisings and served in partisan combat units. Best known of Jewish resistance fighters, poet Hannah Szenes (1921–1944), a Hungarian émigrée to Palestine, parachuted behind Nazi lines to organize Jewish resistance. Though captured and hideously tortured, she refused to divulge her mission secrets and was executed by firing squad.

Many gentile women worked to save the lives of Jews. In Libednik, Poland, Mrs. Bikeviczowa, an illiterate Catholic be-trayed by her neighbors for trying to save Jews, was executed by a local Nazi unit that included her own son. One mother superior of Dominican sisters near Vilna sheltered Jewish resistance fighters in her convent and smuggled grenades into the ghetto; another, from the Warsaw branch of the Order of the Franciscan Sisters of the Family of Mary, hid scores of ghetto children through the entire war.

Among Jewish women who worked to rescue Jews from Europe, best known was Gisi Fleischmann who in 1944 was arrested, deported to Auschwitz, and there sent to the gas chambers. Women staged escapes from concentration camps and organized camp uprisings, even till the last moments of Nazi rule. Only days before Auschwitz was evacuated, Roza Robata, Ella Garter, Estusia Wajsblum, and Regina Sapirstein were hanged after refusing, under torture, to betray others involved in an armed uprising.

	General/ Context	Daily Life/ Customs/ Practices	Humanities/ Fine Arts	Occupations	Education
1945	World War II ends Tupperware, a line of plastic kitchen storage products made of polyethylene, is first marketed to American women Foundation of the Arab League United Nations established	Known as the Blood Angel of Hell, concentration camp guard Irma Grese (1923–1945) is sentenced to death for her brutality to 18,000 female prisoners at Auschwitz Aida De Acosta Breckinridge (1884–1962) founds the Eye-Bank for Sight Restoration in New York Italian women get federal suffrage The women of Guatemala gain the right to vote The women of Japan gain the right to vote	African-American poet Gwendolyn Brooks (b. 1917) publishes her collection of poems, *A Street in Bronzeville* Chilean poet and educator Gabriela Mistral (pen name of Lucila Godoy Alcayaga, 1889–1957) receives the Nobel Prize for Literature French author Françoise Sagan (pen name of Françoise Quoirez, b. 1935) publishes her award-winning *Bonjour Tristesse*	Hélène Gordon-Lazareff (b. 1909) founds and becomes the first editor in chief of *Elle* magazine Lucia Chase begins 40 years as director and patron of the American Ballet Theatre	
1946	The two-piece bikini bathing suit, named by French designer Louis Rénard for Bikini Atoll, site of early atomic testing, debuts in Paris	Canadian Parliament drops its rule requiring women spectators to wear hats The French Constitution recognizes the equality of women in most political areas The women of Mexico gain the right to vote The women of Argentina gain the right to vote	Russian-born French novelist Zoë Oldenbourg (b. 1916) is best known for her historical novels, such as *The World Is Not Enough* American novelist Ann Petry (b. 1911) publishes *The Street* Anna Akhmatova is expelled from the Union of Soviet Writers but reinstated after Stalin's death	Mary Shotwell Ingraham is the first woman to receive a Medal of Merit for her USO work Estée Lauder and her husband found the cosmetics company bearing her name; they also pioneer the free sample technique Dorothy Shaver (1897–1959) is the first woman to assume the presidency of a major department store, Lord and Taylor	Women are permitted to attend Tokyo Imperial University for the first time Foundation of the Women's World Fellowship for Peace in Paris Aileen Osborn Webb starts the School for American Craftsmen
1947	India is granted independence from Great Britain The American Theatre Wing institutes the Tony Awards in memory of the great actress and director Antoinette Perry	Magda Elena Lupescu (1904–1977), mistress of King Carol II of Romania for 22 years, marries him in exile	Russian novelist Vera Panova (1905–1973) publishes *Traveling Companions* American choreographers Virginia Sampler and Valerie E. Bettis are the first to choreo-	The first women graduate from police training school in Buenos Aires, Argentina Stella Charnaud Isaacs (Baroness Swansborough) organizes the Women's Home Industries, Ltd., in Brit-	Concetta Scaravaglione is the first female recipient of an American Academy in Rome fellowship Founded in Paris, the Mouvement Mondiale des Mères (World Movement of Moth-

Performing Arts/ Entertainment/ Sports	Religion/ Philosophy	Science/ Technology/ Discovery	Statecraft/ Military	Reform	
American actress Joan Crawford (1908–1977), born Lucille Fay LeSueur wins an Oscar for *Mildred Pierce* Dancer Agnes de Mille choreographs the musical *Carousel* Peggy Ann Garner (1931–1984) wins a special Oscar as Outstanding Child Performer for her role in *A Tree Grows in Brooklyn*	The Dutch Jewish mystic and diarist Etty Hillesum (b. 1914) loses her life in Auschwitz Doujebamo (b. 1941) becomes a living Buddha in Tibet at age four	British pacifist and scientist Kathleen Lonsdale (1903–1971) is one of the first women to be honored by becoming a Fellow of the Royal Society, for her research into the structure of crystals Computer expert Grace Brewster Murray Hopper (1906–1991) coins the term "bug" to describe a computer glitch when her team discovers a moth caught in the circuitry of a malfunctioning computer A renowned pioneer in mathematical logic and a creator of recursive function theory, Hungarian mathematician Rózsa Péter (1905–1977) publishes *Playing with Infinity: Mathematical Explorations and Excursions,* part of an effort to bring science into the cultural mainstream	Women vote in Panama Kirsten Moe Hansteen becomes Norway's first female minister without portfolio Isabel Arrua Vallejo becomes Paraguay's first woman with diplomatic rank as attaché of the embassy of Paraguay to Brazil "Battling Bessie" Braddock becomes a member of the British Parliament, holding her seat until 1969	Margaret Sanger receives the A. and M. Lasker Award for her maternal health program In Berlin, the Internationale Demokratische Frauenföderation (Women's International Democratic Federation) is founded; its goals are the elimination of fascism, equal rights for women and children, and international cooperation based on a Communist philosophy; by the 1950s, the organization has spread to 62 countries	1945
	Mother Frances Xavier Cabrini (1850–1917), founder of the Missionary Sisters of the Sacred Heart, becomes the first citizen of the US to be canonized by the Catholic Church Mariam Alpert (d. 1976) becomes the first national president of B'nai B'rith Young Adults	Mina S. Rees is made the first female director of the US's largest scientific society, the American Association for the Advancement of Science	Dr. Florica Bagdasar becomes health minister, the first Romanian woman to hold a Cabinet post Italian women vote for the first time in a national election Maria Ulfah Santoso is Indonesia's first female minister of social affairs Eva Duarte (a.k.a. Evita), Perón (1919–1952) co-governs Argentina with her husband, Juan	American Emily Greene Balch (1867–1961), cofounder of the Women's International League for Peace and Freedom, shares the Nobel Peace Prize with fellow American John R. Mott Establishment of the Women's Global Congress for International Peace, Education and Culture, centered in Denmark; it seeks to bring the education of women up to a world standard and works to improve the education of orphans	1946
American puppeteer Frances Allen (1924–1989) stars in *Kukla, Fran, and Ollie,* 1947–1957 American producer Cheryl Crawford (1902–1986), Robert Lewis, and Elia Kazan		Ruth Fulton Benedict (1887–1948) becomes president of the American Anthropological Association, the first American woman to become the leader of a learned profession	Mme. Germaine Peyrolles is the first woman to preside over the French National Assembly Mme. Ludmila Jankovcov is named industry minister of Czechoslovakia, the	The World Association of Mothers for Peace, founded in New York, promotes the enlightenment of mothers of all races and creeds, the elimination of war, and the peaceful upbringing of children	1947

	General/Context	Daily Life/Customs/Practices	Humanities/Fine Arts	Occupations	Education
1947			graph a modern dance for a ballet company Canadian novelist Gabrielle Roy's 1945 novel *Bonheur d'occasion* (*The Tin Flute*) wins France's Prix Femina After many years as a journalist and short story writer, Laura Z. Hobson (b. 1900) writes novels dealing with social issues such as immigration and anti-Semitism; her most famous work, *Gentleman's Agreement,* appears this year	ain to help promote economic recovery after World War II	ers) works for family unity, recognition of women's value, and the rationalization of housework
1948	Israel is created as a homeland for Jews The Universal Declaration of Human Rights, shaped largely by Eleanor Roosevelt, passes the UN General Assembly Creation of Soviet satellite nations	Occupied Japan enacts a "eugenic protection" law authorizing abortion on demand	Welsh-Jewish poet Denise Levertov (1923) immigrates to the US; she publishes such celebrated collections as *Overland to the Islands* (1958) and *The Jacob's Ladder* (1961) American screenwriters Bella and Samuel Spewack write the libretto for *Kiss Me Kate,* a Cole Porter musical based on Shakespeare's *Taming of the Shrew*	Dr. Frances Lois Willoughby is the first female doctor in the regular US Navy Katherine A. Towle becomes the first director of the Women's Marine Corps Matsuyo Yamamoto becomes the first of seven female section chiefs appointed by the Japanese government to start the Home Economics Extension Service; she is awarded the Ceres Medal in 1974	Jacqueline Lelong-Ferrand becomes the first female full professor of mathematics at the University of Paris Cambridge University begins granting full degrees to women
1949	The Bollingen Prize, an annual award for distinguished living poets, is first awarded under the auspices of the US Library of Congress With the explosion of an atomic bomb by the Soviet Union, the nuclear arms race between the US and the USSR begins Ireland becomes a fully independent republic, except for six counties that remain under British control Formation of NATO (North Atlantic Treaty Organization)	In a *New York Times* interview, Dr. M.J.E. Senn claims that the mother's emotional state during pregnancy affects the unborn child's development	Gwendolyn Brooks publishes *Annie Allen* French philosopher Simone de Beauvoir (1908–1986) publishes her groundbreaking essay *The Second Sex;* other important works include *Memoirs of a Dutiful Daughter,* (1954) and *The Prime of Life* (1960) American writer Shirley Jackson (1919–1965) publishes "The Lottery," the often-anthologized short story for which she is best known Hungarian-born Mariska Karasz (1898–	Mrs. Herbert E. Carnes becomes the first female president of the Audubon Society Helene Hoffman becomes the first woman sales manager in the New York City auto industry American pioneer for women's rights, Shelton Burnita Matthews (1894–1988) becomes the first woman to serve as a federal district judge, a position she holds for 34 years	Evelyn Boyd Granville and Marjorie Lee Browne become the first African-American women in the US to be awarded Ph.D.s in mathematics

Performing Arts/ Entertainment/ Sports	Religion/ Philosophy	Science/ Technology/ Discovery	Statecraft/ Military	Reform	
found the Actors Studio Dancer Agnes de Mille choreographs *Brigadoon,* for which she receives a Tony Award Mrs. Finn Ronne completes the first Antarctic-based flight made by a woman		Drs. Gerty and Carl Cori are awarded the Nobel Prize for Physiology and Medicine for their research into carbohydrate metabolism; she is the first female physician to receive the prize Dorothy Crowfoot Hodgkin is awarded a Fellowship of the Royal Society for her work in chemistry	first woman in her country to hold a Cabinet post Women vote for the first time in Bolivia	The World Organization of Mothers of All Nations (WOMAN), based in New York, supports the peacekeeping mission of the UN; it acts as a clearinghouse for all mothers opposed to war	**1947**
American actress Eve Arden (1908–1990) is *Our Miss Brooks* Alicia Alonso (b. 1901) founds her own ballet company and and directs the Ballet Nacional de Cuba Choreographer Agnes De Mille designs the ballet Fall River Legend, based on the celebrated 1892 murder case of Lizzie Borden	Rev. A. Stewart is the first woman to offer prayer at a US House session	Lillian Moller Gilbreth (1878–1972) is depicted in *Cheaper by the Dozen;* with a Ph.D. in industrial psychology, she is known for inventing step-on trash cans and refrigerators with shelves in the doors Hetty Goldman (1881–1972) is the first woman to hold Harvard's Norton Fellowship for her excavation work in Greece and the Near East	Col. Geraldine P. May becomes the first director of the newly organized Women in the Air Force (WAF) Queen Juliana (b. 1909) ascends the Dutch throne Golda Meir becomes the only signatory of Israel's Declaration of Independence to have immigrated from the US and the only woman member of its first provisional legislature, traveling to Moscow as Israel's first minister to the Soviet Union		**1948**
Peggy Wood (1892–1978), American stage, screen, and television actress, undertakes her best-known role in television's *Mama,* which runs for eight years Sara Levi-Tanai founds the improvisational Iubal Dance Company of Israel, bringing folk dance traditions to a high art The life story of Japanese political activist Kageyama Hideko is made into a film, *My Love Has Been Burning*			Syrian women vote for the first time Arab women vote for the first time in Israel Margaret Chase Smith is the first woman elected to the US Senate without first being appointed Stateswoman Alva Reimer Myrdal (1902–1986) is the first woman to hold a high-ranking job in the UN, as principal director of the UN Department of Social Affairs Poet, orator, freedom fighter, and champion of women's rights,		**1949**

	General/ Context	Daily Life/ Customs/ Practices	Humanities/ Fine Arts	Occupations	Education
1949			1960) receives an Institute of Graphic Arts prize for her *Adventures in Stitches*		
1950	Apartheid is established by the white-ruled government in South Africa	In the People's Republic of China, child betrothals, forced arranged marriages, concubinage, female infanticide, and interference in the right of divorced or widowed women to remarry are outlawed; women gain the right to retain their own names, inherit property, and participate in social and work activities By her own request, Agnes Smedley is buried in China; her ashes are honored by being placed in Beijing's National Memorial Cemetery of Revolutionary Martyrs; her memorial reads: "To Agnes Smedley, Friend of the Chinese Revolution"	Gwendolyn Brooks, black poet dedicated to revealing aspects of black urban life, wins the Pulitzer for *Annie Allen* Belgian-French novelist Françoise Mallet-Joris (b. 1930) publishes *The Illusionists,* a novel about the lesbian relationship between a teenage girl and her father's mistress American abstract expressionist Helen Frankenthaler (b. 1928) frequently exhibits her work in one-woman shows	American photographer Constance Gibbs Bannister (b. 1919) gains a worldwide reputation for her pictures of babies The first woman in Nicaragua to get a law degree, Olga Nuñez de Sasallow, also becomes Nicaragua's first female deputy minister of public education Annie Jiagge becomes the first female judge in Ghana	Harvard Law School admits women
1951		Women's hemlines rise to 13 to 15 inches from the ground; they fall to 11.25 inches in 1952, but rise to 16 inches in 1953 Teenage girls in the US wear appliquéd "poodle skirts"; women and girls wear saddle shoes and crinolines	The Pulitzer Prize for Biography goes to Margaret Louise Coit (b. 1922) for *John C. Calhoun: American Portrait* French author Marguerite Yourcenar (1903–1987) publishes her masterpiece, *Memoires d'Hadrien* Political philosopher and theorist who fled Europe to the US when Hitler occupied France, Hannah Arendt (1906–1975) publishes *The Origins of Totalitarianism* (1951); in the same year she becomes the first woman and the first American to receive Denmark's Sonning Prize	Marguerite Higgins (1921–1966) is the first woman to receive the Pulitzer Prize for International Reporting for her work in Korea Dr. Helen E. Meyers is the first female dentist in the US Army Dental Corps	

Balinese woman weaving
Photograph (c. 1950) courtesy Sophia Smith Collection, Smith College

Performing Arts/ Entertainment/ Sports	Religion/ Philosophy	Science/ Technology/ Discovery	Statecraft/ Military	Reform	
			Sarojini Naidu (1879–1949) of India is the first woman to be elected president of the Indian National Congress		**1949**
Greek concert pianist Gina Bachauer (1913–1976) makes her US debut Dutch soprano Elly Ameling (b. 1934) makes her New York City Opera debut American comedian Imogene (Fernandez y) Coca (b. 1908) appears in the pioneer television variety show *Your Show of Shows* with Sid Caesar Italian soprano Anna Maria Alberghetti (b. 1935) makes her debut at Carnegie Hall Former British radio announcer Nancy Spain (b. 1917), one of Britain's first television personalities during the 1950s and 1960s, and her lover, Joan Laurie, found a new type of women's magazine, called *She*	Canonization of St. Bartholomea Capitanio (1807–1833), cofounder with St. Vincentia Gerosa of the Sisters of Charity of St. Vincent de Paul	Yoshi Katsurada becomes Japan's first female Ph.D. in mathematics A. R. Kasturi Bai (b. 1925) is India's leading woman in agricultural research British gardener Frances Perry becomes the Royal Horticulture Society's first female council member Sophie D. Aberle serves until 1957 as the first woman member of the National Science Board, the policy-making body of the US government's National Science Foundation	Women vote for the first time in El Salvador The Cuban House of Representatives passes a bill for equal civil rights for women	From the early 1900s to her death, physician, surgeon, and feminist activist Paulina Luisi (d. 1950) of Uruguay works to change the prostitution laws in Montevideo and Buenos Aires; she also works to destroy white slavery and alcoholism; she is Uruguay's first female holder of a bachelor's degree, its first woman physician, and a member of the Uruguayan diplomatic corps	**1950**
Canadian dancer/choreographer Celia Franca (b. 1921) founds the National Ballet of Canada in Toronto Lucille Ball (1911–1989), the queen of American comedy, stars in the most popular television series of all time, *I Love Lucy*	Mrs. William Ackerman is reported to have taken over the pulpit of a Reform Mississippi synagogue upon her husband's death	Polish historian of logic Sof'ja Aleksandrovna Janovskaja (1896–1966), in her student days a political activist in the Bolshevik wing of the Russian Communist Party, receives the coveted Order of Lenin for her work in mathematical logic British archeologist Jacquetta Hawkes (b. 1910) publishes *A Land*, an account of physical and cultural development of Britain remarkable for the poetic quality of its prose	Japanese women vote for the first time		**1951**

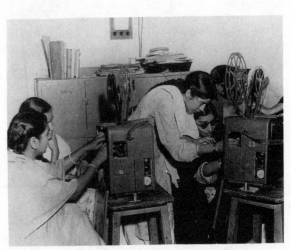

Women learning to use film projectors, Lala Musa, Pakistan
Photograph (c. 1954) courtesy Sophia Smith Collection, Smith College

	General/ Context	Daily Life/ Customs/ Practices	Humanities/ Fine Arts	Occupations	Education
1951			British novelist Doris Lessing publishes the five-volume *Children of Violence* (1951–1969)		
1952	The Mau Mau terrorist movement targets British control of Kenya	Queen Elizabeth II of England is named *Time* magazine's Man of the Year Amy Vanderbilt (1908–1974), American columnist on etiquette whose name becomes synonymous with good manners, publishes *The Complete Book of Etiquette* George W. Jorgensen has the first modern sex-change operation, becoming Christine Jorgensen For the first time in modern Egyptian history, political rights are extended to women; not until 1956, however, are all women eligible to vote	Marianne Moore is awarded a Pulitzer Prize for *Collected Poems* (1951) Swiss novelist Béatrice Beck (b. 1914) wins the Prix Goncourt for *Léon Morin, prêtre* (*Leon Morin, Priest*) Major American novelist Flannery O'Connor (1925–1964) publishes her first book, *Wise Blood;* other important works include the short story collection *A Good Man Is Hard to Find* (1955) and the novel *The Violent Bear It Away* (1960)	After retiring to Los Angeles and going to college, former "madam" Polly Adler (1900?–1962) publishes her autobiography, *A House Is Not a Home* Margaret Bourke-White (1904–1971) serves as UN war correspondent in Korea for *Life* magazine Doriot Anthony Dwyer, the first woman appointed to first chair in a major orchestra, becomes the principal flautist of the Boston Symphony Orchestra Hanya Holm, a choreographer of musicals, is the first choreographer to copyright her works in Washington, DC British flower arranger and culinary expert Constance Spry (1886–1960) is commissioned to decorate Westminster Abbey for the coronation of Queen Elizabeth II	

First Indonesian female pilot Photograph (c. 1950) courtesy Sophia Smith Collection, Smith College

	General/ Context	Daily Life/ Customs/ Practices	Humanities/ Fine Arts	Occupations	Education
1953		Alfred C. Kinsey publishes *Sexual Behavior in the Human Female,* a landmark study of the sexual practices of US women; he concludes that almost half have sex before marriage, a quarter are unfaithful afterward and a quarter of those unmarried have had a homosexual relationship	One of the first modern weavers to present weaving as a fine art, Lenore Tawney (b. 1925) invents a new reed that controls the shape of her weaving, allowing more design possibilities Russian novelist Vera Fiodorovna Panova publishes *Vremena goda* (*Seasons of the Year*), a novel describing life in a Soviet industrial town	American broadcast journalist Pauline Frederick (b. 1908) becomes the first woman to receive a Dupont Award for news commentary; her 30-year career involves political reporting and analysis on both radio and television Jacqueline Lee Bouvier (1929–1994) works as a newspaper photographer before marrying future American president John F. Kennedy	

Performing Arts/ Entertainment/ Sports	Religion/ Philosophy	Science/ Technology/ Discovery	Statecraft/ Military	Reform	

1952

Andrea Mead Lawrence wins a gold medal for the women's giant slalom the first year this skiing event is admitted into Olympic competition; she also wins a gold for slalom, the first American to win two gold medals in skiing

The longest running play in British history, *The Mousetrap,* by British mystery writer Agatha Christie (1890–1976), opens; it runs until 1976

Amalia Hernández, Mexican dancer, choreographer, and teacher, founds the Ballet Folklórico de Mexico to preserve her nation's ethnic dance traditions

Esther Brand of South Africa wins the Olympic gold in the women's high jump at the Helsinki Games, a first in women's track and field for South Africa

Joan Harrison of South Africa wins Olympic gold in the 100-meter backstroke at the Helsinki Games, a swimming first for South Africa

Josephine F. Holmes is the first woman scientist to land on a polar ice cap

Dr. Dorothy Horstmann discovers the presence of the polio virus in the bloodstream of victims at very early stages of the disease

Dr. Virginia Apgar develops the Apgar score, a numerical evaluation of newborn babies' vital signs that can alert doctors to the need for special attention

Romanian foreign minister since 1947, Ana Pauker is ousted by the Communists during a purge of Jewish officials

Elizabeth II becomes Queen of England, head of the British Commonwealth of Nations, following the death of her father, King George VI

Elizabeth Gurley Flynn's leadership of the American Communist party results in her trial and imprisonment under the Smith Act

The UN General Assembly adopts the first international legal statement dealing with women's rights at the Convention on the Political Rights of Women held in New York City

Polling day in Delhi—a blind old woman, carried on her son's back, insists on exercising her franchise and waits in line for her turn to vote
Photograph (1952) courtesy Sophia Smith Collection, Smith College

1953

Lucretia E. Badham patents a combination squirt pistol/spotlight to be used by women who are out alone at night

American flier Jacqueline Cochran becomes the first woman to break the sound barrier

Madame Vijaya Lakshmi Pandit addressing a Congress party meeting, India Information Service of India; photograph (1952) courtesy Sophia Smith Collection, Smith College

Execution of Julius and Ethel Rosenberg (b. 1915), convicted of passing top-secret information on the atomic bomb to the Soviet Union

Vijaya Lakshmi Pandit (1900–1990) is the first female and first Indian president of the UN

Clare Boothe Luce is appointed by President Eisenhower as the first American woman am-

	General/ Context	Daily Life/ Customs/ Practices	Humanities/ Fine Arts	Occupations	Education
1953				this year; during his presidency, 1961–1963, she sets the tone for American women's fashions; she later becomes an editor for Doubleday	
1954	The Battle of Dienbienphu brings about the end of French control over Indochina The first TV dinners are sold in the US, offering American homemakers a quick means of preparing a meal Belize institutes universal adult suffrage	Bigamy is outlawed in India British poet Edith Sitwell, known for such works as *Clown's House* (1918), *English Eccentrics* (1933), and *I Live Under a Black Sun* (1937), as well as for personal eccentricities, such as habitually dressing in medieval costume, is made Dame Commander of the British Empire	Leónie Fuller Adams receives the Bollingen Prize for *High Falcon* (1929); her *Poems: A Selection* appears this year Margaret Hillis (b. 1921) founds and directs the American Choral Foundation American poet and critic Louise Bogan (1897–1970) publishes her *Collected Poems,* a co-winner of the Bollingen Prize	Dr. Leona Baumgartner is the first female health commissioner of New York City Ruth Dayan (b. 1917) is director of Maskit, Israel's center of handicrafts, where she encourages diverse craft skills of Israeli immigrants	
1955	Formation of the Warsaw Pact	As of 1955 in Burma, social security covers maternity benefits Ruth Ellis (1927–1955) is the last woman hanged, for the murder of her lover, in England	Ayano Chiba is chosen one of Japan's highly honored Living National Treasures ("holders of intangible cultural properties"); she is the only living person to understand and practice the 2000-year-old Japanese art of spinning, weaving, and dyeing hemp with indigo	Julia Walsh is the first woman to be accepted to and graduate from the advanced management program at the Harvard Graduate School of Business and one of the first women to hold a seat on the American Stock Exchange State-owned factories, shops, and organizations in the People's Republic of China provide 56-day maternity leave; many provide day care and nursery schools during working hours	Sophie Tucker endows a chair of theater arts at Brandeis University (Waltham, MA)
1956	Sudan, Tunisia, and Morocco gain independence	Dr. Marie-Andrée Lagroua Weill-Hallé founds the French movement for family planning in part to	Elizabeth Bishop receives a Pulitzer Prize for *Poems, North and South*	Mrs. Josephine Bay becomes the first woman to head a New York Stock Exchange member company, as	

Performing Arts/ Entertainment/ Sports	Religion/ Philosophy	Science/ Technology/ Discovery	Statecraft/ Military	Reform	
			bassador to a major power, Italy

Between 1953 and 1964, women in Central Africa participate in large numbers in nationalist political campaigns; they join trade unions and political parties, providing powerful support for strikes and rallies | | **1953** |
| Judy Devlin wins 10 singles titles, the women's record, at the All England Championship Tennis tournament

21-year-old soprano Montserrat Caballé (b. 1933) wins the Liceo Conservatory gold medal, the highest honor for singing in Spain

Swedish actress Greta Garbo (1905–1990) is awarded a special Oscar, though she has won none for any individual performance

Carla Fracci (b. 1936) becomes prima ballerina with Italy's La Scala Ballet, 1954–1967 | | | | American medical doctor Mary Church Terrell (1863–1954) is the founder and first president of the National Association of Colored Women

A Communist organization promoting women's rights, the National Federation of Indian Women is founded | **1954** |
| Marian Anderson is the first black soloist of the Metropolitan Opera, where she appears as Ulrica in *Un Ballo in Maschera* (*A Masked Ball*)

Russian-born filmmaker Maya Deren, known for her avantgarde films, founds the Creative Film Foundation

Ruth Page, choreographer and prima ballerina, founds the Chicago Ballet | | Louise Arner Boyd (1887–1972) becomes the first female counselor of the American Geographical Society; she also becomes the first woman to fly over and around the North Pole | Women vote in federal elections for the first time in Mexico

Honduran women get the right to vote and hold office

Alva Reimer Myrdal becomes Sweden's first female ambassador to India | Rosa Parks (b. 1913), a black resident of Montgomery, AL, is arrested for refusing to take a seat at the back of a public bus; her arrest sparks the first of the great civil rights protests of the next 15 years

British reformer Lilian Charlotte Barker (1874–1955) is best known for her prison reforms, which include establishing a professional service for the care of women and girl offenders | **1955** |
| Signora Minuzzo, the first woman to recite the Olympic oath, formally opens the 1956 Winter Games | | British-born Cecilia Helena Payne-Gaposchkin becomes professor of astronomy at Harvard, one of the | Women in Peru vote for the first time | | **1956** |

Iranian women learning midwifery
Photograph (1950s) courtesy Sophia Smith Collection, Smith College

	General/ Context	Daily Life/ Customs/ Practices	Humanities/ Fine Arts	Occupations	Education
1956	Hungarian revolt against Soviet authority in Hungary	bring down the 1920 law banning the sale of contraceptives The Egyptian Cabinet approves women's suffrage The West German Bundestag passes the Equal Rights Act (Gleichberechitgungsgesetz), "emancipating" German women	British author Nancy Mitford (1904–1973) popularizes the terms "U" (upper class) and "Non-U" Irish novelist Iris Murdoch (b. 1919), known for her witty, psychologically penetrating novels, publishes *The Flight from the Enchanter* British novelist Mary Renault (b. 1905) is best known for her novels based on classical mythology; her compassionate exploration of homosexuality, *The Charioteer* (1953), met with a remarkably favorable reception for its time British playwright Dodie (Dorothy Gladys) Smith publishes the popular children's book *One Hundred and One Dalmatians*	the president and chair of the brokerage house A. M. Kidder and Company Josephine L. Good becomes the first woman to serve as convention director of the Republican National Committee American entrepreneur Bette Clair Nesmith Graham invents Liquid Paper Lee Tai-young is the first female lawyer and judge in Korea Known as the First Lady of Radio, American journalist Mary Margaret McBride (1899–1976) concludes 22 years of regular broadcast interviews	
1957	Ghana gains independence	Young American women adopt ankle bracelets	American burlesque queen Gypsy Rose Lee (Rose Louise Hovick, 1914–1970) writes her autobiography, *Gypsy,* upon which a Broadway musical and a film are based Russian novelist Galina Yevgenyevna Nikolayeva (1911–1963) publishes *Bitva v puti* (*A Battle on the Way*), a novel dealing in part with the workings of the Soviet secret police Italian poet and novelist Else Morante (1912–1986) publishes her most successful novel, *L'Isola di Arturo* (*Arthur's Island*) Sarah Caldwell founds the Opera Group of Boston		

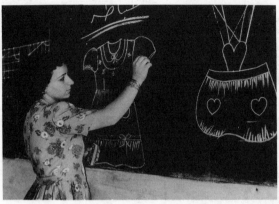

An instructor at the UN-established Embroidery Centre in the Gaza Strip gives a course in dress design, Egypt
Photograph (1954) courtesy Sophia Smith Collection, Smith College

Yemenite woman with baby, late 1950s
Photograph courtesy Sophia Smith Collection, Smith College

Performing Arts/ Entertainment/ Sports	Religion/ Philosophy	Science/ Technology/ Discovery	Statecraft/ Military	Reform	
Billie Holiday (1915–1959), internationally acclaimed jazz singer, publishes *Lady Sings the Blues*		first few women professors at that institution	Nicaraguan women register to vote for the first time		**1956**
Swedish actress Bibi (Birgitta) Andersson (b. 1935), one of director Ingmar Bergman's staple perfomers, appears in his film *The Seventh Seal*		The University of Berlin elects as professor emerita Hilda Geiringer von Mises, a Vienna-born mathematician noted for her contributions to probability theory	The first woman in the Greek Cabinet, Lina Tsaldaris is named Greece's welfare minister		
French actress Brigitte Bardot (Camille Javal, b. 1934) becomes an international sex symbol when she stars in the film *And God Created Woman*			Dr. Josephina Valencia de Hubach is named Colombia's education minister; she is the first woman in the Colombian Cabinet		
			Women vote for the first time in Greece's national elections		
			Golda Meir is appointed Israel's minister of foreign affairs under Prime Minister David Ben-Gurion, serving as Israel's delegate to the UN from 1953 to 1966		
Mrs. L. Mandel becomes the first woman in the history of shooting as a sport to lead men's and women's competitive averages	Teresa Kearney (1875–1957), an Irishwoman known as Mother Kevin, founds religious congregations in East Africa and pioneers higher European education for Catholic African women	Chien-Shiung Wu (b. 1912), professor of physics at Columbia University since 1944, does the experimental proof for two Nobel Prize winners, Dr. Tsung-Dao Lee and Dr. Chen Ning Yang (also Chinese scientists working in the US), who disprove the law of parity with their theory that nuclear particles do not always act similarly	Women vote for the first time in Tunisia		**1957**
Singer and actress Doris Day (Doris von Kappelhoff, b. 1924) becomes popular as Hollywood's All-American girl; films include *The Man Who Knew Too Much* (1955), *The Pajama Game* (1957), and *Pillow Talk* (1959)			Anne W. Wheaton (d. 1977) serves in the Eisenhower administration as the first presidential spokeswoman until 1961		
Country western singer Patsy Cline (1932–1963) scores her first big hit, "Walkin' After Midnight"			Grand Duchess of Luxembourg from 1919 to 1964, Charlotte Aldegonde E. M. Wilhelmine (1896–1985) helps to found the European Common Market		
Cuban dancer Alicia Alonso is the first Western dancer invited to perform in the Soviet Union					

	General/ Context	Daily Life/ Customs/ Practices	Humanities/ Fine Arts	Occupations	Education
1958		Beatnik styles challenge the taste and expectations of the cultural mainstream in the US and Europe; women wear hair and clothing long and loose; men wear leather jackets and jeans; both sexes favor dark colors Aided by the French reforms of the 1950s, Algerian women are granted the franchise, though men obtained this right in 1919; until this point, Algerian women are legally, socially, and politically nonpersons Women are given full political rights under Iran's new constitution	Mary Wells Ashworth shares the Pulitzer Prize for Biography with John A. Carroll for *George Washington,* vol. VII English playwright Shelagh Delaney's witty and bawdy plays about the English lower class include *A Taste of Honey* and *The Lion in Love* (1960) New Jersey-born artist Grace Hartigan (b. 1922) paints large canvases that alternate between abstraction and stylized images of New York City's Lower East Side; in the late 1950s, major museums begin to acquire her work	Hannah Arendt becomes the first female full professor at Princeton University Banker Mary G. Roebling is elected to the board of governors of the American Stock Exchange, the first woman to hold such a position	
1959	Fidel Castro takes power in Cuba, forming the first communist government in Latin America	15-year-old actress Beverly Aadland's love affair with her 50-year-old costar Errol Flynn creates a public scandal; she stars with him in the film *Cuban Rebel Girls*	Lorraine Hansberry (1930–1965) wins the New York Drama Critics Circle Award for *A Raisin in the Sun,* the first play written by a black woman to appear on Broadway Rebecca West (1892–1983) is made a Dame Commander of the British Empire; a committed feminist and social reformer in her youth, she becomes a formidable novelist, critic, and essayist French novelist and filmmaker Marguerite Duras (b. 1914) writes the screenplay for the award-winning film *Hiroshima Mon Amour* British novelist, poet, and critic Muriel Spark (b. 1918) publishes *Memento Mori;* her other works include *The Prime of Miss Jean Brodie* (1961) and *The Abbess of Crewe* (1974)	 *Kurdish woman with elaborately braided hair* Photograph (1958) from *Daughters from Afar,* © State of Israel; courtesy Sophia Smith Collection, Smith College	
1960	Nigeria becomes independent	French fashion designer Coco Chanel introduces her greatest	Poet Gwendolyn Brooks publishes *The Bean Eaters*	Ann Lowe (b. 1898) is the first black couturiere	Nettie Podell Ottenberg, organizer of the US National Child Day Care Association,

Performing Arts/ Entertainment/ Sports	Religion/ Philosophy	Science/ Technology/ Discovery	Statecraft/ Military	Reform	
American actress Susan Hayward (born Edythe Marrener, 1918–1975) wins an Oscar for her performance in *I Want to Live*

Canadian opera singer Teresa Stratas (Anastasia Strataks, b. 1938) sings with the New York Metropolitan Opera; she is the recipient of three Grammys and one Tony Award

Audrey Cooper of Jamaica wins first prize for her piano performance at the Royal Over-Seas League Music Competition | | Pelageya Yakovlevna Polubarinova-Kochina becomes the leading woman in a pioneering group of elite Soviet scientists and mathematicians in Siberia

Physicist Chien-Shiung Wu is the first woman to receive an honorary doctorate in science from Princeton University; she is elected to the National Academy of Sciences | Women in Mauritius vote for the first time

Minister Lindstrom becomes the first female acting premier of Sweden

Mexican women vote in the national elections for the first time

A women's uprising takes place among the Kom people of Cameroon as a result of unpopular colonial policies directed at women farmers; using a traditional form of protest called *anlu*, they stone an official, close down men's stalls at the farmers' market, set up their own court system, and declare that local chiefs are no longer in authority | British birth control pioneer Marie Stopes dies; besides her fame for establishing birth control clinics, she is also the first woman lecturer at the University of Manchester

Mary H. Rutman, a Canadian-born Ceylonese woman, receives the Ramón Magsaysay Award Foundation's Public Service Award for her gift of service to the Ceylonese people | **1958** |
| Maria Bueno of Brazil triumphs at Wimbledon in 1959 and 1960; a Brazilian legend, she is honored after these wins by a statue in São Paulo and a postage stamp; as of 1981, she has 585 tournament wins and is still competing

Cuban ballerina Alicia Alonso founds the Ballet Nacional de Cuba

Radio, television, and stage star Gertrude Berg receives a Tony Award for her role in the Broadway play *Dear Me, the Sky Is Falling* | Revered as the living Buddha, Doujebamo is carried off with the Dalai Lama's retinue when the Chinese force them out of Tibet; they ride until their horses die under them and then continue on foot; upon returning to Tibet four months later, she renounces her position as the living Buddha, marries, and becomes a delegate to the National People's Congress | Paleontologists Mary and Louis B. Leakey discover in Tanzania the fossilized molars of a humanlike creature believed to be 1.75 million years old

Sof'ja Aleksandrovna Janovskaja becomes the first chairperson of the new department of mathematical logic at Moscow State University | Mme. H. E. Anegay becomes the first Moroccan woman representative to the UN General Assembly

Laili Rusad becomes Indonesia's first female ambassador for Belgium and Luxembourg | Helen Suzman (b. 1917) is one of several to form South Africa's Progressive Party; between 1953 and 1974 hers is the only voice in the South African parliament raised on behalf of the blacks; Chief Buthelezi calls her "the one flickering flame of liberty"

Tee Tee Luce of Burma receives the Ramón Magsaysay Award Foundation's Public Service Award for her work with wayward and abandoned boys | **1959** |
| 56-year-old Dr. Barbara Moore (1894–1967), a Russian-born British citizen, is the | Psychiatrists conclude that Shanta Devi is a case of genuine reincarnation; Shanta be- | Englishwoman Jane Goodall (b. 1934) studies the behavior of | Mme. M. Nakayama becomes the first Japanese woman Cabinet member | British women's rights activist Sylvia Pankhurst spends her last years fighting for | **1960** |

	General/ Context	Daily Life/ Customs/ Practices	Humanities/ Fine Arts	Occupations	Education
1960	Belgian Congo (modern Zaire) gains independence	success, the Chanel suit Fashions created by costume designers begin to be popularized by film stars The German city of Erlangen names a street the Noetherstrasse in honor of mathematicians Emmy and Max Noether The Canadian Bill of Rights is amended to prohibit sexual discrimination Establishment of the (US) Federal Women's Award Program in annual recognition of six distinguished women in the federal service for their outstanding contribution to government	Margaret Leech receives her second Pulitzer Prize for History for *In the Days of McKinley* Lillian Hellman publishes the drama *Toys in the Attic*	Dr. Nina Starr Braunwald is the first woman in the US to perform open-heart surgery In the People's Republic of China, special all-women teams, called "Iron Maidens" or "March Eight Teams," undertake heavy jobs, such as reforestation and deep-sea fishing, thought suitable only for men, against whom they compete successfully Irmgard Flügge-Lotz (1903–1974), Stanford University's first woman professor, previously served unofficially as full professor and represented the US as the only woman delegate to the First Congress of the International Federation of Automatic Control in Moscow	obtains the first public money ever allotted to day care in Washington, DC
1961	The self-wringing mop is sold in the US Soviets construct the Berlin Wall to halt defections from East to West Germany Sierra Leone becomes independent from England	The Bahamian Assembly passes a bill giving women the vote and the right to become Assembly members	Harper Lee wins the Pulitzer Prize for Fiction for *To Kill a Mockingbird* Japan Women Writers' Association establishes the Joryu Bungakusha Sho Literary Award, an annual monetary prize and medal to recognize the best novel written by a woman Austrian writer Ingeborg Bachmann (1926–1973) publishes *Das dreiβigst Jahr* (*The Thirtieth Year*); she publishes the experimental novel *Malina* in 1971	Julia McWilliams Child (b. 1912), America's most popular French chef, publishes *Mastering the Art of French Cooking*  *Queen Sirikit of Thailand, opening day of the National Council of Social Work* Photograph (1960) courtesy Sophia Smith Collection, Smith College	

Performing Arts/ Entertainment/ Sports	Religion/ Philosophy	Science/ Technology/ Discovery	Statecraft/ Military	Reform	
first woman to walk across the US, taking 85 days

Judith Anderson (Frances Margaret Anderson, b. 1898) is the first Australian-born actress named a Dame Commander of the British Empire

Janis Joplin (1943–1970) is one of the most successful pop artists in the US and the world; she is immortalized in the film *The Rose* (1979) | gins talking at age three about a husband she had had; she later identifies herself as Lugdi, a young house-wife who died in childbirth; she is brought to meet her husband, and she gives him accurate details of their life together, leaving him in tears | chimpanzees in their natural habitat | Esmeralda Arboleda de Cuevas Cancino becomes Colombia's first female minister of transport

Sirimavo Bandaranaike (b. 1916) of Sri Lanka becomes the first woman head of state in a modern nation upon winning the election following her husband's assassination; although defeated in 1965, she wins again in 1970 and 1975; she is responsible for changing her country's name from Ceylon to Sri Lanka

Yeh Chun is the second of two women in China's politburo during the 1960s | the independence of Abyssinia (later Ethiopia), where she dies in 1960

In the 1960s, German reformer Beate Klarsfeld (b. 1931) dedicates herself to tracking down and bringing to trial Nazi war criminals

Adelaide Casely Hayford (b. 1868), of West Africa's Gold Coast, dies; a prominent cultural nationalist and feminist, she organized a technical school for women, headed the ladies division of the Universal Negro Improvement Association, and made lecture tours in order to refute the stereotype of African barbarism | **1960** |
| American Darlene Hard wins the US Lawn Tennis Association women's singles competition

French soprano Madeleine Grey (b. 1896), appearing in recital and with orchestras in Europe, the US, South America, and Egypt, specializes in modern French and Spanish music and folksongs

Billie Jean King (b. 1943), US tennis player, holds the women's record for winning the most Wimbledon titles: 19 (6 singles, 9 doubles, 4 mixed doubles)

Carla Fracci, Italian ballerina, receives the Anna Pavlova Prize from the Paris University of Dance and is named Woman of the Year by *Mademoiselle* magazine | | Jocelyn R. Gill joins NASA as chief of the In-Flight Sciences Manned Space Program; in 1966 she wins a Federal Women's Award in recognition of her outstanding contributions to the US space program

Dr. Hattie Alexander (1901–1968) discovers the cure for bacterial meningitis | Elizabeth Gurley Flynn succeeds Eugene Dennis as chairman of the US Communist party

G. Wittkowski is appointed deputy premier of East Germany, the first woman to hold that position

Women in Cameroon vote for the first time

West German attorney Elisabeth Schwartzhaupt is appointed health minister, the first woman to hold a Cabinet position in that country | Eleanor Roosevelt is appointed by President John F. Kennedy to the chair of the Commission on the Status of Women

The (US) Women Strike for Peace is founded

Nilawan Pintong of Thailand receives the Ramón Magsaysay Award Foundation's Public Service Award for developing civic enterprises that have given women a new and creative role in Thailand

Beginning in 1961, after Tanzania gains independence, deliberate efforts are made to combat traditional sex discrimination; the United Women of Tanzania become a political force and women begin to participate in the national service, acquiring military, civil, and social service skills | **1961** |

	General/Context	Daily Life/Customs/Practices	Humanities/Fine Arts	Occupations	Education
1962	Uganda gains independence The antiabortifacient thalidomide causes children to be born with deformities	The new constitution of Monaco grants women suffrage and the right to run for parliament The king of Jordan orders political reforms, including women's suffrage The Iranian government suspends its decree giving women the right to vote in order to avert demonstrations by religious leaders	Katherine Anne Porter publishes her masterpiece, the novel *Ship of Fools* With her experimental *The Golden Notebook*, British novelist Doris May Lessing (b. 1919) becomes a major figure among feminist fiction writers Anna Langfus wins the Prix Goncourt for *La pitié de Dieu* (*God's Pity*) American science writer Rachel Carson (1907–1964) publishes *The Silent Spring*, in which she warns against the environmental danger of weed killers and insecticides	Marion Stephenson becomes the first female vice president of the National Broadcasting Company (NBC) Dr. Pierra Hoon Veijjabu is the first female physician of Thailand; under her influence, prostitution is outlawed by the Thai government, which bestows on her the title "Veijjabu," meaning "great woman doctor"	Tayyeba Huq (b. 1921) founds the Bangladesh Housewives Association Felice N. Schwartz founds Catalyst, Inc., a national organization that assists women in choosing and developing their careers; she is also the founder of the National Scholarship Service and Fund for Negro Students (NSSFNS)
1963	The Profumo scandal: British war minister John Profumo resigns when his affair with 21-year-old Christine Keeler, who is also having an affair with a Soviet naval officer, is revealed Kenya gains independence President John F. Kennedy is assassinated in Dallas, TX	The characteristic women's fashions of the 60s appear at about this time: miniskirts, hip-hugging, bell-bottomed pants, and collarless jackets; similar fashions adopted by men make for a unisex look Ellen Sulzberger Straus (b. 1925) founds WMCA Call for Action, a telephone referral with radio broadcasting service responding to citizen complaints	Historian Barbara W. Tuchman wins the Pulitzer Prize for General Nonfiction for *The Guns of August* Publication of *The Feminine Mystique* by Betty Friedan (b. 1921) revitalizes the American feminist movement Indian writer Anita Desai (b. 1937) publishes her first novel, *Cry the Peacock* Photographer Margaret Bourke-White pub-	Jean Slutsky Nidetch (b. 1923), a compulsive eater from Brooklyn, founds the world's most successful diet business, Weight Watchers Inc. Multimillionaire Katharine Graham (b. 1917) becomes president of The Washington Post Company, the only female head of a *Fortune* 500 company	Helen Kim of Korea receives the Ramón Magsaysay Award Foundation's Public Service Award for her role in the emancipation and education of Korean women

WOMEN IN MODERN ISLAM

Since the sixth century Islam has adjusted to a wide variety of climates, cultures, and economic systems. Its holy book, the Koran, like other holy books, has been subject to multiple interpretations. It is, therefore, difficult to make accurate generalizations about such matters as the status of women in Islam, particularly since women of the same modern state who are nomadic as opposed to agricultural, or city dwellers as opposed to village residents can lead very different lives under what seems to be the same religious code.

Still, most experts agree that Islam began as a social reformist movement. Though Muhammad at first limited polygamy and guaranteed married women's property rights, from early Islamic times women have not been considered equal to men in family law. Divorce laws were inequitable, child custody laws favored the father, women inherited only half the men's share in family property, and were subject to special modesty and obedience injunctions.

Many Western feminists and some Islamic critics decry what they see as the inequality—and in some instances brutalization—of women under Islam. But the issue is far more complex: what has no value in one culture may be deeply significant in another. So, for example, while Islamic traditionalists and even some modern reformers have argued that practices such as the seclusion of women and the wearing of the veil protect and

Performing Arts/ Entertainment/ Sports	Religion/ Philosophy	Science/ Technology/ Discovery	Statecraft/ Military	Reform	
American film actress Marilyn Monroe (Norma Jean Mortenson Baker, 1926–1962), star of such films as *Bus Stop* (1956) and *Some Like It Hot* (1959), becomes a cult figure even before her death from a drug overdose Indian dancer Balasarawati makes her US debut at Jacobs Pillow (MA)	American evangelist Kathryn Kuhlman (1910–1976), famed as a faith healer, publishes *I Believe in Miracles* Mother Teresa (b. 1910) receives the Ramón Magsaysay Award Foundation's International Understanding Award for merciful cognizance of the abject poor of a foreign land in whose service she led a new congregation	Marguerite Perey, discoverer of the radioactive 87th element, which she names Francium, becomes the first woman elected to the French Academy of Sciences in its 200-year history Louis and Mary Leakey are awarded the National Geographic Society Hubbard Medal for paleontological research and discovery in East Africa	Chieftainess Gulama is named minister without portfolio of Sierra Leone; she is one of the first women Cabinet members in West Africa	The All-African Organization of Women is founded to discuss the right to vote, activity in local and national governments, women in education, and medical services for women	1962

Russian cosmonaut Valentina Tereshkova Photograph (1963) courtesy *Soviet Life/Novosti*

English actress Dame Margaret Rutherford (1892–1972) wins an Oscar for *The VIP's* German actress Marlene Dietrich is awarded the Chevalier of the Legion of Honor and decorated with the US Medal of Freedom for her work for the Allies in WWII Julia Child's prizewinning TV program brings French cooking styles to millions of American homes		Soviet cosmonaut Valentina Tereshkova-Nikolayeva (b. 1937) is the first woman to orbit the earth in the Soviet spaceship Vostok VI German Maria Goeppert-Mayer, in joint effort with Hans Jensen and Eugene Wigner, receives the Nobel Prize for Physics for work on the unusual stability of various nuclear structures	Dr. van Zeller becomes director general of the health ministry in Portugal, the first woman appointed to such a high post in that country Women vote for the first time in Iran Margot Honecker becomes East Germany's first female minister of education Fannie Lou Hamer (1917–1977), daughter of a sharecropper in rural Mississippi, passes		1963

glorify women, others insist that they are only by degree less degrading than the highly controversial practice of genital mutilation.

As in other modern societies, upper-class Islamic women tend to lead freer lives than their poorer sisters: they may be sent abroad for their education, adopt Western styles of dress, choose their own mates, drive cars, and practice professions. Some, however, have maintained stricter adherence to Muslim codes, retaining their virginity until they marry, seeing men only in the presence of their families, and so forth. The debate about the role of all women in Islam—not just those born into priv-ilege—has so far taken place almost exclusively among women of the upper classes.

Western feminists maintain a vigorous prejudice against Islam's treatment of women. Their disapproval, heightened by propaganda against Islam that has served Western ambitions from the time of the Crusades, continues to be articulated, especially in times of conflict between Middle Eastern interests and Western economic goals. Nevertheless, some feminists have recognized that the social, psychological, and economic ideals of the secularized West do not necessarily answer the needs of women in Islamic societies.

General/ Context	Daily Life/ Customs/ Practices	Humanities/ Fine Arts	Occupations	Education
1963	The US Equal Pay Act is passed	lishes her autobiography, *Portrait of Myself*		
		American poet and novelist Sylvia Plath (1932–1963) publishes the autobiographical novel *The Bell Jar*		
1964	The "topless" bathing suit, designed by Rudi Gernreich, is introduced, but is worn by few women	Hannah Arendt attends the trial of Nazi Adolf Eichmann in Jerusalem and writes *Eichmann in Jerusalem: A Report on the Banality of Evil*	Dorothy H. Jacobson serves as assistant secretary for international affairs, 1964–1968, the first woman to attain such a rank in the US Department of Agriculture's more than 100-year history	
	In *Griswold* v. *Connecticut,* the US Supreme Court rules a Connecticut law banning contraceptives unconstitutional	French artist Françoise Gilot, mistress of Picasso from 1946 to 1953, publishes *Life with Picasso*		
	The death of Kitty Genovese, stabbed to death in full view of 38 neighbors who do nothing to help, makes a tremendous impact on US national consciousness, pointing up the heartlessness of American urban life	Doris Lessing publishes the prizewinning *African Stories* Cosmetics magnate Helena Rubinstein publishes her autobiography, *My Life for Beauty*		
	Passage of the US Civil Rights Act, which prohibits discrimination on the basis of race, sex, religion, or national origin			

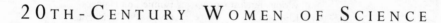

20TH-CENTURY WOMEN OF SCIENCE

The end of the 19th century and the first decades of the 20th were marked by scientific discoveries that changed the way scientists understood matter and energy. The discovery of quantum theory, relativity, radioactivity, X rays, and subatomic particles revolutionized science. For the first time in history hard science had almost immediate and profound effects upon the lives of ordinary people. As the profession of science expanded in the 20th century, so did the role of women in all fields of science.

Many women who made great contributions to science took care to make their discoveries accessible to the public. Margaret Mead's observations of the development of Samoan children in the 1920s, published as *Coming of Age in Samoa,* established her reputation among professionals while introducing the field to a wide lay audience. A pioneer in cultural psychology, Ruth Benedict, as special adviser to the US Office of War Information, wrote *The Chrysanthemum and the Sword,* a book explaining Japanese culture to the West.

Marie Curie received two Nobel Prizes in Science, first in 1906 for her part in the discovery of radioactivity and again in 1911 for chemistry. Her daughter, Irene Joliot-Curie, won the Nobel Prize for Chemistry in 1935.

Emmy (Amalie) Noether, daughter of a mathematician, was first refused a faculty appointment to Göttingen University during World War I on the grounds that returning soldiers would be humiliated to have to learn from a woman. Later, after she formulated Noether's Theorem—a milestone for modern theoretical physics—Albert Einstein called her "the most significant creative mathematical genius thus far produced since the higher education of women began."

Edith Hinkley Quimby helped create radiation physics and determined the precise dosages to be used in radiology. Yale Ph.D. Grace Murray Hopper joined the US Navy in World

Performing Arts/ Entertainment/ Sports	Religion/ Philosophy	Science/ Technology/ Discovery	Statecraft/ Military	Reform	
		Mary L. Petermann (d. 1976) discovers "Petermann's particles," now known as ribosomes, the sites of protein synthesis	her voter registration test in defiance of racial harassment		**1963**
Mickey Wright achieves the best score ever recorded for a woman in golf until this time

The Japanese women's volleyball team wins the Olympic gold medal at the Tokyo Games | | Soviet Jewish engineer Sophia Belkin wins the Lenin Prize, one of the highest honors bestowed by the USSR

British chemist Dorothy Mary Crowfoot Hodgkin is awarded the Nobel Prize for Chemistry for determining the structure of biochemical compounds essential in combating pernicious anemia, the fifth woman ever to receive the Nobel Prize | Women vote for the first time in San Marino

Libyan women vote for the first time

Congresswoman Martha Griffiths presents the argument for including "sex" in the Civil Rights Act

In Zambia and Malawi, women's activism contributes strongly to the success of nationalist movements in winning independence from Britain | Fannie Lou Hamer and Ruby Davis lead the Freedom Democratic Party at the 1964 Democratic Convention | **1964** |

Sylvia Plath, American poet
Photograph (1955) by Eric Stahlberg; courtesy Sophia Smith Collection, Smith College

War II and helped develop the world's first electronic computer, the Mark I. She devised computer programs and developed the first program to translate human-readable symbols into machine-readable language.

Lise Meitner's work on alpha and gamma radiation with Otto Hahn led to the first explanation of nuclear fission. Biophysicists Rosalind Elsie Franklin (1920–1958) and Maurice Wilkins described the probable structure of the DNA molecule, leading to J. D. Watson and F. H. Crick's model of DNA in 1953.

Four more recent Nobelists are Maria Goeppert-Mayer, who received the Nobel Prize for Physics in 1963 for her research on the structure of atomic nuclei; Dorothy Mary Crowfoot Hodgkin, awarded the Nobel in Chemistry in 1964 for discovery of the biochemical structures of penicillin and vitamin B_{12}; Rosalyn S. Yalow, whose 1977 Nobel in Medicine was for the development of radioimmunoassay, a way to measure concentrations of everything from hormones and enzymes to viruses and drugs; and Barbara McClintock, who won the 1983 Nobel Prize for Physiology for her discovery of mobile genes in plants.

In 1973 the reference work *American Men of Science* was renamed *American Men and Women of Science*. Despite their growing and powerful presence, a 1970 National Science Foundation study found that women scientists earned from 15% to 50% less than men working in the same fields.

In the latter part of the 20th century, some feminist scientists have attempted to discover whether women employ approaches to knowledge different from those men have considered necessary for objective thought. If they do, they may offer new ways of teaching and studying science that will open up these vital fields to greater numbers of talented young women and men.

	General/ Context	Daily Life/ Customs/ Practices	Humanities/ Fine Arts	Occupations	Education
1965	Second Vatican Council (1962–1965)	Fashion designer Mary Quant (b. 1934) leads a new generation of British designers, establishing the "Carnaby Street" look of the late 1960s The midthigh-length miniskirt becomes fashionable; in the late 60s, the micromini's hemline creeps even farther up Bolivia's Social Security Code of 1965 provides for maternity leave Women in Afghanistan are enfranchised under the new constitution	*The Keepers of the House* by Shirley Ann Grau wins the Pulitzer Prize for Fiction	Renaude Lapointe (b. 1912) becomes the first woman member of the editorial board of *La Presse* in Montreal	Cavendish College is established as a graduate society at Cambridge University; in addition to providing graduate studies for women, it gives them the opportunity to begin their college studies later in life rather than directly after their school days; named for the British social reformer Lucy Cavendish (1848–1926)
1966	Cultural Revolution in China Suffrage becomes universal for those over 21 in Botswana	Women's fashion increasingly favors the "boy look"; full breasts and hips go out of fashion as women try to make themselves look as androgynous as possible Pierced ears become fashionable among American women Married women in Spain are allowed to vote Barbados's constitution of 1966 provides for an electoral system based on adult suffrage for all persons over the age of 18	Jacqueline Susann (1921–1974) publishes *Valley of the Dolls* German author Nelly Sachs (1891–1970) shares the Nobel Prize for Literature with Shmuel Yosef Agnon of Israel One of the greatest intellectuals of her generation American Susan Sontag (b. 1933) publishes the highly influential essay *Against Interpretation*	Princess Elizabeth Bagaya of Uganda becomes the first African woman allowed to practice law in an African country Constance Baker Motley is the first black woman appointed federal judge Madeline H. McWhinney heads a newly formed Federal Reserve department to monitor the US government securities market Adi Losalini Dovi becomes Fiji's first female minister as the assistant minister for urban development, housing and social welfare	The first class of 100 women graduates from George Washington University's program Developing New Horizons, designed to stimulate housewives' interest in vocational fields Former teacher Margaret C. McNamara founds Reading Is FUNdamental (RIF), an organization dedicated to urging students in innercity schools to read

Women's International League for Peace and Freedom vigil at Times Square to oppose the Vietnam War Photograph (1964) courtesy Sophia Smith Collection, Smith College

WOMEN IN MODERN CHINA

With the development of the People's Republic of China, opportunities and rights unthinkable for women in imperial China became law almost overnight. New laws relating to remarriage of widows, concubinage, forced arranged marriages, child betrothals, and female infanticide were instituted. Like most reforms, though, the new laws had some unexpected negative effects. Infanticide, outlawed under the new dispensation, is again on the rise as popula-tion-control measures permit couples to have only one child.

But the benefits to women are real. They can now participate in work and society outside the home, own and inherit property, and retain their own names. The Chinese state has a manifest concern with sexual equality and also with what is called "women's special conditions." Slogans such as "Times have changed: Anything male comrades can do, women comrades can also do"

Performing Arts/ Entertainment/ Sports	Religion/ Philosophy	Science/ Technology/ Discovery	Statecraft/ Military	Reform	
Ballet dancer Suzanne Farrell (b. 1945) becomes the principal dancer with the New York City Ballet			Marguerite de Reimacker-Legot becomes the first woman in the Belgian Cabinet, as family and housing minister	American civil rights leader Viola Liuzzo (1925–1965) is assassinated while driving protesters from Montgomery to Selma, AL	**1965**
Sheila Scott, British pilot, completes the longest solo flight ever, flying 31,000 miles around the world; she completes the first solo light aircraft flight over the North Pole			K. Nourzai becomes the public health minister of Afghanistan, the first woman in the Cabinet		
Argentinian musician Martha Argerich (b. 1941) takes first prize at the International Frederic Chopin Piano Competition in Warszawie, Poland			Patsy Mink is the first Japanese-American woman to be elected to Congress, representing the state of Hawaii		

Frances Steloff, founder of New York's Gotham Book Mart
Photograph (c. 1965) courtesy Skidmore College Rare Books and Special Collections

Brazilian Maria Bueno wins the US Lawn Tennis Association's women's singles		Austrian physicists Lise Meitner (1878–1968), Otto Hahn, and Fritz Strassmann are awarded the Enrico Fermi Prize for their work in nuclear fission	Mrs. Nguyen Thi Hau is inaugurated as mayor of Dalat, South Vietnam, highest post ever held by a woman in that country in modern times	National Organization for Women (NOW) is founded in the US; Betty Friedan, author of *The Feminine Mystique,* becomes its first president	**1966**
Leontyne Price is the first black female to have the lead role in a world premiere opera, Samuel Barber's *Antony and Cleopatra*			Women in Portugal are allowed to volunteer for military service	Formation in Canada of the Committee for Equality of Women (CEW) and the Royal Commission on the Status of Women (RCSW)	
Joyce Hoffman, US surfer, wins her second straight surfing championship in Sydney, Australia, the only woman to date to win this title twice			Indira Gandhi, daughter of the late Jawaharlal Nehru, becomes prime minister of India		
Anne Burns, British pilot, is the first woman to win the British Gliding Championship			Lusibu Z. N'Kanza becomes the Democratic Republic of the Congo's (later Zaire) first female minister of state, responsible for social affairs		

Prime Minister Indira Gandhi of India
Photograph (1966) by Marcel Sternberger, © Ilse Sternberger

strongly urge acceptance of women in the workforce. State-owned factories, shops, and organizations provide a 56-day maternity leave. Many state enterprises also provide nurseries and day care during working hours. Women civil servants receive pensions and can retire five years earlier than men.

In general, women workers are most numerous in urban light industry. They are well represented in textile and clothing manufacture and in retail and service businesses. One third of college graduates are women. Women work in military service, government administration, and party organizations. The Women's Federation, a national organization with branches in all work units, neighborhoods, and rural villages, provides literacy classes, vocational training, political education, and legal information. Primary schooling is now almost universal in China, and all schools are coeducational.

	General/ Context	Daily Life/ Customs/ Practices	Humanities/ Fine Arts	Occupations	Education
1966					
1967	Compact microwave ovens for home use become available The UN unanimously adopts a declaration opposing discrimination against women The UN establishes the Fund for Population Activities to promote family planning 200,000 in New York City and 80,000 in San Francisco march in the first mass draft-card burning	The USSR marks International Women's Day as a national holiday Extravagant bouffant hairdos become popular among American women In France, the Neuwirth Law permits the sale of contraceptives Death of Ilse Koch (b. 1907), imprisoned for life for her atrocities in Nazi prison camps, including having lampshades made of human skin	Cornelia Otis Skinner (1901–1979) publishes *Madame Sarah,* a biography of Sarah Bernhardt Svetlana Alliluyeva (b. 1926), daughter of Joseph Stalin, publishes *Twenty Letters to a Friend* Anne Sexton's (1928–1974) *Live or Die* is awarded a Pulitzer Prize for Poetry A member of the Argentine Academy of Letters, Victoria Ocampo (1890–1979) is awarded the Desikottama, the highest honor bestowed by the Vishwa Bharati University, India	Super-thin British model Twiggy takes the US fashion world by storm, projecting an affecting image of adolescent androgyny and vulnerability Muriel Siebert puts up a reported $445,000 and becomes the first woman to own a seat on the New York Stock Exchange Phyllis Lamphere becomes the first woman president of the US National League of Cities	
1968	Prague Spring—the Soviets invade Czechoslovakia	Pope Paul VI issues the encyclical *Humanae vitae,* forbidding all artificial means of contraception The British Abortion Act overturns the 1861 law that made abortion illegal under all circumstances; now abortion is legal if two physicians determine that continuing the pregnancy would imperil the physical or mental health of the woman Women in Ireland are granted equal rights to vote and hold office under a UN treaty	Bridget Riley (b. 1931) is the first female British painter to win the Venice Biennial International Prize for painting French feminist journalist Françoise Parturier (b. 1919) publishes *An Open Letter to Men*	Elizabeth Malaise is the first woman appointed director of the Belgian National Bank Mrs. J. Rivera de Vicante becomes the labor secretary of Puerto Rico, the first woman in that country's Cabinet	Alicia Escalante forms East Los Angeles Welfare Rights Organization, the first Chicano welfare rights group

Performing Arts/ Entertainment/ Sports	Religion/ Philosophy	Science/ Technology/ Discovery	Statecraft/ Military	Reform	
			Esmeralda Arboleda de Cuevas Cancino becomes the first Colombian woman to be elected to the Senate		**1966**
The Soviet chess team, headed by Nona Gaprindashvili, wins the Women's International Chess Tournament at Oberhausen, West Germany

Irina Rodnina, Soviet pairs figure skater, wins a total of 10 world champion titles

Innovative percussionist Maureen "Mo" Tucker debuts on the first album released by Velvet Underground, produced by Andy Warhol

Argentinian musician Ana Maria Miranda is awarded the grand prize at Concours International de Chant in Paris

An official attempts to eject Kathy Switzer from the all-male Boston marathon; he is thrown to the sidelines by runner Thomas Miller | | | Mrs. B. M. Jumper becomes the first woman chair of the Seminole Indians Tribal Council of Florida

Yekaterina Furtseva (1910–1974) becomes long-term minister of culture of the USSR, the highest-ranking woman in the Soviet government

The Soviet publication *Women of a New World* proclaims that 43% of the total number of deputies elected to its local government bodies are women | Foundation of Another Mother for Peace (US)

Formation of French feminist groups Féminin-Masculin-Futur and Féminisme-Marxisme

Antiwar protester Alice Herz dies 11 days after immolating herself to protest the Vietnam War

Anti-Vietnam war protester Nhat Chi Mai immolates herself in Saigon

Foundation of NARAL (National Association for the Repeal of Abortion Laws) in the US | **1967** |
| Figure skater Peggy Fleming wins the only US gold medal at the Winter Olympics

Family Planning Association and Women's Council of Thailand at work at the Pah-Pai village
Photograph (1967) courtesy Sophia Smith Collection, Smith College | | | Shirley Chisholm of New York becomes the first black woman elected to the US House of Representatives

Nguyen Thi Binh (b. 1927) leads North Vietnam's National Liberation Front delegation at the Paris peace talks, signing the Paris accords that marked the end of the war

Barbara Watson becomes the first woman and the first black to achieve the rank of assistant secretary in the State Department Bureau of Security and Consular Affairs, a | After the assassination of her husband, Rev. Martin Luther King, Coretta Scott King (b. 1927) takes over the leadership of the American civil rights movement

Protesters at the Miss America Pageant throw bras, girdles, curlers, false eyelashes, and wigs into the Freedom Trash Can

Rosario and Silvino Encarnación of the Philippines receive the Ramón Magsaysay Award Foundation's Community Leadership Award for wise management of a credit cooperative that | **1968** |

	General/Context	Daily Life/Customs/Practices	Humanities/Fine Arts	Occupations	Education
1968					
1969	The Stonewall rebellion in New York City marks the beginning of the gay rights movement; although it takes place at a predominately male bar, it has a profound effect on both the gay and lesbian movements The largest antiwar demonstration ever held in Washington, DC, protests the Vietnam War	The "maxi" look features the longest hemlines since 1915 The American organization Jane is formed, initially to provide an abortion counseling and referral service, but growing into an illegal floating feminist underground abortion service, run for women by women	The Museum of Modern Art in New York purchases the art collection of the late Gertrude Stein for $6 million Lillian Hellman publishes her autobiography, *An Unfinished Woman* American author Joyce Carol Oates (b. 1938) publishes *Them* Elsa Martines is awarded a first prize in the Playwriting, English Division, by the Cultural Center of the Philippines for *In Fragility's Grace*	Charlotte Saikowski is the first female senior editor of *The Christian Science Monitor* Nancy Scannell is the first female sportswriter at *The Washington Post* A. Espinoza becomes the Bolivian labor minister, the first woman in the Cabinet Tina Anselmi becomes the first woman to serve in the Italian Cabinet Aura Celina Casanova becomes Venezuela's first female minister for development	
1970	A subcommittee of the US House of Representatives holds hearings on sex discrimination in education, the first in US history Washington, DC's National Press Club votes to accept women as members	New York City's Mayor John Lindsay signs a bill barring discrimination against women in public places Women are granted suffrage in Andorra A Princeton University Office of Population Control study finds that 20% of all married African-American women have been permanently sterilized; a similar figure is found for Chicana women 50,000 people march in New York City in honor of the first Women's Strike for Equality US Senate subcommittee hearings on the birth control pill are interrupted by protesters claiming that women are being used as "guinea pigs" in testing The first major city in the US to do so, New York City bans sex	Ada Louise Huxtable, architecture critic of *The New York Times,* wins the first Pulitzer Prize for Criticism Playwright Betty Comden (b. 1915) wins a Tony Award for her play *Applause* American screenwriter Carol Eastman wins an Oscar for her screenplay *Five Easy Pieces* *Partisan, année zero,* a journal devoted to writing by women about women, publishes its first issue Publication of the radical (US) feminist journal *Notes from the Second Year* Publication of the first national commercial newsletters serving the US women's movement, *Women Today* and *Spokeswoman* Feminist Kate Millett (b. 1934) publishes *Sexual Politics*, a central document in the	Catherine B. Cleary, becomes the first female president of a bank she did not inherit, the First Wisconsin Trust Company Joan Ganz Cooney becomes president of the Children's Television Workshop, whose productions include *Sesame Street* The City of London's first female merchant banker, Caroline Miles (b. 1929), joins the Anglo-Eastern Bank Ringling Bros. & Barnum and Bailey Circus signs Peggy Williams and Maudie Flippen to join the hitherto all-male Clown Alley Chicana feminists found the National Commission of Mexican Women, which sponsors a service center for working women and two child-care centers Maria Teresa Carcomo Lobo is Portugal's first	Dr. Bernice Sandler of the Women's Equity Action League (WEAL) files the first formal charge of sex discrimination in the US under Executive Order 11246 against the University of Maryland

Performing Arts/ Entertainment/ Sports	Religion/ Philosophy	Science/ Technology/ Discovery	Statecraft/ Military	Reform	
			post she holds until 1974	improves life in their barrio without incurring bad debt	1968
Martha Rockwell, Nordic skier, wins 15 national titles in cross-country skiing Brazilian musician Cristina Ortiz takes first prize in the Van Cliburn International Piano Competition		Research chemist Marguerite Shue-Wen Chang of the (US) Department of the Navy invents a device to trigger underground nuclear explosions	Golda Meir becomes Israel's first female prime minister at age 71 Laurice Hlass becomes Jordan's first and only female ambassador Dr. Angie Elizabeth Brooks becomes president of Liberia, the first female president of an African nation 21-year-old Irish MP Bernadette Devlin becomes the youngest woman elected to the British Parliament	The radical antiwar organization Women Against Daddy Warbucks destroys A-1 files in eight New York City draft boards American social reformer Clara McBride Hale establishes Hale House in Harlem, New York, dedicated to caring for babies of drug-addicted mothers Ruth Weiner founds the Colorado Citizens for Clean Air and helps draft state laws governing air-pollution control	1969
Australian pro Margaret Smith Court wins the grand slam of women's tennis American soprano noted for her Verdi and Rossini roles, Martina Arroyo (b. 1936) joins the Metropolitan Opera At age 17, Sally Younger sets the woman's world speed record on water skiis: 105.14 mph French rider Janou Tissott wins the women's world equestrian championship Russian Natalya Igorevna Bessmertnova (b. 1941), prima ballerina of the Bolshoi Ballet, wins the Lenin Prize for her performance in Spartacus Chi Cheng of the People's Republic of China becomes the first woman to run the 100-yard dash in 10 seconds, and the 220-yard in 22.6 seconds	St. Teresa of Avila is declared a doctor of the Catholic Church —one of only two women to achieve that distinction Normita de la Cruz (b. 1957) is a child faith healer in the town of Agua Dulce, Mexico, attracting huge crowds; she continues until her family mysteriously abandons their home	Death of American physician and reformer Alice Hamilton (b. 1869), known for her pioneering work in industrial toxicology Best known for her contributions to mathematical pedagogy, American mathematician Edna Ernestine Kramer Lassar (1902–1984) publishes her greatest work, *The Nature and Growth of Modern Mathematics*	The first woman to head a political party in Turkey, Mrs. B. Boran is elected head of the Labor party Aileen Hernandez founds Black Women for Action, fighting discrimination and instituting employment opportunity clinics Yadgar Nasriddinova (b. 1920) becomes the presiding officer of the House of Nationalities of the USSR Supreme Soviet	American feminist Ti-Grace Atkinson is instrumental in the passage of New York State's reformed abortion law Founding of the radical group Féministes Révolutionaires, who disrupt public events in order to destroy the patriarchal order The United Auto Workers is the first major national union to endorse the Equal Rights Amendment Foundation of the North American Indian Women's Association, composed of women from 43 tribes At the Congress to Unite Women in New York City, lesbians stage the Lavender Menace Action, one of the first demonstrations to assert the right of lesbians to act publicly Creation of the Canadian National Com-	1970

	General/ Context	Daily Life/ Customs/ Practices	Humanities/ Fine Arts	Occupations	Education
1970		discrimination in public accommodations	American women's movement	woman Cabinet member Anne Thompson becomes the US's first African-American prosecutor	
1971	The US Supreme Court overrules an Idaho statute that gives men preference over women in administering deceased persons' estates The US Supreme Court mandates the removal of all discriminatory barriers to employment not related to job skills in order to end sex discrimination in hiring The US Supreme Court rules that companies may not refuse to hire women with small children if the same policy is not applied to men According to FBI reports, the women's crime rate in the US has risen sharply	Establishment of the Native Women's Association of Canada Hot pants—very short tight pants for women—become a popular, though controversial, fashion The Boy Scouts of America admits girls between 15 and 20 years old into the Explorer Scout division In response to the repeal of antiabortion laws in the US, the Women's National Abortion Coalition is founded The US Senate tax amendment providing that deductions for child day-care costs be treated as a business deduction goes into effect New York State approves a law making it illegal to deny women access to public places	British writer Penelope Gilliatt (b. 1932), film critic for *The New Yorker*, writes the screenplay for *Sunday, Bloody Sunday* First publication of the radical French feminist newspaper *Le torchon brûlé* (*The Burning Dishcloth*) Brazilian artist Maria Bonomi is awarded a Panorama de Arte Atual Brasileira Prize for her woodcuts The Canadian government commemorates the 100th anniversary of the birth of artist and author Emily Carr (1871–1945) with a stamp of her painting Big Raven, naming her Canada's most famous woman artist	Journalist Esther Van Wagoner Tufty (b. 1896) is the first woman elected to the National Press Service when it lifts its 40-year ban against women members Girls are appointed Senate pages for the first time Annabelle Rankin becomes Australia's first woman ambassador Brereton Sturtevant is sworn in as the first woman member of the board of appeals, US Patent and Trade Office	Jean Lowrie (b. 1885) founds the International Association of School Librarians Primary schools in Berkeley, CA, initiate women's studies programs The University of Michigan becomes the first US university to adopt an affirmative action plan to hire and promote women

THE SECOND WAVE OF AMERICAN FEMINISM

The American feminist revolution of the 1960s, or the "second wave" of the women's movement, began among white middle-class educated women who became aware of the many inequalities all women in American society suffered. In 1963 Betty Friedan's book *The Feminine Mystique* articulated the discontent of women caught in a domestic ideology that infantilized them. Frustration with their plight increased that year when the President's Commission on the Status of Women documented widespread discrimination.

Young women activists living in counterculture university communities were becoming disillusioned by their treatment in the civil rights and new left movements. Rarely given leadership positions, they were left traditional female roles of making coffee and doing secretarial tasks. As these young women struggled with their marginalized position, they realized they needed to liberate themselves from conventional ways of thinking and

behaving. They began to understand the limits of sexual freedom without gender equality; they called for a new movement, a women's movement. This group's political style and ideology were shaped by the dissent and violence of the 1960s.

The women's rights group and the women's liberationists complemented each other, merging as the movement matured. The women's rights group, made up of older women with professional experience, formed bureaucratic and hierarchical organizations. In 1966 Betty Friedan founded the National Organization for Women (NOW). Many similar groups, such as the Women's Equity Action League (WEAL), were created by feminists who broke with NOW over the abortion issue. The National Women's Political Caucus was founded in 1971 by Bella Abzug, Shirley Chisholm, Gloria Steinem, and Betty Friedan. These feminists worked to change the legal and political system.

Performing Arts/ Entertainment/ Sports	Religion/ Philosophy	Science/ Technology/ Discovery	Statecraft/ Military	Reform	
Grand prize at the Concours International de Chant in Paris is awarded to South African musician Gerda Hartmann				mittee on the Status of Women (NAC), an umbrella organization that lobbies for women's equality	**1970**
Billie Jean King becomes the first female athlete to win $100,000 in a single year Austrian downhill skier Annemarie Moser Proell, world cup giant slalom champion, is the first person to win the event three times The New York Board of Education votes to permit high school boys and girls to compete with each other in noncontact sports Romanian-born Israeli violinist Miriam Fried (b. 1946) wins first prize at the Queen Elizabeth International Music Competition in Belgium		Ann W. Savolainen becomes the first female member of the American Nuclear Society Standards Committee board of directors	Women are granted the right to vote in Switzerland; L. Gardin, Geneva's first female mayor, wins an office in the first parliamentary election in which women are allowed to vote Danish jurist Helga Pederson is appointed the first female judge at the European Court of Human Rights The American Feminist Party is founded by Florynce Kennedy (b. 1916)	American women's movement leaders announce the formation of the National Women's Political Caucus, whose goal is to put more women who speak for women's and minority issues into elected and appointed political positions Frenchwomen sign the Manifesto of 340 Bitches, declaring that they have had abortions; the radical French feminist group Choisir (Choice) is founded to protect them Nguyen Thi Co immolates herself in protest to the Vietnam War American social reformer Maggie Kuhn (b. 1905) founds the Gray Panthers, an organization of activists for senior citizen rights Gloria Steinem and Brenda Feigen Fasteau	**1971**

Panel discussion with Gloria Steinem, Bella Abzug, Shirley Chisolm and Betty Friedan
Photograph (*Newsweek,* August 16, 1971) courtesy Sophia Smith Collection, Smith College

Meanwhile, the liberationists, or collectivists, were developing a new style of politics. Through consciousness-raising groups, which were personal, informal, and nonhierarchical, they educated women about their own oppression and helped create a momentum for change. Their "the personal is political" stance contributed to the feminist movement, as did their emphasis on egalitarianism and antileadership.

By 1969 the mass media had acknowledged the women's movement. The press often derided "women's libbers," but support for them mounted and such feminist organizations as NOW found their memberships growing. Though women's legal and legislative gains were limited in the 1960s and early 1970s, they laid the groundwork for important victories in subsequent years. Women established feminist services, such as rape-crisis centers, feminist gynecological clinics, production companies, and restaurants. A spate of books on feminist issues profoundly affected women's thinking about themselves: Kate Millett's *Sexual Politics,* Robin Morgan's *Sisterhood Is Powerful,* Shulamith Firestone's *Dialectic of Sex,* and Germaine Greer's *The Female Eunuch.* Scholarly research in women's studies scrutinized aspects of women's lives previously ignored. *Ms.,* a new mass-circulation feminist magazine aimed at a wide audience of women, was founded by Gloria Steinem.

As the second wave of feminism in the US became better established, controversy grew about the inherent racist and classist perspectives of many white middle-class feminists. Women of color and working-class women often formed separate organizations. Such issues as race, class, sexual preference, abortion, and pornography continue to spark debate within the feminist community.

	General/ Context	Daily Life/ Customs/ Practices	Humanities/ Fine Arts	Occupations	Education
1971		The women of Syria gain limited suffrage and the right to hold office			
1972	Disposable diapers are introduced; a very popular labor-saving item, they soon become an environmental hazard Hawaii is the first state to ratify the Equal Rights Amendment The US Congress passes the Equal Employment Opportunity Act, permitting preferential hiring and promotion of women and minorities	The New York City Human Rights Committee widens the ban on sex discrimination to include hotels or residences for only men or women, to "Ladies Day" tickets to ball games and cut-rate drinks for women in bars The age of legal adulthood for women in Spain is lowered from 23 to 21 The jurisdiction of the (US) Civil Rights Commission is extended to sex discrimination but loses its jurisdiction over abortion The *American Heritage Dictionary* for children is the first to define "sexism," to mention "liberated women," and to recognize "Ms." as a title The Ms. Foundation is formed, the only nationwide source of funding for women in the US In one area of Kenya, as many as 60% of the girls have undergone the rite of clitoridectomy	American poet Maya Angelou (b. 1928) is well known for such short pieces as "The Graduation"; she composes and reads a poem at President Clinton's 1993 inauguration French writer Catherine Valabrègue founds Spirale, a group dedicated to studying women's culture and to liberating "smothered creation" American artists Miriam Schapiro, Judy Chicago, and members of the Feminist Art Program at the California Institute of the Arts open a 17-room exhibit, Womanhouse	Feminist leaders Gloria Steinem and Patricia Carbine found *Ms.* magazine; Carbine had been executive editor of *Look,* the highest position attained by a woman in a general interest magazine Foundation of COYOTE (Cut Out Your Old Tired Ethics), an organization of prostitutes founded by activist Margo St. James and others Jean Westwood is elected chairperson of the Democratic National Committee, the first US woman to chair a national political party and manage a presidential campaign Jean Wilkowski (b. 1919) is sworn in as the US ambassador to the Republic of Zambia, the first woman ambassador to Africa	Passage of Title IX of the education amendments, prohibiting sex discrimination in federally assisted education programs; its effect is felt chiefly in the area of sports, where including women and funding for women athletes continue to be hotly debated issues throughout the decade

WOMEN IN SPORTS

When most people think about women athletes, world-class individual-sport champions probably spring to mind: gymnasts, figure skaters, tennis players. Such women have made headlines throughout the 20th century, indeed ever since women began to be admitted, a few sports at a time, into the modern Olympics in 1900. They provide models for aspiring athletes, both girls and boys, and they have sparked an interest in certain sports that many youngsters keep alive between Olympiads. The growth of professional opportunities in tennis, golf, and figure skating means that a significant number of women even get paid to play.

Some nations funnel resources into women's international sports programs, but women from many poorer countries have to train alone. Such a woman is Hassiba Boulmerka, the first Algerian of either sex ever to win an Olympic gold medal. She placed first in the women's 1500-meter race at the Barcelona Olympics in 1992. Social and religious beliefs in many parts of the world also discourage women from competing in sports, another obstacle Boulmerka overcame.

Desire to play sports created opportunity for Boulmerka; opportunity can also create desire. In the US, since passage of Title IX of the educational amendments of 1972 mandating gender-equitable sports programs in schools, the number of

Performing Arts/ Entertainment/ Sports	Religion/ Philosophy	Science/ Technology/ Discovery	Statecraft/ Military	Reform	
				found the Women's Action Alliance, the first national center for women's issues and programs	**1971**
Russian gymnast Olga Korbut is the first person to perform a backward somersault on the uneven parallel bars Galina Kulakova becomes the most decorated Russian cross-country skier Judith Jamison (b. 1944), principal dancer for the Alvin Ailey American Dance Theater, is elected to the board of the National Endowment for the Arts, its first female and first black member American television actress Beatrice Arthur (b. 1926) stars in *Maude,* a television series with a specifically feminist theme Mayumi Aoki of Japan wins the Olympic gold in the 100-meter butterfly at the Munich games Comedian Phyllis Diller (b. 1917) makes her name as a female standup comic, often appearing in bizarre attire satirizing housewives	A group of young Conservative Jewish women, calling themselves Ezrat Nashim ("Help of Women," named after the women's court in the ancient Temple in Jerusalem), lobbies successfully before the annual convention of the Rabbinical Assembly for the right for women to be counted in the minyan (the group of 10 Jews, formerly only men, required to conduct a religious service) and to be called to the Torah Despite its decision, taken in the 1840s, to accept women as rabbis, the first woman to be ordained as a Reform Jewish rabbi is American Sally Priesand	Physician Nawal el Saadawi (b. 1930) publishes *Al-Jins Wa al-Mara* (*Women and Sex*), the first work written by an Arab woman to examine scientifically questions about women and sex in traditional Arab society	Dr. Hildegard Hamm-Brücher is appointed the second-highest ranking political official in Germany's ministry of foreign affairs Jeanne Martin Cissé of Guinea becomes the first woman president of the UN Security Council and the only woman in its history to serve as a representative on the council Margrethe II (b. 1940) becomes the first real queen of Denmark following the death of her father, King Frederik IX; her namesake, Margrethe I, who ruled in the late 14th century, was not granted the title of queen, as the right of female succession was not introduced in Denmark until 1953	Erin Pizze founds the first battered-women's shelter in England, Women's Aid The French women's group Ecologie-Féminisme holds that the destruction of the planet originates in an inherent aspect of male power, the profit motive Carmen Rosa Maymi and others organize the National Conference of Puerto Rican Women in Washington, DC Carol Burris founds the Women's Lobby, Inc., to promote women's issues in Congress Second wave feminism in Australia brings about a proliferation of feminist newspapers, rape-crisis centers, women's health centers, women's studies courses; the Women's Electoral Lobby (WEL) lobbies on feminist issues, and feminists become active in trade unions	**1972**

girls and young women participating in school-based sports has grown sixfold. Many girls now begin team sports before high school, either in elementary school or in church or community leagues: soccer, softball and baseball (Little League began accepting girls in the 1970s), and basketball are especially popular. Girls who have grown up in the era of Title IX and other social changes have come to expect that sports are open to them, and their drive to participate in sports now has a life of its own.

Still, many schools do not comply with Title IX. Nationwide, women account for under one third of college athletes. Women often have to face more serious funding cuts, poor-quality equipment, and a shortage of facilities. Most universities offer far fewer athletic scholarships to women than to men and fewer women's varsity sports. There are few professional leagues in which talented women can continue their commitment to team sports.

In recent decades, despite the obstacles, many women are participating in sports throughout their lifetimes, in the US and elsewhere. With the example of committed pathfinders like Boulmerka, more and more young girls around the world will undoubtedly challenge themselves in athletic competition. The drive to run ever faster, jump higher, play better, or perform with greater courage and grace seems to be contagious.

	General/Context	Daily Life/Customs/Practices	Humanities/Fine Arts	Occupations	Education
1972		Black militant Angela Davis (b. 1944), on the FBI's 10 Most Wanted list in 1970, is acquitted of murder conspiracy charges			
1973	In the Bahamas universal suffrage over age 18 is constitutionally provided; women hold key judicial, civil service, and elective positions The US Supreme Court bans sex-segregated classified ads The US Supreme Court bans discrimination against female officers and their husbands in the distribution of military benefits	The US Public Health Service announces that there is strong evidence that pregnant women who smoke cigarettes increase the risk of infant mortality The landmark US Supreme Court decision *Roe* v. *Wade* invalidates state laws prohibiting abortion for women up to six months pregnant MLAC (Movement for the Freedom of Abortion and Contraception) is founded in France Two African-American sisters, Minnie Lee, age 12, and Mary Alice Relf, age 14, are sterilized without their or their mother's consent; their case opens the eyes of some to the existence of sterilization abuse in the US The US Government Printing Office style book accepts the title "Ms." The (US) Federal Home Loan Bank Board prohibits sex	*Up Country* by Maxine Winokur Kumin receives the Pulitzer Prize for Poetry Eudora Welty wins a Pulitzer Prize for Fiction for *The Optimist's Daughter* Awarded an honorary doctorate of literature from the University of Nebraska in 1935, Bess Streeter Aldridge is elected into the Nebraska Hall of Fame The feminist bookstore Des Femmes, run by the French women's group Politique et Psychanalyse, opens in France, selling and eventually publishing only women's works Ruth Elynia S. Mabanglo is awarded a First Prize Literary Award by the Cultural Center of the Philippines for *Ang Pilipinasasyon Ni Suan* in the playwriting division Brazilian painter Wanda Pimentel wins the prestigious Panorama de Arte Atual Brasileira Prize for her work	In Northern Ireland, women police reservists go on duty for the first time Foundation of Musidora, a union of French feminist actresses and filmmakers The American Stock Exchange adopts an affirmative-action hiring policy Foundation of (US) Stewardesses for Women's Rights, to address issues of rights on the job, public image, and health The (US) Civil Service Commission revises discriminatory height and weight requirements that have kept women out of jobs in park police work, fire prevention, and narcotics control The South African Navy trains 21 women—its first female personnel Tan Sri Fatimah becomes Malaya's first female holder of the portfolio for social welfare	Women are admitted for the first time to the US Coast Guard officer candidate program Sports scholarships are made available to women for the first time at the University of Chicago

WOMEN IN MODERN JUDAISM

In the last half of the 18th century, as Jews became more fully integrated into European society, their greater access to secular learning led them to examine their religious tradition in a modern context. As a result, Judaism began to reconsider the status of women, and reformers began to extend to women the rabbinical principle of *kabod habriyot,* the dignity of human beings. The ensuing controversy helped 19th-century Judaism evolve into three movements, Orthodox, Conservative, and Reform, as well as the Reconstructionist movement in the 20th century.

The Reform movement eliminated the separation between men and women at synagogue and changed the symbolism of the marriage ceremony to equalize the consecration of husband and wife. In the 1920s women gained equal opportunity in synagogue lay leadership, and in the 1940s for the first time women could be called up to the Torah at worship services. In the 1950s the bat mitzvah, a confirmation ceremony for girls based on the traditional bar mitzvah, began being celebrated. With the advent of the women's movement, Jewish women began to challenge the lack of leadership roles women played in the faith. While Regina Jones had been privately ordained as the first woman rabbi in Germany in the late 1930s, she served

Performing Arts/ Entertainment/ Sports	Religion/ Philosophy	Science/ Technology/ Discovery	Statecraft/ Military	Reform	
The First International Festival of Women's Films is held in New York City					**1972**
In a tennis match billed as the "battle of the sexes," Billie Jean King defeats Bobby Riggs 6–4, 6–4, 6–3

Linda Meyers becomes the US's first archer to win the world championship

Joan Lind wins the national title for single skulling, becoming the first woman to make the finals in the World Rowing Championships in Moscow; she is the first Olympic female single skuller representing the US to win a silver medal

The African-American, Washington, DC-based, women's a capella group Sweet Honey in the Rock is founded by Bernice Johnson Reagon; the group performs politically charged songs dedicated to social change

US swimmer Lynn Cox swims from England to France in 9 hours 36 minutes, the fastest time recorded for a woman | Mother Teresa receives the Templeton Prize for Progress in Religion from the Bahamas' Templeton Foundation for founding the Missionaries of Charity in India | Wife of Tai, the world's most perfectly preserved woman, is discovered by archeologists 2100 years after her burial; the ancient Chinese noblewoman is on display in the Changsha Museum in China

National Observer reporter Barbara Katz publishes the first exposé of the IUD the Dalkon shield, resulting in its eventual withdrawal from the market | Argentinian ex-President Juan Perón and second wife, Isabel Martinez de Perón (b. 1931), elected president and vice president of Argentina

Pakistan announces that all women will have military training as part of the nation's defense plan

Portuguese feminist writers Maria Horta, Maria Veilho da Costa, and Maria Barreno go on trial for "offending public morals" with the publication of their book, *New Portuguese Letters*

The all-male Grand Council of the Republic of San Marino adopts a law ending some traditional discrimination against women

Begum Ra'Ana Liaquat Ali Khan becomes the first woman governor of a state (Sind) in Pakistan

The first black woman elected to Congress | Michiko Ishumure of Japan receives the Ramón Magsaysay Foundation's Award in Journalism, Literature, and Creative Communication Arts in the Philippines for being "the voice of her people" in their struggle against the industrial pollution that is destroying their lives

Foundation of the (US) National Black Feminist Organization, to address the double problem of racism and sexism

The first National Lesbian Feminist Conference takes place in Los Angeles

Foundation of the abortion-rights organization Catholics for a Free Choice | **1973** |

only briefly before dying in a Nazi concentration camp. In 1972 the first woman rabbi in the US was ordained.

Although a liberal denomination, the Conservative movement bridges tradition and modernism, and so change for Conservative women has come more slowly, with the first Conservative woman rabbi ordained in 1985. The Reconstruction movement, a branch within the Conservative movement until it broke away in the 1960s, promotes the equality of women with fervor. The movement ordained its first woman rabbi in 1974, and in 1980, it facilitated the first divorce initiated by a Jewish woman. In traditional Judaism, only the husband may initiate a divorce.

Women in Orthodox denominations embrace the traditional belief that their primary purpose in life is marriage and child rearing, although in recent years women have won more privileges, such as limited study of religious texts.

Betty Friedan, a pioneer of the late-20th-century women's movement, claimed that her passion for equality for women "was really a passion against injustice, which originated from my feelings of the injustice of anti-Semitism." The women's movement has helped many Jewish women redefine their religious roles. Thus, Judaism continues to adapt itself to the modern world.

	General/ Context	Daily Life/ Customs/ Practices	Humanities/ Fine Arts	Occupations	Education
1973		discrimination by savings-and-loan institutions Foundation of the first Feminist Credit Union, in Detroit, MI		Finland's Helvi Linnea Sipila is the highest-ranking woman in the UN Secretariat as assistant secretary general for social development and humanitarian affairs	
1974	Mandatory maternity leave for teachers is outlawed by the US Supreme Court The US Passport Office allows married women to use their maiden names The (US) Equal Credit Opportunity Act makes discrimination in credit on the basis of sex or marital status illegal	The string bikini, a much tinier version of the two-piece bathing suit introduced in 1946, becomes a popular fashion; Brazilian women are the first to wear it, though the government tries to ban it Divorce by mutual consent is made legal in France The women of mainland China gain the right to vote Tennis star Renée Richards, born Richard Raskind, is the recipient of a sex-change operation Jailed for shoplifting, Joan Little (b. 1954) attracts national attention when she kills the white jailer who sexually abuses her In Connecticut, married women are permitted to register to vote under their maiden names The Three Marias, Portuguese feminist writers, are acquitted by the new revolutionary government in Portugal, following internationally organized demonstrations on their behalf	Poet Adrienne Cecile Rich (b. 1929) wins the (American) National Book Award for *Diving into the Wreck: Poems 1971–72* South African author, chiefly of books for children, Jenny Seed (b. 1930) publishes the historical novel *Bushman's Dream* French feminist Luce Irigaray publishes *Speculum de l'autre femme* (*Speculum of the Other Woman*) The Frenchwomen's group Politique et Psychanalyse begins publication of the newspaper *Le quotidienne des femmes* (*Women's Daily*) Publisher McGraw-Hill, Inc., issues non-sexist guidelines for nonfiction writing	Barbara Allen [now Rainey] is the first female aviator in the US Navy Dr. Pauline Jewett, Canada's first female college president, becomes president of Simon Fraser College Simone Weil (b. 1927) becomes France's first minister of health and social security; largely due to her efforts the law prohibiting abortions is repealed Ruth Johnson becomes the first woman to join the US Marine Corps Band in its 175 years of existence Mary Sullivan Simons is the first female senior editor of *The New York Times Sunday Magazine* Dr. Mary Ellen Avery (b. 1927) is the first woman appointed to head Children's Hospital of Boston	Women are admitted into the US Merchant Marine Academy
1975	The UN declares 1975–1985 the Decade for Women, Equality, Development, and Peace	The Equal Pay Act and the Sex Discrimination Act go into effect in Great Britain The Italian parliament passes a new family	Founder of the first research group on the theory of femininity at the University of Paris, French feminist critic Hélène Cixous (b. 1938) publishes the	First Women's Bank opens in New York City Commander Lucille R. Kuhn is the first female officer to head	Rugby, a 408-year-old English private school, accepts women for admission Alice Frey Emerson becomes Wheaton College's first female president

Performing Arts/ Entertainment/ Sports	Religion/ Philosophy	Science/ Technology/ Discovery	Statecraft/ Military	Reform	
Robyn Smith becomes the first female jockey to win the Aqueduct Stakes

In New Jersey, girls are permitted to join the Little League | | | from California is Yvonne Braithwaite Burke (b. 1934)

Simone A. Poulain becomes the first woman to act as official spokesperson for the US government in foreign policy affairs | | 1973 |
| Little League Baseball, Inc., votes to allow girls to play on its team

Reita Clanton is voted the US's top female college athlete for basketball, volleyball, and softball

The first professional female tennis player in Japan, Kazuko Sawamatsu becomes the first Japanese tennis player in 41 years to win a major title at Wimbledon

13-year-old Abla Khairi of Egypt is the youngest person to swim the English Channel, in 12 hours 36 minutes

Judith Somogi (b. 1941) is the first woman to conduct the New York City Opera

Colleen Dewhurst (1926–1992), the foremost interpreter of the plays of Eugene O'Neill, wins a Tony Award for her performance in *Moon for the Misbegotten*

Formation of the (US) National Women's Football League | Pope Paul VI canonizes Teresa Ibars, a 19th-century Spanish nun

Four US Episcopal bishops defy church law and ordain 11 women as priests | Mary Beth Stearns invents the high-revolution electron spectrometer (HRES) used to study the structure, behavior, and properties of the electron | Juan Perón, president of Argentina (1946–1955, 1973–1974), dies and is succeeded in office by his wife, Isabel Martinez de Perón

Mary Louise Smith becomes the first woman to be named chair of the Republican party

Janet Gray Hayes (b. 1926) becomes the first woman elected mayor in a large US city, defeating six men in San Jose, CA

The French government creates a secretariat of state for the status of women; Françoise Giroud is appointed its head

Mme. Elizabeth Domitien is appointed prime minister of the Central African Republic by President Jean Bokassa; she is removed from office and placed under house arrest for opposing Bokassa's monarchial tendencies after he names himself emperor in 1976 | The French feminist revolutionary Communist paper *Les pétroleuse* (*The Women Incendiaries*) is first published

The French Ligue du Droit des Femmes (Women's Rights League), headed by Simone de Beauvoir, is founded

Fusaye Ichikawa of Japan receives the Ramón Magsaysay Award Foundation's Community Leadership Award for lifetime labors advancing Japanese women's freedom

Foundation of the Mexican American Women's Association

Men are admitted as members of the (American) League of Women Voters | 1974 |
| Beverly Sills (b. 1929) sings Rossini's *The Siege of Corinth* in her Metropolitan Opera debut | Four women are ordained to the Episcopal priesthood in Washington, DC; the earlier ordination of 11 women in Philadelphia | Frederica de Laguna and Margaret Mead are the first women anthropologists to become members of the (US) National Academy of Sciences | Jeanne Sauvé becomes Canada's first female minister of communications

Ella Grasso (1919–1981) is both the | The International Women's Year World Conference in Mexico City adopts a 10-year plan to improve the status of women around the world | 1975 |

	General/ Context	Daily Life/ Customs/ Practices	Humanities/ Fine Arts	Occupations	Education
1975	Khmer Rouge Communists take over Cambodia The US Supreme Court declares unconstitutional a Social Security law authorizing benefits to widows with children but denying them to widowers in the same position Different ages of majority for women (18) and men (21) is prohibited by the US Supreme Court	code giving wives full equality with their husbands Boston obstetrician Dr. Kenneth C. Edelin is found guilty of manslaughter in the death of a male fetus in a legal abortion he performed in 1973 The life expectancy for women in Argentina is 72.12 years The first black to hold the Girl Scouts of America presidency is Gloria Dean Scott The automatic exclusion of women from jury duty is banned by the US Supreme Court Federal employees in the US are granted the right to sue on the grounds of sex discrimination Korean jurist Lee Tai-young receives the Ramón Magsaysay Award Foundation's Community Leadership Award in honor of her sustained commitment to the improvement of family law in Korea The automatic discharge of pregnant women from the US armed services is outlawed by the Pentagon Great Britain passes the Sex Discrimination Act in order to comply with European Economic Community equal pay and equal treatment directives	seminal article *"Le rire de la méduse"* ("The Smile of the Medusa") The Jane Addams Peace Association awards Elizabeth Sutherland Martinez and Enriqueta Longeaux y Vasquez the Jane Addams Children's Book Award for *Viva La Raza* (*Long Live the Race*) American author Frances Moore Lappé, cofounder of the World Food Movement, writes *Diet for a Small Planet,* which sells 1.5 million copies Ruth Elynia S. Mabanglo wins the Cultural Center of the Philippines' Literary Award in the Poetry Division for *Supling* Chavda Vidadhar and Alka Shah of Ahmedabad, India, are awarded the Prix UNESCO d'Architecture The influential journal of feminist scholarship *Signs*, founded by Catharine R. Stimpson, begins publication The New York Philharmonic, sponsored by *Ms.* magazine, performs a "Celebration of Women Composers," conducted by Sarah Caldwell	the naval officer candidate school Robin Herman is the first female sportswriter at *The New York Times* Lynn Young is the first female senior editor of *Newsweek* Joellen Drag becomes the first woman helicopter pilot in the US Navy; she later files a successful class-action suit against the navy, overturning its rule prohibiting women pilots from landing at sea	Jill Ker Conway becomes Smith College's first female president Jacquelyne Johnson Jackson becomes the first black female faculty member at Duke University A bill requiring all service academies to admit women is passed by the US Congress Chilean educator Amanda Labarca (1917–1975) is concerned with upgrading education for all Chileans, but primarily with the improvement of women's status

Performing Arts/ Entertainment/ Sports	Religion/ Philosophy	Science/ Technology/ Discovery	Statecraft/ Military	Reform	
Tatiana Averina, Soviet speed skater, sets six world records in 18 days, twice lowering the 500 meter record and three times the 1000 meter	is invalidated by the House of Bishops The Anglican Church in Canada approves ordaining women to the priesthood	Physicist Chien-Shiung Wu (b. 1912) is named the president of the American Physical Society	first woman governor of Connecticut and the first woman governor in US history not to follow her husband into office	Co-coordinators of the NOW task force on older women and of the National Alliance for Displaced Homemakers, Tish Sommers and Laurie Shields lobby the US First Displaced Homemaker Act into California law	**1975**
Anita Wold of Norway jumps 321′5″ at Okura Sapporo, Japan, the longest jump recorded in women's skiing	Elizabeth Ann Seton (1774–1821) is the first US citizen to be canonized by the Roman Catholic Church	Mathematicians Evelyn Boyd Granville and Jason Frand publish *Theory and Application of Mathematics for Teachers*	Bernadette Olowo of Uganda becomes the first woman ambassador to the Vatican, breaking with a 900-year-old tradition of keeping female envoys out of the Holy See	The Soviet delegation to the International Women's Year meeting in Mexico City is led by Valentina Tereshkova, the first woman astronaut	
Barbara J. Kopple (b. 1946) directs and produces the first feature-length documentary about a labor dispute, for which she is awarded an Oscar		Julia Bowman Robinson (1919–1985), famed for her work in mathematical logic, becomes the first woman mathematician to be elected to the (US) National Academy of Sciences	Elected to the British House of Commons for the first time in 1959, Margaret Hilda Roberts Thatcher (b. 1925) is selected to head the Conservative party in Great Britain, the first woman to head a major political party and the first potential female prime minister in that country in 700 years	The Angolan Women's Organization, formed within the Movimento Popular de Libertação de Angola (MPLA), the country's single legitimate political party, gives women the opportunity to serve at all but the highest levels of the party	
US swimmer Diana Nyad is the first person to swim across Lake Ontario, 32 miles in 20 hours		Mina S. Rees is elected the first woman president of the US's largest scientific society, the American Association for the Advancement of Science			
The death of the most popular Egyptian singer of the 20th century, Umm Kulthum (1898–1975), is mourned by millions; the radio broadcast commemorating her is followed by solemn readings from the Koran, an honor usually reserved for heads of state; famous for her huge four-hour-long outdoor concerts, her rich, reverential, hypnotic voice, and her quiet way of life			Toure Aissata Kane is appointed minister for the protection of the family and for social affairs in Mauritania, the first woman to attain Cabinet rank in this Islamic republic		
Junko Tahei is one of 15 Japanese women to make an assault on Mt. Everest, and only she reaches the top; the first woman to conquer the 29,028 foot mountain			Former child star Shirley Temple Black (b. 1928), the first US woman ambassador to Ghana, is made the first woman chief of protocol in US history		
			Nguyen Thi Binh is appointed minister of foreign affairs and is appointed minister of education in 1976, one of the few South Vietnamese to hold a government post since the North Vietnamese victory		

	General/ Context	Daily Life/ Customs/ Practices	Humanities/ Fine Arts	Occupations	Education
1976	The UN proclaims International Women's Year Cuisinart introduces the food processor The Continental Walk for Disarmament and Social Justice begins in California and ends in Washington, DC Direct, universal, and secret suffrage is provided by the Algerian constitution	Jinx Melia founds the Martha Movement for those who consider homemaking their primary role but "want to feel better about it" Dr. Connie Uri testifies to a US Senate committee that by 1976, 24% of the Native American women of childbearing age have been sterilized; the Indian Health Services Hospital in Oklahoma has been sterilizing one out of every four women who come into the federal facility to give birth	Chinese-American author Maxine Hong Kingston publishes *The Woman Warrior* The first annual conference of the International Women's Writing Guild at Skidmore College, Saratoga Springs, NY Diane Claire Sorber Dillon (b. 1933) and her husband, Leo, win a Caldicott Medal for their illustration of the children's book *Ashanti to Zulu* American cartoonist Cathy Lee Guisewite (b. 1950) creates the syndicated Cathy cartoon strip Carolyn Forché is the winner of the Yale Series of Younger Poets Award for her first book, *Gathering Tribes;* in 1982 she wins the Lamont Prize for her second book, *The Country Between Us*	Naomi Sims (b. 1949) is the first black model of international repute; she is also the first to design wigs and hairpieces for black women Suzanne Kennedy is the first female veterinarian at the National Zoological Park in Washington, DC 23-year-old nuclear engineer Roberta A. Kankus becomes the first woman and youngest person to be licensed as a nuclear power plant operator in the US French prostitutes hold a nationwide strike Barbara Walters joins ABC, where she later becomes the first female anchor to earn $1 million a year	Hélène Ahrweiller (b. 1916) becomes the first female president of the Sorbonne in Paris The Arthur and Elizabeth Schlesinger Library on the History of Women in America at Radcliffe College is the largest library on women in the US The British Rhodes Scholarship program opens its applications to women; they accept 13 women and 19 men in 1977 The US Air Force Academy admits 155 women, ending the all-male tradition at US military academies 87% of the world's Muslim women are illiterate The French Cabinet appoints Alice Saunier-Seite (b. 1925) the first secretary of state for universities

NOBEL PEACE PRIZE WINNERS

Women have won the Peace Prize more than any other Nobel award. In fact, historians credit a woman with the establishment of the category. Baroness Bertha von Suttner was an Austrian novelist and pacifist whose popular 1889 novel, *Die Waffen nieder!* (*Lay Down Your Arms!*), inspired an international pacifist journal of the same name, which she edited. She is believed to have been the driving force behind her friend Alfred Nobel's endowment of a prize for peace in his will. For her lifetime of peace activism, Baroness von Suttner became the first woman to win the Nobel Prize for Peace in 1905.

The two American women recipients of the Peace Prize had more in common than nationality. Jane Addams's charity settlement known as Hull House, founded in 1889, helped Chicago's immigrant poor adjust to life in the US. During and just after WWI, Addams organized women's international peace conferences and aided war victims, and in 1920 she helped to found the American Civil Liberties Union. In 1931 she was awarded to the Nobel Prize for Peace. Another settlement founder, Emily Greene Balch, went on to work as a union organizer, sociologist, and economics professor at Wellesley College. After the Women's International League for Peace and Freedom was formed in 1919, and Balch served in many of its top posts over the next two decades. Her 1946 Peace Prize thus also rewarded the efforts of the league.

The 1976 Nobel Prize for Peace was shared by two women who were jolted into peace activism in an instant. When British troops in Belfast shot a member of the Irish Republican Army behind the wheel of a car, the car went out of control and killed three children. The children's aunt, Mairead Corrigan-Maguire, a Catholic, witnessed the accident, as did a Protestant, Betty Williams. Within days, the two formed the Peace People Community. Thousands of Catholic and Protestant women joined the organization, calling for integration of schools, neighborhoods, and playgrounds.

Mother Teresa was born Agnes Gonxha Bejaxhia, daughter of Albanian parents in what later became Yugoslavia. She served as a nun and teacher in Calcutta, India, for nearly 20 years before founding her own order, the Missionaries of Charity, in 1948. Providing schooling and medicine to the poor, the Missionaries of Charity now operates over 200 cen-

Performing Arts/ Entertainment/ Sports	Religion/ Philosophy	Science/ Technology/ Discovery	Statecraft/ Military	Reform	
Sarah Caldwell (b. 1924) is the first woman conductor of the Metropolitan Opera	The Anglican Church of Canada ordains six women as priests	Dr. Allene R. Jeanes is honored as the first in the chemistry bureau to receive the USDA's Distinguished Service Award	Karin Söder is appointed the first female minister for foreign affairs in Sweden	Mairead Corrigan (b. 1944) and Betty Williams (b. 1944) of Northern Ireland share the Nobel Prize for Peace	**1976**
Nadia Comaneci, 14-year-old Romanian gymnast, is the first athlete in Olympic history to score a perfect 10.0 in any event	The general convention of the Episcopal Church votes to ordain women, to recognize those already ordained illegally, and to consecrate women bishops	Anna J. Harrison becomes president of the American Chemical Society, the first woman in the society's 102 years of existence to hold that office	Sakado Ogata becomes Japan's first female diplomat of ministerial rank	Soviet dissident Yelena Bonner organizes a group of dissidents for which she is sentenced to internal exile in 1984	
Christine Scheiblich of East Germany collects the first Olympic gold medal awarded in women's single skulling		Canadian Elsie Gregory MacGill is the first woman in North America to become chief aeronautical engineer of any company, the first to design, build, and test her own plane, and the first fellow of the Canadian Aeronautical and Space Institute	Barbara Mikulski becomes the first Polish-American woman in Congress and the first woman to serve on the House Interstate and Foreign Commerce Committee	The International Tribunal on Crimes Against Women takes place in Brussels	
Christine Stueckelburger is the only female medalist at the Olympic equestrian competition			Jiang Quing (b. 1913), a former actress and wife of Mao Zedong, is sentenced to death as a member of the Gang of Four	Problems facing Mozambican women are defined by the 1976 national conference of the Mozambican Women's Organization (OMM): illiteracy, unemployment, tribalism, racism, prostitution, and forced marriage	
US car driver Kitty O'Neil achieves the women's land/speed record of 612 mph; she is not permitted to beat this and is told that she is not supposed to be competing against men (the men's record is 627.287 mph)		The National Science Foundation names Eloise E. Clark assistant director of biological, behavioral, and social sciences, the first woman to hold that post	Annemarie Renger (b. 1919) is elected the first woman president of West Germany's Bundestag		

ters worldwide. Mother Teresa was awarded the Nobel Prize for Peace in 1979.

Alva Reimer Myrdal represented her native Sweden as a diplomat and served as a member of the Swedish parliament and Cabinet. She also stood out as an early advocate of decolonization, a director of UN social welfare agencies, and an author of several books before becoming a world-renowned expert on all aspects of disarmament. She received the Nobel Prize for Peace in 1982, four years before her death.

Like Williams and Corrigan-Maguire, two recent winners of the Peace Prize have focused on political conflicts in their native countries. In Burma, Daw Aung San Suu Kyi organized the National League for Democracy, which won the support of 80% of the Burmese people in 1988 elections. But the brutal military regime simply disavowed the results and arrested the leaders. Suu Kyi has been under house arrest since then, unable to communicate with her husband in England, perhaps unaware that she was awarded the 1991 Nobel Prize for Peace for her brave resistance to Burma's repressive and unwanted government.

Guatemalan Indian-rights activist Rigoberta Menchu lost several members of her family to torture and assassination by the Guatemalan military, and others to the grinding poverty of peasant existence. Despite her poor education, Menchu published her autobiography in 1983; it was later translated into 11 languages. She also led international opposition to the celebration of the 500th anniversary of Christopher Columbus's arrival in the New World, with its disastrous results for indigenous peoples throughout Latin America. The announcement of her Nobel Prize for Peace in 1993 in the same week as the quincentenary pointedly acknowledged those grim results.

The women who have received the Nobel Prize for Peace have come from diverse backgrounds and served the cause of peace in many ways. Taken as a group, the stories of the female Peace Prize winners do not support the notion that women naturally work for peace because they are mothers, since few of the recipients have had children. Instead, this group suggests the range and impact of women's contributions to solving the world's problems on scales large and small.

	General/ Context	Daily Life/ Customs/ Practices	Humanities/ Fine Arts	Occupations	Education
1976			Brazilian painter Wilma Martins is awarded a Panorama de Arte Atual Brasileira Prize		
1977	Roman Catholicism loses its status as the state religion in Italy Divorce is legalized in Brazil The parliament of South Australia makes rape within marriage a criminal offense, the first such ruling in the world	A British court declares a man's mistress has the same rights to protection against abuse as a wife Janelle Penny Commissiong (b. 1953) of Trinidad-Tobago is the first black Miss Universe Eleanor Cutri Smeal (b. 1939) becomes the first housewife to be president of NOW, and its first paid leader, at a salary of $17,500 The Hyde Amendment is passed, disallowing Medicaid funding for abortions, making abortions inaccessible to women of the lower economic classes in the US; a 27-year-old Chicana from Texas is the first victim of this amendment 19-year-old Princess Misha'al and her 20-year-old lover are publicly executed in Saudi Arabia for adultery	Australian author Colleen McCullough (b. 1937) publishes *The Thorn Birds* Nelly Guillerm, a.k.a. Violette Verdy (b. 1933), is named director of the Paris Opera Ballet, the first woman to hold that position *Histoires du MLF (Stories of the MLF)* is published by Annie de Pisan and Anne Tristan Maïté Albistur and Daniel Armogathe publish *Histoire du féminisme français (History of French Feminism)* French critic Luce Irigaray publishes *Ce sexe qui n'en est pas un (This Sex Which Is Not One)* Foundation of the feminist journal *Questions féministes,* edited by Simone de Beauvoir African-American playwright Ntozake Shange receives a Tony Award for her play *for colored girls who have considered suicide/when the rainbow is enuf*	Maria Pia Esmeralda Matarazzo (b. 1942) becomes Brazil's only female executive of a major enterprise, Reundas F. Matarazzo, Brazil's 10th largest private company Marie Geoghegan Quinn becomes Ireland's first woman parliamentary secretary of industry and commerce Joan S. Wallace becomes the first woman and first black to direct the US Department of Agriculture's management programs Salwa Saleh manages a branch of the Khalij Commercial Bank in Abu, Saudi Arabia; women depositors can remove their veils and complete their own transactions, in contrast to past banking practices where Saudi women had either to use banks' back doors or let their male relatives handle their banking needs	Adele Simmons becomes the first president of Hampshire College Mayra Buvinic becomes director of the International Center for Research on Women Carolyn R. Payton becomes the Peace Corps's first female director Foundation of the (US) National Women's Studies Association

Performing Arts/ Entertainment/ Sports	Religion/ Philosophy	Science/ Technology/ Discovery	Statecraft/ Military	Reform	
Clare Francis is the first woman to sail solo across the Atlantic, in 29 days		Brazilian-born Sarah Kerr Myers (b. 1940) becomes the first woman director of the 130-year-old American Geographical Society The tomb of Fu Hao, a "royal consort and lady general," is found in Anyang in Hunan Province, China; found in her tomb is an intact royal burial with hundreds of objects dating from the 12th century B.C.	Monique Bégin (b. 1936) is appointed Canada's minister of national revenue Sweden's Prime Minister Thorbjörn Fälldin appoints six women to his Cabinet British economist and environmentalist Barbara Ward (b. 1914) is honored with life peerage in the British House of Lords, where she demonstrates her commitment to sensible and humane economics		**1976**
Cindy Nicholas of Canada becomes the first woman to complete a round-trip nonstop swim across the English Channel Chantall Langlace, world's fastest marathoner, wins a marathon in San Sebastian, Spain, in 2:35:15; as Frenchwomen were not allowed to compete in long-distance events until 1976, Langlace's victory was the result of years of unsupported training Working-class women in Jamaica form a group called Sistren to politicize culture through theater, often dealing with issues of violence against women	Jacqueline Means becomes the first woman to be officially ordained a priest in the Episcopal Church in America Dr. Pauli Murray is the first black female priest ordained by the Episcopal Church in America Beverly Messenger-Harris (b. 1949) is the first female rector to the Episcopal Church in America	Ilya Prigogine of Belgium wins the Nobel Prize for Chemistry Rosalyn S. Yalow shares the Nobel Prize for Physiology or Medicine with Roger Guillemin and Andrew Schally	Women vote for the first time in Liechtenstein The US Army restores Civil War surgeon Dr. Mary Edwards Walker's Medal of Honor, revoked in 1917 for insufficient evidence of "gallantry" Dr. Elisabeth Blunschy-Steiner is elected president of the Swiss National Council Rika de Backer-Van Ocken becomes Belgium's first woman minister for Flemish cultural affairs The US Navy assigns women as permanent shipboard crew Black South African activist Winnie Mandela (b. 1936) is banished from her home in Soweto, where she founded the Black Parents' Association; her husband is imprisoned for most of their married life, and she spends no more than eight months free from imprisonment or banning orders from 1969 to at least 1981	3000 women march in Washington, DC, on Women's Equality Day to support the Equal Rights Amendment Doris Royal, farm wife from Springfield, NB, files with Congress 231,261 signatures from 49 states to fight outmoded estate tax laws that fail to recognize a woman's equitable status in joint tenancy should her husband's death precede her own Mothers in Argentina hold the first Rally for the Disappeared at the Plaza de la Mayo in Buenos Aires The Third World Women's Committee of the Abortion Action Coalition is formed; they issue the statement, "The right to abortion can be a woman's right to life" Ela Ramesh Bhatt of India receives the Ramón Magsaysay Award Foundation's Community Leadership Award for spreading Gandhian principles of truth, nonviolence, and self-help among the most depressed of the female workforce	**1977**

Australian antinuclear activist Helen Caldicott
Photograph courtesy Wide World

	General/Context	Daily Life/Customs/Practices	Humanities/Fine Arts	Occupations	Education
1978	The Muslim fundamentalist revolution in Iran ousts the shah and establishes the rule of Ayatollah Khomeini, who opposes the modernization of Iran In England the first successful test-tube-fertilized infant is born The Longest Walk begins, as Native Americans march from San Francisco to Washington, DC New York is the first state to pass a bill to locate the children of women who have taken the cancer-linked hormone diethylstilbestrol (DES) In Connecticut, police agree to arrest husbands who beat their wives, even if the wife does not bring charges National Cancer Institute reports that lung cancer in women increased 30% between 1973 and 1976	Italy legalizes abortion within the first 90 days of pregnancy Faye Wattleton becomes the first woman and first African American elected president of Planned Parenthood The US Congress bans the use of a victim's reputation in cases of rape and attempted rape Monsanto Textiles Company pays Barbara Taibi $10,000, the largest individual settlement to date of a sexual harassment suit John Rideout, the first US man to be charged with marital rape, is acquitted by an Oregon circuit court	British dramatist Caryl Churchill's (b. 1938) award-winning play *Cloud Nine* explores the effects of male domination Novelist Toni Morrison (b. 1931) is the first black woman to win the National Book Critics Circle Award for *Song of Solomon* Indian activist and anti-Communist physician Gandhi Marg publishes *A Political Dissenter's Diary,* which airs her criticism of Indira Gandhi and her own political convictions *F,* a French feminist magazine, begins publication	American activist Byllye Avery and friends establish an alternative birthing center, Birthplace, where they stress the importance of women being involved in their own health care The National Aeronautics and Space Administration (NASA) accepts women for astronaut training The Coal Employment Project is organized by Appalachian women's and citizens' groups to encourage the hiring of women and minorities in coal mines After American Cyanamid Company declares that women of reproductive capability will be barred from jobs with exposure to lead compounds, five women at the West Virginia plant are sterilized in order to keep their jobs	A report by the (US) National Association of Secondary School Principals finds the percentage of women high school principals has declined from 10% in 1965 to 7% in 1978 Hanna Holborn Gray is appointed president of the University of Chicago For the first time in American history, more women than men enter college
1979	National Lesbian and Gay Rights march on Washington, DC, takes place Foundation of the Moral Majority, a US political action group	The Department of Health, Education, and Welfare is pressured to release sterilization guidelines; till now 100,000 women have been sterilized annually in the US under the	Indian politician Vijaya Lakshmi Pandit publishes her autobiography, *The Scope of Happiness: A Personal Memoir*	American producer Marcia Carsey (b. 1944) becomes senior vice president of all prime-time series on the ABC network	The National Archives for Black Women's History and the Mary McLeod Bethune Memorial Museum open in Washington, DC

RAPE

The question "Can a man rape his wife?" has been answered in the negative from the time Augustine of Hippo asked it in the 5th century until the 1970s in the US. California first acknowledged spousal rape, and several other states have done the same. The slow progress toward the legal protection of wives from forcible intercourse illustrates the high degree of social tolerance for rape. On the other hand, Western tradition has also held it to be a despicable, even heinous, crime. Countless literary and artistic renderings of the rape of Lucrece, the Sabine women, Helen of Troy, and various heroines of classical mythology testify to society-destroying implications of violating a woman's body. For female Christian martyrs and saints, rape is equated with loss of spiritual integrity; many achieved immortal glory by dying to avoid it.

In literature, art, and real life, rape may be common, but it is never simple. The victim, long assumed by the popular imagination to have caused her own violation by seductive dress or behavior, often does not report her rape. Even when it is reported, rape has the lowest rate of apprehension and conviction of any violent crime. The victim's credibility is still tainted with the notions that women cry rape simply because they can. Meanwhile, men are not held responsible for their sexual aggression once their sexual drive has been aroused.

Statutory rape, i.e., sexual intercourse with an underage fe-

Performing Arts/ Entertainment/ Sports	Religion/ Philosophy	Science/ Technology/ Discovery	Statecraft/ Military	Reform	
Naomi James of England becomes the first woman to sail around the world alone	Sara Berenice Mosely of Sherman, TX, becomes the first woman elected to head the governing body of the Presbyterian Church	Lesley Brown of England gives birth to the first "test-tube baby"—a girl; she is the first human baby conceived outside of a woman's body	Nicaraguan revolutionary Nora Gadea Astorga (1949–1988) takes part in the assassination of Reynaldo Perez Vegas	The US Congress extends the ratification of the Equal Rights Amendment from March 22, 1979 to June 30, 1982	**1978**
Marina Legcuno of Argentina wins in four of the nation's horse racing classics		Johanna Dobereiner is awarded the Bernard A. Houssay Inter-American Science Prize by the Organization of American States (OAS), The Inter-American Council for Education, Science, and Culture	A US district court ruling states that women sportswriters may not be barred from major league baseball locker rooms	Australian Helen Caldicott (b. 1938) leads the antinuclear coalition Physicians for Social Responsibility	
Golfer Nancy Lopez sets the record for rookies, both men and women, winning $161,235			Margaret A. Brewer becomes the first female brigadier general in the US Marine Corps	The National Lesbian Feminist Organization is formed in Los Angeles	
Beverly Johnson becomes the first woman to climb the face of Yosemite's 3000-foot El Capitán		Mathematician Julia Bowman Robinson becomes the first woman president of the American Mathematical Society		Acquittal of Maria Elaine Pitchford, the first US woman ever to be tried for performing an illegal abortion on herself	
Dolly Parton (b. 1946), the first C&W singer to bridge the gap between country and pop, earns her first gold record for "Here You Come Again"		Durga Agarwal, the world's second test-tube baby, is born to Pravat Kumar and Bella Agarwal in Calcutta, India		Women Against Violence in Pornography and Media in San Francisco sponsors the first national feminist conference on pornography	
				Foundation of the (US) National Coalition Against Domestic Violence	
Joan Benoit completes the Boston Marathon in a record time of 2:35:15	In spite of wide support for women Conservative rabbis, the rabbinical assembly of the Jewish Theological Seminary refuses to admit women or allow them to be ordained	Alexandra Moreno Toscano of Mexico is awarded the Premio de Investigación Científica (Prize for Scientific Research) of the Academia de la Investigación Científica	Lidia Gueiler Tejada becomes the prime minister of Bolivia, the second Western Hemisphere nation to have a woman head of state; she governs until being over-	Judie Brown (b. 1944) founds the American Life League, a lobbying organization whose goal is to prohibit abortion by constitutional amendment	**1979**
Diana Nyad becomes the first person to swim from the Baha-					

male, need not include a victim's resistance to be a criminal act. The definition of rape now includes oral and anal penetration, and rape of men by either sex has now been acknowledged by law. Rape by familiars—e.g., family members, dates, coworkers—has been found as much as twice as common as rape by strangers. Upper-class women are likelier to be raped than middle- or lower-class women. African-American women are statistically less likely to be raped than white women; Latina women are even less likely to be raped; and Asian women are the least likely of all to be raped. Women in the US are at a greater risk than in any other Western nation. Rape occurs only infrequently in tribal societies.

In wartime, though, the violation of women symbolizes for the aggressors the conquest of the land they seek to vanquish. Moreover, as the recent Serbian rape camps demonstrated, wartime rape dishonors the male relatives of the victim, contaminates lines of descent, and demoralizes the enemy.

Rape, rage, fear, and humiliation are inseparable in violent sexual aggression. Rape-crisis centers and better enforcement of law have drawn public attention to the fact of rape as a widespread criminal phenomenon, and victims have been more forthcoming as a result. The feminist movement is largely responsible for these positive developments. In spite of our heightened awareness of the problem, though, the incidence of rape is on the rise.

	General/ Context	Daily Life/ Customs/ Practices	Humanities/ Fine Arts	Occupations	Education
1979	that seeks to block passage of the ERA, fight abortion liberalization, and institute other ultraconservative reforms The US Treasury issues the Susan B. Anthony dollar coin The US Supreme Court rules that a minor has a constitutional right to abortion, but requires her to persuade the judge that she is mature enough to make the decision Egyptian law governing the People's Assembly is amended, legislating that a woman be elected in addition to the usual two male members of each constituency	auspices of Medicaid and family planning agencies Iowa City officials prohibit firefighter Linda Eaton from nursing her infant son at the firehouse The US National Weather Service begins naming storms for men, alternating with women's names The Family Law of Egypt is codified, taking precedence over Islamic law; it stipulates the right of women to seek divorce, their right to child custody, and retention of the family residence The US Supreme Court rules that welfare benefits must be paid to families in need because of the mother's loss of her job, just as they are to families with an unemployed father Women's magazine *Emma* brings suit against the West German newsmagazine *Stern* to stop it from	Publication of *Les écrits féministes de Simone de Beauvoir (The Feminist Writings of Simone de Beauvoir)* Folklorist Francesca Reyes Aquino is awarded the Ramón Magsaysay Award Foundation's Government Service Award for her original research on Filipino folk dance and music Lucila Hosillos is awarded the Grand Prize by the Cultural Center of the Philippines for *Originality as Vengeance: The Filipino Cultural Achievement in Literature* in the criticism section, English division Clara Medeiros Ramos receives the Premio Literario Nacional from Brazil's Instituto Nacional do Livro for an unpublished biography, *Mestre Graciliano, confirmaçao humana de uma obra* Victoria Ocampo publishes the journal *Sur*, which provides com-	More the 290 women hold seats on the boards of major US corporations, almost double the number in 1975 Debbie Shook smashes her Miss North Carolina crown after state Jaycees retract her title for saying that being a beauty queen is not "a bed of roses" The US Air Force and Navy introduce maternity uniforms for pregnant military women; Rear Admiral James Hogg says: "The people in the Navy look on motherhood as being compatible with being a woman" A US court of appeals rules that employers may not require their female employees to wear uniforms if male employees in comparable jobs can wear customary business attire	

CONTEMPORARY THIRD WORLD LEADERS

In the 1980s, a number of women rose to become world leaders, not only in industrialized countries where women had considerable freedoms but also in developing nations. Corazon Aquino (b. 1933) of the Philippines, Violeta Barrios (b. 1929) of Nicaragua, and Pakistan's Benazir Bhutto (b. 1953) have proved that women can direct the affairs of a nation and suffer the slings and arrows of high-stakes politics as well as men.

Corazon Aquino was a quiet mother of five until her husband, an opposition politician, was jailed in 1972. She gained political savvy during his eight-year prison stay by serving as his mouthpiece to supporters and the press. When he was released from jail, she lived peacefully, a housewife again, with her husband and children in exile near Boston.

Returning to the Philippines in 1983, her husband was assassinated as he stepped off the plane, and Corazon found herself left to carry on his work. She gathered more than a

million petition signatures and ran for president in 1986 against 20-year dictator Ferdinand Marcos. She lost the election due to rampant fraud and violence. But, backed by an anti-Marcos military faction, Aquino led massive peaceful demonstrations that succeeded in ousting the entrenched president. Throughout the 1980s, she fought off coup attempts, coped with natural disasters, and tried to bring reform to her troubled country. In 1991, she decided not to run for a second presidential term.

Nicaragua's Violeta Barrios de Chamorro shares with Aquino a tragic reason for entering politics: in 1978 her husband, too, was assassinated. A Conservative opposition figure and editor of his family's newspaper, *La Prensa,* he ran afoul of the dictator Anastasio Somoza. Somoza was overthrown in 1979, but Violeta soon broke with the ruling Sandinistas. She used *La Prensa* to protest government policies and support the US-backed contra rebels. Her grown children were also in-

Performing Arts/ Entertainment/ Sports	Religion/ Philosophy	Science/ Technology/ Discovery	Statecraft/ Military	Reform	
mas to Florida; she is in the water 27 hours 38 minutes

Immensely popular British nightclub and vaudeville entertainer Gracie Fields (Grace Stansfield, 1898–1979) is best known for singing "The Biggest Aspidistra in the World" | Her support of the Equal Rights Amendment leads to Sonia Johnson's excommunication from the Mormon Church; she writes on the subject in *From Housewife to Heretic* (1981)

In a revival of an ancient appeasement ritual, the women of Uttar Pradesh, India, are sent nude to till the soil at night in order to appease the rain god Varuma and end the worst drought in 40 years; rains come in a month, saving 40% of the autumn crop

Sister Theresa Kane, president of the Leadership Conference of Women Religious, calls on Pope John Paul II to "regard the possibility of women being included in all ministries of the church"

Mother Teresa of India is awarded the Nobel Prize for Peace | The US National Institutes of Health endorse a two-stage breast biopsy procedure, enabling women to have a choice in breast surgery for cancer | thrown by a coup in July 1980

Chen Muhua becomes deputy prime minister of the People's Republic of China

Violeta Barrios de Chamorro becomes a member of the provisional junta that governs Nicaragua after Anastasio Somoza's expulsion

The market in Accra, Ghana, is razed by the government, which encourages persecution of the market women as scapegoats for food shortages; the public views women traders as wealthy and powerful and support the government actions; in reality, women have little means of fighting back

US President Carter dismisses Bella Abzug as cochair of the National Advisory Committee for Women; cochair Carmen Delgado Votaw and more than half the committee resign in protest | Parivash Khajehnouri, Farzeh Nouri, and Kathe Vafardi lead a successful protest to repeal the Iranian Revolutionary Council's 1975 edict ordering all women to wear the chador in public; the edict is repealed in 1979

Women's rights activist Begum Ali Khan of Pakistan receives a human rights award from the UN

The Inter-American Institute for Cooperation on Agriculture establishes the Inter-American Award for the Participation of Women in Rural Development, presented annually to women who have made important contributions to the rural development process

The National Coalition Against Sexual Assault is formed by rape-crisis centers in 20 American states

Sponsored by more than 50 organizations, Abortion Rights Ac- | **1979** |

volved in politics and the press, but not all on the same side: two worked for *La Prensa,* one for a moderate paper, and one for a Sandinista daily. Another daughter had been ambassador to Costa Rica.

When 14 political parties formed a coalition to oppose the Sandinistas in 1989, they chose Violeta as their presidential candidate. She won the election and became president of Nicaragua in April 1990. Since then, she has kept her promises to end the nine-year civil war and to stop the draft, and she has begun to revive the war-ravaged economy. But she has received vocal criticism at home and abroad for appointing family members and retaining Sandinistas in high posts. Some claim she is only a figurehead for her powerful son-in-law, whom she named her chief minister.

Like Aquino and Barrios, Benazir Bhutto's political career was sparked by a family assassination: her father, the prime minister of Pakistan, was overthrown in a 1977 military coup and hanged in 1979. Becoming the head of the opposition Pakistan People's Party, Benazir spent 1977–1984 under house arrest until her release into exile. Allowed to return in 1986, she received a joyful welcome. Upon the death of the prime minister in a suspicious plane crash in 1988, she ran for and won his post. Only 35, she was the first woman prime minister in any Muslim country.

Although the urbane Harvard and Oxford graduate had many supporters in the West, her leadership of Pakistan soon came under sharp attack at home. In the first year in power, her government, preoccupied with its political rivals, submitted no major legislation except a budget. Meanwhile, corruption and nepotism charges dogged Bhutto, her husband, and her hand-picked ministers. Within two years, she fell from power (her husband was jailed by the president with the support of the military). She ran again in the elections of November 1990, but her party lost by a landslide.

	General/ Context	Daily Life/ Customs/ Practices	Humanities/ Fine Arts	Occupations	Education
1979		portraying nude women on its cover	mentaries on the lives and works of such prominent Indian figures as Mahatma Gandhi and Rabindranath Tagore		
1980	Iran–Iraq War (1980–1989) begins Cape Verde holds its first national elections, with suffrage for all over age 18; by 1986 women comprise 14% of the only party's membership	In Zimbabwe, the election of President Robert Mugabe brings women new legal rights and expanded opportunities for education and jobs Revisions to the Marriage Law in China increase the minimum marriage age for women from 18 to 20 and stress family planning Among the Nzema in Ghana, practices of contraception and abortion are still primarily based on the use of plants Mothers Against Drunk Driving (MADD) is founded by Candy Lightner	American artist Betty Beaumont builds a sculpture reef off the coast of New York using 17,000 blocks made from 500 tons of stabilized coal waste byproduct, forming a thriving marine ecosystem Marguerite Yourcenar becomes the only woman ever admitted to the Académie Française Senegalese writer Mariama Bâ becomes the first African to win the prestigious Japanese literary prize the Noma Award for her novel *Une si longue lettre* (*A Very Long Letter*)	Mahnaz Afkhami, the former Iranian minister of state of women's affairs, is the head of the Iranian Organization of Women	
1981	The Solidarity strike in Poland results in imposition of martial law The Canadian constitution is amended to guarantee equality for women Spain legalizes divorce	Soraya Khashoggi, born Sandra Jarvis-Daley, sues her husband of 13 years—an Arab arms dealer—after he divorces her without her knowledge, for $2.54 billion for business services she performed while they were married, probably the largest personal suit ever made in a marital case	Caryl Churchill's Off-Broadway play *Top Girls* wins an Obie Award British artist Winifred Nicholson (1893–1981) paints throughout her life, often depicting the wild- and garden flowers and rainbows of the Cumbrian countryside, Greece, and the Hebrides	Japan's first female tycoon, Hanae Mori, presides over 15 companies, including restaurants and clothing and linen productions, bringing her annual sales of $100 million; she is responsible for bringing Western fashion into Japan's industrial miracle In the Islamic absolute monarchy of Brunei, 23.8% of the econom-	In the Central African Republic the female literacy rate is 19.2%, male is 43.3%; girls constitute 37% at primary school enrollment, 26% at secondary, and 11% at tertiary; work at home and in the fields prevents education for many

Performing Arts/ Entertainment/ Sports	Religion/ Philosophy	Science/ Technology/ Discovery	Statecraft/ Military	Reform	
			British politician Margaret Thatcher is elected Europe's first female prime minister	tion Week is held nationally across the US WOMEN, USA is formed by Bella Abzug, Patsy Mink, and others to work for equality and economic justice	**1979**
Turkish dancer Ozcan Tekgul is awarded a certificate of honor by the National Turkish Cinema Council; she says, "I win this prize not for my belly dancing . . . but because of my contribution to the Turkish Oriental dance"; the award is denied by the Islamic minister of culture Maria Colón of Cuba wins an Olympic gold in the women's javelin throw at the Moscow Games, a first in women's track and field for Cuba Zimbabwe's women's field hockey team wins its first Olympic gold medal at the Moscow Games	Ita Ford, Maura Clarke, Dorothy Kazel, and Jean Donovan, American religious workers in El Salvador, are victims of politically motivated murder Three Maryknoll nuns and a lay missioner are murdered in Nicaragua by a government death squad	Marie-Thérèse Basse, director of the Institute of Food Technology in Dakar, helps to develop *pain de mill,* a millet bread made from locally grown millet instead of imported wheat flour, thus helping to avert food crises in the Sahara Desert region The first contour map of planet Venus is released in May 1980 by NASA; every feature of the planet is named for a woman, subject to approval by a committee of the International Astronomical Union, including Hather, the Egyptian goddess of love; Ishtar, the Babylonian goddess of love; Lakshimi, the Hindu mother of all life; and Eve, the Judeo-Christian first woman	Vigdis Finnbogadottir (b. 1930) takes office as Iceland's first female head of state Farrokhrou Parsa, the first female member of parliament in Iran and the minister of education, is executed after a secret trial Member of Israel's Knesset, Geula Cohen has a reputation for repudiating policies of the prime minister of her own party Princess Ashraj Pahlavi is the several-time head of Iran's delegation to the UN and serves as chair of the Commission on the Status of Women and the Commission on Human Rights Queen Juliana of the Netherlands abdicates; she is succeeded by her daughter, Beatrix, whose marriage to a former SS officer outrages Dutch citizens, who mount mass demonstrations in several major cities	The UN World Conference on Women opens in Copenhagen; the US and 52 other nations sign an agreement to end discrimination against women The Women's Pentagon Action and protesters of patriarchy and war making rally at the Pentagon in Washington, DC Anilu Elias and Marta Acevedo are leaders of the women's liberation movement in Mexico Organization of Cape Verdean Women is founded to sensitize the government and community on issues affecting women Namibian Ida Jimmy is sentenced to seven years' imprisonment for making a speech at a SWAPO (South West African People's Organization) meeting; deputy secretary of SWAPO's Women's Council Gertrude Kandanga is also arrested and held for a year without charge or trial	**1980**
Tai Ai-lien, director of the Beijing Ballet, restores her company after it is closed by China's Cultural Revolution Golfer Hisako Higuchi Matsui is the most celebrated woman athlete in Japan, known there as the queen; took the European Open and the Japanese title in 1976 and the Ladies Professional	Dame Cicely Saunders receives the Templeton Prize for Progress in Religion from the Bahamas' Templeton Foundation for being the originator of the hospice movement in England		President Ronald Reagan creates a federal task force on legal equality for women; Carol Dinkins is appointed chair Sandra Day O'Connor (b. 1930) becomes the first woman named to the US Supreme Court At this time, Burundian women are not discriminated against	The Women's Peace Camp at Greenham Common Airbase is set up as an antinuclear arms peaceful demonstration; women can visit the camp and join the protesters for as long as they like The deadline for the ratification of the Equal Rights Amendment expires with only 35 of the 38 nec-	**1981**

393

	General/ Context	Daily Life/ Customs/ Practices	Humanities/ Fine Arts	Occupations	Education
1981		Women of Bangladesh receive unequal treatment before the law; there is a publicly recognized pattern of murder, rape, domestic violence, and breach of matrimonial contract; the suicide rate among women is triple that among men In Burundi women cannot inherit land or work if forbidden by their husbands and fewer women attain education than men	In her open letter to third world women writers, Chicana poet Gloria Anzaldúa counsels, "Forget the room of one's own—write in the kitchen, lock yourself up in the bathroom. Write on the bus or the welfare line, on the job or during meals, between sleeping or waking," addressing the situation of many modern women writers	ically active population is female In Bhutan, every adult is required to contribute 23 days of labor per year to public projects, and almost all the women work beside men in the fields Despite the code of the family, sex discrimination exists in Cape Verde, with women being traditionally banned from certain types of work and often receiving less pay for comparable work	
1982		Jane Fonda publishes *Jane Fonda's Workout Book*	Sylvia Plath is posthumously awarded a Pulitzer Prize for her *Collected Poems*	The Federación de Mujeres Profesionales y de Negocios de Costa Rica establishes the Honor al Mérito to recognize women who have served the business and professional women of Costa Rica in an outstanding way	The 100th anniversary of mathematician Emmy Noether's birth is marked in her native city of Erlangen by the rededication of her girlhood school as a full-fledged high school, emphasizing mathematics, sciences, and modern languages, and named the Emmy Noether School By 1982, almost half of university graduates in Colombia are women
1983	The government of São Paulo creates the first Brazilian state commission on the status of women The life expectancy for women in Bangladesh is 49 years	A constitutional amendment makes voting compulsory for all Argentinian citizens, including women In Bangladesh, a law is passed to deter murder and trafficking in women; the death penalty is instated for the many notorious "dowry killings"	Soviet poet Irina Ratushinskaya (b. 1954) becomes a political prisoner of the KGB Grace Nichols of Guyana is awarded the Commonwealth Poetry Prize of the Commonwealth Institute in the UK for her *I is a long memoried woman*	Connie (Constance Yu-Hwa) Chung (b. 1946) becomes one of the first female minority news anchors in the US; she wins Emmys for her work in 1978, 1980, and 1987	
1984	Discovery of genetic fingerprinting The International Tribunal and Meeting on	Popular singer Karen Carpenter dies of anorexia nervosa	Nora Ephron writes the screenplay for *Silkwood*, based on Karen Silkwood whose efforts to hold her com-	In Burma, women constitute 4% of the labor force; the average monthly earnings of a female industrial	The literacy rate for females in Bahrain is 73.7%; girls comprise 46% of enrollments in primary, 46% in sec-

Performing Arts/ Entertainment/ Sports	Religion/ Philosophy	Science/ Technology/ Discovery	Statecraft/ Military	Reform	
Golf Association (LPGA) in 1977; as of 1981, there are 200 women playing tournament golf in Japan, 175 of them on the US tour; in 1979 four played along with Higuchi on the LPGA tour			by the government in respect to jobs and hiring; women are represented at all political levels; however, their main political expression is the women's movement, affiliated with a party dominated by men	essary states having voted their approval Maria Tereza Jorge Padua is awarded the J. Paul Getty Wildlife Conservation Prize of the World Wildlife Fund	**1981**
American ballet dancer Darci Kistler is made a principal dancer in the New York City Ballet, becoming the last of the Balanchine ballerinas Colombian musician Martha Senn takes first prize in the Concours International de Chant in Paris				Ruth First (1920–1982), a prominent South African Marxist radical and writer, is assassinated; First had been arrested and detained in the 1950s and 60s in South Africa, later going into exile and working to build socialism in Mozambique	**1982**
The troubled life of stage and screen actress Frances Farmer (1914–1970), who spent most of the 1940s in a mental institution, is the subject of the film *Frances*	The faculty of the Jewish Theological Seminary votes to admit women to the rabbinical school, opening the way for women's ordination as Conservative rabbis	America's first female astronaut, Sally K. Ride (b. 1952), is launched into space in the shuttle *Challenger* for over six days with three male crew members Publication of mathematician Emmy Noether's *Collected Papers,* heralded as long overdue, "since she was by far the best woman mathematician of all time, and one of the greatest mathematicians (male or female) of the XXth century"	Jiang Quing, the widow of Mao Zedong, tried as a member of the Gang of Four in 1980, is given a suspended death sentence In Cameroon's National Assembly 14% of the positions are held by women	The Women's Peace Encampment begins in Seneca Falls, NY Environmental activist Petra Kelly (1948–1992) is elected to the German parliament as a representative of the Green party	**1983**
Sylvie Guillem (b. 1965) becomes a featured dancer with the Paris Opera Ballet Company			Prime Minister Indira Gandhi is assassinated by two Sikh members of her bodyguard	A group of working-class women meet in Brazil and demand sex education	**1984**

	General/ Context	Daily Life/ Customs/ Practices	Humanities/ Fine Arts	Occupations	Education
1984	Reproductive Rights is held in Amsterdam The Sex Discrimination Act is passed in Australia		pany accountable for radioactive contamination led to her death	worker is about 89% of those of her male counterpart Canadian women earn on the average 63% of male wages	ondary, and 39% in postsecondary education; one of the country's three institutions of higher education is a women's teacher training college
1985	The Egyptian supreme court strikes down the Personal Status Amendment of 1979 because Muslim fundamentalists oppose this liberalizing legislation as inconsistent with Islamic religious tradition Mikhail Gorbachev takes power in the Soviet Union and advocates glasnost and perestroika, policies of openness and restructuring Canada passes the Divorce and Corollary Relief Act, which eliminates the concept of fault from divorce and authorizes courts to issue support orders where a dependent wife is unable to be self-sufficient Egypt enacts a law guaranteeing women's rights without, however, touching on the issue of polygamy In the Central African Republic female life expectancy is 44.6 years and male is 41.4 years; polygamy is common, but the legal system and traditional practices support the rights of wives and all children of such marriages; women are generally accorded lower status than men	The Brazilian federal government follows São Paulo's lead in establishing a commission on the status of women, the Conselho Nacional des Direitos da Mulher Columnist Ann Landers runs a sex survey; 72% of female respondents report themselves dissatisfied with their sexual relationships The state of Montana passes legislation requiring unisex insurance rates Sterilization is the most widespread form of birth control throughout the world	Special Agent Robin L. Ahrens, shot while making an arrest, is the first female FBI agent to be killed in the line of duty Carolyn Kizer wins the Pulitzer Prize for Poetry for *Yin* *Foreign Affairs* by Alison Lurie wins the Pulitzer Prize for Fiction Valquiria Chiarion of Brazil is awarded a Panorama de Arte Atual Brasileira Prize for sculpture and objects Pamela Kelley with Earl W. Wallace and William Kelley receive the Edgar Allan Poe Award for *Witness;* she is the only woman from 1945 until 1987 to get the award Gertraude Schultz Steigleder receives the Premio Literario Nacional from Brazil's Instituto Nacional do Livro for the biography *Imperatriz Sob um ven de lagrimas* Pamela Cohen and José Ponce of El Salvador receive the Philafilm Award at the Philadelphia International Film Festival for their film, *In the Name of Democracy* Publication of *Trabajos Monográficos: Studies in Chicana/Latina Research,* a scholarly (US) journal put out by Mujeres Activas en Letras y Cambio Social (MALCS)	According to the US Department of Labor, 53% of all married women are part of the labor force In Portland, OR, Capt. Penny Harrington becomes the first woman to head the police department of a major US city Studies show that few women reach the top of the journalism industry; a University of Maryland study suggests that journalism's pay and prestige may be lowered as women become the majority of journalism majors in college A Rand Corporation study shows that contrary to popular belief, young blue-collar working women do not quit their jobs more often than their male counterparts According to Women's World Banking President Michaela Walsh, credit extended to third world businesswomen has proved profitable Former TV newscasters Christine Craft and Cecily Coleman join with the legal unit of NOW to fight sexual discrimination and harassment in employment; Coleman launches a $15 million lawsuit against former ABC network executive James D. Abernathy for sexual harassment; ABC pays her $500,000 in an	Death of Bitu, a Muganda woman from southern Uganda who attacked the problem of teenage pregnancy by starting a center for pregnant girls and young unmarried mothers that allowed them to continue their schooling In Cape Verde the national literacy rate is 49.3%: female is 40.8%, and male is 59.2%; girls comprise 49% of primary school enrollment and 50% of secondary The South African Association of University Women establishes the Hausi Pollack Fellowship awarded biennially to provide postgraduate study in the field of social sciences to ameliorate social conditions in South Africa Nelson and Winnie Mandela of South Africa are awarded the Third World Prize by the Third World Foundation for Social and Economic Studies, located in the United Kingdom

Performing Arts/ Entertainment/ Sports	Religion/ Philosophy	Science/ Technology/ Discovery	Statecraft/ Military	Reform	
Nawal el Moutawakii of Morocco wins the Olympic gold in the 400-meter hurdles at the Los Angeles Games, a first in women's track and field for Morocco			US Democratic presidential nominee Walter F. Mondale chooses Geraldine Ferraro as his running mate	Women Working for a Nuclear-Free and Independent Pacific forms "to support indigenous people's struggles to be independent and nuclear free"	**1984**
Libby Riddles becomes the first woman to win the Iditarod Trail International Race, the 1827-kilometer dogsled event in Alaska	Amy Eilberg (b. 1955) becomes the first Conservative woman rabbi	Baltimore teachers Kathleen A. Beres and Judith M. Garcia are selected as space shuttle finalists	Wilma Mankiller becomes principal chief of the Cherokee Nation of Oklahoma, the first woman in history to lead a major Native American tribe	The UN Conference on the Status of Women takes place in Nairobi, Kenya, attended by more than 13,500 women from over 100 countries; the meeting concludes the UN Decade for Women	**1985**
University of Kansas basketball star Lynette Woodard signs on as the Harlem Globetrotters' first woman player	The first female African-American pastor of the American Lutheran Church, Rev. Maria-Alma Copeland, is ordained in St. Paul, MN	At 26, Tamara Elizabeth Jernigan is the youngest US astronaut candidate	Suffrage in Bangladesh is universal for citizens over the age of 18		
Japanese singer Chihiro Bamba is awarded first prize at Concours International d'Execution Musicale in Geneva; she had previously won the women's award at the International Singing Competition of Toulouse in 1984	In a pastoral letter on women, opposed by many Catholic women in the US, Cardinal Bernardin of Chicago notes the frustration caused by the Catholic Church's ban on women priests, but encourages women's involvement in other leadership positions, such as in new ministries		The USSR amends the draft to allow women into the armed forces	The General Arab Women Federation in Baghdad establishes the Medal of Distinction to be awarded annually for recognition of distinguished efforts in support of the Arab women's movement	
Wang Yan-Yan of China wins the grand prize for her soprano performance at the Rio de Janeiro International Singing Contest	Adventists debate the ordination of women as ministers			Black South African women describe life under apartheid in an unofficial forum at the UN World Conference on Women	
	A growing number of black women clergy press against the traditional barriers imposed by their churches			Right-to-Life groups meet with opposition at the UN World Conference on Women	
				Nearly 400 delegates representing over 100 women's organizations from all parts of India participate in the National Conference on Perspectives for Women's Liberation in Bombay, India	

General/ Context	Daily Life/ Customs/ Practices	Humanities/ Fine Arts	Occupations	Education
1985			out-of-court settlement	
			Icelandic women go on a 24-hour strike to protest unequal wages and male privilege	
1986 The space shuttle *Challenger* explodes during liftoff at Cape Canaveral, FL, killing seven astronauts, including elementary school teacher Christa McAuliffe The life expectancy of women in developing countries outstrips that of men by an average of a few years, in spite of a higher incidence of childhood and adult malnutrition among females, the risks of childbirth, and the often heavier burden of physical labor women undertake The US Supreme Court upholds affirmative-action hiring quotas promoting the hiring of women and minorities as a remedy for past discrimination Canada's Employment Equity Act requires equal employment and remuneration for	The American Psychiatric Association considers labeling PMS (premenstrual syndrome) as a mental illness *Newsweek* magazine cites a Yale University study suggesting that single women over 35 have only a 5% chance of getting married *The New York Times* adopts the use of the term "Ms." A Stanford University study shows that American women are no better off economically than they were in 1959 A House select committee on children, youth, and families report predicts one million teen pregnancies in the US annually, about half of them to unwed mothers; it also notes the inadequacy of funding and services of preg-	Poet Adrienne Rich receives the first annual Ruth Lilly Poetry Prize, at $25,000 the largest award to poets in the US Elizabeth Frank receives the Pulitzer Prize for Biography for *Louise Bogan: A Portrait* Donna Gold, American writer and journalist, writes her poem "Nicaraguita Rose" after joining the International March for Peace through Central America *This Bridge Called My Back, Writings by Radical Women of Color,* edited by Cherríe Moraga and Gloria Anzaldúa and first published in 1981, is the winner of the Before Columbus Foundation American Book Award Honor Ford Smith and "Sistren," a politi-	In developing countries, women generally constitute between a fifth and a third of the labor force in such areas as agriculture, commerce, manufacturing and handicrafts, construction and transport, and services Working women in Algeria are entitled to maternity leave under national security schemes Women are well represented in public service in the island nations of Antigua and Barbuda New, but contested, figures suggest that women comprise the majority of workers in professional occupations in the US The US Navy's only female jet test pilot is Lt. Beth Hubert Nelly Speerstra, NATO's first female	The literacy rate for women in developing countries varies greatly by region: in Afghanistan it is as low as 5.8% while in Antigua it is 88%; in Argentina it is 94%, equaling that of males; in Barbados, the literacy rate is 99.3% for males and females Argentina's prison system places emphasis on rehabilitation, prison farms, open-door institutions, and homes for women and minors

THE FEMINIZATION OF POVERTY AND HOMELESSNESS

Just as there has always been poverty, there have always been poor women. But recent developments have thrown the economic conditions of women into bold relief. In the US, women constitute an increasing proportion of poor adults, and children in female-headed households often end up living in poverty, too.

Certain factors leading to poverty affect women more than men. Now that half of all marriages end in divorce, many women find themselves raising children on one income. Only a small fraction of divorced fathers pay child support, whether court ordered or voluntary. The percentage of unwed fathers who support their children is miniscule. These concerns vary by race: 62% of poor blacks live in households headed by women, in contrast with 28% of poor whites. Unlike men, many women both with and without children face sharp economic decline in situations of divorce, widowhood, or abandonment. Women

who leave husbands or boyfriends to escape domestic violence confront the same economic problems. In fact, these household composition factors are more closely linked to poverty than to such common explanations as a poor education or a negative attitude.

Finding a good job is crucial for single women, especially single mothers, but a shortage of affordable child care can make it difficult to hold a job. Women also consistently earn less than men. Concentrated in low-skill jobs, women are denied equal pay for equal work or prevented from promotion due to persistent, often unconscious, job discrimination. Many women in the inner cities find that the jobs once located there have gone overseas or moved to the suburbs; even when jobs are available and accessible, the wages might not support a family.

The number of women among the homeless has risen no-

1985

1986

Susan Butcher wins the Anchorage-to-Nome Iditarod dogsled race, only the second woman to do so in the traditionally all-male sport; she wins again in 1987

National Women in Sports Day is created by a joint congressional resolution; its purpose is to fight gender discrimination in sports

Debi Thomas becomes the first African-American woman to win the Senior Singles US Figure Skating Championship; she also wins the women's World Figure Skating Championship

The Harlem Globetrotters hire Jackie White as their second female player

Air acrobat Susan King performs wing-walking stunts on her father's plane at the Fauquier (VA) Air Show

Edward A. McCarthy, Roman Catholic bishop of Miami, FL, issues a pastoral letter offering absolution to women who have had abortions and to those who have assisted abortions

Pennsylvania Roman Catholic women protest a bishop's directive banning them from participation in Holy Thursday "washing of the feet" services

2400 Catholic women assemble in a Washington, DC, conference to press for an expanded role for women in the Church

At a conference of US Catholic women activists, Canadian Bishop Remi J. De Roo urges the ordination of women

The first female Episcopalian dean is appointed to Christ Church Cathedral in Louisville, KY

Founder of the laboratory of cell biology of the National Research Council of Rome, Rita Levi-Montalcini shares the 1986 Nobel Prize for Physiology or Medicine with Stanley Cohen for the discovery of nerve growth factor; she also receives the Albert Lasker Basic Research Award

US astronaut Sally Ride serves as a special aide to the NASA administrator

Corazon Aquino, widow of Filipino opposition leader Benigno Aquino, becomes president of the Philippines as former president Ferdinand Marcos flees

The exiled daughter of former Pakistani president Zulfikar Ali Bhutto, Benazir Bhutto returns to Pakistan and revitalizes the Pakistan People's Party

Lucia Garcia de Solar becomes the Argentinian ambassador to Washington, DC

The military dictatorship of Burkina Faso has at least two female Cabinet members between 1981 and 1986: Beatrice Damiba is the minister of environment and tourism; Josephine Ouedreogo is the minister of family affairs and national solidarity

In *Meritor Savings Bank* v. *Vinson*, the US Supreme Court rules that sexual harassment of employees violates federal law

British peace activist Dora Russell remains active right up until her death, advocating for disarmament, women's rights, and world peace

The Women's Social Pioneer Foundation and other private organizations are engaged in medical welfare in Brazil

The Affirmative Action (Equal Opportunity for Women) Act is passed in Australia

---

ticeably. The deinstitutionalization of the mentally ill in the late 1970s left many single women homeless. A severe decrease in affordable housing, both for single adults and for families, has compounded the employment problems of the urban poor. The number of homeless families has grown faster than the number of homeless single people, and the majority of homeless families are headed by women, struggling to support children on at most one income. By the mid-1980s, as many as 84% of homeless families in Boston were headed by women.

Government assistance often fails to help families in this dire situation. Along with reductions in federal spending for poor relief, the bureaucratic problems brought on when recipients lack a stable address often block eligible candidates from benefits. In many cases, saving money for a deposit on an apartment causes ineligibility for continued relief, so that women are forced to choose between receiving assistance and finding housing. Homeless shelters have been opened in many cities, but many are overcrowded or just as unsafe as the streets. With shelters often closed during the day, little access to day care for younger children, and difficulties in school attendance for older children, homeless single mothers face special obstacles to keeping a steady job. And they and their children often lack medical care.

The increasing presence of women among the poor—the working poor, the unemployed, and the homeless—has led many people to speak of the "feminization of poverty." That phrase recognizes that poverty now affects women in higher proportions than men. Although opinions vary widely on how to solve the problems of poverty and homelessness among women and children, most agree that a solution has not been found and that these problems are, unfortunately, getting worse.

	General/Context	Daily Life/Customs/Practices	Humanities/Fine Arts	Occupations	Education
1986	women, the disabled, aboriginals, and minorities The US Census Bureau reports that women own 25% of the nation's businesses The European Economic Community (EEC) approves an action program from 1986 to 1990 to encourage progress toward equality between men and women in employment, training, advancement, working conditions, and pay	nant teens and teenage mothers According to a study published by Harvard University, women who exercise regularly run a significantly lower risk of developing breast and reproductive cancers In the Central African Republic, social welfare includes prenatal allowances, a lump-sum payment at the birth of each of the first three children, and a recuperation allowance of 14 weeks for employed mothers	cocultural women's collective in Jamaica, publish *Lionheart Gal: Life Stories of Jamaican Women* Paulina Matta of Chile receives the Premio de Novela Andres Bello for her *Album de Fotografías*	combat pilot, graduates from a US training facility and serves in the Dutch Air Force	
1987	A strike by black workers in South Africa triggers violent unrest in South Africa that lasts into the 1990s US Senator Gary Hart withdraws from the presidential race when his relationship with model Donna Rice is revealed AIDS (acquired immune deficiency syndrome) is the leading cause of death of women aged 25–34 in New York City The high court of Rajastan, India, upholds an ordinance banning widow burning Polls find that most US voters say that female political candidates are as capable as men; 57% believe that a woman president would do as well or better than a man	Studies show that two thirds of the elderly poor in the US are women Bypass surgery is recommended for men with heart disease symptoms 10 times more often than for women with the same symptoms The US Census Bureau reports that the average woman earned 64% of median male income in 1984 Soviet leader Mikhail Gorbachev claims that Soviet women have greater rights than men, but admits that their social obligations have also increased The US Supreme Court rules that states retain the right to deny unemployment benefits to women who leave work because of pregnancy	Rita Dove's *Thomas and Beulah* receives the Pulitzer Prize for Poetry Maria Bonomi of Brazil is awarded the Wilson M. Caldeira Junior Prize for art on paper by the Panorama de Arte Atual Brasileira Diane Ying of Taiwan receives the Ramón Magsaysay Award Foundation's Journalism, Literature, and Creative Communication Arts Award for her work as an editor and publisher	Celebrity television host Yue-Sai Kan (b. 1949) produces *One World*, the first Western life-style magazine-format broadcast in China Gayle Sierens becomes the first woman to broadcast a play-by-play account of an NFL game on NBC The US Commission on Civil Rights rejects a staff report criticizing the US Supreme Court's opinion upholding affirmative-action plans to offer job opportunities to women and minorities The Washington, DC, police department secretly tests policewomen for pregnancy, using urine samples taken for drug tests; when this is revealed, the department agrees in future to inform applicants of the results	The Indian Adult Education Association of New Delhi establishes the Tagore Literacy Award, an annually awarded plaque with citation and a shawl to recognize outstanding contributions to women's literacy and adult education in India More women than men are enrolled in Australian colleges; they comprise 47.4% of university students and receive 35.5% of master's and 29.3% of doctoral degrees In Maryland, the legislative women's caucus and the University of Maryland's women's studies department set up legislative internships in the state's general assembly to help interest young women in politics

Performing Arts/ Entertainment/ Sports	Religion/ Philosophy	Science/ Technology/ Discovery	Statecraft/ Military	Reform	
			Between 1981 and 1986, Botswana has two female members of parliament; one is also minister of external affairs, the other is executive secretary of the majority political party; though there is little overt discrimination, social custom elevates the rights of men; political rights of women are generally observed Mrs. Euphrasie Kandecke is the minister of women's affairs in Burundi A record number of women run for statewide office in the US; at the same time, women hold more elective city offices than ever before Denmark allows women sailors to volunteer for naval combat duty		**1986**
American pilot Lois McCallin sets the endurance and the closed-course records for women, flying an experimental pedal-powered plane, the 92-pound *Eagle* The Associated Press names tennis champion Martina Navratilova Female Athlete of the Year (1986) The Association of Track and Field Statisticians of Salisbury, England, establishes the Jan Popper Memorial Prize to recognize the author of the publication that, having appeared in the previous four years, is adjudged by the executive committee to contribute the most to the statistical history of women's track and field Basketball player Nancy Lieberman signs	Roman Catholic Bishop Rembert Weakland says that the Church should give women more authority in liturgy and leadership An informal panel of Catholic bishops agrees to permit altar girls to serve at mass While condemning discrimination against women, a synod of Catholic bishops rejects proposals for new roles in the Church for women	NASA's new astronaut candidates include the program's first black woman, Dr. Mae Jemison	US authorities reject a proposal to build a memorial for women who served in the Vietnam War Nora Gadea Astorga, a revolutionary known for her role in the 1978 assassination of Reynaldo Perez Vegas, becomes Nicaraguan ambassador to the US, 1987–1988 A four-year study of women in the Danish military shows that mixed-gender crews outperform traditional male-only units Barbara A. Mikulski becomes the first Democratic woman elected to a Senate seat not previously held by her husband; she is also the first Democratic woman to serve in the House and the Senate 10% of Iceland's parliament seats are held by	The first Eleanor Roosevelt International Caucus of Women Political Leaders takes place in San Francisco, CA; attended by more than 60 women leaders from nearly 50 countries, the meeting is chaired by Geraldine A. Ferraro The fifth International Women and Health Conference is held in Costa Rica Saudi Arabian feminists begin to demand more rights though the society remains segregated League of Women Voters workers picket the organization's Washington, DC, headquarters, demanding the right to form a union Molly Yard (1910–1991) becomes the president of NOW	**1987**

401

	General/ Context	Daily Life/ Customs/ Practices	Humanities/ Fine Arts	Occupations	Education
1987					
1988	The number of women in US jails is on the rise; experts claim that most are led into crime by men 42% of US female federal civil servants claim that they have been sexually harassed, though few file complaints Sweden adopts a five-year plan to attain equality for women in the economy, the labor force, education, the family, and in general influence	Surveys show that uninsured women receive markedly less preventive medical care than women with health insurance The Boy Scouts of America drop its ban on women as troop leaders Despite their high level of education and prosperity, Japanese women's primary role remains that of housewife and mother In response to complaints about abusive behavior toward women in military service, the US Navy bans topless dancers and sexually oriented entertainment at base clubs	*Beloved* by Toni Morrison wins the Pulitzer Prize for Fiction Irina Ratushinskaya publishes a memoir of her years as a KGB prisoner, *Grey Is the Colour of Hope* American artist Kiki Smith has her first solo commercial gallery show in New York City; working in many mediums, she explores issues surrounding the body; her work can be seen in major international galleries and museums Dina Malhotra of India receives the International Book Award from UNESCO The (US) National Museum of Women in the Arts buys its first painting, Traute Washing, by Lotte Laserstein	The South Carolina legislature elects its first woman to the state's supreme court Only seven women work in upper levels of major US newspapers, in spite of the growing numbers of female journalists A Disclosure, Inc., survey shows that women make up only 3.4% of the directors of publicly traded US companies Studies show that female faculty members in medical schools are rarely promoted to top positions	Christian relief agencies working in Bangladesh focus their efforts on women, helping them overcome their low status by making them employable Former First Ladies Rosalynn Carter and Lady Bird Johnson host a two-day symposium on the place of women in America's past and future
1989	The Berlin Wall is torn down US pro-life groups challenge the legal status of abortion following a reinterpretation of the *Roe* v. *Wade* decision 133 of Sweden's 349 Riksdag (parliament) members are women	Alexandria Biryukova, the highest-ranking female Soviet official, speaks out on abortion and the lack of contraceptives in the USSR during her first news conference An increasing number of women in Teheran replace the full-length black chadors with colorful scarves and pants; they are criticized by Muslim fundamentalists In response to the gang rape and brutal beating of a female jogger in New York's Central Park, RunHers is formed to alert female runners to the dangers they face The FDA proposes that tampon manufac-	Vietnamese American filmmaker and writer Trinh T. Minh-ha publishes her book, *Woman, Native, Other: Writing Postcoloniality and Feminism* Aboriginal lesbian playwright Eva Johnson writes and produces her plays in Australia *Volevo i Pantaloni* (I Wanted to Wear Pants) by 19-year-old author Lara Cardella causes an uproar in her native Sicily The Folger Shakespeare Library (Washington, DC) mounts an exhibit entitled "Women of the Renaissance"	The Canadian Job Strategy sets targets for women's participation in job entry, job development, skill investment, and skill shortages programs US women's rights groups hail a Supreme Court ruling that once a woman presents direct evidence of having been denied promotion because of illegal sex stereotyping, her employer must prove that there were other legitimate reasons for denying the promotion Women begin to be accepted as chefs in some of France's great kitchens	Betty Friedan conducts research for her book *The Fountain of Age* at the Gerontological Center at the University of Southern California; feminist activists unite to disseminate her findings among aged poor women Women's advocacy groups charge that the SAT (Scholastic Aptitude Test), a standard predictor of success in college, is biased against women Kristin Baker becomes the first woman in the 187-year history of the US Military Academy to be selected captain of the corps of cadets at West Point

Performing Arts/ Entertainment/ Sports	Religion/ Philosophy	Science/ Technology/ Discovery	Statecraft/ Military	Reform	
with a men's team in the US Basketball League			members of the country's feminist political party		**1987**
American stand-up comic and actress Roseanne Barr (later Arnold) stars in a groundbreaking television comedy series, *Roseanne,* featuring a plain-speaking working-class family	Rev. Barbara C. Harris is elected the first female bishop in the 450-year history of the Anglican Church	The French government approves the drug RU-486, the infamous "abortion pill" that raises a storm of controversy when women push for its approval in the US	President Reagan signs a bill authorizing a monument honoring the 10,000 women who served with the US armed forces in Vietnam	Boston hosts the Women and AIDS conference	**1988**
The Women's Sports Foundation (US) lobbies for the Civil Rights Restoration Act to ensure equality of funding for women's sports	The House of Bishops of the (US) Episcopal Church establishes a system of substitute bishops for parishes that object to female bishops		Spain's Prime Minister Felipe González gives two Cabinet posts to women	African-American health activist and feminist Beverly Smith, along with others, forms the Black Women's Council on AIDS	
Hulda Crooks, 91-year-old mountain climber, climbs the US Capitol steps in celebration of National Women in Sports Day	Pope John Paul II condemns sex discrimination against women, but reiterates his opposition to their ordination as priests		Black reformer Lenora B. Fulani runs as an independent candidate in the US presidential election	US women's groups work with the AARP (American Association of Retired People) to secure a system of long-term health care for the infirm	
The National (baseball) League (US) decides against hiring its first female umpire, Pam Postena, in spite of her superior experience and qualifications	Members of the Cantors Assembly, a professional organization of Conservative Jewish cantors, vote against admitting female cantors		While fighting as soldiers in the rebellion against Ethiopia, Eritrean women gain equal rights with men	A coalition of women's groups marches on Washington, DC, in an attempt to secure passage of the Family and Medical Leave Act	
			The ouster of former Tunisian president Habib Bourguiba helps to reopen the question of women's role in the country's Islamic society		
Xiaoxuan Wu of the People's Republic of China wins the Olympic gold for the small bore rifle, three positions, at the Los Angeles Games	The Catholic Church and conservative forces introduce a bill into the Philippine congress advocating the death penalty for abortion	A long-acting contraceptive that protects women from pregnancy for up to five years when implanted under the skin is approved by the FDA	Canada abolishes laws banning women from military service	The congressional agenda of the Council of Presidents, an organization representing 49 national US women's organizations, includes family and medical leave, child care, health care, pay equity, and reproductive rights	**1989**
African-American dancer Judith Jamison becomes artistic director of the Alvin Ailey American Dance Theater			During the US invasion of Panama, Army Capt. Linda L. Bray becomes the first woman to lead a platoon into battle		
June Croteau is the first woman on record to play in an NCAA varsity baseball game; she plays first base for St. Mary's Seahawks			Japan's Prime Minister Toshiki Kaifu appoints two women to his Cabinet—a record number—in response to his party's problems with female voters	Mothers Embracing Nuclear Disarmament sponsors a delegation of 10 Soviet women to the US	

Author Tillie Olsen holding a plaque for the Elizabeth Cady Stanton House
Photograph (1990) courtesy Sophia Smith Collection, Smith College

Among the first acts of the new Romanian government are the repeal of the ban on abortion and the easing of access to contraception

Some 300,000 people march on the US Capitol to demand the preservation of women's right to legal abortions in a March for Women's Equality/ Women's Lives, Apr. 10

	General/ Context	Daily Life/ Customs/ Practices	Humanities/ Fine Arts	Occupations	Education
1989		turers be required to label their products using standard absorbency ratings in order to reduce the risk of toxic shock syndrome 75% of the women in America with AIDS are women of color			
1990	Namibia gains independence French Prime Minister Edith Cresson suggests in an interview that 25% of Americans, Germans, and British men are homosexual, and that Englishmen in particular are not interested in women; the remark opens her up to ridicule in the international press Discrimination against girls in Asia appears to be on the rise; the disappearance of 60 million to 100 million females—abandoned, aborted, killed at birth, or neglected—is attributed to the cultural preference for boys Between 40% and 90% of urban-based male and female prostitutes in Central, East, and West Africa are infected with the AIDS virus	In Cairo, Egypt, the first car on each subway train is reserved for women only, to prevent harassment by men Clitoridectomies for girls is debated all across Africa; a means of discouraging intercourse outside of marriage, the practice is plagued with medical hazards including infection, loss of fertility, and even death Studies show that the leading cause of death of American women in the workplace— 42%—is homicide A government-funded national family-planning campaign in South Africa targets black women, administering contraceptive injections, often without their knowledge, or pressuring them into sterilization R. J. Reynolds Tobacco Company targets young poorly educated white women, whom they describe as "virile females," in their marketing strategy for a new brand of cigarettes Alarmed by the country's low fertility rate, Japanese officials encourage women to have more children	The Guerrilla Girls, a group of masked women proclaiming themselves the conscience of the art world, crusade to end discrimination against female and minority artists; they mount their campaign by means of posters, personal appearances, and performances	Black women in South Africa and Namibia who work rarely receive maternity leave, paid or unpaid; nor do they receive maternity benefits The institution of equal pay for work of equal value in Canada's Public Service results in $317 million in retroactive equal-pay adjustments The US State Department settles a 14-year-long sex discrimination suit by giving some female Foreign Service officers priority in obtaining assignments or honors previously denied them because of their sex Young Japanese women are emigrating in record numbers because of the demoralizing expectation of marriage and limited employment opportunities Death of India Edwards (b. 1896), former vice-chair of the Democratic National Committee (US) who worked to advance the role of women in politics for more than 30 years; under her influence, President Truman appointed more women to top jobs than any other president before him	Middlebury College (VT) fraternities are ordered to admit women or close down; the college has had no Greek system for women since 1960 Derrick A. Bell, Jr., is named Feminist of the Year by the Feminist Majority Foundation for having refused to teach his classes at Harvard Law School until a woman from a minority group was hired as a professor; a second winner is Dr. Jean Jew, who successfully sued the University of Iowa Medical School for sexual and racial harassment The Woman's Project of New Jersey establishes a permanent women's archive at Rutgers University US educators regard the California Institute of Technology's doubled enrollment of freshmen women a significant advance for women's science education
1991	According to a UN report, the number of rural women living in poverty in developing countries has increased	American law professor Anita Hill brings sexual harassment charges against Supreme Court nominee	American Pulitzer Prize-winning journalist Susan Faludi publishes her examination of women's status in	The Feminist Majority Foundation reports that less than 3% of top jobs in *Fortune* 500 companies were	

Performing Arts/ Entertainment/ Sports	Religion/ Philosophy	Science/ Technology/ Discovery	Statecraft/ Military	Reform	
					1989
Tennis champion Billie Jean King is inducted into the (US) National Woman's Hall of Fame

Tracy Edwards and her all-woman team aboard the *Maiden Great Britain* compete in the Whitbread Round the World Race, the most grueling sailing competition in the world

Kelly Craig becomes the first girl to start as pitcher in the history of the Little League world series; the third girl to play in the event at all, she plays for the Canadian team of British Columbia

Sailor Florence Arthaud sets a record time in the solo transatlantic Route de Rhum race from France to Guadaloupe | After a two-day meeting at the Vatican, the US Roman Catholic hierarchy indicates that it will again have to revise its draft pastoral letter on women's concerns to incorporate views from other continents

Islamic fundamentalists in Algeria step up efforts to suppress women's rights and to make them adhere to strict Islamic practices

In a revolutionary move, Ireland's main Protestant church agrees to the ordination of women, potentially blocking the Church's reconciliation with Roman Catholics

In the face of a 150-year tradition, the Christian Reformed Church votes to permit churches to "use their own discretion in utilizing the gifts of women"

Representatives to the Seventh-Day Adventist world conference turn down the ordination of women to gospel ministry by a vote of 1173 to 337 | | Ertha Pascal-Trouillot (b. 1944), the first woman to sit on the Supreme Court of Haiti, becomes the provisional president of that country for a year

The US deploys more women to the Middle East in combat support roles than ever before—about 10% of all forces

Pakistani president Benazir Bhutto, the first woman to head a Muslim state, is ousted

In response to women's demonstrations, the Saudi goverment reinforces the ban on licensing women drivers, declaring that driving a car violates Islamic tradition by denegrating women | As of this year, the treaty adopted by the UN at the 1979 convention on the Elimination of All Forms of Discrimination Against Women has been ratified by only 101 countries, of which only a few have made any attempt to eliminate discrimination

Delegates to NOW assemble in San Francisco to express outrage over the recent US Supreme Court decision to limit access to abortion

About 50 Saudi women in Riyadh take to the streets in automobiles to protest the country's ban on women drivers

NOW calls for an immediate withdrawal of US troops from the Persian Gulf to protest the Saudis treatment of women and the restrictions put on female military personnel | **1990** |
| The Women's International Bowling Congress holds the "world's largest participatory sports event" | The Vatican urges US bishops to modify their draft pastoral letter, which urges more decision-making roles | The Baltimore Orioles considers installing history-making plumbing in their women's restrooms; the new | Juliane Gallina is named brigade commander by the US Naval Academy, the | Hundreds of Iraqi and Jordanian women protest against the Persian Gulf War in front of | **1991** |

	General/ Context	Daily Life/ Customs/ Practices	Humanities/ Fine Arts	Occupations	Education
1991	50% over the last two decades, far outstripping the number of impoverished rural men Studies of heterosexual couples indicate that women have a 20% chance of contracting the AIDS virus from their male partners; men have a slightly more than 1% chance of contracting it from women Reports indicate that in many cultures throughout the world rape is viewed as a man's prerogative or as a crime against a woman's family or husband, not as a violation of the woman herself	Clarence Thomas; her accusation causes an uproar in all reaches of American society Worldwatch Institute reports that at least one million women worldwide die each year and over 100 million suffer disabling illnesses from pregnancy complications, unsafe abortions, and childbirth Female infanticide persists in China US President George Bush vetoes legislation allowing abortion to be discussed in federally financed family planning clinics	contemporary American life, *Backlash* A three-day Women's Caucus for the Arts in Washington, DC, addresses racism and ecological activism in the arts, biases against artists with disabilities, and lack of recognition of women's contributions to art history	held by women in 1990 Studies indicate that some 60% of female lawyers have experienced sexual harassment—over twice the national average Soviet women begin to lose their jobs in greater numbers than men as the economy takes on new forms; women's rights, too, begin to disintegrate	
1992	Despite the Chinese Communist party's claim to have stopped the practice, the abduction and sale of women as prostitutes and wives has increased in response to economic reforms; some women are sold by their own families; local villagers violently resist efforts of police to rescue these women At the Earth Summit Conference in Rio de Janeiro, Brazil, experts blame overpopulation in Rwanda on the fact that Rwandan husbands forbid their wives to use birth control pills, under the assumption that it weakens the women so that they cannot work in the fields	Dancer and choreographer Katherine Dunham goes on a hunger strike to protest the deportation of Haitian refugees In response to the prevalence of domestic violence in the US, the American Medical Association issues guidelines recommending that physicians routinely ask female patients whether they have been abused Scientific studies show that women who carry extra body fat in the upper body and abdomen risk getting cancer A study in the British medical journal *Lancet* indicates that deaths among women who smoke are on the rise and projects that they will nearly double between 1965 and 1995 New Zealand researchers find that calcitriol can reduce women's risk of a broken backbone from osteoporosis	32-year-old Leslie Harris writes, directs, and coproduces *Just Another Girl on the IRT,* becoming the first African-American woman to release her own feature film A boom in Latin American literature brings such writers as Elena Castedo, Isabel Allende, and Claribel Alegría into international prominence	Chinese businesswoman Yue-Sai Kan founds a cosmetic company In Japan, a district court decision marks the first successful legal action against a company and one of its employees for sexual harassment in Japan; the court declares the woman's rights were violated by crude comments that made her quit her job Severe unemployment in the former East Germany, where two thirds of the jobless are women, causes some women to have themselves sterilized in order to make themselves acceptable to employers	

Performing Arts/ Entertainment/ Sports	Religion/ Philosophy	Science/ Technology/ Discovery	Statecraft/ Military	Reform	
in Cedar Rapids, IA; about 45,000 women take part

The first Women's World Cup competition for soccer is held in China | for women and speaking out against sexism in the Roman Catholic Church | equipment would be the first public toilet facilities to allow women to urinate standing up | first in its 146-year history

Semra Ozmal is elected head of the Istanbul branch of the ruling Motherland party in Turkey, representing a major challenge to the male-dominated Muslim society

The US House Armed Services Committee votes to allow women to fly combat missions in the Air Force, Navy, and Marines

Final approval is given for the erection of a memorial honoring the women who served in the Vietnam War | the US Embassy in Amman, Jordan

Because of women's active role in the Persian Gulf War, a confrontation between women's rights activists and Muslim fundamentalists develops over the issue of women's suffrage in Kuwait | **1991** |
| Paraskevi Patoulidou of Greece wins the Olympic gold in the 100-meter hurdles, capturing her country's first medal in track and field since 1912

Gao Min of the People's Republic of China wins her second Olympic gold in springboard diving

Athletic performance researchers say that the speed of female champion runners has increased so much more rapidly than that of top male runners in recent years that by 1998 both sexes could reach parity in marathon competition | Roman Catholic bishops struggle with the Vatican's prohibition of women's admission to the priesthood, which is favored by most Catholics, according to surveys; the bishops take a historic decision to reject a pastoral letter that reaffirms traditional roles for women in the Church and issue a draft statement calling sexism a "moral and social evil"—though they assert that a male priesthood is God's will

The Church of England votes by a narrow margin to ordain women as priests; the move threatens to cause the deepest split since the Church's foundation by King Henry VIII | All female athletes competing in the Olympics must submit to a gene test to prove that they are women; dozens of false results persuade Olympic officials to switch to a new test

Development of a female condom, the vaginal pouch, which offers women more protection from sexually transmitted diseases and as much protection from pregnancy as male condoms | In a fund-raising letter opposing a proposed equal rights amendment to the Iowa constitution, evangelist Pat Robertson writes that feminist women want to kill their children and practice witchcraft

Pacifist Maria Elena Meyano, deputy mayor of Villa El Salvador in Peru, is assassinated by Shining Path revolutionaries

Afghanistan's new Islamic government imposes greater restrictions on women

Political observers in the US call 1992 "The Year of the Woman," reflecting the large number of women who run successfully for higher political office

At a conference in Seoul, South Korea, representatives of women's groups from six Asian countries discuss the Japanese army's procurement of women from their countries as prostitutes during WWII | A conference on the plight of poor rural women is held at the UN in Geneva, Switzerland

Guam's abortion law, the most restrictive in all US territories, is turned back in a US court of appeals; it declares it a felony for any doctor to perform an abortion unless a woman's life is in danger; women who have abortions and anyone who advises them to do so are guilty of a misdemeanor

A mass march on Washington, DC, to keep abortion legal reflects a new level of activism among younger American women

22 Native American women leaders from 20 tribes meet for the fourth annual Leadership Conference of Female Chiefs | **1992** |

INDEX

Entries in the index are indicated by the year and the first three letters of the subject, such as 1865SCI (Science/Technology/Discovery). Those in essays are indicated by a page number in **boldface**.

Jurisdictions (nations, regions, cities) are listed without indication of the relation between one and the other; e.g., Illinois and Chicago or France and Paris.

Alonso, Alicia, 1948PER, 1957PER, 1959PER

Alpert, Mariam, 1946REL

Alphabet, see Writing

Alphabetical Compendium of the Various Sects, An (Adams), 1784HUM

Alpha Kappa Alpha sorority, 1908EDU

Alphonsa, Mother Mary (Rose Hawthorne), 1897HUM, 1901EDU

Alpine Club (US), 1897PER

Altamsh, sultan of Delhi slave dynasty, 1236STA

Altrusa International (Chicago), 1917DAI

Aluminum pans, 1890GEN

Aly, Muhammad, 1930EDU

Alyona (warrior), 1670STA

Amalswinthe, regent of Ostrogoths, 520STA

Amanerinas, queen of Meroë, −100STA

Amanikhatashan, queen of Meroë, 60STA

Amanishakete, queen of Meroë, −50STA

Amanitere, queen of Meroë, −10STA

Amazones, Les (Chaminade), 1888HUM

Amazons, **48**, −2000STA, −1200SCI, −500DAI; French, 1792STA

Ambassadors, see Diplomats

Ameling, Ellie, 1950PER

Amenhotep IV, king of Egypt, −1374REL

America the Beautiful (Bates), 1895HUM

American Academy in Rome, 1947EDU

American Anthropological Association, 1947SCI

American Antislavery Society, 1833GEN

American Association for the Advancement of Science, 1848SCI, 1859SCI, 1885SCI, 1946SCI, 1975SCI

American Association of Retired People (AARP), 1988REF

American Association of University Women, 1882EDU, 1923EDU

American Astronomical Society, 1938SCI

American Athletic Union, 1922PER

American Ballet Theatre, 1940PER, 1945OCC

American Bar Association, 1917OCC

American Chemical Society, 1940SCI, 1976SCI

American Choral Foundation, 1954HUM

American Civil Liberties Union (ACLU), 1920DAI, 1927REF

American College for Girls (Istanbul), 1890REL

American Committee for the Prevention of Legalizing Prostitution, 1877REF

American Craftsmen's Education Council, 1943OCC

American Cyanamid Company, 1978OCC

American Drama Society, 1897HUM

American Equal Rights Association, 1866REF, 1869STA

American Family (Baldwin), 1935HUM

American Federation of Labor (AFL), 1934GEN

American Feminist party, 1971STA

American Genetic Association, 1937SCI

American Geographical Society, 1955SCI, 1976SCI

American Heritage Dictionary for Children, 1972DAI

American History and Its Geographic Conditions (Semple), 1903SCI

American Institute of Architects, 1887HUM

American Jewish Congress, 1931DAI

American Journal of Nursing, 1884EDU

American Jubilee (Littlefield), 1939PER

American Library Association, 1911OCC

American Life League, 1979REF

American Mathematical Society, 1978SCI

American Medical Association, 1992DAI

American Men and Women of Science, **367**

American Museum of Natural History, 1926SCI

American Music Society, 1897HUM

American Nuclear Society, 1971SCI

American Ornithologists' Union, 1885SCI, 1929SCI, 1931SCI

American Pediatric Society, 1930SCI

American Physical Education Association, 1923EDU

American Physical Society, 1975SCI

American Psychiatric Association, 1986DAI

American Red Cross, 1821OCC, 1881EDU

American Repertory Theatre, 1926PER

American Revolution, women in, **131**, 1775STA, 1776HUM, 1778STA, 1780OCC, 1782STA

American School of Opera, 1885HUM

American Social Hygiene Association, 1914REF

American Society of Psychical Research, 1859DAI

American Stock Exchange, 1955OCC, 1958OCC, 1973OCC

American Theatre Wing, 1947GEN

American Weekly Mercury, 1742HUM

American Welding Society, 1940SCI

American Woman Suffrage Association (AWSA), **235**, 1869REF, 1890REF

American women, see African-American women; Asian-American women; Chicana women; Feminism; Frontier women; Suffrage, women's; Women's rights; *and specific occupations*

American Women's Medical Association, 1915SCI

American Youth Hostels, Inc., 1934OCC

Ames, Fanny Baker, 1877STA, 1891STA

Ames, Jessie Daniel, 1931PER

Ames, Mary E. Clemmer, 1866OCC, 1869OCC

Amin, Qasim, 1899STA

Amina, Hausa queen, **49**, 1536STA

Ammers-Küller, Johanna van, 1925HUM

Amoss, Harold, 1918SCI

Amra, 640DAI

Amuhia, queen of Babylon, −600SCI

Anabaptists, **146, 147**

Anarchists, 1869REF, 1871EDU, 1906REF

Anastasia (of Pomerania), 1240REL

Anatomy, female, see Physiology, female

Ancrum, Battle of, 1545STA

Andely (France) monastery, 690REL

Anderson, Elizabeth Garrett, 1869OCC, 1877OCC, 1885EDU, 1916STA

Anderson, Dame Judith (Frances Margaret), 1960PER

Anderson, Louisa Garrett, 1915OCC

Anderson, Lucy, 1802PER

Anderson, Marian, 1939PER, 1955PER

Anderson, Mary, 1920OCC

Anderson, Mary Antoinette, 1875PER

Anderson, Mary MacArthur, 1906EDU

Anderson, Violet Neatly, 1926OCC

Andersson, Bibi (Birgitta), 1956PER

And God Created Woman (film), 1956PER

Andorra, 1970DAI

Andover, MA, 1821EDU

Andrássy, countess, 1909REF

Andrews, Eliza Frances, 1908HUM

Andrews, Jane, 1833EDU

Andrews Sisters (Laverne, Maxine, and Patti), 1941PER

Anecdotes of the Late Samuel Johnson (Thrale), 1786HUM

Anegay, Mme. H. E., 1959STA

Angela Merici (saint), **138**, 1535REL

Angel of the Waters (Stebbins), 1873HUM

Angelou, Maya, 1972HUM

Anglican Church, see Anglican Church (Canada); Church of England; Episcopal Church (US)

Anglican Church (Canada), priests, 1975REF, 1976REL

Angolan women, 1975REF

Anguissola, Sofonisba, **148**, 1546HUM

Animal Crackers (film), 1930PER

Animal Mind, The (Washburn), 1908SCI

Anna (biblical figure), 1REL

Anna Comnena, **94–95**, 1140HUM

Anna Ivanovna, czarina of Russia, 1730STA

Anna Magdalena Notebooks (Bach), 1721DAI

Annapolis, MD, see US Naval Academy

Anne, queen of Great Britain and Ireland, 1702STA

Anne of Austria, 1602STA

Anne of Bohemia, queen of England, 1382STA

Anne of Brittany (Anne de Bretagne), 1491STA, 1514REL

Anne of Cleves, 4th wife of Henry VIII, 1540STA

Anne of Green Gables (Montgomery), 1908HUM

Annie Allen (Brooks), 1949HUM, 1950HUM

"Annie Laurie" (Spottiswoode), 1900HUM

Anning, Mary, 1811SCI

Ann of the Word, see Lee, Ann

Another Mother for Peace (US), 1967REF

Anselmi, Tina, 1969OCC

Antarctica, 1947PER

Antheil, George, 1942SCI

Anthony, Susan Brownell, **234, 235**, 1820REF, 1852REF, 1853REF, 1854REF, 1863REF, 1866REF, 1869REF, 1869STA, 1872REF, 1881REF, 1900REF, 1904REF, 1906REF, 1921HUM, 1979DAI

Anthropologists, 1893SCI, 1928SCI, 1934SCI, 1947SCI, 1975SCI; see also Ethnologists and ethnology

Antiabolitionists, 1838REF

Antiabortion movement (US), 1967REF, 1979REF, 1985REF

Anticolonialist Women's Association (Vietnam), 1930REF

Antiguan women, 1986EDU, 1986OCC

Antin, Mary, 1899HUM

Antinuclear movement, 1981REF, 1984REF

Antioch (OH) College, 1833EDU

Anti-Semitism, **379**, 1935GEN

Antislavery, see Abolition (of slavery) and abolitionists

Anti-Slavery Convention of American Women (Philadelphia), 1838REF

Antislavery Society (England), 1823GEN